D1082781

Natural Justice

Natural Justice

Ken Binmore

OXFORD

UNIVERSITY PRESS

2005

OXFORD
UNIVERSITY PRESS

Oxford University Press, Inc., publishes works that further
Oxford University's objective of excellence
in research, scholarship, and education.

Oxford   New York
Auckland   Cape Town   Dar es Salaam   Hong Kong   Karachi
Kuala Lumpur   Madrid   Melbourne   Mexico City   Nairobi
New Delhi   Shanghai   Taipei   Toronto

With offices in
Argentina   Austria   Brazil   Chile   Czech Republic   France   Greece
Guatemala   Hungary   Italy   Japan   Poland   Portugal   Singapore
South Korea   Switzerland   Thailand   Turkey   Ukraine   Vietnam

Published by Oxford University Press, Inc.
198 Madison Avenue, New York, New York 10016

www.oup.com

Oxford is a registered trademark of Oxford University Press

Library of Congress Cataloging-in-Publication Data
Natural justice / Binmore, K. G., 1940–
p. cm.
Includes bibliographical references and index.
ISBN-13 978-0-19-517811-1
ISBN 0-19-517811-4
1. Justice. 2. Fairness. 3. Social ethics.   I. Title.
JC578.B54 2004
320'.01'1—dc22   2004057639

1 3 5 7 9 8 6 4 2

Printed in the United States of America
on acid-free paper

Natural Justice

is dedicated
to my son

Daniel

Preface

In 1984, I impulsively accepted a late invitation to speak at a prestigious conference on social choice in Canada. Having nothing relevant in my research file, I immediately set about throwing together a paper on a subject to which I had previously given only an idle thought or two.

John Rawls' celebrated *Theory of Justice* proposes an imaginary scenario in which the citizens of a society meet to plan a new social contract. Rawls suggests that the social contract on which they agree would be fair if the citizens are kept in ignorance of their identities while bargaining. Each citizen will then have equal reason to fear being the victim of any injustice built into the final deal. My idea was to apply Ariel Rubinstein's recently invented theory of rational bargaining to the negotiation problem created by such a Rawlsian veil of ignorance.

Four weeks later, on the morning of my arrival at the conference, I presented a paper on this subject to a large audience consisting almost entirely of strangers. After the talk, a tall gentleman rose from his seat, and introduced himself as John Rawls. Given that I had been speaking more or less impromptu on a subject about which he knew a great deal and I knew essentially nothing, his kindness went way beyond the call of duty—especially since I now know that he had by then lost faith in economic theory as a tool for investigating political philosophy. However, his continuing encouragement made me think it worthwhile to put my material into publishable form after tying up the philosophical loose ends I had left blowing in the wind.

In 1994, I was still tying up loose ends, having come close to despair along the way, as attempt after attempt to create adequate foundations for a scientific theory of fairness norms simply revealed new loose ends of whose existence I had been unaware. Those who have grappled with Immanuel Kant will get some feeling for the immensity of the struggle, when I say that I even read every book by Kant that was available in the library of the University of Michigan in an attempt to get to the bottom of Rawls' assertion that he was merely operationalizing Kant's categorical imperative. But this effort was to prove my salvation. It eventually dawned upon me that I was reading the work of an emperor who was clothed in nothing more than the obscurity of his prose.

Kant never provides any genuine defense of his claims—not even in his *Grundwerke*. His categorical imperative is simply a grandiloquent rendering of the folk wisdom which says that it is immoral to lay oneself open to my mother's favorite reproach: "Suppose everybody behaved liked that?" Kant's assertion that one should honor this principle for *rational* reasons is conjured from the air. But Kant is widely regarded as the greatest philosopher of all time. Could it really be that his claim to fame as a moral philosopher is based merely on his having invented one of the fallacies of the Prisoners' Dilemma before anyone else?

If I hadn't once held the chair in mathematics at the London School of Economics, and so had the opportunity to interact a little with Karl Popper, I would probably have rejected this suggestion as being too outrageous to consider seriously. I can't say that I found Popper's manner very charming, but one has only to read his quotes from Plato's *Republic* to recognize that Popper's *Enemies of the Open Society* is right on the ball in denying that the received opinion of Plato as the founder of rational liberalism can be squared with what Plato actually believed. In modern terms, Plato was a fascist who thought that we all so need a leader that nobody should even "get up, or move, or wash, or take his meals" without permission! If philosophical scholarship could convert such adolescent authoritarianism into a model of civilized debate, might it not have done the same for Kant's attempts to evade the rules of deductive reasoning?

My mathematical friends and colleagues were of no help, because their training in logic had led them to abandon Kant much sooner than I. So I began to approach philosophers with my heretical thoughts. Those willing to talk to me fell into three classes. Philosophers in the first class agreed that the categorical imperative calls for cooperation in the Prisoners' Dilemma, and dismissed game theory as misguided and irrelevant. Those in the second class explained that Kant's conception of a maxim and a universal law are too subtle to allow a definite yes or no as to whether it is rational to cooperate in the Prisoners' Dilemma. However, I struck gold with philosophers in the third class, who told me to read the works of David Hume.

I can't say that I realized immediately that I was reading the author who genuinely deserves to be called the greatest philosopher of all time. Like most people, I allowed the fact that he is one of the great stylists of the English language to cloud my appreciation of his creative genius. As though merely making conversation, he would today be explaining quantum physics to someone he met on a bus without either party feeling any sense of incongruity. But the tendency to assess the quality of a good by its price carries over into philosophy. Surely the hours spent struggling to make sense of Kant must be a measure of the depth and originality of his thought? How could the insights bought at such a low price from Hume be comparable in value?

However, a game theorist ought to have recognized from the start that Hume is the original inventor of reciprocal altruism—the first person to recognize that the equilibrium ideas now studied in game theory are vital to an understanding of how human societies work. He understood that one must look to evolution for a solution of the equilibrium selection problem—a conclusion that modern game theorists have reached only after fifty years of fruitless attempts to tackle the difficulty by inventing high-flown definitions of rationality in the style of Kant. He even anticipated modern game theorists in seeing legal reform as a problem in mechanism design.

Reading Hume gave me the courage to throw off the dead hand of Kantian metaphysics and to seek naturalistic foundations for Rawls' powerful intuitions about the way human fairness norms work. My background as a mathematician-turned-economist seemed to put me in an ideal position to translate his pregnant thoughts into simple mathematical models using the language of game theory invented by Von Neumann and Morgenstern.

The time was particularly apt, since Hamilton, Maynard Smith, and others had also recently applied the language of game theory to evolutionary biology, and so made it possible to understand the role of the family in the evolution of human morality. For a long time, I was held up by the necessity of coming up with a theory of interpersonal comparison of utility, but this problem eventually solved itself when I realized that Rawls' egalitarian theory wasn't so distant as it looked from the utilitarian theory of John Harsanyi. Once Harsanyi's metaphysical theory of interpersonal comparison had been reinterpreted in naturalistic terms, and then recycled through a Rawlsian filter, I was led to a formulation of fairness that is very close to the psychological law of equity, for which a measure of empirical support has been obtained in the laboratory.

Putting this material into publishable form proved a nightmare. Nearly everything I had to say was controversial to somebody, and it was therefore necessary to be very precise about the basic framework. But how can one explain things in precise terms to people who are untrained in mathematics? In the end, I compromised by writing a two-volume work for MIT Press called *Game Theory and the Social Contract* that contains long expository passages but makes free use of formulas and equations, although I did the best I could to keep them to a minimum.

The first volume, *Playing Fair*, which appeared in 1994, attempted to clear the air by expounding the widely misunderstood ideas from economic theory that I needed to call upon. For example, the third chapter lists all the fallacies of the Prisoners' Dilemma that I had come across at that time, explaining in detail the various errors in reasoning involved. A long delay then ensued before the second volume *Just Playing* appeared in 1998 with the beef of the theory. Between the publication of the two volumes, I read so much anthropology, biology, economics, philosophy, and psychology that my previous reading of Kant's works pales into insignificance by comparison. The experience was immensely rewarding, but I have to confess to times when my heart sank as I realized that there was yet another whole literature of which I knew nothing at all.

Not being sufficiently original to fall "deadborn from the press" like David Hume's first great work, my *Game Theory and the Social Contract* sold reasonably well. But it isn't a book for the general reader. It is an academic work with long footnotes and earnest asides considering abstruse objections. As always in such books, it discusses much literature of marginal relevance in the hope of disarming critics who would otherwise challenge its author's scholarly credentials. Worst of all are the equations—each of which halves a book's readership, if Stephen Hawking is to be believed.

Natural Justice has been written to try to bring my ideas to a wider audience. The previous publication of *Game Theory and the Social Contract* leaves me free to adopt the conventions of popular science books without feeling too guilty. In *Natural Justice*, I don't hedge my speculations about with reservations and qualifications. My claims aren't proved, but illustrated with examples. Scholarly references are rare. Above all, there are no algebraic equations at all. If Hawking is right and my audience doubles for each equation removed from *Game Theory and the Social Contract*, I shall be the most successful author of all time!

But I will be satisfied if *Natural Justice* is able to make at least some converts to the view that debate on public morality and political reform needn't be confined to those would-be philosopher-kings who continue to write footnotes to Plato. Two thousand years of such moral punditry has got us nowhere, and never will. Surely we now know enough about human nature to begin to restrict our attention to aspirations for our societies that have some chance of working.

Finally, I want to thank all the many people who have helped me with this book, especially John Weymark and Terry Vaughn, whose faith in the project was a constant source of comfort and support.

Ken Binmore
Monmouth, Wales

Contents

Natural
Justice

Chapter 1

Moral Science

He who understands *Baboon* would do more towards metaphysics than John Locke.

Charles Darwin

1.1 Evolutionary Ethics

II:2.4

What should we be aiming for? Wherein lies our duty? How ought we to live? Such questions have been debated for millenia, but to so little effect that moral philosophers commonly agree that the sum of their endeavors should count as no more than a footnote to Plato. How could so little have been achieved in such a long time?

I think that orthodox moral philosophy has gotten nowhere because it asks the wrong questions. If morality evolved along with the human race, then asking how we ought to live makes as much sense as asking what animals ought to exist, or which language we ought to speak.

The authority claimed by gurus who argue to the contrary is conjured from nowhere. They no more have access to some noumenal world of moral absolutes than the boy who delivers our newspapers. Like the rest of us, they actually get their intuitions from observing the *real* rules that govern our moral behavior. These are not the absurdly impractical moral principles we teach to our children, but which they quickly learn to classify alongside Santa Claus and the Tooth Fairy. As every parent knows, it is a waste of time preaching to children unless you also practice what you preach.

The moral rules that really govern our behavior consist of a mixture of instincts, customs, and conventions that are simultaneously more mundane and more complex than traditional scholarship is willing to credit. They are shaped largely by evolutionary forces—social as well as biological. If one wishes to study such rules, it doesn't help to ask how they advance the Good or preserve the Right. One must ask instead how they evolved and why they survive. That is to say, we need to treat morality as a science.

1.2 Mudslinging

The idea that morality is best understood from an evolutionary perspective goes all the way back to Charles Darwin, but progress in developing this most controversial of his many insights has been painfully slow. People are so reluctant to surrender traditional ways of thinking about morality that they actively place obstacles in the path of those who are more adventurous by ridiculing or misrepresenting their views.

This task was made easier by the appearance of an early school of would-be moralists who argued that the strong ought to be allowed to trample on the weak because only the fit survive. The philosopher Moore lampooned their views as the proposition that "we ought to move in the direction of evolution simply because it is the direction of evolution". Although the idea that Darwinism is teleological is manifestly absurd, their unpleasant creed is nowadays called Social Darwinism in an attempt to discredit anyone who uses the words evolution and ethics in the same sentence. Critics of Edward Wilson's *Sociobiology* contrived to sling this kind of mud so successfully that some of his followers now prefer to call themselves behavioral ecologists or evolutionary psychologists rather than stand accused of being sociobiological fascists.

The same eggshell sensitivity to mudslinging is also to be found in the popular books on evolutionary theory that are now endemic in airport bookstores. Such books commonly present the evidence that our minds and bodies evolved from less complex organisms with such consummate skill that one has to doubt the sincerity of the dwindling band of brothers who continue to insist that evolution is just a theory. However, when it comes to evolutionary ethics, the eloquence of popular authors dries up, and all we usually get on the subject is a few inoffensive platitudes toward the end of the last chapter.

Even if I wanted to, there is no way that I can similarly walk on eggshells. If I am taken seriously, I know that I will therefore be attacked from all sides as an ignorant teller of just-so stories. It is true that one can't write about human morality with the same authority as the life cycle of the parasitic worm *Dicrolium dendriticum* or the leaf-cutting ant *Acromyrmex versicolor*, but the importance of the subject surely licenses a certain amount of informed speculation. After all, nobody complains when cosmologists speculate that most of the universe consists of dark energy and matter of which we have no direct evidence at all. So why should similar theorizing be forbidden when studying morality? Only, I think, because moral and religious zealots see it as a challenge to their spurious sources of authority.

In any case, I plan to brave the inevitable brickbats by taking the basic facts of evolution for granted, and devoting the whole of this book to a sustained line of speculation on the evolutionary origins of the human fairness norms that lie at the root of our notions of justice.

My past efforts in this direction have all involved mathematical modeling, but there is no algebra in this book. Nor is there any heavy philosophizing. Nor yet scholarly references and learned asides on why I differ from others. My plan is to get on with telling my story with as few apologies as possible. Anyone sufficiently interested can look for documentation in my two-volume *Game Theory and the Social Contract*, to which the marginal notes refer.

1.3 Social Contracts

I:1.2.3

A social contract is the set of common understandings that allow the citizens of a society to coordinate their efforts.

The common understandings or conventions that make up a social contract are many and various. They range from the arcane table manners we employ at formal dinner parties to the significance we attach to the green pieces of paper we carry round in our wallets bearing pictures of past presidents. From the rules that govern how we drive our cars in heavy traffic to the meaning of the words in the language we speak. From dietary and sexual taboos to the standards of integrity and truthfulness expected of honorable folk. From the vagaries of fashion to the criteria that we fondly suppose secure ownership of our possessions. From the amount that we think it appropriate to tip in restaurants to the circumstances under which we are ready to submit ourselves to the authority of others.

The seemingly profound half of each of these pairings is usually attributed to iron laws of morality derived from an ineffable source into which we are not encouraged to look too closely. But I think the differences between the trivial and the profound halves in the pairings are differences only of degree. There are no iron laws beyond those encoded in our genes. Like Gulliver in Lilliput, we are bound only by a thousand gossamer threads woven from our own beliefs and opinions.

Everybody believes this of fashion and etiquette, where it is necessary that the rules change sufficiently fast that outsiders are always just far enough behind that they can be distinguished from insiders. There are those who would claim otherwise of dietary taboos, but most of us know perfectly well that we would be as unwilling to eat a cow or a pig if we had been brought up in another society as we currently are to eat a dog or a caterpillar. Sexual mores are particularly fluid. In Nigeria, a woman guilty of adultery can be stoned, whereas a chaste woman in Beverly Hills would be at risk of social exclusion if found out.

The same goes for the different standards of honesty and fair play that operate in different societies. The myth that there are universal standards doesn't even begin to hold water. We even think it right to operate different standards ourselves in different contexts. Would you, for example, blow the whistle on a colleague if you learned that he was cheating on his tax returns? But what if he had falsified his results in reporting a scientific experiment?

It is true that some of our cultural conventions are codified as laws, but the legal system and the constitution of a modern society are relevant to a social contract only to the extent that they are actually honored in practice. If it is customary to give and take bribes, then giving and taking bribes is part of the social contract—whatever the law may say.

As for the authority of constitutions, all of us would be delighted to enjoy the civil rights supposedly guaranteed by the constitution of the old Soviet Union. Nor are popes, presidents, kings, judges, or the police exempt from the social contract of the society in which they officiate. Far from enforcing the social contract, they derive what power they have from a social convention which says that ordinary citizens should accept their direction. If they were ignored in the same way that the citizens of Naples ignore traffic signals, they would be totally powerless.

How do social contracts work? What is the glue that holds a society together? It isn't the law or the constitution. These are just words on a piece of paper. It isn't the officers of state. They are just people like you or me. Is it our sense of moral obligation? But there is honor of a sort even among thieves. Is it God? Some social contracts are so horrendous that even fundamentalists must sometimes entertain doubts.

None of these answers fit the bill, because we asked the wrong question. A stable social contract doesn't need any glue.

Dostoyevsky's autobiographical *House of the Dead* makes this point very clearly when describing his experience as a political prisoner in a Czarist concentration camp: "The majority of these men were depraved and hopelessly corrupt. The scandals and the gossip never ceased; this was a hell, a dark night of the soul. But no-one dared to rebel against the endogenous and accepted rules of the prison; everyone submitted to them. To the prison came men who had gone too far . . . the terror of whole villages and towns . . . [but] the new convict . . . imperceptibly grew resigned and fitted in with the general tone." Dostoyevsky's fellow convicts didn't follow the social contract that had evolved in the camp for moral reasons, or because they feared the prison guards. They unknowingly followed its precepts because their fellow prisoners punished them if they didn't.

When punishment is mentioned, one's mind naturally turns to the kind of institutionalized violence that put Dostoyevsky behind bars in the first place. But the punishments that deter us from cheating on the social contract are nearly always so mild that we scarcely notice them at all. In my own country, I find it hard to codify the subtle use of body language and shades of verbal expression that my neighbors use to hint that my current behavior is likely to result in more positive forms of social exclusion if I don't start mending my ways. One is so habituated to responding appropriately, that such subliminal signals are automatically translated into behavior without any conscious control. Only when some social gaffe in a foreign country is greeted by an unfamiliar signal does the mechanism become apparent.

In David Hume's metaphor, a social contract holds together like a drystone wall or a masonry arch. Each stone supports and is supported by its neighbors, without any need for cement or glue. In modern game theory, we express the same idea by saying that the rules of a stable social contract succeed in coordinating our behavior on an *equilibrium* in the game of life. With this idea under our belts, we can give up the search for the social equivalent of the angels invented by medieval philosophers to explain what keeps the planets in their orbits. Like the solar system, our societies work all by themselves.

Much of this book explores the consequences of David Hume's insight that a social contract can be seen as a largely unrecognized consensus to coordinate on a particular equilibrium of the game of life that we play together. As Hume explains: "Two men, who pull the oars of a boat, do it by an agreement or convention, tho' they have never given promises to one another. Nor is the rule concerning the stability of possessions the less derived from human conventions, that it arises gradually, and acquires force by a slow progression . . . In like manner are languages gradually established by human conventions without any promise. In like manner do gold and silver become the common measures of exchange."

So what is an equilibrium? How does it capture Hume's big idea? How come a society finds itself at one equilibrium rather than another?

Writing on this subject is like juggling with numerous slippery balls while being pelted with rotten vegetables by a surly audience. Critics are particularly impatient at the necessity of getting the balls in the air one at a time. Whatever ball they are first shown is taken to be the whole of the theory, which can then be dismissed as naive on the grounds that it doesn't take account of all the other balls.

In this chapter and the next, I try to head off such hasty criticism by giving broad-brush answers to some of the more immediate broad-brush questions in the course of distinguishing three levels of priority made necessary by an evolutionary approach to social contract theory. The three levels of priority are:

- Stability
- Efficiency
- Fairness

A social contract must be internally stable, or it won't survive. It needs to be efficient, or it won't compete successfully with the social contracts of other societies. Conventional moral philosophy pays little or no attention to either of these issues, but we shall find that they are essential to making sense of the question that arises at the third level: How and why are social contracts fair?

I know that the danger in beginning a book with such an extended introduction is that critics will assume that I am unable to provide a detailed defense of the claims that are being made. However, these details are provided in later chapters as I work up through the three levels of priority, justifying the claims made in the current overview along the way. Some patience is therefore necessary on the part of those who don't think that it possible that social justice can have a natural origin, since I only really get going on this subject in chapter 9.

1.4 Stability

I:2.2

After the movie *A Beautiful Mind*, everybody has heard of John Nash, who was awarded a Nobel prize after recovering from a schizophrenic illness that left him on the sidelines of intellectual inquiry for more than forty years. He got his prize both for his work on bargaining theory, and for formulating the idea of an equilibrium in a game. The movie makes a feeble attempt to give an example of a Nash equilibrium, but gets it hopelessly wrong, although the basic idea isn't hard to understand.

A game is any situation in which people or animals interact. The plans of action of the players are called strategies. A Nash equilibrium is any profile of strategies— one for each player—in which each player's strategy is a best reply to the strategies of the other players.

A very simple example is the Driving Game we play each time we get into our cars in the morning to drive to work. Shall we drive on the left or on the right? If all we care about is avoiding accidents, the game has three Nash equilibria. In the first, we all choose the strategy of driving on the left. In the second, we all choose the strategy of driving on the right. In the third, we each toss a coin to decide whether to drive on the left or on the right. The third alternative may seem dubious, but if everybody else is randomizing their choice, your chances of ending up in an accident are going to be the same whatever you do. So tossing a coin is just as much a best reply as doing anything else.

Why should anyone care about Nash equilibria? There are at least two reasons. The first is that if a game has a rational solution that is common knowledge among the players, then it must be an equilibrium. If it weren't, then some of the players would have to believe that it is rational for them not to make their best reply to what they know the other players are going to do. But it can't be rational not to play optimally.

The second reason why equilibria matter is even more important. If the payoffs in a game correspond to how fit the players are, then evolutionary processes—either cultural or biological—that favor the more fit at the expense of the less fit will stop working when we get to an equilibrium, because all the survivors will then be as fit as it is possible to be in the circumstances.

Much of the power of game theory as a conceptual tool derives from the possibility of moving back and forward between the rational and evolutionary interpretations of an equilibrium. Since this is an idea which is easily misunderstood, the first priority is to explain why switching interpretations in this way can be legitimate.

Selfish genes?   Because evolution stops working at an equilibrium, biologists say that Nash equilibria are evolutionarily stable.[1] Each relevant locus on a chromosome is then occupied by the gene with maximal fitness. Since a gene is just a molecule, it can't *choose* to maximize its fitness, but evolution makes it seem as though it had. This is a valuable insight, because it allows biologists to use the rational interpretation of an equilibrium to predict the outcome of an evolutionary process, without following each complicated twist and turn that the process might take.

The title of Richard Dawkins' *Selfish Gene* expresses the idea in a nutshell, but it also provokes a lot of criticism. It is easy to be tolerant of critics like the old lady I heard rebuking Dawkins for failing to see that a molecule can't possibly have free will, but tolerance is less easy in the case of critics like Lewontin or Gould, who chose to whip up public hostility against Edward Wilson and his followers on similar grounds. As Alcock's *Triumph of Sociobiology* documents, they willfully pretend not to understand that sociobiologists seek explanations of biological phenomena in terms of *ultimate* causes rather than *proximate* causes.

Why, for example, do songbirds sing in the early spring? The proximate cause is long and difficult. This molecule knocked against that molecule. This chemical reaction is catalyzed by that enzyme. But the ultimate cause is that the birds are signalling territorial claims to each other in order to avoid unnecessary conflict. They neither know nor care that this behavior is rational. They just do what they do. But the net effect of an immensely complicated evolutionary process is that songbirds behave *as though* they had rationally chosen to maximize their fitness.

---

[1] John Maynard Smith defines an evolutionarily stable strategy (ESS) to be a best reply to itself that is a better reply to any alternative best reply than the alternative best reply is to itself, but biologists seldom worry about the small print involving alternative best replies.

When studying the social behavior of songbirds and other animals, evolutionary biologists seldom know any more about the proximate causes of what they observe than the animals themselves. But only the most prejudiced critic can deny them the successes they have enjoyed in explaining social behavior in terms of ultimate causes in the manner dear to the hearts of game theorists.

1.5 Efficiency

I:1.2.8

The first priority for a social contract is stability, which is to be crudely modeled using the idea of an equilibrium in a game. The next priority is efficiency, which means that nothing gets wasted. Economists follow Vilfredo Pareto in taking the absence of waste to be equivalent to the requirement that nobody can be made better off without someone else being made worse off.

Adam Smith famously explained that an "invisible hand" steers a perfectly competitive market to an efficient outcome. This invisible hand is yet another metaphor like the selfish gene. What actually happens is that sellers from whom people are reluctant to buy gradually lower the prices at which they are willing to sell, and buyers to whom people are reluctant to sell gradually raise the price at which they are willing to buy. When this process stops, there is no waste, because demand equals supply. No genes compete for survival in such economic adjustment processes, but I shall still call them evolutionary, because they work by themselves, without planning or supervision, until an equilibrium is reached.

Traditional economists sometimes forget that perfectly competitive markets are the exception rather than the rule, and hence come on as though we should expect the equilibria of all the games that people play with each other to be efficient.[2] But this is very far from the truth.

I:2.2.5

The Tragedy of the Commons is a stylized game that illustrates why equilibria are often inefficient. A hundred families keep goats that graze on some common land. Total milk production is maximized with a thousand goats in all. How many goats should each family keep to maximize its own milk production?

At first sight, the answer seems to be ten, but it isn't an equilibrium for each family to keep ten goats. If all the other families keep ten goats, your family's optimal strategy isn't to do the same. You will do better by grazing one goat more, because your family will enjoy all the benefit from the extra goat, while its cost in terms of less grass for the other goats to eat will be shared by the whole community. Families will therefore add extra goats to their herd until the common is reduced to a desert. But this outcome is very inefficient indeed.

The Tragedy of the Commons captures the logic of a whole spectrum of environmental disasters that we have brought upon ourselves. The Sahara Desert is relentlessly expanding southward, partly because the pastoral peoples who live on its borders persistently overgraze its marginal grasslands. We jam our roads with

---

[2]For competition to be perfect, a whole list of conditions must be satisfied, even when frictions in the adjustment process are ignored. We need a large numbers of buyers and sellers, none of whom is big enough to have market power on their own. Nobody must have any secrets. Returns to production need to be decreasing. And so on.

cars. We poison our rivers and pollute the atmosphere. We fell the rainforests. We have plundered our fisheries until some fish stocks have reached a level from which they may never recover.

Game theorists get a lot of stick for saying this kind of thing. Our critics ask how it can possibly be *rational* for a society to engineer such disasters. Can't we see that everybody would be better off if everybody were to grab less of the common resource? The error in this kind of reasoning is elementary. A player in the human game of life isn't some abstract entity called "everybody". We are all separate individuals, each with our own aims and purposes. Even when our capacity for love moves us to make sacrifices for others, we each do so in our own way and for our own reasons.

In biology, the mistake of confusing the aims of individuals with aims attributed to the collectives of which they form a part is called the group selection fallacy. One can't help feeling sorry for the biologist Wynne-Edwards, who is endlessly denounced for originating the fallacy, but it can't be right that genes will be favored that benefit the survival of the species at the expense of their own fitness. For example, starlings don't flock together in the evenings to estimate their numbers in order that each starling can selflessly restrict its breeding opportunities so as to keep the population at an optimal level. If they did, mutant starlings programmed to take advantage of the chastity of their fellows by breeding without restraint would soon predominate.

II:3.1   **Reciprocal altruism.**   The invisible hand can only be counted on to take a population to an efficient outcome of a game in the exceptional case when all of its equilibria happen to be efficient. Perfectly competitive markets are one such case, but markets didn't exist when our species separated itself from the other apes. So how did our unique style of cooperation evolve?

Because relatives share genes, it is easy to explain the evolution of cooperation within the family. For example, any of my genes has half a chance of being present in the body of my sister. If I were genetically programmed to maximize the average number of copies of my genes that are transmitted to the next generation, I would therefore count each of my sister's children as being worth half of one of my own. This is presumably why some birds help bring up their nephews and nieces when their own chances of raising a family are not very promising.

But human cooperation is more complex. The fierce loyalties that sometimes develop in street gangs or army platoons can perhaps be explained in terms of the collective serving as a surrogate family, but we often manage to cooperate very successfully with total strangers, or with people whom we actively dislike or despise. What is the secret of this seeming contradiction to the doctrine of the selfish gene?

In 1976, Robert Trivers offered "reciprocal altruism" as the solution of the mystery, but David Hume was already on the ball in 1739.

As Hume explains: "I learn to do service to another, without bearing him any real kindness, because I foresee, that he will return my service in expectation of another of the same kind, and in order to maintain the same correspondence of good offices with me and others. And accordingly, after I have serv'd him and he is in possession of the advantage arising from my action, he is induc'd to perform his part, as foreseeing the consequences of his refusal."

Vampire bats provide an exotic example of reciprocity in action. The bats roost in caves in large numbers during the day. At night, they forage for prey, from whom they suck blood if they can, but they aren't always successful. If they fail to obtain blood for several successive nights, they die. The evolutionary pressure to share blood is therefore strong.

The biologist Wilkinson reports that a hungry bat begs for blood from a roost-mate, who will sometimes respond by regurgitating some of the blood it is carrying in its own stomach. This isn't too surprising when the roostmates are related, but the bats also share blood with roostmates who aren't relatives. The behavior is nevertheless evolutionarily stable, because the sharing is done on a *reciprocal* basis, which means that a bat is much more likely to help out a roostmate that has helped it out in the past. Bats that refuse to help out their fellows therefore risk not being helped out themselves in the future.

Although vampire genes are selfish, reciprocal sharing turns out to be sustainable as an equilibrium in the vampire game of life. We therefore don't always need to assume that people are selfless to explain cooperation in the human game of life. A society of Mr. Hydes can use reciprocal altruism to sustain an efficient social contract just as effectively as a society of Dr. Jekylls. We may not like their motives for avoiding waste, but it is enough for a social contract to be efficient that waste is avoided.

Warm glow? To say that reciprocal altruism is important to the survival of *I:1.2.2* human social contracts is usually taken as a wicked denial of the existence of selfless altruism, so let me insist that I too derive a warm glow from my occasional selfless acts. I give money to charity like other bourgeois folk. If I could swim better, perhaps I would be one of those who are willing to risk their lives by plunging into a raging torrent to save a stranger from drowning.

However, it is necessary to face up to the fact that such selfless altruism survives because it either doesn't cost us very much, or else is called for only rarely. Apart from a few saints, who gives so much of their income to charity that it really hurts? Who would keep on plunging into the river if there were always a stranger struggling for his life when you took the dog out for a walk? If taxes were replaced by voluntary contributions, how would the resulting Tragedy of the Commons eventually get played? If there were no policemen, who would walk safe at night?

We are all mixtures of the selfless Dr. Jekyll and the selfish Mr. Hyde. It would be nice if human nature had more Jekyll and less Hyde, but no amount of abusing sociobiologists is going to change what evolution has made of us. History is full of failed utopias in which Jekyll was going to displace Hyde as soon as the conditions were right. If we are to avoid repeating these mistakes, we need to be realistic about the relative amounts of Jekyll and Hyde that are mixed into the human cocktail.

I was brought up in a tough neighborhood that taught me not to rely very much on the milk of human kindness. Outside my immediate circle, there was a lot of Hyde and not much Jekyll. Most of those who read this book will have been luckier, and grown up with a gentler social contract. But everybody can read about the downside of human nature in newspapers and history books.

Who were those southern gentlemen who once got their kicks from lynching uppity blacks? What of the ordinary German housewives who turned to savagery when recruited as guards at Ravensbrück? How about the subjects in Milgram's experiments who inflicted apparently painful electric shocks on a helpless victim when told to do so by an authority figure? Those people are us—or who we might have been if we had lived their lives in their cultures. Perhaps you or I would have been one of the brave exceptions, but who would want the survival of our social contract to rely on this being true of everybody?

The folk theorem.   Game theorists don't talk about altruism at all when dis-
I:2.2.6   cussing reciprocity. Perhaps this explains why the world paid no attention to their discovery of the secret of how reciprocal altruism works some twenty-five years before Trivers introduced the idea to biologists. This secret seemed so obvious after John Nash's formulation of an equilibrium in the early fifties that nobody knew to whom the idea should be attributed. It is therefore called the folk theorem.

Rational reciprocity can't work unless people interact repeatedly, without a definite end to their relationship in sight. If the reason I scratch your back today is that I expect you will then scratch my back tomorrow, then our cooperative arrangement will unravel if we know that there will eventually be no tomorrow.

The simplest kind of game in which reciprocity can appear is therefore a *repeated* game with an indefinite time horizon. The simplest of the folk theorems characterizes all the equilibria of such a game in the case when nobody can conceal any information, and everybody always cares about tomorrow nearly as much as they care about today. The important point is that any efficient outcome of the original game on which the players might like to agree approximates an *equilibrium* outcome of the repeated game.

For example, in the Tragedy of the Commons, the efficient outcomes are those in which exactly one 1,000 goats graze the common. If the 100 families got together in a conclave, they might agree on what share of the 1,000 goats each family should be allowed to keep. But without an external enforcement agency to police the deal, it won't hold together, because nothing prevents a family cheating on the deal by keeping more goats than they were assigned at the conclave.

But if the Tragedy of the Commons is repeated indefinitely often, the folk theorem says that the deal reached at the conclave can be sustained as a *self-policing* social contract. In equilibrium, no family will try to improve their lot by cheating on the deal today, because they see that other families will respond by nullifying today's gain in the future.

In later chapters, we shall find that the folk theorem improves on David Hume's insight that a social contract is like a masonry arch or a drystone wall by allowing us to examine the details of the equilibrium strategies that sustain it. We can thereby break with the tradition that takes concepts like authority, duty and trust as axiomatic when *explaining* social contracts, and see them rather as words that have evolved to *describe* different social contracts.

For example, it is fashionable nowadays to attribute our current social woes to a lack of the "social capital" our grandparents enjoyed. The implication is that the cure is to inject more social capital into the body politic. But looking around for more social capital is like sending a rookie out for a pint of elbow grease. Social capital isn't a *thing*—it's just a word we use when talking about the properties of an equilibrium that has evolved along with our game of life. Similarly, if we want to know why a citizen obeys an officer of the state, it isn't an explanation to say that the citizen respects the authority of the officer. One might as well say that the stones in a masonry arch stay where they are because they don't move.

Just as it is held to be wicked to say that cooperation is possible without people acting selflessly, so the idea that the folk theorem can explain the workings of supposedly difficult ideas like authority, duty, and trust is held to be naive. Let me therefore hasten to explain that nobody thinks that the ways these notions operate in any given social contract are simple. The detailed workings of real social contracts are complex beyond our capacity to imagine. But traditional moral pundits are too busy making easy things difficult to come anywhere near addressing these fundamental issues. They are right that it would be naive to think that the folk theorem teaches us more than one small secret about human sociality, but we shall find that only one small secret is needed to settle much of the dust that these same pundits kick around so furiously.

Evolution of cooperation. Darwin commented on our similarity to baboons. *II:3.3.8* More recently, chimpanzees have been recognized as closer cousins. Not only do we share nearly all our genes, but we also behave like chimpanzees in many respects. De Waal's *Good Natured* even offers convincing evidence that chimpanzees empathize with each other, putting themselves in the position of their fellows to see things from their point of view. The foundation stones for our sense of justice must therefore have been in place long before humans appeared on the scene.

Such relevations about chimpanzees and other primates have led some authors to insist that humanity is nothing more than another species of ape. This is a natural reaction to the popular Cartesian claim that we are somehow endowed with a divine spark that elevates us above mere automata like dogs and cats. But to adopt a perspective that minimizes the distinctions between us and other animals is to abandon any hope of explaining the gulf between the sharing of food that is common in chimpanzee societies and the extreme egalitarianism of some of the human hunter-gatherer bands that survived into modern times.

We are indeed naked apes, but it doesn't follow that the way to find out about human table manners is to watch baboons dining. Our brains are also pieces of biological machinery, but we won't learn French by listening to a vacuum cleaner. Like etiquette and language, justice is exclusively a human phenomenon. To understand it, we need to pay as much or more attention to what makes us different from other animals as to what makes us the same. I think that part of the answer lies in the unique ability of our species to use culture as a means of solving equilibrium selection problems.

Games commonly have many equilibria. For example, the Driving Game has three. The equilibrium in which everybody drives on the left and the equilibrium in which everybody drives in the right are both efficient. The equilibrium in which people decide on which side of the road to drive at random is inefficient, because everybody could get a higher payoff by driving on the same side of the road.

Such a multiplicity of equilibria in the game of life creates an equilibrium selection problem for evolution to solve if she is to get the players organized into a properly functioning society. In the Driving Game, for example, how is she to replace the inefficient social contract in which drivers randomize by an efficient social contract in which everyone drives on the same side of the road?

The folk theorem tells us that this problem of multiple equilibria was much worse in the repeated games played by our prehuman ancestors. Not only are all the efficient outcomes on which rational players might like to agree available as equilibrium outcomes, but so are large numbers of inefficient equilibria. Why should we expect evolution to succeed in selecting one of the efficient equilibria rather than one of the many inefficient alternatives?

The answer postulates competition among groups. Suppose that many identical small societies are operating one of two social contracts, a and b. If a makes each member of a society that operates it fitter than the corresponding member of a society that operates b, then here is an argument which says that a will eventually come to predominate.

To say that a citizen is fitter in this context means that the citizen has a larger number of children on average. Societies operating social contract a will therefore grow faster. Assuming societies cope with population growth by splitting off colonies which inherit the social contract of the parent society, we will then eventually observe large numbers of copies of societies operating social contract a compared with those operating contract b.

This retelling of the standard evolutionary story is unusual in two respects. The first is that selection takes place among groups. So why isn't it an example of the group selection fallacy?

The reason is that a social contract is identified with an *equilibrium* of the game of life played by each of the competing societies. But selection among equilibria doesn't require that individuals sacrifice anything for the public good, because every individual in every group is already optimizing his or her fitness by acting in accordance with the social contract of his society. The paradigm of the selfish gene is therefore maintained throughout.

The second unusual feature of the story is that the social contract of a parent society is transmitted to its colonies by *cultural* rather than genetic means.

This observation confuses critics of sociobiology, because they have convinced themselves that sociobiologists are "genetic determinists". An aside on the subject of coevolution is therefore necessary to press home the point that sociobiologists don't subscribe to the patently silly view that everything which matters about human beings is determined by their genes. Just like everyone else, they believe that culture matters.

Coevolution. What distinguishes us from other animals? The naive answer is that evolution somehow endowed us with bigger brains, which we use to create the arts and sciences that allow us to dominate the world. However, I think the sociobiologists are much more likely to be right when they deny the simplistic assumption that our big brains came first, and hence are entitled to a primary role in explaining the success of our species.

Although their critics accuse them of believing that nothing but biology is relevant to human behavior, the mainstream sociobiological position adopted in books like Laura Betzig's *Human Nature* or Boyd and Richerson's *Culture and the Evolutionary Process,* is that we are a product of both biological and cultural evolution operating in tandem. Edward Wilson went so far as to adopt the term *coevolution* to emphasize that what we learn from the culture in which we grow to maturity is as important to us as the instincts written into our genes.

As the various wild boy stories suggest, our big brains are useless to us unless we grow up in a culture that provides them with appropriate inputs at the correct development stage. Rather than simply substituting a big brain theory for Descartes' divine spark, the lesson is that we need to treat culture as an autonomous phenomenon in its own right.

How does our culture separate us from other animals? After all, chimpanzees and baboons are also social, and hence maintain a culture of sorts. Even songbirds learn what songs it is fashionable to sing by listening to their neighbors. Apart from our peculiar sexual behavior, the obvious answer is that we have a highly flexible language, whereas other animals are restricted to a limited menu of signals that relate only to events that are immediately at hand. But to understand the origins of human social contracts, I think we need to go back to a time *before* human signalling systems were recognizable as languages to ask what made human societies such a fertile ground for the growth of language. My guess is that coevolution had by then already made the large step that separates us from other apes.

Our species somehow learned to use culture as a form of collective unconscious or group mind within which to store the fruits of trial-and-error experimentation from the past, and to incorporate new discoveries made by individuals in the present. Such a cultural resource allows a group to react flexibly in the face of new challenges or opportunities, and hence creates a larger metaphorical cake for the group than would be possible if everybody only knew what they could find out by themselves.

A great deal of our culture is concerned with how we get along with each other; how we split the cake we have jointly created without wasteful conflict. It is this aspect of our social contract with which I am most concerned. Many anthropologists still maintain that only our cultural heritage is relevant to such questions, but it seems obvious to me that human biology must impose constraints on what social contracts can evolve, just as human biology imposes constraints on the deep structure of the languages that can evolve.

David Hume was making a similar point when he observed that the "natural laws" that govern our societies are actually artificial, but are called "natural" because everyone can see that it is natural to the human species that we should have such laws. Similarly, it is natural that a human society should have a language, but its actual language is an artifact of its cultural history. I think that the same is true of social contracts in general. It is natural that a human society should have a social contract, but its actual social contract is an artifact of its cultural history.

If we want to look for *universals* in the morals of the human species, we therefore have to look beneath the differing cultures of different societies. We must look at the deep structure of human social contracts written into our genes.

Traditionalists are virulently hostile to this suggestion, because they think that nothing is written in our genes but the savagery of nature, red in tooth and claw. I think they are right to the extent that the only social contracts available to us are equilibria in our game of life, but wrong in supposing that such equilibria must necessarily resemble Hobbes' state of nature—in which life is "solitary, poor, nasty, brutish and short". On the contrary, the folk theorem tells us that constraining our prehuman ancestors to social contracts that correspond to equilibria in their repeated game of life would have been no bar at all to the evolution of efficient cooperation in their societies.

1.6   Fairness

Stability tells us that social contracts need to be equilibria of the game of life. But most games have many equilibria, and so we face an equilibrium selection problem. Efficiency takes us some way toward solving this problem, but the folk theorem tells us that many efficient equilibria are available as possible social contracts. To operate successfully, a society needs to single out one of these on which to coordinate.

For example, in the Tragedy of the Commons, the efficient number of goats is 1,000. These can be divided up among the 100 families in many ways, each of which can be supported as an equilibrium outcome of the repeated version of the game. Since we know nothing about the special circumstances of the families in the story, one of these outcomes shrieks for special attention—that in which each family gets to keep 10 goats. Why? Because something tells us it is the *fair* outcome.

Why do we care about fairness? I think we care because fairness is evolution's solution to the equilibrium selection problem for our ancestral game of life.

What evidence is there for this conjecture? All the societies studied by anthropologists that survived into modern times with a pure hunter-gathering economy had similar social contracts with a similar deep structure. This applies across the world—to Kalahari bushmen, Greenland eskimos, Australian aborigines, and Brazilian indians. They tolerate no bosses, and they share on a very egalitarian basis.

I will have more to say about this fascinating fact, but right now I want only to emphasize that although this global behavior is presumably genetically determined, we are obviously not helpless victims of a genetic predisposition to live in utopian anarchies in which each contributes according to his abilities and receives according to his need. As the economic means of production of a society becomes more complex, its social contract must necessarily adapt if the potential gains from improved technology and the division of labor are to be efficiently exploited. But all the many adaptations that history records are almost certain to have a cultural origin, since the time spans are too short for a biological explanation to be plausible.

Anthropologists started gathering quantitative evidence about food sharing only when pure hunter-gathering societies were on their last legs. So we don't know how important culture was in determining precisely how much was thought to be fair for different people in different societies. But if the general assessment of the way that fairness norms work in modern societies offered in such books as Elster's *Local Justice* or Young's *Equity* is a reliable guide, then there is currently a great deal of cross-cultural variation. So it can't be that the fairness norms we use are determined entirely by our genes.

What counts as fair in different societies can vary as much the languages spoken. Just as different dialects may be used in different regions of a basically monoglot country, so different views of what counts as fair may operate in different societies, or in the same society at different places or times. Individuals of a particular society even operate different standards when interacting with different groups, or with the same group in a different context—just as schoolkids speak a teenage argot to each other, but communicate with their parents quite comprehensibly.

I have been arguing that what we count as fair depends both on our culture and on our genes. Since cultures vary, any *universal* principles of justice—its deep structure—must presumably be written into the genes that we all share as members of the same species. If I am right in guessing at the existence of such a deep structure, the next question asks itself. What shape does the deep structure of fairness take?

The original position. The thesis I defend in this book is that the common deep structure of human fairness norms is captured in a stylized form by an idea that John Rawls called the device of the *original position* in his celebrated *Theory of Justice.*

Rawls uses the original position as a hypothetical standpoint from which to make judgments about how a just society would be organized. Members of a society are asked to envisage the social contract to which they would agree *if* their current roles were concealed from them behind a "veil of ignorance". Behind this veil of ignorance, the distribution of advantage in the planned society would seem determined as though by a lottery. Devil take the hindmost then becomes an unattractive principle for those bargaining in the original position, since you yourself might end up with the lottery ticket that assigns you to the rear.

Rawls defends the device of the original position as an operationalization of Immanuel Kant's categorical imperative, but I think this is just window-dressing. The idea certainly hits the spot with most people when they hear it for the first time, but I don't believe this is because they have a natural bent for metaphysics. I think it is because they recognize a principle that matches up with the fairness norms that they actually use every day in solving the equilibrium selection problem in the myriads of small coordination games of which daily life largely consists.

It is important to emphasize that I am not following Rawls here in talking about the grand coordination problems faced by a nation state. Our sense of fairness didn't evolve for use on such a grand scale. Nor am I talking about the artificial and unrealistic principles of justice promoted by self-appointed moral pundits, to which people commonly offer only lip service. Nor am I talking about the kind of moral pathology that led Osama bin Laden to believe that thousands of innocent New Yorkers should die to compensate for the humiliations that he thought Islam had received at the hands of the West. I am talking about the real principles that we actually use in solving everyday coordination problems.

The sort of coordination problems I have in mind are those that we commonly solve without thought or discussion—usually so smoothly and effortlessly that we don't even notice that there is a coordination problem to be solved. Who goes through that door first? How long does Adam get to speak before it is Eve's turn? Who moves how much in a narrow corridor when a fat lady burdened with shopping passes a teenage boy with a ring through his nose? Who should take how much of a popular dish of which there isn't enough to go around? Who gives way to whom when cars are maneuvering in heavy traffic? Who gets that parking space? Whose turn is it to wash the dishes tonight? These are picayune problems, but if conflict arose every time they needed to be solved, our societies would fall apart.

Most people are surprised at the suggestion that there might be something problematic about how two people pass each other in the corridor. When interacting with people from our own culture, we commonly solve such coordination problems so effortlessly that we don't even think of them as problems. Our fairness program then runs well below the level of consciousness, like our internal routines for driving cars or tying shoelaces. As with Molière's Monsieur Jourdain, who was delighted to discover that he had been speaking prose all his life, we are moral in small-scale situations without knowing that we are moral.

Just as we only take note of a thumb when it is sore, we tend to notice moral rules only when attempts are made to apply them in situations for which they are ill-adapted. We are then in the same position as Konrad Lorenz when he observed a totally inexperienced baby jackdaw go through all the motions of taking a bath when placed on a marble-topped table. By triggering such instinctive behavior under pathological circumstances, Lorenz learned a great deal about what is instinctive and what is not when a bird takes a bath. But this vital information is gained only by avoiding the mistake of supposing that bath-taking behavior confers some evolutionary advantage on birds placed on marble-topped tables.

Similarly, one can learn a lot about the mechanics of moral algorithms by triggering them under pathological circumstances—but only if one doesn't make the mistake of supposing that the moral rules are adapted to the coordination problems they fail to solve. However, it is precisely from such sore-thumb situations that I think traditional moralists unconsciously distill their ethical principles. We discuss these and only these situations endlessly, because our failure to coordinate successfully brings them forcefully to our attention.

This isn't to say that we shouldn't talk about such games. On the contrary, it is partly because we need to extend the class of games that our social contract handles adequately that it is worth studying the problem at all. But we won't learn how natural morality works by confining our attention to situations where it doesn't.

I:1.2.6   **Egalitarian or utilitarian?**   In arguing that Rawls' original position is built into the deep structure of human fairness norms, I have two tasks. The first task is to offer a plausible account of the evolutionary pressures that might have resulted in such a mechanism being written into our genome. The second task is to explain how this biological mechanism interacts with our cultural heritage to generate a specific choice of equilibrium in some of the games of life we play.

The first task will have to sit on a back-burner until Chapter 9, but the second task needs more immediate attention, because the orthodox literature on the original position points in two directions that are commonly thought to be diametrically opposed. John Rawls argues that, after the basic rights and liberties of each citizen have been secured, using the device of the original position will lead to an egalitarian distribution of goods and services. John Harsanyi—who independently proposed the device of the original position around the same time as Rawls—argues that its use will lead to a utilitarian distribution.[3]

My naturalistic approach reconciles Harsanyi's and Rawls' conclusions to some extent, but the reconciliation is achieved at the expense of de-Kanting their ideas into a Humean bottle—an activity which both viewed with only cautious sympathy. However, adopting such a new perspective not only allows us to dispense with all metaphysical reasoning, it also allows us to relate the human capacity for empathy to our use of fairness as a coordinating device.

Empathy and interpersonal comparison. The original position might be said to be a do-as-you-would-be-done-by principle that takes account of the objection that you shouldn't do unto others as you would have them do unto you, because they may not have the same tastes as yours. For example, Adam may be a keen jogger who likes to be woken before dawn for a ten-mile run through the ice and snow, but Eve is unlikely to respond well if he shakes her awake before the sun has risen on the grounds that this is what he would like her to do for him.

The original position forces Adam to take account of Eve's tastes in such situations by requiring him to consider how it would be if he were to emerge from behind the hypothetical veil of ignorance occupying her role in life. He must therefore have the capacity to empathize with her by putting himself in her position to see things from her point of view. She must simultaneously be able to empathize with him by putting herself in his shoes to see things from his point of view.

John Harsanyi saw that to get a grip on what it means for two rational people to empathize with each other is to solve the long-standing puzzle of how interpersonal comparisons of utility can sensibly be made. He thereby created a simple theory in which Adam and Eve's welfare can be measured in a way that makes fairness comparisons possible. He sought to explain the standard of interpersonal comparison that arises in metaphysical terms, but I think that this standard is an artifact of the cultural history of a society.

This claim that our standards of interpersonal comparison of utility are culturally determined is the second pillar of my analogy between fairness and language. Elster's *Local Justice* and Young's *Equity* document how widely fairness norms can differ in different times and places, but the implicit assumption in describing the differing norms is that the standard of interpersonal comparison is unproblematic, and it is the basic structure of the norm that varies. My alternative explanation for at least

---

[3] Harsanyi attributes the idea to William Vickrey. The philosopher, Robert Hare, gives credit for his own version of the idea to C. I. Lewis.

some of the variation is that our biology guarantees that the deep structure is always the device of the original position, leaving differences in the observed norms to be explained largely by cultural or contextual variations in the standards of interpersonal comparison.

But how are we to incorporate such considerations into our analysis of how Adam and Eve will bargain in the original position? What relevance do they have for the debate between Harsanyi and Rawls? Should we expect everyday fairness norms to be egalitarian or utilitarian? Even a broad-brush account requires some knowledge of the economic theory of bargaining, but before moving on to this task in the next chapter, I want to summarize where we have got to so far.

1.7   Reform

The feature of my theory of fairness previewed in this chapter is the claim that all fairness norms in actual use share the deep structure of Rawls' original position. This deep structure is biologically determined, and hence universal in the human species, but the standards of interpersonal comparison that the original position needs as inputs are culturally determined, and hence vary with time and place.

The analogy with language is close. Like language, I think that our capacity to resolve coordination problems using fairness criteria is one of those few characteristics of our species that separates us from other animals. I know the speculation is bold, but I hope I have made the idea seem plausible enough that it seems worth pursuing its implications in the following chapters.

Karl Marx might respond that it is all very well seeking to understand society, but the point is to change it, and I don't disagree. I hope very much that the scientific study of how societies really work will eventually make the world a better place for our children's children to live in, by clarifying what kind of reforms are compatible with human nature, and which are doomed to fail because they aren't.

As an example, consider the pragmatic suggestion that we might seek to adapt the fairness norms that we use on a daily basis for settling small-scale coordinating problems to large-scale problems of social reform. This is one of the few things I have to say that traditional moralists find halfway acceptable. But they want to run with this idea without first thinking hard about the realities of the way that fairness norms are actually used in solving small-scale problems. In particular, they are unwilling to face up to the fact that fairness norms didn't evolve as a substitute for the exercise of power, but as a means of coordinating on one of the many ways of balancing power.

This refusal to engage with reality becomes manifest when traditionalists start telling everybody how they "ought" to make interpersonal comparisons when employing the device of the original position. But if I am right that the standards of interpersonal comparison we actually use as inputs when making small-scale fairness judgments are culturally determined, then these attitudes will necessarily reflect the underlying power structure of a society. One might wish, for whatever reason, that these attitudes were different. But the peddling of metaphysical arguments about what would be regarded as fair in some invented ideal world can only muddy the waters for practical reformers who actually have some hope of reaching peoples' hearts. Nobody is going to consent to a reform on fairness grounds if the resulting distribution of costs and benefits seems to them unfair according to established habit and custom, whatever may be preached from the pulpit.

It is true that facing up to such facts requires recognizing that it is sometimes pointless or counter-productive to urge reforms for which a society isn't ready. What would anyone have gained by urging the abolition of slavery in classical times, when even Aristotle thought that barbarians were natural slaves? What of the emancipation of women at a time when even the saintly Spinoza took time out to expound on their natural inferiority? Instead of tilting at such windmills, I think reformers need to make a hard-nosed assessment of the nature of the current social contract, and all the possible social contracts into which it might conceivably be transformed by pushing on whatever levers of power are currently available. Only when one has seriously thought through this feasibility question is there any point in asking what is optimal.

This pragmatic attitude mystifies traditional moralists, who pretend not to understand how a naturalist like myself can talk about optimality at all. How do I know what is best for society? What is my source of authority? Where are my equivalents of the burning bush and the tablets of stone?

The answer is that I have no source of moral authority at all—but I think everyone else is in precisely the same boat. I know perfectly well that my aspirations for what seems a better society are just accidents of my personal history and that of the culture in which I grew up. If my life had gone differently or if I had been brought up in another culture, I would have had different aspirations. But I nevertheless have the aspirations that I have—and so does everyone else.

The only difference between naturalists and traditionalists on this score is that naturalists don't try to force their aspirations on others by appealing to some invented source of absolute authority. We don't need a source of authority to wish that society were organized differently. If there are enough people with similar aspirations sufficiently close to the levers of power, they can get together and shift the social contract just because that is what they want to do—and for no other reason.

We naturalists think that this is what always happens anyway when reforms are consciously implemented, whatever the accompanying rhetoric may be. We would doubtless be more successful in recruiting others to our way of thinking if we too followed the traditional line of looking around for whatever line of rhetoric is currently most persuasive, but intellectual honesty is one of the artificial virtues that cultural history has somehow lodged in our heads.

How and why we got stuck with this inconvenient meme is a mystery that I am at a loss to explain, but we bear up under the handicap as best we can by making fun of the castles in the air built by our opponents. However, my attempt to join in the fun will have to wait until chapter 3, since the next item on the agenda is a whirlwind tour of bargaining theory.

Chapter 2

Bargaining

When I suggested twenty-five, a nicer-looking number than his thirty, he shook his grey head regretfully, and so we went on haggling, and he haggled better than me, so that eventually we settled on thirty-five.

P. G. Wodehouse, *Aunts Aren't Gentlemen*

2.1 Realistic Bargaining

II:1.1

This chapter continues the broad-brush survey of my theory of fairness begun in chapter 1 by looking at the bargaining questions that arise when discussing the original position.

When two people use fairness to resolve an everyday coordination problem, I believe they are implicitly calculating the agreement that they would reach if they were to bargain on the assumption that their identities would be reassigned at random after the negotiation was over. Although such hypothetical bargaining usually operates beneath our level of consciousness, we are sufficiently aware of what is going on that most of us feel a thrill of recognition when the mechanism is described to us for the first time in terms of John Rawls' original position.

I would like to see the original position used as Rawls envisaged to focus the reforming zeal of those among us who think our children's children would lead more satisfying lives in a fairer society. But I differ from most people with similar aspirations in believing that its potential for solving social problems will evaporate if we fail to use it for large-scale purposes in the same way that we currently use it when settling picayune fairness questions.

It is particularly important to be realistic about the bargaining we imagine taking place behind the veil of ignorance. If the hypothesized bargaining were outside the experience of the players using the device of the original position, how could they be using it at present—albeit only for such petty matters as deciding who should wash the dishes tonight?

Progress therefore depends on having access to a sound economic theory of bargaining. Not only must such a theory be realistic about the rules it postulates to govern how the bargainers negotiate, it must also put aside the temptation to attribute motives to bargainers in the original position beyond the urge to advance their own self-interest. Fairness criteria therefore have no place in the theory to be used in predicting how people would bargain in the original position. Aside from other considerations, there wouldn't be any point in proposing the original position as a final court of appeal on fairness questions if it couldn't itself be used without making fairness judgments. Nor would the use of nonstrategic bargaining fit the evolutionary origins for the original position that I shall be proposing in chapter 9.

This isn't to say that theories of fair bargaining are meaningless or devoid of interest. On the contrary, one of the objectives of this book is to defend a particular view of what constitutes a fair bargain. But such a view should emerge as one of the outputs of the theory rather than being subsumed among its inputs.

2.2 The Meeting Game

Thomas Schelling conducted some instructive experiments in the fifties on how people manage to solve coordination problems. In his best known experiment, the subjects were asked what two people should do if they had agreed to meet up in New York tomorrow without specifying a place and time in advance. The standard answer was that they should go to Grand Central Station at noon. In London, it would have been Piccadilly Circus.

When people commonly agree on how to resolve such coordination problems, Schelling says that the consensus they report constitutes a focal point. I think it significant that people seem to have little advance insight into what will turn out to be relevant in determining what counts as focal, but that they are nevertheless rather good at recognizing what other people will regard as focal in any particular coordination problem. This book is about the kind of focal points that people call fair. Fairness doesn't arise in Schelling's New York example because the protagonists don't care where they meet up as long as they meet up somewhere. However, in the Meeting Game that I plan to use as a numerical example when discussing bargaining issues, Adam and Eve have opposing views on where it would be best to meet.[1]

location	1	2	3	4	5	6	7	8	9	10
Adam's payoff	0	6	16	19	22	28	34	40	44	46
Eve's payoff	36	36	34	32	30	26	22	18	8	0

Table 1: Adam and Eve's payoffs at each location in the Meeting Game.

Each player independently chooses one of the locations in Table 1 at which to

---

[1] A politically incorrect version of the Meeting Game is traditionally called the Battle of the Sexes. Adam and Eve are a pair of honeymooners who failed to agree on whether to meet up at the ballet or a boxing match. Eve prefers the former and Adam the latter.

await the other. If they choose the same location, each receives the corresponding payoff, measured in the notional units of utility that economists call utils. If they choose different locations, Adam gets a small payoff of 4, and Eve a small payoff of 2. They therefore have a common interest on coordinating on the same location, but Adam prefers locations to the right, and Eve prefers locations to the left.

How should Adam and Eve resolve this archetypal coordination problem? Two locations can be ruled out immediately. Adam would rather not meet at all than meet at location 1. Eve would rather not meet at all than meet at location 10. However, each of the other eight locations is an efficient equilibrium of the Meeting Game, and so Adam and Eve are faced with the kind of equilibrium selection problem that I believe fairness evolved to solve.

How does fairness work in such situations? Numerous theories compete for attention, but the two leading contenders are the egalitarian and the utilitarian concepts of a fair outcome. I believe the literature is right to focus on these two alternatives, but which applies in what circumstances? I think we can decide this question in any particular case by appealing to the device of the original position. However, to predict the deal that Adam and Eve would reach if they were to bargain behind the veil of ignorance, we need a realistic theory of strategic bargaining.

What would be the result of applying such a theory of strategic bargaining *directly* in the Meeting Game? That is to say, if Adam and Eve were selfish players offered the opportunity to bargain face-to-face, on which location would it be rational for them to agree? The rest of this chapter compares the answer that game theory offers to this question with the result of applying various egalitarian and utilitarian fairness norms to the same problem.

2.3 Bargaining Problems

Figure 1 shows a general bargaining problem stripped down to its essentials. The shaded set X represents the set of all feasible agreements. The two coordinates of a point in X represent the payoffs that the two players will receive if they agree on this point. As in the Meeting Game, these payoffs are measured in notional units of utility called utils. The boundary of the feasible set X consists of all the efficient agreements that are available.

II:1.2

The point within the feasible set marked with the letter D represents the status quo—the outcome that will result if Adam and Eve fail to reach an agreement at all. The thickened part of the boundary shows all the efficient agreements that both players agree are at least as good as the disagreement point D. It is generally accepted that rational players will agree on one of these points, but we shall need to say more than this.[2]

If the disagreement point D is placed at the point $(4, 2)$, a bargaining problem can be regarded as a generalization of the Meeting Game in which inefficient points of the feasible set X are available as agreements as well as the efficient points on

---

[2]Economists refer to the claim that rational players will agree on an efficient outcome as the Coase theorem, although Edgeworth made the same proposal as far back as 1881.

the boundary of X that correspond to locations in the Meeting Game.

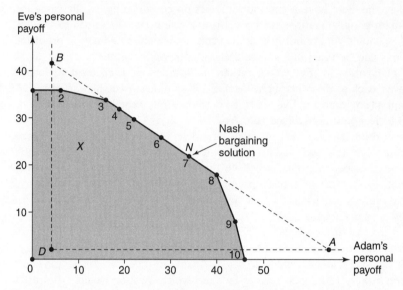

Figure 1: A bargaining problem that generalizes the Meeting Game, whose ten locations have been numbered. To find the Nash bargaining solution N, draw the tangent that touches the boundary of X halfway between A and B.

Social contracts. In this book, social contract questions are nearly always simplified by restricting attention to just two players, whom I romantically envisage as Adam and Eve after their expulsion from the Garden of Eden.

When offering a social contract interpretation of a bargaining problem, each point in the feasible set X is identified with the pair of utilities or payoffs that Adam and Eve will receive if they coordinate on one of the many equilibria in the repeated game of life that they must now face. The set X represents the set of all their feasible social contracts—all the stable forms of social and economic organization that are possible within the human game of life. The disagreement point D in a bargaining problem represents the inefficient social contract that Adam and Eve are assumed to be operating at present.

It is easy to lose sight of how much significant social activity is being packed away in a black box when all that is retained of the rich structure of a social contract is a pair of payoffs in the set X. In particular, the stability issues that commonly monopolize the attention of right-wing thinkers are abstracted away almost entirely—but they are not therefore to be forgotten.

Nobody denies that the wealth of a society depends on the freedom it offers to its entrepreneurs and the incentives it offers to its workers, but such considerations are built into the structure of an equilibrium in the game of life. We need to take them into account when determining what payoffs to assign each equilibrium when constructing the set X. In particular, social contracts that make proper use of markets will tend to generate higher payoffs than command economies. However, after the set X has been constructed, such issues will be visible only to the extent that they determine the size and shape of X.

Of course, after a social contract has been chosen from the feasible set X, it is necessary to unpack the black box so that everyone can be told what strategy they need to play in order that society can implement the agreed outcome. All the issues that right-wing thinkers suspect are being neglected when we are discussing what efficient outcome it would be fair to choose from X then come to the fore.

The state of nature. When talking about social contracts, it is traditional to refer to the disagreement point as the *state of nature*, but my state of nature doesn't at all resemble Thomas Hobbes' "war of all against all". Nor is it related to John Locke's pastoral idyll, in which everybody enjoys natural rights, according to which: "No one ought to harm another in his life, health, liberty or possessions", and property rights are acquired by mixing one's labor with a good, provided that there be "enough and as good left in common for others". These seem to me to be mere fictions, invented to generate conclusions that favor a particular prejudice.[3]

I:1.2.1

Nor do I see much point in following the utilitarians in pretending that a new Jerusalem can be established without paying any attention to the current social contract at all. You may recall the old Irish joke of the peasant who explained that if he were going to Dublin, he wouldn't start from here. He is right that we would perhaps do better if we were able to start from somewhere else, or from nowhere at all. But here is where we are at. Like it or not, we are what history has made of us.

2.4 The Nash Bargaining Solution

II:1.3.1

How are bargaining problems solved when two parties negotiate face-to-face, bringing to bear whatever bargaining power they may have at their disposal? In such strategic bargaining, fairness has only a rhetorical function. For example, Jon Elster counted 24 different fairness norms proposed in Swedish wage negotiations. Instead of crude demands for this hourly rate or that, the bargainers could then discuss whose "fairness norm" would apply!

Game theory has made substantial advances in analyzing strategic bargaining among rational players when the characteristics of the players and the nature of the bargaining problem are common knowledge. I therefore always stick with this case, although it is sometimes less than realistic. The reason is that a number of different lines of enquiry then converge on identifying the *Nash bargaining solution* as the

---

[3]Hobbes was seeking to legitimize the monarchy after the chaos of the English Civil War. Locke was similarly conjuring up an argument that would legitimize the morality of the new commercial classes that was replacing the medieval Christian tradition in his time.

rational agreement when the players have equal bargaining power.[4]

The Nash who first proposed the Nash bargaining solution is the same as the Nash who formulated the concept of a Nash equilibrium, but it will be obvious that the two ideas are very different. There are few takers for this point of view, but I think Nash deserves his Nobel prize more for his bargaining solution than for his equilibrium concept, since his contribution to bargaining theory is entirely original, whereas his equilibrium idea had a number of precursors.

Locating the Nash bargaining solution in numerical examples is simple. It occurs where the product of the players' gains over their disagreement payoffs is largest. The Nash bargaining solution in the Meeting Game is therefore location 7, because the product of gains there is $(34 - 4) \times (22 - 2) = 600$, which exceeds the product of gains at any other location.[5] Its nearest rivals are locations 6 and 8, where the product of gains are $(28 - 4) \times (26 - 2) = 576$ and $(40 - 4) \times (18 - 2) = 576$.

Geometrically minded folk may prefer to note that the Nash bargaining solution lies at the point marked with the letter N in figure 1. This point is halfway between the points A and B on the tangent to the boundary of X at N.

Why the Nash bargaining solution?   The Nash bargaining solution is game theory's best shot at predicting the agreement that will be reached when two rational players with equal bargaining power negotiate face-to-face without any appeals to fairness being made. It has rivals, like the version of the Kalai-Smorodinsky bargaining solution reinvented by David Gauthier in his *Morals by Agreement*, but none of these rivals allow the same defense in depth as the Nash bargaining solution. However, this isn't a book on strategic bargaining, and so I only give the most naive of the arguments that can be offered in its support.

The point N is halfway between A and B in figure 1. If the bargainers have equal bargaining power, N is therefore the natural candidate for the outcome of a rational negotiation when the feasible set is everything under the straight line through A and B. Now throw away outcomes from this notional feasible set until we get the feasible set with which we started. These discarded alternatives are "irrelevant", since the bargainers chose to reject them in favor of N when they were available. The agreed outcome should therefore continue to be N after they are thrown away, because "nothing that matters" in the negotiation has changed.

Nash supplemented this argument by looking at a specific bargaining model in which the two players make simultaneous take-it-or-leave-it demands (Section 4.7). Such bargaining games always have many equilibria, but a natural resolution of the equilibrium selection problem yields the Nash bargaining solution. Ariel Rubinstein studied the more realistic case in which the players alternate in making demands until someone gives in. A natural resolution of the equilibrium selection problem again yields the Nash bargaining solution, provided that the time interval between

---

[4]I focus on the case of equal bargaining power because the available bargaining strategies behind the veil of ignorance are the same for both players.

[5]It remains largest if we allow Adam and Eve to toss a coin or cut cards to settle any disputes, but I don't plan to worry much about the use of random devices as instruments of compromise in this chapter.

successive demands is sufficiently small.

These and other arguments supporting the Nash bargaining solution are strong but not entirely overwhelming. What would happen if some sensible alternative were substituted for the Nash bargaining solution in my theory? The details of the theory would then become more complicated, but I think it unlikely that there would be substantive qualitative changes in the conclusions.

Why not bargain directly? The Nash bargaining solution has been introduced to help predict the outcome of bargaining in the original position. But why not use it to solve Adam and Eve's bargaining problem directly? There are two reasons.

The first reason is that fairness evolved for use in situations in which face-to-face bargaining isn't an alternative option. My guess is that it probably predates language. After all, we had to have some way of coordinating with each other to create the conditions under which true language could evolve. Nowadays, we mostly use fairness norms in everyday situations in which it is either impossible to negotiate, or in which the benefits of negotiating are outweighed by the costs in time or money.

The second reason is that the Nash bargaining solution has no fairness content whatsoever. This becomes obvious when one notes that the outcome it generates doesn't depend at all on the scales we use to measure Adam and Eve's utilities. For example, if we double Adam's utils so that each new util is worth half an old util, the new Nash bargaining solution simply doubles the number of utils that Adam gets. Thus, in the Meeting Game, the Nash bargaining solution selects location 7 both before and after we double all of Adam's payoffs (including his disagreement payoff). It similarly selects location 7 both before and after we add 3 to all of Eve's payoffs. How could matters be otherwise in strategic bargaining? Players can't alter their bargaining power by changing the scale they choose to measure their utility, any more than a physicist can change how warm a room is by switching from degrees Celsius to degrees Fahrenheit.

2.5   Interpersonal Comparison of Utility

The Nash bargaining solution doesn't even begin to qualify as a fairness norm, *I:4.3*
because a minimal requirement for a fairness criterion is that it somehow compares Adam and Eve's welfare.

Economics textbooks commonly say that such interpersonal comparisons of utility are impossible. Taken literally, this is just a piece of dogma without any theoretical justification, but the textbooks are right to the extent that one can't just assume that Adam's utils can be traded against Eve's at some commonly understood rate, in the manner almost universal among those philosophers who address the issue at all. I therefore think it important to register that I follow John Harsanyi in basing a theory of interpersonal comparison of utility on the ability of human beings to empathize with each other.

Empathetic identification. If Adam and Eve are autistic or unable to empathize successfully with each other for other reasons, then the device of the original position won't work for them. When our attempts to use fairness norms in everyday games go awry, as they do every now and then, I think it is largely because of such failures in empathetic identification. But, in attempting to make a first stab at explaining how fairness norms work, I follow Harsanyi in looking at the idealized case in which Adam is totally successful in his attempts at empathizing with Eve.

It may be that Adam is modest, and so would prefer a fig leaf to an apple if forced to choose between them. But if Eve is a brazen hussy who would choose the apple in the same situation, then our idealized Adam will accept that *if he were Eve*, then he would take the apple too. With this assumption, Harsanyi gave a simple argument which implies that people in the original position will bargain as though they think that Adam's utils can be traded against Eve's utils at some fixed rate.

Culture. I don't suppose anyone but the most diehard of neoclassical economists denies that we actually do have standards for making interpersonal comparisons of utility, and that these are widely shared within a particular society. However, people don't commonly ask *why* evolution should have equipped our brains with the unconscious capacity to make the complicated calculations necessary to determine who is worth how much in this or that situation.

It is easy to guess that the origins of the capacity lie in the need for members of an extended family to recognize how closely they are related to each other. But why do we need to make interpersonal comparisons of utility outside the family? One reason is that such comparisons are necessary as inputs to the device of the original position. It is a strong claim, but I think this is the *only* reason that evolution provided us with the capacity to compare our welfare with the rest of humankind.

But why should everyone in a particular context employ the *same* standard of interpersonal comparison, as Harsanyi and Rawls assume? I think that we must look at the cultural history of a society for the answer. That is to say, the standards of interpersonal comparison that are current in a society are determined by social or cultural evolution, with the result that any differences in the standards being operated tend to be ironed out in the long run (chapter 8).

As noted in the previous chapter, the second pillar of my analogy between fairness and language is therefore the claim that standards of interpersonal comparison of utility are *culturally* determined. This is why what counts as fair differs in different places or times or contexts. Just as Japanese is different from French, so the fairness norms of modern New York operate differently from those of classical Athens. For example, women count for a great deal more in the New York of today than they did in Athens, but suckers no longer get an even break.

2.6 Social Indices

When making fairness judgments using the device of the original position, Adam and Eve don't actually negotiate at all. They coordinate on the deal on which they *would* agree if they *were* to bargain behind the veil of ignorance. But what would this deal be? Harsanyi and Rawls independently asked this question, but came up with very different answers. Harsanyi argues that the final outcome will be utilitarian. Rawls argues that it will be egalitarian.

For the utilitarian and the egalitarian bargaining solutions to be meaningful, we need to be given a *social index* for each player. I hope this term is sufficiently neutral that it won't trigger any preconceptions about whether having a high or a low social index is necessarily 'good' or 'bad'. Just as you like the price to be small when you are buying and large when you are selling, so the significance of a high or a low social index depends crucially on the context.

We need social indices because nothing says that the personal payoffs used in specifying a bargaining problem can be compared directly in a way that is meaningful for a fairness calculation. For example, if the payoffs in the Meeting Game were given in dollars, nobody would want to say that Adam is better off than Eve at location 10 after learning that he is a billionaire and she is a beggar.

We therefore rescale each player's personal payoffs by dividing them by the player's social index. The result of this rescaling or *weighting* can be thought of as society's assessment of the worth of each possible outcome of the bargaining problem to the player in question. More precisely, to say that Adam's social index is three and Eve's is two is to proceed as though three of Adam's personal utils are worth the same as two of Eve's.

Such a social judgment will reflect a kaleidoscope of factors determined by the historical context in which a coordination game like the Meeting Game has been played in the past. Is Adam rich or poor? Is Eve fat or thin? Is Adam an illegal immigrant? Does Eve have a ring through her nose? Are they man and wife? Are they brother and sister?

The list of possible cultural and contextual factors is obviously endless, but both the utilitarian and egalitarian bargaining solutions cut through all the complexity by insisting that only their effect on Adam and Eve's social indices matters. In fact, only their effect on the ratio of their social indices is significant, since we will get the same answer by taking their social indices to be 100 and 50 as from taking them to be 2 and 1.

2.7 The Utilitarian Bargaining Solution

A utilitarian assesses the worth of any outcome by adding up the weighted payoffs obtained by dividing Adam and Eve's personal payoffs for that outcome by their social indices. The utilitarian bargaining solution is therefore the outcome at which the sum of the weighted payoffs is largest.

II:1.3.3

Numerical examples. It may be helpful to work out the utilitarian solution in the Meeting Game for different pairs of social indices.

If Adam's social index is twice Eve's—so that two of his personal utils are deemed to be worth one of hers—then the utilitarian bargaining solution selects location 3 in the Meeting Game. Taking his social index to be 2 and hers to be 1, the sum of the weighted payoffs at location 3 is

$$\frac{16}{2} + \frac{34}{1} = 42\,,$$

which is larger than the corresponding sum at any other location. The nearest rival is location 4, where the weighted utilitarian sum is

$$\frac{19}{2} + \frac{32}{1} = 41\tfrac{1}{2}\,.$$

If Eve's social index were twice as large as Adam's—so that two of her personal utils are deemed to be worth the same as one of his—the utilitarian bargaining solution would select location 8 instead. At this location, the utilitarian sum with the new weighting is

$$\frac{40}{1} + \frac{18}{2} = 49\,,$$

which is larger than the corresponding sum at any other location. The nearest rival is location 9, where the weighted utilitarian sum is

$$\frac{44}{1} + \frac{8}{2} = 48\,.$$

Notes. We can obviously make the utilitarian outcome anything we like in the Meeting Game by choosing the social indices appropriately. It therefore doesn't make any sense to talk about the utilitarian outcome without first specifying what social indices are to be used. In particular, there is nothing special about the case when Adam and Eve have equal social indices. To suppose otherwise would be to take for granted that we have already scaled Adam and Eve's payoffs up or down to make them properly comparable.

Just as we aren't entitled to assume that we can compare Adam and Eve's raw payoffs, so we can't simply assume that we can compare the utilitarian sums obtained using different weightings. For example, it would be absurd to say that we could make a society that assigned Adam and Eve the same social index worse off by halving Eve's social index. In fact, both societies will end up at location 8.

Finally, there may be multiple locations at which a utilitarian sum is maximized. For example, when Adam's social index is three and Eve's is two, the corresponding utilitarian sum is maximized at all the locations between 3 and 8 inclusive. Location 7 is then both a utilitarian bargaining solution and the Nash bargaining solution.

Geometry. I find the geometry of figure 2 easier than such numerical examples. It features a line of slope $-\tfrac{1}{2}$ (which means that a point on the line moves down one unit for each two units that it moves across). All points on such a line have the same weighted utilitarian sum when Adam's social index is twice Eve's. Utililitarian sums that correspond to lines that don't cut the set X are infeasible. The utilitarian bargaining solution is therefore located at a point U where a line with slope $-\tfrac{1}{2}$ just touches the boundary of X.

If Adam's social index were three and Eve's were two, then the utilitarian outcomes would occur at the numerous points where a line of slope $-\tfrac{2}{3}$ touches the boundary of X.

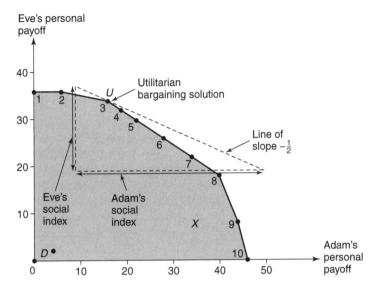

Figure 2: The utilitarian bargaining solution U when Adam's social index is twice Eve's. No point with a larger weighted utilitarian sum than U is feasible, because lines corresponding to larger sums don't have a point in common with the feasible set X. The social indices shown can be scaled up or down without altering anything.

2.8   The Egalitarian Bargaining Solution

Each player's personal payoffs are first rescaled by dividing them by the player's social index. The kind of egalitarian with whom we are concerned then assesses an outcome by comparing the gain over the status quo it confers on each player in terms of these weighted payoffs. The egalitarian bargaining solution is the efficient outcome at which each player's weighted gain is equal.[6]

II:1.3.3

In the Meeting Game, Adam's personal payoff at the status quo is 4 and Eve's is 2. When Adam's social index is the same as Eve's, the egalitarian bargaining solution therefore selects location 6, since this is where

$$\frac{28-4}{1} = \frac{26-2}{1}.$$

If Eve's social index is twice Adam's, then the egalitarian bargaining solution will select location 4, because

$$\frac{19-4}{1} = \frac{32-2}{2}.$$

---

[6]Rawls' difference principle reduces to this egalitarian outcome when the players' personal payoffs at the status quo are taken to be zero. Rawls only advocates an appeal to his difference principle after the players' basic rights and liberties have been secured.

If Adam has social index three and Eve has social index two, the egalitarian bargaining solution coincides with the Nash bargaining solution at location 7, because

$$\frac{34 - 4}{3} = \frac{22 - 2}{2} \, .$$

If we make Adam's social index twice as large as Eve's, there is no location at which the weighted gains are exactly equal. The best Adam and Eve can do is to randomize between locations 7 and 8. If the day of the week on which they are meeting is randomly chosen, it might perhaps be conventional for them to go to location 7 at weekends and location 8 on weekdays.[7]

The geometry is illustrated in figure 3. The egalitarian bargaining solution for the case when Adam's social index is twice Eve's is labeled with the letter E. It lies where the line of slope $\frac{1}{2}$ through the disagreement point D cuts the boundary of the set X.

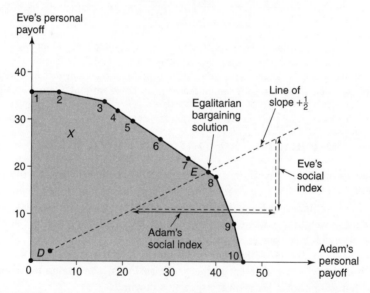

Figure 3: The egalitarian bargaining solution E when Adam's social index is twice Eve's. The social indices shown can be scaled up or down without altering anything.

2.9   Utilitarianism versus Egalitarianism

II:4.6.9   What distinguishes utilitarians and egalitarians? Two differences in their positions are especially worth noting.

---

[7]Meeting at location 7 with probability 2/7 makes their weighted gains equal on average.

Utilitarians ignore the current status quo D. They think that where we are now and how we got there is irrelevant to where we should go next. Egalitarians care about history, since the location of the status quo D matters a great deal to who gets how much at the egalitarian bargaining solution. To this extent, egalitarians therefore side with Edmund Burke, and utilitarians with Thomas Paine in their great debate over the French Revolution.

The second difference relates to their understanding of the significance of a social index. Decreasing a player's social index *increases* his or her contribution to a weighted utilitarian sum. A utilitarian therefore favors giving more help to citizens with a lower social index. Decreasing a player's social index *decreases* the utility he or she will be awarded by the egalitarian bargaining solution. An egalitarian therefore favors giving more help to citizens with a high social index.

Utilitarians and egalitarians therefore have diametrically opposed views on the significance of a social index. Utilitarians think folk with lower social indices deserve a larger share of the pie. Egalitarians think that those with higher social indices deserve a larger reward.

2.10 Enforcement

Who is right about the outcome of rational bargaining in the original position: Harsanyi or Rawls?

Both Harsanyi and Rawls postulate an enforcement agency that somehow compels Adam and Eve to honor the hypothetical deal they would have made if they had bargained in the original position. Rawls invents an agency called "natural duty". Harsanyi proposes a similar agency called "moral commitment". I reject such fictions. I think that the only plausible candidate for an effective enforcement agency consists of human beings other than Adam and Eve, who will punish them if they don't play fair. However, if there were an enforcement agency of the type postulated by Harsanyi and Rawls, game theory endorses Harsanyi's claim that Adam and Eve would agree on a utilitarian social contract behind the veil of ignorance.

I:4.6

It isn't very remarkable that game theorists should agree with John Harsanyi, since he shared the Nobel prize for game theory in 1992 along with John Nash and Reinhard Selten, but we don't agree out of a misplaced loyalty to our own kind, but because this is where the logic leads. The implication is that if Rawls had analyzed the bargaining problem in the original position correctly, he would have been led to the same utilitarian conclusion as Harsanyi.

Game theorists think that Rawls' error is easy to detect. He claims that ordinary decision theory doesn't apply in the case of the original position, and proposes instead the use of the maximin criterion that Von Neumann showed is optimal in two-person, zero-sum games. It is then no great surprise that the fairness norm Rawls comes up with should require applying the maximin criterion. But why should we treat a bargaining game like that played behind the veil of ignorance as though it were a game of pure conflict?

Since Rawls explicitly wrote his *Theory of Justice* to provide a well thought-out alternative to the utilitarianism that was riding high at the time, this may seem a devastating criticism, but Rawls' moral intuition was better than his game theory. He wrote at length on the "strains of commitment" that would be involved in sustaining a social contract that isn't an equilibrium in the game of life.

So what happens if we abandon the assumption that some real or fictional agency is available to enforce the hypothetical agreements made in the original position? Perhaps Adam and Eve are the whole of society. Or perhaps nobody else notices or cares whether they play fair with each other—as must have been the case when our sense of fairness was evolving. Since there is then nobody else to do any policing, any conventions that Adam and Eve adopt must therefore police themselves.

As we shall see in chapter 11, imposing such a self-policing requirement reverses our previous conclusions. Harsanyi's utilitarian social contract can no longer be sustained as the appropriate bargaining outcome, and we end up with something much nearer to Rawls' egalitarian social contract instead. Lest it be thought that something deep is involved in this reversal, let me hasten to add that little more is involved than observing that one can't settle issues by tossing a coin when nothing prevents the loser from repudiating his or her agreement to abide by its fall.

2.11   Cultural Evolution

II:2.7   Attributing the standard of interpersonal comparison embedded in a fairness norm to the cultural history of a society makes it possible to discuss why one sees different standards operating at different times and places. In chapter 8, I make a crude first attempt at this task by arguing that we should expect cultural evolution to mould the empathetic preferences of the citizens of a society until the system reaches what I call an empathy equilibrium.

Both in the case when we assume an external enforcement agency and when we don't, it turns out that Adam and Eve's social indices will then evolve until the effect of their appealing to the original position is simply to implement the Nash bargaining solution.

A certain kind of critic needs no further excuse to reject the theory, root and branch. After all, what else would you expect from an economist than the conclusion that all talk of fairness is merely a cosmetic veneer concealing the application of naked power? However, such critics aren't entitled to leap to such a conclusion.

They are right to the extent that it would be true that the action of cultural evolution would eventually erode all moral content from a fairness norm if each norm were specific to a particular coordination game. But we never play exactly the same coordination game twice. Each norm is therefore used to solve the equilibrium selection problem in a whole class of games. Moreover, the class of games develops over time at a rate that can sometimes be too fast for cultural evolution to keep pace. The relevance of this timing issue is discussed at length in chapters 10 and 11, but I shall simply offer a numerical example at this point to illustrate why the fact that each norm is used in a variety of games can be significant.

Meeting many times.   The easiest way of exploring the consequences of applying the same fairness norm to many coordination problems at once is to consider what would happen if Adam and Eve often had to play the Meeting Game—but with different disagreement payoffs each time. Since the location of the disagreement point is irrelevant to a utilitarian fairness norm, I shall take for granted that we are talking about the more interesting case of an egalitarian fairness norm.

To make things easy, suppose that Adam and Eve's *average* disagreement payoffs are 4 and 2. However, each time they play the Meeting Game, their actual disagreement payoffs are chosen independently by chance so that they will sometimes be quite distant from their average values.

Whenever they play the Meeting Game, the choice of disagreement payoffs made by chance today is assumed to be common knowledge, but the social indices which characterize their fairness norm are taken to be the same no matter what the disagreement payoffs turn out to be. Although this is not quite so obvious as it sounds, cultural evolution will then eventually shape Adam and Eve's social indices so as to make the egalitarian bargaining solution of their *average* bargaining problem coincide with the Nash bargaining solution of the average problem.

We already know what these adapted social indices will turn out to be, because the average bargaining problem was carefully chosen to be the version of the Meeting Game introduced at the beginning of the chapter. The Nash bargaining solution happens to coincide with the egalitarian bargaining solution in this game when Adam's social index is three and Eve's is two. If nothing left out of the model intervenes, we must therefore expect that cultural evolution will eventually lead to three of Adam's personal utils being regarded as equivalent to two of Eve's.

What happens if Adam and Eve now play the Meeting Game when the disagreement payoffs are 32 and 0? The egalitarian bargaining solution with social indices three and two then selects location 9, since

$$\frac{44 - 32}{3} = \frac{8 - 0}{2}.$$

But location 9 is definitely not the Nash bargaining solution of Adam and Eve's current problem, because its Nash product is only $(44 - 32) \times (8 - 0) = 96$, whereas the Nash product at location 8 is $(40 - 32) \times (18 - 0) = 144$.

It follows that Adam and Eve don't resolve their coordination problem when the disagreement payoffs are 32 and 0 as they would if they were able to bring their bargaining power to bear. Their use of an egalitarian fairness norm results in Eve doing substantially worse than at the Nash bargaining solution.

Context. The coordination problem that arises when two people are trying to meet up is a useful example with which to introduce bargaining solutions because of the innocence of its context. Our culture hasn't equipped us with such strong feelings about what is fair in such situations that we aren't willing to consider other possibilities. But our ability to take a detached view begins to erode if we look at other possible interpretations of what is strategically the same coordination problem.

Suppose, for example, that Adam and Eve have fallen out after running a flower shop together for a number of years. What is the fair way to divide the assets of the business?

It may be that when the problem is formulated as an abstract bargaining problem, it turns out to have exactly the same payoff table as the Meeting Game, but nobody would think it appropriate to pontificate on what is fair without finding out a lot more information than is reflected in the payoffs. Who invested how much when the business was set up? How many hours did each partner work per day? Who has children to support? Who brought what skills to the enterprise? Who attended the rotary luncheons? Who made unwelcome advances to the customers?

Such questions are asked because we know that the *context* in which a coordination problem arises somehow determines the social indices our culture tells us to use when deciding what is fair. Most of us have little or no idea of precisely how our cultural programming allows us to translate a set of contextual parameters into appropriate social indices, because the process operates beneath the conscious level, but we can hope to investigate the question scientifically.

I make a crude beginning on the problem in chapter 11 by investigating how need, effort, ability, and social status might affect Adam and Eve's social indices after cultural evolution has had the opportunity to adjust their values to a particular context. However, the final court of appeal is the psychology laboratory.

2.12   Signifying Nothing?

The common practice in philosophy is to treat the problem of interpersonal comparison of utility as an uninteresting sideshow. I want to close this chapter with an illustration of why such an attitude is a bad mistake.

It is easy to check that when Adam and Eve's social indices are chosen to make any two of the three bargaining solutions mentioned in this chapter coincide, then all three bargaining solutions coincide. In the Meeting Game, this happens when Adam's social index is three and Eve's is two.

If we restrict our attention to our unique game of life, the workings of social evolution are therefore likely to lead both utilitarians and egalitarians to end up assigning the *same* social indices to Adam and Eve—and advocating precisely the *same* reforms. Indeed, although Harsanyi and Rawls were philosophical rivals, I found that they expressed strikingly similar views when conversing on matters of practical politics.

The moral is that there are situations in which all the sound and fury of the traditional dispute between utilitarians and egalitarians can be just so much hot air, because both sides are simply saying the same thing in different ways. Their fundamental differences would become apparent if they were to envisage a change in the current standard of interpersonal comparison, but such an act of imagination isn't possible if you think that the standard is somehow irrevocably determined by metaphysical considerations.

Chapter 3

Battle of the Isms

Instead of ethics, they have generally written satire.

Benedict de Spinoza

3.1   Kicking up Dust

In all fields of inquiry, much of the activity consists of people kicking up dust and then complaining that they can't see very far. In philosophy, the confusion is often sustained at a high level by turning the meaning of words upside down. Here, for example, is Immanuel Kant: "Man therefore needs a master who can break man's will and compel him to obey a general will under which every man could be free."

Such Humpty-Dumpty reasoning is to be found under almost any stone you turn over in standard moral philosophy books. Scientists are understandably reluctant to engage with such gibberish, but are nevertheless prone to fall victim to its products. For example, several biologists have explained to me that the "naturalistic fallacy" prevents their extending their thoughts to moral questions. But how many are aware that the naturalistic fallacy was actually formulated by David Hume—the champion of a scientific approach to morality—to demonstrate that the Oughts of the antiscientific schools of philosophy are conjured from nowhere?

I therefore think it necessary to devote this chapter to a battle of the isms, in which I hope to persuade others to join me in proudly wearing some of the labels that antiscientific philosophers pin on us with derogatory intent. But one label I am not ready to have pinned on me is that of an enemy of philosophy. David Hume is only one of many scientific philosophers for whom I have the greatest admiration. It is only bad philosophy from which I think we need to shrug ourselves free.

3.2   Empiricism

Philosophers love to attach labels to their various schools of thought, but the meaning they attach to these labels can seldom be deduced from what dictionaries say.

In seeking to categorize the scientific approach to morality advocated in this book, the first labeling question is whether it should be called *rationalist* or *empiricist*.

Most moral philosophers are rationalists. This doesn't mean they think other philosophers are irrational. It means they believe it possible to find out things about the world without the need to collect any data. In particular, they believe that we can decide what people ought to do by playing around with words, or consulting our gut feelings. Immanuel Kant is the most famous of the rationalists. As such, he is commonly held to be the greatest philosopher of all time. However, if the approach taken in this book is even halfway right, it is necessary to face up to the fact that he gets pretty much everything upside down and back to front.

I:2.4.1 **The categorical imperative.** Kant distinguishes between hypothetical and categorical imperatives. A hypothetical imperative tells you what you ought to do to achieve some objective. For example, "Eat your spinach if you want to grow up big and strong." A categorical imperative is an "ought" without an "if." It tells you what you ought to do independently of what your personal objectives may be.

Kant claimed that a truly rational individual will necessarily observe one particular categorical imperative: "Act only on the maxim that you would at the same time will to be a universal law." My mother had similar views. When I was naughty, she would say, "Suppose everybody behaved like that?" Even to a child, the flaws in this line of reasoning are obvious. It is true that things would be unpleasant if *everybody* were naughty, but I'm not everybody—I'm just myself.

Kant isn't very keen on giving practical advice, but it seems that always telling the truth is an example of a maxim to which one is led by applying his categorical imperative. To emphasize his belief that rationality demands *always* telling the truth regardless of the consequences, he insists that one shouldn't even lie to a homicidal axman asking for the whereabouts of your neighbor. It is supposedly *irrational* to lie because, if everybody were to lie all the time, then lying would cease to be a meaningful activity. But it simply isn't true that Kant's categorical imperative implies that I should therefore *always* tell the truth. As any schoolboy can see, all we can legitimately deduce is that people must *sometimes* tell the truth.

If Kant's logic is bad when applying his categorical imperative, it is worse when he seeks to justify the categorical imperative itself. He starts with the obviously false claim that each human capacity is ideally suited to its purpose, and then asks for the purpose of our capacity to reason. According to Kant, its purpose can't be to advance our welfare or happiness, because such material aims would be better served by eliminating our reasoning powers altogether in favor of a system of reflexes designed to respond optimally to each possible stimulus.

Our capacity for reason must therefore exist for some other purpose. But what could this purpose be? Kant's answer is that its "true function must be to produce a will which is good, not as a means to some further end, but in itself". Why its purpose should be this, and not one of the infinite number of other possibilities is left unexplained. Nor are we offered any hint as to why having a good will entails honoring Kant's categorical imperative, and not some other categorical imperative that you or I might dream up.

The scientific tradition. Fortunately, there is a long and venerable philosophical tradition within which such Alice-in-Wonderland reasoning has no place. This scientific tradition begins with presocratic philosophers like Antiphon and Xenophanes, and embraces Aristotle and Epicurus on its way to Thomas Hobbes and such luminaries of the Scottish Enlightenment as David Hume and Adam Smith.

Through Adam Smith and Thomas Malthus, it exerted a direct influence on Charles Darwin's formulation of the theory of natural selection. Bertrand Russell and Karl Popper famously carried the standard of scientific philosophy forward into modern times, but perhaps the most thoughtful recent works by moral philosophers working in this tradition are John Mackie's *Inventing Right and Wrong*, Peter Singer's *Expanding Circle*, and Brian Skyrms' *Evolution of the Social Contract*.

I refer to the tradition of scientific philosophy that insists on looking at the data before reaching any conclusions as *empiricism*. Its great spokesman is David Hume. He has no time for the kind of wordplay for which Kant is celebrated. If a book tries to convince us of something, Hume suggests that we ask ourselves two questions. Does it say something about the logical consequences of the way we define words or symbols? Does it say something that has been learned from actually observing the way the world works? If not, we are to commit it to the flames, for it can contain nothing but sophistry and illusion.

As for categorical imperatives and the like, Hume tells us that reason is merely the "slave of the passions". Only hypothetical imperatives can therefore make any sense. In brief, it isn't enough to announce that we have a duty to do this or that; it needs to be explained why we should pay any attention when told to do our duty. As Hume put it: "What theory of morals can ever serve any useful purpose, unless it can show that all the duties it recommends are also the true interest of each individual?"

In this quotation, Hume isn't advocating a morality of blind selfishness. He is making the practical point that it is a waste of time contemplating reforms that won't work. Considerthe case of lying. Everybody would prefer to live in a society in which people tell the truth most of the time, but how could such a society be created from one in which lying is endemic? Insofar as Kant's ideas are relevant to such practical questions, he would presumably favor going round explaining to anyone who will listen that it is irrational not to honor his categorical imperative. But such a utopian strategy won't work, because it ignores the realities of human nature. A charismatic preacher might temporarily succeed in persuading people to trust each other's word without reserve, but backsliding would commence more or less immediately as deviants saw the advantages to be gained by betraying the trust of their fellows.

One might object that we do teach our children to tell the truth, and the consequence is that people don't actually lie to each other very much. But this objection neglects the fact that the rules of our current social contract make our reputation for being trustworthy very valuable to us. If it becomes known that you have betrayed the trust of a partner in some serious way, who will trust you enough to take you as a partner in the future?

When we teach our children not to lie, we are therefore teaching them something that will accord with their own self-interest most of the time. Of couse, as they grow up, they learn to modify the rule they were taught as children, and start to lie more freely when they aren't likely to be found out, or when the people they let down are too unimportant for their opinions to matter. Lying therefore survives in our society, and doubtless always will.

Ring of Gyges?   The idea that utopia is beyond our reach comes very hard to some people, but I am by no means the first to suggest that such utopian do-gooders represent a far greater threat to the stability of our social contracts than those of us who try to be realistic about human nature.

Rationalists who use magical reasoning to convince themselves that the impossible is possible make the same mistake as Santayana's Lucifer when he rebelled against God's decision to create only the best of all *possible* worlds. But if we follow Lucifer in over-reaching ourselves by trying to implement reforms that won't work, then we are condemning ourselves to live in whatever hell evolves after our new social contract has broken down. Empiricists like Hume therefore think it wiser to begin by using the scientific method to determine what reforms are feasible before worrying about what is optimal.

The chief stumbling block in gaining acceptance for this view is that it requires being realistic about power. People find it more comfortable to think of justice as a substitute for power than as means of balancing power. However, there are good reasons why we personify Justice as a blindfolded maiden bearing a pair of scales and a sword. In my theory, her blindfold is the veil of ignorance. Her scales are used to weigh Adam and Eve's worth. Her sword is necessary because, as Thomas Hobbes observed, "Covenants without the sword are but words."

Such talk of power is shocking to the modern ear. Overlooking the fact that the Socrates of Plato's *Republic* ends up advocating a stifling authoritarian state in which all power is invested in the philosopher-king and his guardians, traditional philosophers tend to assume that anyone who thinks that power matters agrees with Thrasymachus that justice is simply what the powerful are able to get away with. The mythical Gyges, with his magic ring of invisibility, is the classical icon of such an unprincipled exercise of power.

However, although it would be foolish to deny Thrasymachus his point that power corrupts, my hero in the *Republic* isn't Thrasymachus, but Plato's brother, Glaucon—who gets short shrift from Socrates for putting a view close to the social contract ideas defended in this book. I think that a modern Glaucon would be agreeing with me that fairness norms evolved to select one of the many ways to *balance* power in a group.

But we have moved on so little since classical times that the immediate reaction is still to detect a paradox. What have jackboots and the iron fist to do with justice and fair play? However, a Thrasymachian free-for-all is only one of many ways in which power can be exercised. For our purposes, the most significant examples are the hunter-gatherer bands that have survived into modern times. Anthropological reports from all over the world show that these bands often operate remarkably similar social contracts, in which food is shared broadly according to need, and no bosses are allowed to emerge.

The fact that modern hunter-gatherers can get by without bosses is liable to provoke commentary of the noble savage variety. The idea that the natural state of man is a pastoral idyll in which all is sweetness and light is certainly attractive, but one needs to start thinking more complex thoughts once it is revealed that our noble savages often murder each other at an alarming rate. So why doesn't a mighty hunter establish a tyranny? It isn't because hunter-gatherers don't want to dominate their fellows, or because their mothers are better at persuading them not to do things that would be bad if everyone did them. As individuals, hunter-gatherers are no different from the rest of us. They differ only in operating a social contract that holds the power of any individual in check by bringing to bear the power of the group *as a whole* whenever someone shows signs of getting bossy. At first the bossy character is mocked. If he persists, he is ostracized. In extreme cases, he may be expelled from the group altogether—in which case he will be lucky to survive at all. As a consequence, mighty hunters are careful not to throw their weight around too much.

In trying to understand fairness, we therefore can't afford to throw the works of writers like Nietzsche or von Clausewitz out of the window.[1] Their macho posturing is unpleasant, but it nevertheless serves a useful end. It reminds us to look beneath the civilities of ordinary life to the realpolitik that lies below. We aren't usually conscious of using our social skills to keep the scales of power in balance, but this is what we are doing when we play our part in sustaining an equilibrium in the game of life. Denying this fact would be like failing to take account of the traffic when crossing the road on the grounds that you have lived all your life so far without being run over.

In brief, lovers of freedom can't afford to take their eyes off the power ball. If we relax our vigilance, we will do no better than the French revolutionaries of 1789 who thought they were abolishing slavery in their Declaration of the Rights of Man, but merely paved the way for the reintroduction of slavery under the military dictatorship of Napoleon Bonaparte that succeeded their unstable regime.

Asymmetries of power. Power is built into the rules of the game of life, which say who can do what, and when they can do it. Since the rules of a game determine what outcomes can be sustained as equilibria, it follows that power is reflected in the size and shape of the set X of feasible social contracts.

Inequities in power therefore translate into asymmetries in the set X of feasible social contracts. For example, if Gyges were a player in our game of life, his possession of the ring of invisibility would shift the set X so as to include outcomes more favorable to him than if he were just like everyone else.

Two caveats are important here, especially after Hobbes, Nietzsche, and von Clausewitz have been mentioned. The first is that the kind of power exercised by a

---

[1]Which doesn't mean that I agree with Nietzsche when he says that justice is merely "good will operating among men of roughly equal power". If I thought this were true, I would be advocating the direct use of the Nash bargaining solution. Nor do I agree with von Clausewitz when he describes war as the "continuation of diplomacy by other means". In a bargaining problem, the outbreak of a war would be modeled as a disagreement!

capitalist or a king won't be reflected in the shape of X. The right to hold property or to command obedience aren't properties of individual players, but of the social contract that a society operates. They are relevant to the extent that they figure in the current social contract D, but we needn't preserve such powers when we make a new choice from the set X of all possible social contracts. Even the ring of Gyges would be of little use to its current owner if he were unable to prevent its being confiscated by the combined strength of his neighbors. As we have seen, the same applies to the strength of body enjoyed by mighty hunters in foraging societies.

The second caveat is that it isn't so much the strength of some individuals that creates important asymmetries in the set X, but the weakness of others. After all, to a blind person, what are the rest of us if not embodiments of Gyges? And much the same goes for the old and the sick, or the very young—especially those who have yet to be born or conceived.

Rawls referred to such handicaps as "inequalities of birth or natural endowment" requiring redress in a just society. Critics who insist on pretending that power doesn't matter to justice may care to reflect that if X were taken to be symmetric, we would have no way of identifying those whom Rawls thought deserving of compensation.

3.3   Naturalism

If you favor a scientific approach to morality, you are not only an empiricist; you are also a naturalist, a relativist, and a reductionist. All of these epithets will be directed at you with derogatory intent, because it is assumed that accepting one of these labels commits you to believing all sorts of nonsense that philosophers have invented over the years. If you refuse to be labeled, then you are said not to have a position at all.

For example, if you aren't a rationalist, you don't have much choice but to acquiesce in being called an empiricist, since this label at least captures the idea that you favor the empirical methods of science. However, philosophers are liable to interpret your acceptance of the label as meaning that you believe in the demonstratively false *tabula rasa* theory commonly attributed to John Locke, according to which we are born with minds that are blank slates on which only experience can write. As a consequence, biologists sometimes refer to the fact that some of our knowledge comes prepackaged in our genes as Kantian epistemology—although it was actually David Hume who first pointed out that we aren't always able to justify how we think about the world, but nevertheless have no choice but to think as we are programmed to think.

Juggling with words.   In biology, a naturalist is someone who gathers facts about living creatures, and tries to organize them into a framework that avoids speculative hypotheses about supernatural ormetaphysical entities. When I call myself a naturalist, my use of the term differs from this biological usage only to the extent that I focus on the moral behavior of the particular living creatures called human beings.

In moral philosophy, a naturalist is someone quite different. He is a philosopher who tries to find naturalistic definitions for the words people use when talking about morality. For example, G. E. Moore held that the Good is a transcendental concept that we all intuitively perceive, but which is incapable of being defined in naturalistic terms. To maintain otherwise is to fall to prey to a fallacy—the naturalistic fallacy.

In defense of this view, Moore argues that no naturalistic definition of the Good can ever be adequate, because one can always ask of any complex of natural phenomena said to embody the Good whether it is indeed Good. As with Kant, it is difficult to get to grips with the fact that such arguments are taken seriously. If I am told that the man in the blackraincoat is Smith, am I to deduce that he can't really be Smith because I have doubts about whether he has been correctly identified?

A quite different argument that is more commonly said to be the naturalistic fallacy derives from my hero, David Hume. With the intention of discrediting rationalists by pointing out that they conjure their categorical imperatives from nowhere, he observed that philosophers always cheat when they pretend to deduce an *ought* from an *is*. But modern rationalists have turned the tables on him by claiming that his dictum shows that moral naturalism is untenable, because categorical imperatives have to be derived from somewhere!

However, naturalists think that only *hypothetical* imperatives make any sense, and there is no difficulty about deducing an *ought* of this kind from an appropriate *is*. For example, it is now half past three, and so you ought to leave now if you want to catch your train.

Kant played the same trick with the definition of ought when he deduced that we have a transcendental variety of free will from the dictum: *ought* implies *can*. It is true that I wouldn't tell you that you ought to leave now if you want to catch your train unless I thought that you would indeed catch your train by leaving now. The ought-implies-can principle therefore works fine for hypothetical imperatives, but Kant applies it to *categorical* imperatives. He then deduces the existence of a supernatural unmoved mover in our heads, who can somehow suspend the laws of physics when necessary, from the fact that philosophers say that there are things we ought to do regardless of the circumstances!

The rationalist idea that one can find out things about the world by juggling with words is curiously persistent. So firm a grip does it have on the minds of some philosophers that it usually doesn't even occur to them that the data relevant to a naturalist might be something more than the things people *say* when talking about moral phenomena.

But what if the same approach had been taken to physics? Instead of following Torricelli in experimenting with a mercury barometer, teams of philosophers would still be at work analyzing the law which says that Nature abhors a vacuum. Who is Nature, and why does she so dislike empty spaces? Did she fall into a hole in her youth? How does she eliminate vacua? Is she omnipotent as well as ubiquitous?

Notice that the mistake doesn't lie in the fact that predictions based on the principle that Nature abhors a vacuum are normally wrong. The mistake is to assume that the *explanation* built into the words we use when expressing the law is correct. Philosophers make a similar mistake when they devote their attention to analyzing the meaning of the sentences we use when discussing moral questions.

This isn't to say that such sentences don't often embody good advice, but there is no particular reason why the explanation builtinto the language used in expressing the advice should be the real reason that the advice is good.

Skyhooks.   One reason why rationalists try to define moral naturalists out of existence is because we refuse to recognize the sources of authority to which they lay claim.   Jeremy Bentham had their measure when he called them ipsedixists: preachers who dress up their own prejudices as categorical imperatives for the rest of us to follow.

When asked why their vision of a satisfactory society should prevail, ipsedixists invent supernatural or metaphysical entities to trump the cards played by their rivals. Daniel Dennett aptly characterizes their sources of authority as *skyhooks* that they invent to hold aloft their philosophical castles in the air.

Gods were once popular as skyhooks, but history has exposed this particular fraud by showing that each culture somehow ends up with whatever divine ordinances happen to support the social contract currently being operated. Beliefs about the will of God therefore vary in both space and time. In England, where many babies are now born out of wedlock, the Archbishop of York recently reassured us that even living in sin is no longer sinful!

Naturalists want to see some evidence before believing that those who preach in the name of God know anything more about the wishes of a supreme being than the rest of us. Everybody laughs at the authority claimed by the witch doctors of darkest Africa who once worshiped the great god Mumbo-Jumbo, but only our childhood conditioning prevents our seeing that the traditions on which our own priests of Jehovah rely have no firmer foundation. As with the shabby political compromise at the Council of Nicaea that established the incoherent doctrine of the Trinity, we can sometimes even document how the Church came to pass off a newly invented skyhook as the Word of God.

If ipsedixists always wore their collars back to front, they would be easy to recognize. But in the guise of philosophers or political scientists, they are usually less crude than their priestly brethren when inventing sources from which their authority supposedly flows. Instead of Mumbo-Jumbo being personified as a god, he is reified as some abstract Platonic form. We are told that we must adopt the prejudices of famous philosophers like Kant, Moore, or Rousseau because of the demands of Practical Reason, Moral Intuition, or the General Will. A metaphysical Nature, unrelated to the natural world of plants and animals, is sometimes wheeled on to provide a justification for our having Natural Rights, and being subject to Natural Law.

In seeking an appropriate supernatural successor to the gods of old, many people favor one of the innumerable varieties of an absolute Good or Right that have been invented to capture the one-and-only universal moral truth. However, the race is by no means over, and new runners are being proposed all the time. A popular new contender is an idealized notion of Community, to which appeal is made by right-wingers who need a magic spell to counter the social collapse that would follow if the myopic selfishness they otherwise advocate were actually consistent with human nature. The parallel between their new god and the fallen gods of the Marxist pantheon is striking, but seems to escape their attention altogether.

The ancient Greeks used to introduce actors playing gods onto the stage using some kind of machine. The demon king of British pantomime similarly pops up through a trapdoor in a puff of smoke. Naturalists think the supernatural entities of the rationalists are introduced onto the philosophical stage by similar means. In other words, the whole enterprise is a gigantic confidence trick, which survives only because it is customary to supend disbelief during the performance in order not to spoil the fun. But if morality is to be investigated seriously, it is necessary to put away these childish fancies.

Blank slates? The only viable alternative to the essentially supernatural explanations of human morality offered by rationalists is the theory of evolution. Such an appeal to evolution is frequently taken to be the obviously false claim that only biology matters—that we are merely creatures of instinct—but it is clear that *social* evolution has been at least as important as biological evolution in shaping us as social animals.

The most telling example is the evolution of language, as documented in Stephen Pinker's magnificent *The Language Instinct*. Everybody knows of Chomsky's discovery that all human languages share a common deep structure. Evolutionary psychologists explain this fact by postulating an innate capacity for language that is carried in our genes. This isn't to argue that Frenchmen carry genes for speaking French, or that an American baby adopted by Japanese parents would find it any harder to learn Japanese than the natural children of his adoptive parents. Just as our immune system isn't just a stockpile of specific antibodies, but a piece of biological hardware that enables our bodies to create antibodies as and when required, so the language instinct is a hardwired learning device that makes it relatively easy for toddlers to learn languages structured according to certain innate principles. But this mental hardware is very far from tying down all the details of a language. On the contrary, French and Japanese are such different languages because our genes leave a great deal to be determined by social evolution.

The idea that we are born with deep structures hardwired into our brains is greeted with knee-jerk hostility by those social scientists who have been brainwashed with the idea that a baby's mind is a blank slate upon which experience can write anything whatever. Part of the reason for this insistence on this *tabula rasa* theory is that it can then be argued that we are all born equal. As Edward Wilson observes, "This country is so seized by our civic religion, egalitarianism, that it just averts its gaze from anything that would seem to detract from the central ethic we have that everybody is equal."

I am so far from sharing Wilson's skepticism about egalitarianism, that I am writing this book in an attempt to show that egalitarian social contracts of the kind practiced in the early years of the American republic are better suited to what evolution has made of the human species than the authoritarian alternatives with which most societies have been saddled in the past. However, I am at one with Wilson when he attacks those idealists who are so enamored with equality that they deny the brute facts of biology. They do us no favor when they peddle utopias that are incompatible with human nature, and hence are doomed to fail. They simply obstruct the path of realists who advocate workable reforms.

Nor can they be genuine in their professed belief that we are so different from other animals that we are born without instinctive behavioral traits. Does anybody really deny that the human sexual drive is innate? Or the panic reflex? Or the disgust we feel when offered tainted food?

The robotic character of our behavior when in the grip of such strong emotions as love, disgust, fear, or anger is surely too transparent for serious doubt to arise on such questions. It is less obvious that our capacity to empathize with our fellow human beings has an instinctive basis, but the evidence on chimpanzees and brain-damaged humans offered in books like de Waal's *Good Natured* and Damasio's *Descartes' Error* seems overwhelming. The autistic heroine of Sachs' *An Anthropologist on Mars* even offers an inside view on how it feels to be born without instinctive access to the social tools that the rest of us take entirely for granted.

As far as I know, nobody at all subscribes to the theory that social evolution isn't at least as important in shaping human social contracts as biological evolution. That is to say, genetic determinism has no takers at all. Social scientists therefore needn't fear being left high and dry when asked to modify the traditional *tabula rasa* theory. Nature has made our species flexible in the face of changing circumstances by endowing us with the ability to learn from our own experience, and the experience of other members—past and present—of the society in which we grow to maturity.

Although our genes preempt much of the space on our mental slates, we are nevertheless born with large blank spaces for experience to fill. It follows that the hostility from some sociologists and anthropologists to the intrusion of biology into their domain is misplaced. It is true that their training sometimes leads biologists to underestimate the size of the blank spaces on our slates when comparing us with chimpanzees or baboons, but this is an error open to correction. Far from preempting the traditional role of social science, evolutionary biology heralds a potential renaissance in which we no longer vainly seek to explain how social evolution created the deep structures written into our genes, but redirect our efforts to explaining how it contrives to fill the part of our slates left blank at birth.

No preaching.   Social scientists may have reason to rejoice as moral naturalism invades their fields, but the same isn't true of traditional philosophers. For them, it is bad news that questions they thought lay in their domain are actually scientific; but worse is to come. Whether something is held to be right or wrong in a given society at a given time is a matter of objective fact, but different societies don't always have the same standards of right and wrong.

For example, Herodotus tells us of two parties of Greeks and Indians who were summoned to the court of Darius in an early anthropological experiment. The Greeks were horrified to learn that the Indians ate their dead fathers. The Indians were no less horrified to learn that the Greeks burned theirs!

The customs of the Greeks seem more civilized to me. After all, my parents were cremated rather than eaten. Nor am I at all enthusiastic about consuming human flesh. If asked my opinion, I would therefore say that I prefer the Greek custom to the Indian custom. I might go on to comment on the recent discovery that certain societies in New Guinea which held it to be polite to eat a little of the brains of deceased relatives contrived to keep certain diseases alive that would otherwise have died out. But if I were to insist that my personal preferences for cremation deserved privileged treatment on ethical grounds for this or any other reason, then I would have fallen into the ipsedixist error. To say that one custom is better or worse than another makes sense only in relation to a specific social contract. Naturalists are therefore *moral relativists* who think it meaningless to use the language of ethics when comparing different social contracts, without first specifying the culture whose standards are to be adopted.

This returns us to the bitter pill that evolutionary ethics forces us to swallow. It undercuts the authority claimed by utopians who feel they have a mission to convert the world. It can offer a culture-free assessment of the kinds of social contract that are feasible for a human society, but it denies the existence of some privileged culture-free way of choosing an optimum point from this feasible set.

Moral naturalists can tell their fellow human beings about the sort of society in which they would like to bring up their children. They can seek to infect others with the enthusiasm they feel for their personal vision of the good life. They can urge others to join them in reforming society in order to realize those aspirations that are sufficiently widely shared. What naturalists cannot honestly do is to claim that their knowledge of evolutionary science converts their personal preferences over social contracts into a privileged set of social or moral values that somehow trumps the personal preferences of others.

3.4 Relativism

Long ago, Xenophanes made an empirical observation which says everything that needs to be said about the supposedly universal nature of the various supernatural entities that have been invented down the ages: "The gods of the Ethiopians are black and flat-nosed, and the gods of the Thracians are red-haired and blue-eyed."

But in spite of its ancient provenance and the intellectual distinction of the great philosophers who have recognized its validity, moral relativism remains the big turn-off for most modern philosophers. They are therefore particularly creative when inventing absurdities to which moral relativists must supposedly subscribe. I consider five calumnies, of which three can be disposed of in short order.

Circularity?   Relativism is sometimes held to be vulnerable to a piece of sophistry used by Socrates in demolishing Euthyphro. According to relativists, people think an action is right or good because this is generally held to be the case in their society. But how does one tell that a view is generally held? By observing that this is what most people think!

I wonder whether the philosophers who think that such circularities are necessarily fatal realize that their argument entails rejecting all the sciences that depend on the notion of an equilibrium. The concept of a Nash equilibrium in game theory would be the first idea that would have to go, because the circularity on which it is based lies immediately on the surface. Why did Adam do that? Because Eve did this. Why did Eve do this? Because Adam did that.

Postmodernism?   Moral relativists believe that moral facts are true because they are generally held to be true within a particular culture. Postmodernists claim to believe that the same holds for *all* facts. A postmodernist must therefore be a moral relativist, but nothing says that a moral relativist must be a postmodernist. For example, I am as premodern as it is possible to be, but I am nevertheless a moral relativist.

John Stuart Mill accused David Hume of being condemned to play a Tory tune because his skepticism supposedly made it impossible for him to place any reliance in reason as an instrument for planning reform. Postmodernists are ready to apply the same argument to any attempt to argue scientifically about the world, but they miss their target for the same reason that Mill missed his. Hume was indeed skeptical about our reasons for being confident that we know how to reason correctly, but that didn't stop him giving reasons why society should be reformed—usually in a Whiggish direction.

We need to respond to the extreme skepticism of postmodernists in the same pragmatic style. Perhaps there are indeed no genuine absolutes, but the theorems of mathematics and the laws of physics and biology will serve as acceptable substitutes when we are talking about human morality. In particular, I believe that the genetic differences between historical human beings are sufficiently slight that it makes sense to think of human nature as an absolute when comparing different cultures.

Inconsistency?   Moral relativists are said to be inconsistent in asserting the moral absolute that there aren't any moral absolutes. But why would should it be thought that denying the existence of moral absolutes is a *moral* assertion? Nobody would say it was magical to deny the existence of magic.

In any case, I don't claim to know for sure that there aren't any moral absolutes. I simply think it irrational to believe in something for which no evidence exists. My denial of the existence of culture-free moral judgments therefore has no grander status than a denial that there are fairies at the bottom of the garden.

Anything goes?   The next calumny confuses a moral relativist with a moral subjectivist—someone who thinks that morality is just a matter of personal taste. The confusion in conflating the words *relative* and *subjective* is compounded by a similar conflation of their opposites, *absolute* and *objective*. Even John Mackie tells us that there is no objective morality, when I think he means that there is no absolute morality.

Relativists are said to maintain the wishy-washy liberal doctrine that all social contracts are equally good. It is then a short step to various emotive slanders. For example, I have been accused of holding that pedophiles are justified in disregarding the law when pursuing their claim that prepubic sex is good for children. Similarly, relativists supposedly see nothing wrong in keeping slaves or wife-beating, since both activities have been endorsed as morally sound by past societies. Even more absurdly, relativists are charged with believing that it makes no sense to teach children the difference between right and wrong.

But relativists don't maintain that all social contractsare equally good. We deny that *any* culture-free comparison across social contracts is meaningful—including the assessment that they should all be ranked at the same level. There are biological universals, but the concepts of good or right that figure in moral disputes are always *cultural* artifacts. If we could somehow free ourselves of all cultural influences, we would be as helpless when asked to make moral judgments as a Kalarahi bushman asked to to adjudicate a game of chess.

Even in the unlikely event that a culture were to appear in which all social contracts were held to be equally good, there is no reason whatever why its citizens would be moral subjectivists. For example, most cultures wouldn't value two societies differently just because they drove on different sides of the road. But someone who says that it doesn't matter on which side of the road a society drives isn't saying that we should all be free to consult our individual fancy in deciding whether to drive on the left or the right when setting out each morning. It doesn't matter whether the Japanese all drive on the left or whether they all drive on the right, but it obviously matters a great deal that everybody in Japan drives on the *same* side of the road.

As the driving example illustrates, moral subjectivism is absurd because it overlooks the fact that moral rules evolved to help human beings *coordinate* their behavior. But successful coordination depends on everybody operating the *same* moral rules. If everybody in a society made up their own standards, there wouldn't be any point in having moral rules at all. Individuals who talk of having moral values that transcend those of their society are simply dramatizing the fact that they would prefer to live under a different social contract. As Bertrand Russell says of Nietzsche: "His doctrine might be stated more simply and honestly in the sentence, 'I wish I had lived in the Athens of Pericles or the Florence of the Medicis'."

Far from being subjectivists, moral relativists argue that the moral values of a society are *objective* features of its culture. As with all important scientific facts, children can usefully be taught that different cultures have different standards of right and wrong. But this is far from saying that children should not simultaneously be taught the importance of observing the standards of right and wrong that hold *in their own society*. On the contrary, the facts of history suggest that a society falls apart when its citizens so lose faith in its social contract that children cease to be given clear guidance on how it works.

Affirming that there have been societies in which it wasn't considered wrong to keep slaves or beat your wife doesn't entail teaching children the lie that is legitimate to treat other human beings like property in a modern democracy. It is a matter of historical record that the moral absolutists of Plato's circle thought that making love to underage boys was entirely admirable. Presumably they thought it always would be. But moral relativists insist that it is also an objective fact that pedophilia is no longer acceptable in any of today's societies—and that we therefore have a duty to punish those who abuse children whenever we can catch them.

All change is bad?   Karl Marx famously said that philosophers have tried to understand society, but the point is to change it. As usual, he got things back to front. Philosophers have traditionally been so busy inventing reasons why their plans for changing society should triumph that they have devoted little or no attention to understanding how real social contracts actually hold together. Indeed, so ingrained is this attitude, that most traditionalists simply cannot get their minds around the idea that moral relativism is about understanding societies rather than changing them. Their inability to grasp that there could be an approach to morality that denies its adherents any authority to preach in its name is made manifest in the reasons they invent to discredit what they see as a rival tribe of ipsedixists.

When relativists aren't thought to hold that anything goes, it is said that our creed requires resisting any reform that is currently unpopular. For example, I have been told that my relativist views would have forced me to oppose liberalizing the laws on homosexuality. The misconception is that one can only advocate a reform because it is Good or Right, and relativists are supposedly stuck with identifying the Good or the Right with whatever society currently holds to be good or right.

However, those of us who follow the strait and narrow path of naturalism never advocate a reform because it conforms to some abstract conception of the Good or the Right. When traditionalists invoke the Sanctity of Life or the like as a reason for inflicting suffering on babies who have yet to be conceived, the temptation to fight fire with fire by inventing some rival Mumbo-Jumbo like Humanism or Gaia or Science is admittedly sometimes very strong. Adam Smith, for example, contradicts the basic naturalism of his *Moral Sentiments* when he appeals to an invented Impartial Spectator. Peter Singer's otherwise admirable *How Are We to Live?* similarly goes astray when he invents the Viewpoint of the Universe in urging his ultragreen views upon us. Such rhetorical expedients may well be more persuasive than the plain truth, but to tread this primrose path is to abandon all pretension at trying to create a *science* of morals.

The truth is that moral preachers are just expressing their personal opinions about how they would like the current social contract to change. This is no less true of the pundits who claim privileged access to the wisdom of the ages than of a drunk sounding off in a neighborhood bar. It is because relativists recognize this truth that it is possible to get away with misrepresenting us as subjectivists. However, to affirm that people are expressing their subjective views when advocating a reform isn't the same thing as being a moral subjectivist.

A real-life instance of the driving example may help. Sweden switched from driving on the left to driving on the right on September 1st, 1967. If I had been a Swede before this decision was made, I would have lent my voice to those advocating the change. Since relativists hold that it was wrong to drive on the right in Sweden before September 1st, 1967, and wrong to drive on the left afterwards, the words *bad* or *wrong* would have been useless to me when urging reform. It might have helped the cause to argue that driving on the left is intrinsically Bad or Wrong, but it would be intellectually dishonest for a relativist to take this line. Still less would I have argued that Swedish citizens should be left to make their own subjective judgments when choosing on which side of the road to drive. I would simply have argued that enough Swedes would benefitfrom driving on the same side of the road as the rest of continental Europe to make it worthwhile for us all joining together to get the reform adopted.

To capture the analogy with a gene in biological evolution, Richard Dawkins suggests using the word *meme* when speaking of a practice or idea that may take over a population through imitation or education. It is in some such manner that relativists believe that social evolution contrives to change a culture over time. Most frequently, cultures change without any individual consciously aiding and abetting the change, or even being aware that a change is in the air. But a culture can sometimes be changed as a consequence of an individual deliberately injecting a well-engineered meme into the system at a pivotal moment.

Far from being trapped like a fly in amber by the concepts of right and wrong that we have inherited from the past, relativists revel in this knowledge. Perhaps you or I might be the lucky individual whose newly minted meme eventually colonizes sufficiently many minds that our society's perception of what counts as right or wrong is changed.

However, relativists don't make the mistake of thinking that our ideas for reform *are* Good or Right because we would like them to *become* good or right. Nor do we make the absolutist mistake of imagining that our own minds are somehow immune to the cultural process by means of which memes propogate through a society.

Feet of clay?   There is good deal of innocent fun to be had in observing the antics of absolutists when one can locate the time at which one of their eternal verities was invented. For example, no classical author ever mentions Natural Rights or Free Will. Along with Romantic Love, these memes appeared in medieval times. More topically, I learned in today's newspaper that the definition of a saint is to be brought up to date. One can only hope that the special place in Heaven preserved for those canonized by the Catholic Church is adequate to cope with the increased immigration rate!

I particularly enjoyed a recent conversation with a modern Sir Roger de Coverley, who earnestly assured me that the convenience of having British clocks show the same time as French and German clocks counts as nothing against the iniquity of abandoning the one true time. Nothing I could say came anywhere near shaking his apparent belief that God drew the Prime Meridian through the former Royal Observatory in Greenwich at the same time that He fashioned the globe.

But there is also a serious lesson for relativists in the fact that absolutists see gold when they look at their all-too-obvious feet of clay. We must be careful to see only what is really there when looking at our own feet. Our preferences over social contracts are no less shaped by our culture than those of our absolutist critics. We too have feet of clay that will be washed away by the river of time.

If I had been brought up in classical Greece, I would no doubt have joined Aristotle in regarding the enslavement of barbarians as entirely right and proper.[2] In Chaucer's

---

[2] The art of war is in some sense a natural mode of acquisition. Hunting is part of that art: and hunting ought to be practised, not only against wild animals, but also against those human beings who are intended by nature to be ruled by others and refuse to obey. War of this kind is naturally just—Aristotle's *Politics*.

time, I would have classified clinical depression as the sin of *accidie*. Lending money at interest would have struck me as being little different from selling my body in a brothel. In Victorian times, I might easily have been a homophobe. Perhaps I would have disowned my daughter if she gave birth to an illegitimate child, although I find this particular possibility hard to envisage. However, history shows that human beings are capable of finding justifications for far more inhumane behavior than this. The torturers of the Spanish Inquisition thought they were saving their victims' souls. The ordinary housewives of Hitler's Germany who turned to savagery when recruited as concentration camp guards thought that they were purifying the human race.

Future societies will doubtless look back on the morality of contemporary social contracts with a similar mixture of horror and incredulity.   My guess is that a particularly bad press eventually awaits those who believe that life is always an unmitigated good, and hence must be inflicted even on those whose suffering is so great that they beg for an easy death. Those who sabotage birth control initiatives for similar reasons have even less prospect of being remembered kindly.

The idea that each human life is infinitely valuable will surely seem absurdly quaint in a world in which the Malthusian nightmare has become a reality. Our descendants will ask how western societies could sustain such a bizarre notion while simultaneously accepting the need to ration health care at home, and refusing to pay more than a tiny fraction of their domestic product to alleviate starvation abroad.

However, I wouldn't care to put my money on much else when predicting the shape of future social contracts. Who would have guessed that the British would turn into a race of sex-crazed football hooligans? History not only tells us that the past is another country—it also tells us that the future is always unimaginably foreign to those who live in the past.

Summary.   Moral absolutists believe that relativists make a damaging admission when they acknowledge their feet of clay. If relativists agree to being no more than a mouthpiece for the cultural memes that have taken over their minds, why should anybody pay attention when they urge reform? The answer to this question will serve to summarize what this section has to say about relativism.

Any decision problem can be split into two parts. One first determines what is feasible, and then chooses the optimal alternative from the set of feasible possibilities. Feasibility is a scientific question that can be settled independently of our cultural biases if we try sufficiently hard. It is only when we get to choosing an optimal social contract from those that are feasible that science ceases to guide our path. This book suggests that we can usefully employ the device of the original position for settling large-scale problems of social justice, but the reasons for making this suggestion are entirely pragmatic. Since people already use this social tool to solve small-scale coordination problems, perhaps it won't be so hard to persuade them to use it to solve large-scale problems.

I can justly be accused—as Rawls has been accused—of favoring the original position because it accords with my cultural prejudices. But there isn't any point in looking around for some supposedly culture-free alternative of the type that absolutists peddle. The rock of certitude on which they imagine they stand exists only in their own minds. They too are merely mouthpieces for the memes that hold them in thrall. In this respect, they differ from relativists only in being unaware of the source of their inspiration.

3.5 Reductionism

A famous example of the reductionist fallacy was Mrs Thatcher's denial that there is such a thing as the society she was doing her best to dismantle: "I don't believe in society: there is no such thing—only people and families." One might equally say that a wave is "nothing but" the molecules of which it is made up at any given instant. Or that an animal is "nothing more" than the cells that make up its body.

Scientists seldom fall prey to the reductionist fallacy, because their business is to study the very phenomena whose existence the reductionist fallacy denies. For example, this book is devoted to studying the structure of the social contracts that Mrs. Thatcher thinks exist only in the minds of empty-headed sociologists. But those of us who take such a scientific line on moral issues are nevertheless regularly dismissed as naive reductionists. I think that the criticswho react with this knee-jerk response don't even begin to understand what scientific modeling is all about.

For example, Isaac Newton treated the heavenly bodies as points when using his new theory of gravitation to explain the orbits of the planets. Nowadays, we would call his theoretical construct a *model* to emphasize that it only captures some particular aspect of a natural phenomenon.

However, the idea that one can slowly make progress by studying one aspect of a problem at a time is alien to the kind of critic who has no experience of solving any problems at all. Such virginal minds think that a model has to explain everything all at once to be useful. They would therefore reject Newton's astronomical model on the grounds that everybody knows that the planets are solid bodies. If they were consistent, they would similarly reject the use of maps on the grounds that maps are flat, and everybody knows that the world is round.

Of course, modelers often do claim that their models apply morewidely than is justified by the evidence. But it isn't because they sometimes make such errors that scientists are categorized as naive reductionists by their holist critics. The accusation commonly appears even before the critic knows for what purpose the model was constructed. But how can one judge whether a model serves its purpose well unless one knows what its purpose is?

Of course, if holists were ever to produce a model of everything that were useful for something, it would be necessary to sit up and listen. But as long as they confine their activities to complaining about the overlapping patchwork of sometimes inconsistent models that scientists use in trying to understand the world, there seems no reason why anyone should take them seriously. As it says in the Book of Matthew, by their fruits ye shall know them.

Emergent phenomena. The principal reason that critics seek to discredit game-theoretic models of social relationships by calling them reductionist is the absence of primitives within the model that correspond to such notions as authority, blame, courtesy, dignity, envy, friendship, guilt, honor, integrity, justice, loyalty, modesty, ownership, pride, reputation, status, trust, virtue, and the like.

In our everyday lives, we all manipulate informal models in which such concepts appear as primitives when seeking to make sense of the behavior of those around us. We therefore all know that such models work to some extent. When a new model appears in which such concepts don't appear as primitives, holistic critics see it as a rival to the old model, since the idea that different models of the same phenomenon might usefully be maintained simultaneously is too difficult for them. The value of maintaining a model that postulates a proximate cause alongside a model that postulates an ultimate cause for the same phenomenon is a case in point. But if one inhabits an intellectual straitjacket within which only one model can be right at a time, then those who propose new models that are inconsistent with old models that work well enough appear as irresponsible meddlers.

Of course, meddlers like myself don't see things this way at all. Authority, blame, courtesy, and the like may not appear as primitives in our models, but that isn't the same as saying that they don't exist. They appear as *emergent phenomena*. That is to say, they appear as necessary consequences of the *relationships* between the primitives that the model does postulate.

For example, a physical model of an ocean is unlikely to postulate waves as a primitive notion. More likely, it will model water molecules as little billiard balls that obey certain laws when they knock against each other. But if the initial conditions are right, waves will necessarily appear as an emergent phenomenon when the implications of the postulated laws are explored. A sea captain accustomed to thinking of waves as primitives of his world may accuse the modeler of being a naive reductionist, who claims that the sea is nothingbut molecules. But, in doing so, he makes two mistakes. The first is to neglect the overwhelming importance of the relationships between the molecules postulated by the model. The other is to imagine that the physical model is necessarily a threat to his own model.

The same applies when game theorists try to use the folk theorem to make sense of how social contracts work. The theorem says nothing about reputation, status, trust, and the like, but it doesn't follow one little bit that we think Mrs. Thatcher is right in claiming that such considerations don't matter. On the contrary, we hope to put our understanding of such social concepts on a firmer basis by treating them as emergent phenomena.

3.6   Nil desperandum!

The naturalistic views expressed in this book are often attacked as dehumanizing or dispiriting. Do our lives really have no meaning? Are we no more than soulless beasts, like apes or robots? People often refuse to believe that anyone could really hold such supposedly bleak views on the nature of human existence. What would be the point of going on with life if such things were true?

One answer is that Nature doesn't care whether we like her truths or not. For example, I am unenthusiastic about Einstein's theory of relativity because it means we may never reach the stars, but this isn't a good reason for returning to Newton!

But to reply in such a vein is like saying yes or no when asked if you have stopped beating your wife. The right response is to deny the premise. The things one has to believe if one takes a naturalistic viewpoint seriously are neither dehumanizing nor dispiriting. In particular, the idea that telling ourselves the truth about ourselves will somehow throw a wrench into the works seems to me quite ridiculous—rather like the claim I once read in a popular science book that our bodies would fly apart if the quantum theory were false. Of course they wouldn't! They would continue to operate exactly as before. All that would change is that we would need to find a better explanation of how the universe works.

The loss of religious faith provides a good example. While holding onto their belief in God, people typically think that life would be impossible for them without their faith. With no God at the helm, life would lose its point, society would fall apart, wickedness would prevail, and so on. But after apostates have recovered from the trauma of losing their faith, they find that daily life goes on just as before. Nor are irreligious people noticeably less caring or good-hearted than their churchgoing brethren—they simply find it possible to get on with their lives without the need to invent simplistic stories that supposedly explain everything around them. And so it is with those of us who have given up the secular fairy stories that attribute a divine spark to human nature. Do we seem to have lost our zest for life? Are we any less kind to those around us? Not as far as I can see.

As the ancient skeptics taught, contentment is possible without the need to cling to comforting beliefs. As proof, we have the example of David Hume who lived an entirely admirable life without any belief in the supernatural. His personal example shows that nobody need feel gloomy because life has no ultimate purpose, or because conventional conceptions of moral responsibility are built on foundations of sand. So what if our fine feelings and intellectual achievements are just the stretching and turning of so many springs or wheels, or our value systems are mirrored by those of chimpanzees and baboons. Our feelings are no less fine and our values no less precious because the stories we have traditionally told ourselves about why we hold them turn out to be fables. In discarding the metaphysical baggage with which the human race bolstered its youthful sense of self-importance, Hume taught us that we throw away nothing but a set of intellectual chains.

Far from being dehumanized or dispirited, Hume was the most civilized, companiable, and contented of men—especially when compared with neurotic oddities like Rousseau or Kant, from whom the human race usually seeks inspiration on how best to live. Even on his deathbed, Hume retained his good humor, totally disarming Samuel Johnson's biographer, James Boswell, when he tactlessly quizzed him on how it felt to be at death's door without a belief in the afterlife. As Boswell reports, "Mr Hume's pleasantry was such that there was no solemnity in the scene, and death for the time did not seem so dismal."

In a less ghoulish deathbed conversation, Hume told Adam Smith that he had been reading Lucian's *Dialogues of the Dead*, in which various notables offer reasons to Charon why they shouldn't be ferried across the Styx. When his own time came, he proposed to say, "Have a little patience, good Charon, I have been endeavouring to open the eyes of the Public. If I live a few years longer, I may have the satisfaction of seeing the downfall of some of themore prevailing systems of superstition." But then, says Hume, Charon would lose all patience, "You loitering rogue, that will not happen these many hundred years. Do you fancy I will grant you a lease for so long a term? Get into the boat, you lazy, loitering rogue."

David Hume was right to predict that superstition would survive for hundreds of years after his death, but how could he have anticipated that his own work would inspire Kant to invent a whole new package of superstitions? Or that the incoherent system of Marx would move vast populations to engineer their own ruin? Or that the infantile rantings of the author of *Mein Kampf* would be capable of bringing the whole world to war?

Perhaps we will one day succeed in immunizing our societies against such bouts of collective idiocy by establishing a social contract in which each child is systematically instructed in Humean skepticism. Such a new Emile would learn about the psychological weaknesses to which *Homo sapiens* is prey, and so would understand the wisdom of treating all authorities—political leaders and social role-models, academics and teachers, philosophers and prophets, poets and pop stars—as so many potential rogues and knaves, each out to exploit the universal human hunger for social status. He would therefore appreciate the necessity of doing all of his own thinking for himself. He would understand why and when to trust his neighbors. Above all, he would waste no time in yearning for utopias that are incompatible with human nature.

Would Adam and Eve be happy in such a second-best Garden of Eden? On this subject at least, Hume's own experience is immensely reassuring. We don't need to tell ourselves lies to be content. We don't need to believe that utopia can be achieved by some quick fix. It isn't even necessary to be optimistic that things will get better in the long run. We need only the freedom to create a stable microsociety within which we can enjoy the respect of those whose respect we are able to reciprocate. As Hume's example shows, even death can then be faced with equinamity.

Chapter 4

Equilibrium

Remember always to study power as it is, and not as you would wish it to be.

Niccoli Machiavelli

4.1 Inventing Right and Wrong

The previous chapter takes the views of scientific philosophers like John Mackie to their logical extreme. As he explains in his *Inventing Right and Wrong*, a close examination of the arguments of the rationalist tradition shows them to be specious. So why should we continue to buy tickets for this long-running flop? Let us turn instead to the scientific tradition represented in the Socratic dialogues by Protagoras, and continued into modern times by Hobbes and Hume.

Human morality is an artifact of human evolutionary history. To study it, Mackie tells us to look at the facts presented in such pioneering studies as Westermarck's *Origin and Development of the Moral Ideas*. And for a framework within which to make sense of such anthropological data, he directs our attention to Von Neumann's theory of games.

It is at this point that scientific philosophers tend to falter. Game theory books are mostly written by economists, who use an exotic vocabulary and complicated mathematical equations. Is it really necessary to master this arcane discipline to make progress?

I think this is another when-did-you-stop-beating-your-wife question. If you think it likely that morality evolved as a means of balancing power in human communities, then it is obviously necessary to know some game theory, because game theory is the study of how power is balanced. However, there is nothing arcane about game theory. On the contrary, what has to be explained in this chapter is embarrassingly easy. The exotic vocabulary and the fancy equations of game theory books are just more of the dust that scholars always kick up lest it be found out that what they have to say isn't very profound.

4.2 Toy Games

Nobody denies that it is worthwhile to study rational interaction within human communities, but why call it game theory? Don't we devalue our humanity by reducing our struggle for fulfillment to the status of mere play in a game?

I think that such comments miss the point altogether. The more deeply we feel about issues, the more important it is that we don't allow ourselves to be misled by wishful thinking. It is for this reason that game theorists follow John Von Neumann in making a virtue out of using the language of parlor games like chess or poker. People are usually able to think dispassionately about the strategic issues that arise in parlor games. That is to say, they are willing to follow the logic wherever it goes, without throwing their hands up in horror if it leads to an unwelcome destination. But logic is the same whatever the context in which it is applied.

The same principle applies to the absurdly simple toy games that are used as examples in this chapter. It is tempting to brush them aside on the grounds that the world is too complicated to be captured by such simple models, but whoever learned to solve complicated problems without practicing on simple problems first? Indeed, the crucial step in solving a real-life strategic problem nearly always consists of locating a toy game that lies at its heart. Only when this has been solved does it make sense to worry about how its solution needs to be modified to take account of all the bells and whistles that complicate the real world.

4.3 Cooperation and Conflict

One sometimes still reads dismissive commentaries on game theory in which Von Neumann is caricatured as the archetypal cold warrior—the original for Dr. Strangelove in the well-known movie. We are then told that only a crazed military strategist would think of applying game theory in real life, because only a madman or a cyborg would make the mistake of supposing that the world is a zero-sum game.

Von Neumann was an all-round genius. Inventing game theory was just a sideline for him. It is true that he gave advice on developing the atom bomb, but far from being a mad cyborg, he was a genial soul, who liked to relax and have a good time. It is also true that the first half of his famous book with Oskar Morgenstern was about two-player, zero-sum games, but one can only sustain the fiction that Von Neumann thought that the whole world was a game of pure conflict by air-brushing out the second half of the book, which is devoted to the study of cooperative games.

Game theory is actually about both conflict and cooperation, because realistic games usually contain the potential for both. Just like anyone else, game theorists prefer cooperation to conflict, but we don't think the way to achieve cooperation is to pretend that people can't sometimes profit by causing trouble. We believe that cooperation and conflict are two sides of the same coin, neither of which can properly be understood without taking account of the other.

Figure 4 illustrates this point by showing the payoff tables of a toy game of pure coordination and a toy game of pure conflict alongside each other. The game of pure coordination is the Driving Game that we met in chapter 1. The game of pure conflict is Matching Pennies, which most people play as children. In this game, each of two players shows a coin. One player wins if they are both the same, and the other if they differ.

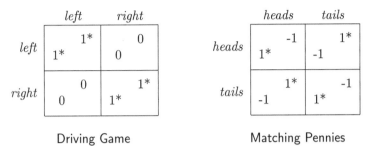

Driving Game   Matching Pennies

Figure 4: Cooperation and conflict.

I call the players Alice and Bob. In both the Driving Game and Matching Pennies, Alice has two strategies that are represented by the rows of the payoff table. Bob also has two strategies represented by its columns. The four cells of the payoff table correspond to the possible outcomes of the game. Each cell contains two numbers, one for Alice and one for Bob. The number in the southwest corner is Alice's payoff for the corresponding outcome of the game. The number in the northeast corner is Bob's payoff. Notice that the payoffs in each cell of Matching Pennies add up to zero. One can always fix things to make this true in a game of pure conflict, which is why such games are said to be zero sum.

Each player is assumed to seek to maximize his or her expected payoff in a game. This would be easy if a player knew what strategy the other were going to choose. For example, if Alice knew that Bob were going to choose *left* in the Driving Game, she would maximize her payoff by choosing *left* as well. That is to say, *left* is Alice's best reply to Bob's choice of *left*, a fact indicated in figure 4 by starring Alice's payoff in the cell that results if both players choose *left*.

A cell in which *both* payoffs are starred corresponds to a Nash equilibrium, because each player is then simultaneously making a best reply to the strategy choice of the other. As explained in chapter 1, Nash equilibria are of interest for two reasons. If it is possible to single out the rational solution of a game, it must be a Nash equilibrium. For example, if Alice knows that Bob is rational, she would be stupid not to make the best reply to what she knows is his rational choice. The second reason is even more important. An evolutionary process that adjusts the players' strategy choices in the direction of increasing payoffs can only stop when it reaches a Nash equilibrium.

Since both payoffs are starred in two cells of the payoff table of the Driving Game, we have found two Nash equilibria for the Driving Game. It is an equilibrium if everyone drives on the left. It is also an equilibrium if everyone drives on the right.

The Meeting Game of chapter 2 is similar to the Driving Game, but its strategic form has ten strategies for each player instead of two. Eight of the cells on the main diagonal correspond to equilibria, but now the players aren't indifferent about which is nominated as the solution of the game.

II:3.8   **Personal tastes or social values?**   All this is very straightforward, but there is nevertheless a lesson to be learned about modeling human conventions as equilibrium selection devices. Imagine an anthropologist from Mars who asks why the Japanese drive on the left and the French drive on the right. The naive answer is that the Japanese like driving on the left and the French like driving on the right. But this isn't true in the Driving Game. If Alice or Bob had the opportunity to choose between the social contracts in which everybody drives on the left and everybody drives on the right, they would be indifferent between the two choices. They don't give a damn about left or right—they only care about avoiding accidents.

One can say, of course, that the Japanese like driving on the left because they expect the oncoming traffic to be on the left. Or one can say that the French like driving on the right, because this is what they are accustomed to. But these descriptive observations are just ways of saying that Japan and France operate different social contracts. One can't bend them back on themselves to explain how and why their social contracts got established in the first place.

We are similarly in the position of an anthropologist from Mars when we ask ourselves why we play fair. The easy answer is that we play fair—insofar as we do—because we like playing fair. There is even a small academic industry in which behavioral economists rationalize the fair behavior observed in psychological laboratories by attributing utility functions to the subjects that incorporate a "taste for fairness". But there is a reason that they always seems to need a new utility function for each new experiment. I think it is because their putative explanation of the data is really only a *description* of the data. It might sometimes be a good description of the data—as with the dictum that Nature abhors a vacuum—but even the very best of descriptions is only a description and not an explanation.

If we want a genuine explanation, we have to dig deeper. It isn't true that we just happen to like playing fair. Fairness isn't a piece of random flotsam that somehow washed up on our evolutionary beach. I think it evolved as an equilibrium selection device—like driving on the left or right.

4.4   Mixed Strategies

Sherlock Holmes was playing a variant of Matching Pennies when he had to decide at which station to leave a train when pursued by the evil Professor Moriarty. However, Edgar Allan Poe offers a more thoughtful discussion than Conan Doyle of the strategic problem in such games. In Poe's *Purloined Letter,* the villain has stolen a letter, and the problem is where to look for it. Poe argues that the way to win is to extend chains of reasoning of the form "He thinks that I think that he thinks that I think. . ." one step further than your opponent.

But what if both Alice and Bob attempt this feat? The idea of a Nash equilibrium short circuits the apparent infinite regress, because any pair of strategies that isn't a Nash equilibrium will be destabilized as soon as the players start thinking about what the other players are thinking. But we are still left with a problem, because the trick of starring best replies that we used successfully to find two Nash equilibria for the Driving Game doesn't work for Matching Pennies. None of the cells of its payoff table has both payoffs starred.

But John Nash won his Nobel prize partly for showing that all finite games have at least one equilibrium. So what is going on? The answer is that we have to look beyond the pure strategies we have studied up to now, and consider *mixed* strategies, in which the players randomize their strategy choice. Critics often respond to the idea of mixed strategies by saying that someone who makes serious decisions at random must be crazy, but people use mixed strategies all the time without realizing it. You don't need to toss coins or roll dice for this purpose. All that is necessary is to make your choice unpredictable. After all, if Bob can't predict Alice's choice, she is a randomizing device as far as he is concerned.

The use of mixed strategies isn't at all surprising in Matching Pennies, where the whole point is to keep the opponent guessing. As every child knows, the solution is to randomize between *heads* and *tails,* choosing each with probability one half. In the playground, Alice sometimes even makes a performance of tossing her coin to make it clear to Bob that she is equally likely to show *heads* or *tails.* If both players use this mixed strategy, the result is a Nash equilibrium. Both players win half the time, which is the best each can do given the strategy choice of the other.

Similarly, it is a Nash equilibrium in the Driving Game if both players choose *left* and *right* with probability one half. The Driving Game therefore has three Nash equilibria, two pure and one mixed. The mixed equilibrium isn't at all efficient, since players who use it will end up in a stand-off half the time. But it is an equilibrium nevertheless, and hence might emerge as part of the set of conventions that make up a social contract. I used to say that it is a convention that has never actually emerged anywhere in the world, until corrected by some Turks, who observed that I had obviously never visited Turkey. But I have now, and I see what they mean.

Mixed strategies in evolutionary models.   In the simplest models of evolutionary game theory, chance is assumed to pick animals or people every so often from one or more large populations to play a game. The players aren't usually rational. Instead, they are assumed to be programmed with a strategy that they use mindlessly whenever called upon to play.

Evolution operates between successive plays of the game to increase the frequency of strategies in the population that get high payoffs at the expense of strategies that get low payoffs. The precise mechanism depends on the context. In biological evolution, fitter players pass on their strategies to more children. In cultural evolution, players who get high payoffs are more likely to be imitated than those who get low payoffs.

Mixed strategies are used to label a population state. The probabilities a mixed strategy assigns to the available pure strategies are identified with the frequencies with which animals or people in the population currently use these pure strategies. We can then track the evolutionary process by seeing how the mixed strategy that represents the current population state moves over time.

Figure 5 shows all the possible population states for Matching Pennies and the Driving Game when both players are drawn from the same population. The arrows in figure 5 show how a deterministic evolutionary process will move the population

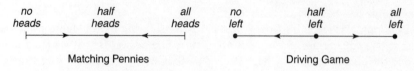

Figure 5: Evolutionary dynamics with one population.

state in the direction of whatever pure strategy is currently a best reply. Figure 6 shows how things might work when chance chooses Alice and Bob from two separate populations that evolve independently.

In the long run, the system will end up at one of the population states to which one is led by following the arrows. These all correspond to Nash equilibria of the game, for the reasons given in chapter 1. But the converse isn't true. For example, the mixed Nash equilibrium in the Driving Game is unstable, because arrows lead away from it. It isn't therefore enough that a strategy profile be a Nash equilibrium for it to be evolutionarily stable.

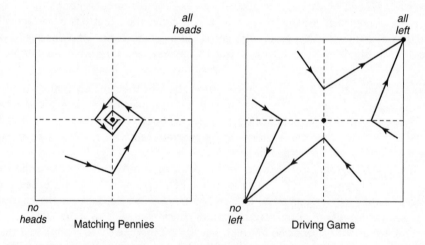

Figure 6: Best-reply dynamics with two populations. The best-reply dynamic assumes that the population state moves in a straight line toward whichever pair of strategies are currently best replies. This isn't very realistic with more than one population. The replicator dynamics of figure 10(b) are more realistic but less easy to explain.

4.5 The Prisoners' Dilemma

I:2.2.3

As the simplest of all possible variants of the Tragedy of the Commons, the Prisoners' Dilemma of figure 7 is the most famous of all toy games. A whole generation of scholars swallowed the line that this trivial game embodies the essence of the problem of human cooperation. The reason is that its only Nash equilibrium calls for both Alice and Bob to play *hawk*, but they would both get more if they cooperated by both playing *dove* instead. The hopeless task that scholars set themselves was therefore to give reasons why game theory's resolution of this supposed "paradox of rationality" is mistaken.

	dove	*hawk*
dove	2 2	3* 0
hawk	0 3*	1* 1*

Prisoners' Dilemma

	dove	*hawk*
dove	6* 6*	3 6*
hawk	6* 3	3 3

Prisoners' Delight

Figure 7: Paradox of rationality?

Game theorists think it just plain wrong to claim that the Prisoners' Dilemma embodies the essence of the problem of human cooperation. On the contrary, it represents a situation in which the dice are as loaded against the emergence of cooperation as they could possibly be. If the great game of life played by the human species were the Prisoners' Dilemma, we wouldn't have evolved as social animals! We therefore see no more need to solve some invented paradox of rationality than to explain why strong swimmers drown when thrown in a lake with their feet encased in concrete. No paradox of rationality exists. Rational players don't cooperate in the Prisoners' Dilemma, because the conditions necessary for rational cooperation are absent in this game.

Fortunately the paradox-of-rationality phase in the history of game theory is just about over. Insofar as they are remembered, the many fallacies that were invented I:3.1
in hopeless attempts to show that it is rational to cooperate in the Prisoners' Dilemma are now mostly quoted as entertaining examples of what psychologists call magical reasoning, in which logic is twisted to secure some desired outcome. The leading example remains Kant's claim that rationality demands obeying his categorical imperative. In the Prisoners' Dilemma, rational players would then all choose *dove*, because this is the strategy that would be best if everybody chose it.

The following argument is a knock-down refutation of this nonsense. So as not I:2.2.4
to beg any questions, we begin by asking where the payoff table that represents the players' preferences in the Prisoners' Dilemma comes from. The economists' answer is that we discover the players' preferences by observing the choices they make (or would make) when solving one-person decision problems.

Writing a larger payoff for Alice in the bottom-left cell of the payoff table of the

Prisoners' Dilemma than in the top-left cell therefore means that Alice would choose *hawk* in the one-person decision problem that she would face if she knew in advance that Bob had chosen *dove*.[1] Similarly, writing a larger payoff in the bottom-right cell means that Alice would choose *hawk* when faced with the one-person decision problem in which she knew in advance that Bob had chosen *hawk*.

The very definition of the game therefore says that *hawk* is Alice's best reply when she knows that Bob's choice is *dove*, and also when she knows his choice is *hawk*. So she doesn't need to know anything about Bob's actual choice to know her best reply to it. It is rational for her to play *hawk* whatever strategy he is planning to choose. In this unusual circumstance, we say that *hawk dominates* Alice's alternative strategies.

Nobody ever denies this utterly trivial argument. Instead, one is told that it can't be relevant to anything real, because it reduces the analysis of the Prisoners' Dilemma to a tautology. But who would say the same of $2 + 2 = 4$?

What are the payoffs?   The main reason for giving the knock-down argument that shows defection to be rational in the Prisoners' Dilemma is to counter the misapprehension that payoffs are necessarily measured in money. One commonly reads that only the kind of mean-minded, money-grubbing misfits attracted into the economics profession would fail to notice that people aren't always miserly egotists. That we are all members one of another. That no man is an island. That when the bell tolls, it tolls for thee. And so on.

But game theory assumes nothing whatever about what people want. It only says what Alice or Bob should do if they want to maximize their expected payoff. It doesn't say that we have to identify these payoffs with money. Even when the payoffs are identified with money, why should it be assumed that the players want the money for selfish purposes? Perhaps Alice is a pseudonym for Mother Teresa.

For example, it may be that Alice and Bob are so much in love that they regard a dollar for their lover as being worth twice as much as a dollar for themselves. If we tried to make them play the Prisoners' Dilemma with dollar payoffs, we would then fail, because their actual preferences would convert the game into the Prisoners' Delight of figure 7, in which it is now *dove* which is the dominant strategy. Such examples show that utopians who think that human beings are basically altruistic go astray when they accuse game theorists of analyzing of the Prisoners' Dilemma wrongly. What they should be saying is that the Prisoners' Dilemma isn't a good representation of our game of life—in which they would be right, albeit for the wrong reason.

A somewhat more sophisticated error is to suppose that payoffs are measured in notional units of happiness, as in the utilitarian theories of Jeremy Bentham and John Stuart Mill. Perhaps neuroscientists will eventually discover some kind of metering device wired into our brains that registers how many utils of pleasure or pain we are experiencing, although it doesn't seem likely that our motivational wiring will turn

---

[1] The common response that Alice wouldn't behave like this is silly. If Alice would choose *dove* in this situation, then we would have to write the larger payoff in the top-left cell. But then the game wouldn't be the Prisoners' Dilemma any more!

out to be so simplistic. However, nothing in game theory hinges on the details of how our brains are organized. All that is necessary for the theory to apply is that people behave *consistently*. It can then be shown that they necessarily behave as though maximizing the expected value of *something*, whether they are intending to or not. Whatever this abstract something may be in a particular context, we call it *utility*.

In some contexts, Alice's utility may correlate very closely with money. In others—especially within the family—her utility will correlate with some index of the well-being of her loved ones. I think that a major error made by utopian critics of economics is that they fail to recognize that there are good reasons why the spirit of good fellowship that usually reigns within families and circles of close friends quickly evaporates when strangers try to muscle in. But this is an empirical question. Game theory remains the same whatever view one takes on the nature of human nature.

An especially useful interpretation of the payoffs in a game arises in an evolutionary context. We can sometimes take the payoffs to be the extra fitness that an animal enjoys on average as a consequence of using a particular strategy. To measure fitness, we look at an animal's reproductive success. How many animals in the next generation will inherit the instinct to use the strategy?

This idea of William Hamilton is another of those stunningly simple insights that turns the way people think upside-down. With this interpretation of the payoffs in a game, we can cease to agonize about where evolution will take us. It becomes almost a tautology that if evolution stops anywhere, it has to be at a Nash equilibrium of whatever game is being played. We can then focus on the question that really matters: what is the game that is being played?

It is important for this book that Hamilton's insight can be applied to cultural evolution as well as biological evolution. Richard Dawkins speculates that, just as genes are biological replicators, so there are entities he calls memes that are cultural replicators. Their mode of replication is largely via imitation and education. A nice example is provided by the melodies sung by birds. Young songbirds can only sing some primitive snatches of song. Only later do they learn the complex melodies of their culture by imitation.

I was more enthusiastic about the idea of memes at one time, but I now feel that the story pushes the analogy between cultural and biological evolution too far. On the other hand, it doesn't push the analogy very far if we only ask that cultural evolution share with biological evolution the property of directing a population toward an equilibrium of the underlying game of life.

However, the utils in which the payoffs of the game of life are measured then become very distant from the units of money or happiness to which our critics think we are restricted. In the case of cultural evolution, payoffs measure the extent to which the players' strategy choices make them the locus for imitation of the way they choose their strategies.

Experiments and simulations. One sometimes hears that it doesn't matter that it may be rational to play *hawk* in the Prisoners' Dilemma, because experiments show that real people play *dove*. It is certainly true that inexperienced and unmo-

tivated subjects cooperate a lot, but the evidence is overwhelming that the rate of
defection increases steadily in games like the Prisoners' Dilemma, as the subjects
gain experience and as the value of the payoffs is increased, until only about 10%
of subjects continue to cooperate.[2]

Evolutionary computer simulations are similarly said to generate cooperation in
the Prisoners' Dilemma. They certainly generate cooperation in the *indefinitely
repeated* Prisoners' Dilemma, but this no surprise, since we have seen that the folk
theorem shows that efficient outcomes can be sustained as equilibria in such games.
But the one-shot Prisoners' Dilemma isn't its indefinitely repeated cousin, and only
confusion can result from blurring the distinction between them.

I:2.3.1   **Changing the rules?**   It is sometimes argued that the state of nature in a social
contract problem should be identified with a *game*. The Prisoners' Dilemma is
popular in this role with political philosophers who are influenced by the misanthropy
of Thomas Hobbes. Our task is then seen is as changing the rules of the Prisoners'
Dilemma so that cooperation becomes an equilibrium in the new game.

This approach makes sense if some external agency is available to enforce the
new rules, but when the Prisoners' Dilemma is intended as a toy version of our
game of life, there isn't anybody to act as an external enforcer, because we are all
players in the game of life. If the players themselves could change the "rules" of the
game they are playing, then we would have to list what the players can do to change
the "rules" among the available strategies of the old game. But the rules of this
augmented game wouldn't then be the "rules" that we are talking about changing.

The point here is that the rules of the game of life must embody all the factors
over which we have no control at all—like the laws of physics, the facts of geography,
and the accidents of our evolutionary history—but none of the factors over which
we do have control. All we can then hope to do is to shift our social contract
from one equilibrium in the game of life to another, as Sweden switched overnight
from driving on the left to driving on the right. The Prisoners' Dilemma therefore
represents a hopeless case, because it only has one Nash equilibrium.

4.6 Multiple Equilibria

Modern economic textbooks usually have little to say about fairness. Sometimes they
promote the myth that there is a necessary trade-off between equity and efficiency,
but they mostly brush the problem of distribution under the carpet altogether by
defining *any* efficient outcome to be "socially optimal". Complaints that a particular
efficient outcome is unfair needn't then be considered because the outcome is already
as good as it can get!

This kind of double-think can only be sustained by peering through the wrong end
of a telescope at models that have only one equilibrium—with the neoclassical ideal

---

[2]See the highly professional survey of the experimental literature on the private provision of
public goods carried out by John Ledyard for Roth and Kagel's *Handbook of Game Theory*,
Princeton University Press, 1995.

of a perfectly competitive market as the leading example. But games that are at all realistic commonly have large numbers of equilibria, among which a selection must somehow be made. I think our sense of fairness evolved to resolve this equilibrium selection problem in certain contexts. If I am right, then it is no wonder that neoclassical economists see no role for fairness in their modeling. If your models have only one equilibrium, what do you need fairness for?

No attempt is made in this chapter to explain how we use fairness to solve the equilibrium selection problem. Instead, I simply plan to use some examples to draw attention to the difficulty of the problem.

Stag Hunt Game. Kant absurdly idolized Jean-Jacques Rousseau as the "Newton of the moral world". Perhaps it was because he agreed with me that Rousseau's story of a stag hunt should be acknowledged as the first time anyone claimed it was rational to cooperate in a version of the Prisoners' Dilemma. However, as in Brian *I:2.3.2* Skyrms' book *The Stag Hunt*, kinder game theorists have interpreted his story in terms of the Stag Hunt Game of figure 8, which illustrates how one social contract can be better for everybody than another.

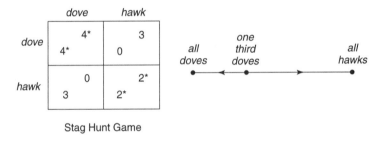

Stag Hunt Game

Figure 8: Hunting stags.

In Rousseau's stag-hunt story, Alice and Bob agree to cooperate in hunting a stag, but when they separate to put their plan into action, each may be tempted to abandon the joint enterprise by the prospect of bagging a hare for themselves. The starred payoffs in the payoff table show that there are two Nash equilibria in pure strategies, one in which the players cooperate by both playing *dove*, and one in which they defect by both playing *hawk*.

If a society found itself at a social contract corresponding to the inefficient equilibrium in which everybody plays *hawk.* why wouldn't they just agree to move to the efficient social contract in which everybody plays *dove*?

As the biologist Sewell-Wright explained, this may not be so easy if the task of moving from one equilibrium to another is left to evolution. In the evolutionary dynamics for one population shown on the right of figure 8, the basin of attraction of the inefficient equilibrium is large, and that of the efficient equilibrium is small. We therefore need a lot of random mutations coming all at once to bounce us from the inefficient equilibrium into the basin of attraction of the efficient equilibrium.

But we aren't animals who have to wait for the slow forces of evolution to take them to a new social contract. We can talk to each other and agree to alter the way we do things. But can we trust each other to keep any agreement we might make? The Stag Hunt Game is used by experts in international relations under the name of the Security Dilemma to draw attention to the problems that can arise even when the players are rational.

Suppose that Alice and Bob's current social contract in the Stag Hunt Game is the equilibrium in which they both play *hawk*. However hard Alice seeks to persuade Bob that she plans to play *dove* in the future and so he should follow suit, he will remain unconvinced. The reason is that whatever Alice is actually planning to play, it is in her interests to persuade Bob to play *dove*. If she succeeds, she will get 4 rather than 0 if she is planning to play *dove*, and 3 rather than 2 if she is planning to play *hawk*. Rationality alone therefore doesn't allow Bob to deduce anything about her plan of action from what she says, because she is going to say the same thing no matter what her real plan may be! Alice may actually think that Bob is unlikely to be persuaded to switch from *hawk* and hence be planning to play *hawk* herself, yet still try to persuade him to play *dove*.

This Machiavellian story shows that attributing rationality to the players isn't enough to resolve the equilibrium selection problem—even in a seemingly transparent case like the Stag Hunt Game. If Alice and Bob continue to play *hawk* in the Stag Hunt Game, they will regret their failure to coordinate on playing *dove*, but neither can be accused of being irrational, because both are doing as well as they can given the behavior of their opponent.

The standard response is to ask why game theorists insist that it is irrational for people to trust one another. Wouldn't Alice and Bob both be better off if both had more faith in each other's honesty? But nobody denies that Alice and Bob would be better off if they trusted each other, any more than anybody denies that they would be better off in the Prisoners' Dilemma if they cared more for each other's welfare. Nor do game theorists say it is irrational for people to trust each other. They only say that it isn't rational to trust people without a good reason: that trust can't be taken on trust. Who trusts a used-car dealer or a dean? What wife doesn't keep an eye on her husband? Who doesn't count their change?

If we want a better social contract, there is no point in bleating that people should be more trusting or honest. We need to try and understand how and why it makes sense to be trusting or honest in some situations, but not in others. We can then hope to improve our social contract by doing what we can to promote the former situations at the expense of the latter.

II:0.4.1   **Ultimatum Game.** A second example of a game with a difficult equilibrium selection problem is called the Ultimatum Game. In this game, a sum of money is donated to Alice and Bob by a philanthropist on condition that they can agree on how divide it. The rules specify that Alice makes a proposal on how to divide the money, to which Bob can only respond by saying *yes* or *no*. Experiments that have been replicated by many people (including me) show that Bob will end up with somewhat less than half the money on average. This result is said to show that game theory is wrong in predicting that Alice will end up with nearly all the money.

The Ultimatum Minigame is a simplified version in which the sum of money is four dollars. Alice is restricted to making a *high* offer of two dollars to Bob, or a *low* offer of one dollar. If Bob receives the high offer, he automatically accepts. If he receives the low offer, he is free to say *yes* or *no*.

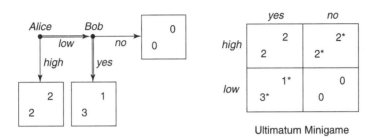

Ultimatum Minigame

Figure 9: Making an ultimatum.

The diagram on the left of figure 9 shows the extensive form of the game, which sets out the sequential structure of the moves. The diagram on the right shows the more familiar strategic form of the game.

The starred payoffs in the strategic form show that there are two Nash equilibria in pure strategies: one in which Alice makes the low offer and Bob accepts; and one in which Bob plans to refuse the low offer, and so Alice makes the high offer. The former is often wrongly said to be the "game theory prediction," because it is a *perfect* equilibrium. This means that the players' strategies remain best replies to each other even in subgames that won't be reached when the strategies are played.

One can work out perfect equilibria by working backward through the extensive form of some games. For example, in the subgame of the Ultimatum Minigame that is reached when Alice makes a low offer, Bob has to decide whether to say *yes* or *no*. The line representing *yes* in figure 9 is doubled to indicate that this choice gives him a higher payoff. The line representing Alice choosing *low* is then doubled to indicate that this choice gives her a higher payoff—given that Bob will choose rationally in the ensuing subgame. We therefore have an argument that favors the Nash equilibrium (low, yes) over the Nash equilibrium $(high, no)$.

One can reach the same conclusion in this simple case by deleting dominated strategies in the strategic form. The story is that it is irrational for Bob to play *no*, because *yes* dominates *no*. If Alice knows that Bob is rational, she can therefore deduce that he won't play *no*. It is then optimal for her to play *low*, because this strategy dominates *high* after Bob's *no* strategy has been deleted.

Throwing out Nash equilibria that aren't perfect, or which fail to survive the successive deletion of (weakly) dominated strategies was admittedly once popular with game theorists as a means of "solving" the equilibrium selection problem in those few cases where it applies.[3] But most game theorists now understand that we are *never* justified in throwing away one Nash equilibrium on the grounds that it is somehow less rational than another. In particular, it isn't true that "game theory predicts" that the perfect equilibrium will necessarily be observed when the Ultimatum Game is played rationally.

It is for this reason that Ariel Rubinstein's analysis of strategic bargaining with repeated offers mentioned in chapter 2 isn't regarded as a knock-down defense of the Nash bargaining solution. His argument only applies if we restrict our attention to perfect equilibria. Weaker assumptions suffice to generate the same result, but we will never get back to the subject of fairness norms if I get started on this subject!

The understanding that all Nash equilibria may matter is especially important in evolutionary game theory, where adjustment processes often converge on weakly dominated Nash equilibria. The phenomenon is particularly striking in the Ultimatum Minigame. As figure 10 shows, nothing very exciting happens with the best-reply dynamics of figure 6, but it is a different story with the replicator dynamics, which captures more of what actually goes on in real evolutionary processes.

We then have to take account of the many mixed Nash equilibria in which Alice plays *high* because Bob is planning to say *no* with a sufficiently high probability. Each of these weakly dominated Nash equilibria is a possible destination of the replicator dynamics. Taken together, their basin of attraction is large.

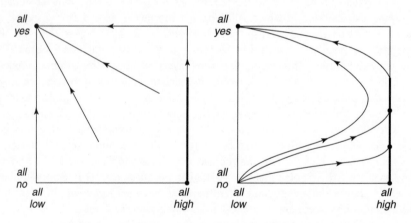

Figure 10: Dynamics in the Ultimatum Minigame.

None of this is meant to imply that I think the results of Ultimatum Game

---

[3]Nobody has doubts about the iterated deletion of *strongly* dominated strategies. For example, in the Prisoners' Dilemma, *hawk* strongly dominates *dove*. This means that a player always gets *strictly* more by playing *hawk* rather than *dove*. However, one can never lose a Nash equilibrium when only strongly dominated strategies are deleted.

experiments can be explained by saying that the subjects are playing one of its many dominated Nash equilibria. I think the experiments simply trigger conventions that evolved for our real game of life, but which aren't adapted to the anonymous environment in which the Ultimatum Game is played in laboratories. Subjects often learn to adapt to a new laboratory game quite quickly, but studies of toy dynamics in the Ultimatum Game suggest that convergence to any equilibrium by trial-and-error adjustment will be very slow. So it would be surprising if subjects learned to play an equilibrium after a few trials, even if we were sure that they were actually trying to maximize their payoffs in money.

Centipede Game. The Ultimatum Minigame shows that one shouldn't be in too much of a hurry to throw away imperfect Nash equilibria. The version of the Centipede Game to be studied next shows that one also should be cautious about throwing away *approximate* Nash equilibria.

II:1.6.2

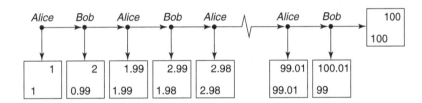

Figure 11: The Centipede Game.

As a small child, I remember wondering why shopkeepers hand over the goods after being paid. Why don't they just pocket the money? This is a simple version of the hold-up problem that arises in the economic theory of incomplete contracts. In the case of shopkeepers, they hand over the goods after receiving the money because their reputation for honest dealing is too important to lose in the repeated game they play with their customers.[4] But what of transactions in which neither party has reason to trust the word of the other?

As an example, consider the case of two criminals who agree to exchange a quantity of heroin for a sum of money. Alice is to end up with Bob's heroin and Bob with Alice's money. But how is this transition to be engineered, if each is free to walk away at any time carrying off whatever is currently in his or her possession? In real life, matters are complicated by the threat of physical violence, but we shall assume that neither player can be forced to act against their will. Nor are they fearful of losing their reputations or their lives should either go back on their word.

There is obviously no point in Alice handing over the agreed price and waiting

---

[4] I notice that filling stations increasingly demand payment up front, because many customers aren't similarly incentified.

for the goods. Somehow the criminals have to arrange a flow between them, so that the money and the drug change hands *gradually*.

Suppose that Alice has $100, each dollar of which is worth only one cent to her if not spent on heroin. Each grain of heroin that Alice buys for one dollar at the agreed rate of exchange is worth only one cent to Bob if not sold to Alice. Figure 11 shows the extensive form of a game with alternating moves that represents a procedure which the players might use to facilitate the exchange. At each decision node, the player whose turn it is to move can choose *across* or *down*. To choose *across* is to make a gift to the other player which is worth one cent to the donor, but one dollar to the recipient. To choose *down* is to cheat on the arrangement by exiting with what one currently has. Cognoscenti will recognize that this game of exchange has the same structure as the much studied Centipede Game.

If the last node of the game is reached, Bob must choose between 100.01 and 100. He will therefore cheat by choosing the former. If the penultimate node is reached, Alice will predict that Bob will cheat if the final node is reached and so realize that her choice is between 99.01 and 99. She will therefore cheat by choosing the former. The same argument then shows that Bob will also cheat if the preceding node is reached, and so on. The conclusion is that the agreement to exchange unravels completely.

This backward induction argument differs from the similar argument used with the Ultimatum Minigame only in having 100 steps rather than two. It therefore shows that the only perfect equilibrium is for Alice and Bob to plan to cheat whenever it is their turn to move. There are lots of other Nash equilibria, but these all require that Alice always cheats by exiting at the very first move.

Does this mean that trustless exchange is impossible? To draw such a conclusion would be to put more weight on the mathematical model proposed above than it can bear. The real world is imperfect in many ways. The Centipede Game takes account of the imperfection that money isn't infinitely divisible. But real people are even more imperfect than real money. In particular, they aren't infinitely discriminating. What is one cent more or less to anybody?

To capture this idea, suppose that players are satisfied to get within a nickel of their optimal payoff. With this assumption, the Centipede Game suddenly has large numbers of "approximate" Nash equilibria—including the trusting equilibrium in which both players always plan to honor their agreement. If the players are more discriminating so that they achieve satisfaction only when they get within some fraction of a cent of their optimal payoff, we can retain the same result by altering the Centipede Game to make each transfer worth even less to the donor than this fraction of a cent.

As the size of each transfer becomes vanishingly small, we therefore retain the trusting equilibrium, even though each player becomes infinitely discriminating in the limit. That is, trustless exchange is feasible between rational players provided that the goods flow continuously between the two players at an agreed rate.

Biology offers the exotic example of sex among the hermaphroditic sea bass. Eggs are expensive to produce, but sperm is cheap. When two sea bass mate, each therefore takes turns in laying *small* batches of eggs for the other to fertilize. A sea bass that laid all its eggs at once would be outperformed by an exclusively male mutant that fertilized the eggs, and then swam off without making an equivalent investment in the future of their joint children.

4.7 Nash Demand Game

II:1.5.1

John Nash's demand game applies to a bargaining problem like that of figure 1. Alice and Bob each simultaneously demand a payoff. If the pair of payoffs demanded is in the feasible set, both players receive their demands. If not, both players receive the disagreement payoff. It is therefore an analogue of the Meeting Game that also admits inefficient outcomes.

The game poses the equilibrium selection problem in an acute form, because every efficient outcome that assigns both players no less than their disagreement payoffs is a Nash equilibrium of the game. For this reason, the game has become a standard testbed for trying out equilibrium selection ideas.

Nash proposed dealing with the equilibrium selection problem by looking at a smoothed version of the game in which the players aren't certain where the boundary of the feasible set starts and stops. As one moves out along a curve from the disagreement point, the probability that the current payoff pair is feasible declines smoothly from one to zero in the vicinity of the boundary. All the Nash equilibria of the unsmoothed game are still approximate equilibria of the new game, but the exact Nash equilibria of the smoothed game all lie near the Nash bargaining solution, which is one of several reasons why it is studied.

Other authors have studied evolutionary equilibrium selection in the demand game. Brian Skyrms' *Evolution of the Social Contract* is a friendly introduction to these ideas. The Nash bargaining solution again does well. For example, if we add tiny random mutations to the best-response dynamics, we find that the population will end up close to the Nash bargaining solution with high probability after a long enough time has gone by—a result that survives if any disagreement isn't final, but merely leads to another bargaining round with a slightly smaller feasible set.

What is fair? An experiment on the smoothed demand game that I ran with some colleagues at the University of Michigan will perhaps serve to press home some of the points made in previous chapters about how I believe fairness works.[5]

The feasible set in the experiment is shown in figure 12, with serious money substituting for utility. The disagreement payoffs were zero.

The exact Nash equilibria correspond to points on the thickened line. (The reason they don't all approximate the Nash bargaining solution N is that our computer implementation didn't allow the players to vary their demands continuously.) The letters E and U refer to the egalitarian and utilitarian outcomes that we found to be rival candidates for a fairness norm in chapter 2, on the assumption that all players have the same social index. The letter N corresponds to the Nash bargaining solution. The letter K refers to an alternative bargaining solution proposed by Kalai and Smorodinsky.

---

[5] *International Journal of Game Theory* 22 (1993), 381–409.

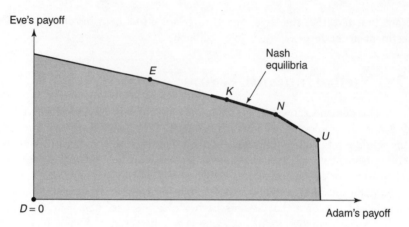

Figure 12: What is fair?

The experiment began with ten trials in which different groups of subjects know-ingly played against robots programmed to converge on one of the focal points E, N, K, and U. This conditioning phase proved adequate to coordinate the play of a group on whichever of the four focal points we chose. The conditioning phase was followed by thirty trials in which the subjects played against randomly chosen human opponents from the same group. The results were unambiguous. Subjects started out playing as they had been conditioned, but each group ended up at an *exact* Nash equilibrium.

In the computerized debriefing that followed their session in the laboratory, subjects showed a strong tendency to assert that the equilibrium reached by their own group was the fair outcome of the game. But different groups found their way to different exact equilibria. Indeed, for each exact equilibrium of our smoothed demand game, there was some group willing to say that this was near the fair outcome of the game!

In a situation that doesn't match anything to which they are habituated, people therefore show little sign of having some fairness stereotype built into their util-ity functions. On the contrary, money works well as a putative motivator in this experiment—as in many others. Instead of attributing fair behavior to a built-in "taste for fairness", I think we need to regard the subjects in each experimental group as the citizens of a minisociety in which a fairness norm evolved over time as a device to select among the efficient equilibria.

It is striking that the different fairness norms that evolved in the experiment se-lected only exact Nash equilibria, even though some groups were initially conditioned on the egalitarian and utilitarian solutions, which were both approximate equilibria from which the players would have no incentive to deviate if they neglected amounts of less than one dime. But the fact that E and U were nearly stable wasn't enough to keep groups at these focal points—an observation that accords with the claim in chapter 1 that we should rank stability at the top of our list of priorities that a social contract needs to satisfy.

Why doesn't the experiment refute both Rawls' claim that fairness norms are egalitarian, and Harsanyi's claim that they are utilitarian? Apart from the fact that E and U aren't Nash equilibria in the experiment, there is also the fact that calling them the egalitarian and utilitarian outcomes begs the question of how interpersonal comparisons are made. Why should we assume that one extra dollar in Alice's pocket should be regarded as equivalent to one extra dollar in Bob's pocket?

4.8 Out-of-Equilibrium Behavior

There is a school of behavioral economists who seem to believe that real people always behave as though maximizing some utility function, albeit one that depends on parameters that are commonly neglected in traditional economics. Since this book has the word *equilibrium* in nearly every sentence, it would be easy to get the impression that I similarly think that real people never do anything but rationally play their equilibrium strategy in some exotic game. However, I believe that trying to explain human behavior in this kind of way is rather like trying to explain the orbits of the planets with Ptolemaic epicycles. You can get a really good fit if you juggle with enough epicycles, but what would be the point?

I believe that both behavioral economists and game theorists need to face up to the fact that human behavior is often downright irrational. When this happens our standard theories don't apply. Perhaps we will one day develop adequate theories of bounded rationality, but current efforts in this direction have made little progress—and are only hindered by those behavioral economists who fail to see that the problem isn't that boundedly rational people maximize something unusual, but that they don't maximize anything at all. So where does that leave a theory like mine in which everything significant is an equilibrium?

My answer is that, even if the theory were souped up a great deal so that the toy games considered were replaced by games a lot closer to our real game of life, it would still have to put aside any aspiration to predict human behavior all the time. The best that one could hope for is a theory that would predict human behavior in games in which the players have had enough time for their behavior to adjust to their incentives through trial-and-error learning. But how long would this take?

Research on this front is progressing steadily, but it still has far to go. However, it is at least clear that the answer depends very much on what game we are talking about. In some market games, convergence on an equilibrium can be very fast. In games like the Ultimatum Game, it can be glacially slow. In the one-shot Prisoners' Dilemma, the truth is somewhere in between.

None of this is very satisfactory, but what can we do but make out what we can by the flickering light of the only candle we currently have at our disposal?

Chapter 5

Reciprocity

Give to him who gives, and do not give to him who does not give.

Hesiod, 5th Century BC

5.1 Tit-for-Tat

II:3.1

The idea that reciprocity is the mainspring of human sociality goes back nearly as far as there are written records. When Confucius was asked to encapsulate the "true way" in a single word, he is said to have replied *reciprocity.*

David Hume already understood how reciprocity works in 1739, but I don't suppose that Bob Aumann or any of the other game theorists who independently formulated the folk theorem in the fifties knew anything about his approach. Robert Trivers was equally ignorant of Aumann's work when he proposed the idea of reciprocal altruism twenty years later. It was only with the publication of Bob Axelrod's *Evolution of Cooperation* in 1984 that the idea finally stopped being rediscovered—in much the same way that America ceased being discovered after the voyage of Columbus in 1492.

Axelrod's book focuses on the strategy TIT-FOR-TAT for the infinitely repeated Prisoners' Dilemma. This strategy requires that a player begin by playing *dove* and continue by copying whatever action the opponent chose last time. If both Alice and Bob play TIT-FOR-TAT, the result will be that they both choose *dove* each time the Prisoners' Dilemma is repeated.

Observers who see Alice and Bob cosily cooperating all the time may be tempted to deduce that they have put aside the Machiavellian scheming that game theorists supposedly promote in favor of an open-hearted policy of trust and good fellowship. But we are now looking at a case where there is no contradiction between what game theory recommends and the yearnings of utopians. It isn't rational to cooperate in the *one-shot* Prisoners' Dilemma, but two TIT-FOR-TAT strategies constitute a Nash equilibrium for the *infinitely repeated* Prisoners' Dilemma.

To see this, we need to check that neither Alice nor Bob can profit by deviating from TIT-FOR-TAT if the other doesn't. Suppose, on the contrary, that Alice does deviate at some time by playing *hawk*. If Bob sticks with TIT-FOR-TAT, he will therefore respond by playing *hawk* until Alice signals her repentance by switching back to *dove*. Alice's income stream during her period of deviance will then be $3, 1, 1, \ldots, 1, 0$ instead of $2, 2, 2, \ldots, 2, 2$. So her deviation was unprofitable.

The essential point is that TIT-FOR-TAT has a built-in provision for *punishing* deviations. If both players believe that the other is planning to use TIT-FOR-TAT, neither has a motive for using an alternative strategy.

There are an infinite number of strategies for the infinitely repeated Prisoners' Dilemma that share this property. The simplest is the GRIM strategy, which plays *dove* until the opponent plays *hawk*, whereupon it switches *permanently* to *hawk* itself. Any deviation from cooperation by the opponent is then punished remorselessly to the maximal extent. Two GRIM strategies are a Nash equilibrium in the infinitely repeated Prisoners' Dilemma for the same reason that the same is true of two TIT-FOR-TAT strategies.

Both TIT-FOR-TAT and GRIM are "nice" strategies in that they are never the first to defect, but we also need to take account of "mean" strategies that begin by playing *hawk*. For example, the strategy TAT-FOR-TIT begins by playing *hawk* and thereafter switches its action if and only if the opponent played *hawk* last time. Two TAT-FOR-TIT strategies are a Nash equilibrium in the infinitely repeated Prisoners' Dilemma, in which cooperation is achieved only after the first round of play.

II:3.3.7   **Axelrod's Olympiad.** Axelrod was led to TIT-FOR-TAT by a competition he ran in which he invited various social scientists to submit computerprograms to be matched against each other in an indefinitely repeated version of the Prisoners' Dilemma. After learning the outcome of a pilot round, the contestants submitted computer programs that implemented 63 of the possible strategies of the game.

In this competition, TIT-FOR-TAT was the most successful strategy. Axelrod then simulated the effect of evolution operating on all 63 strategies. The fact that TIT-FOR-TAT was the most numerous of all the surviving programs at the end of the evolutionary simulation clinched the question for Axelrod, who then proceeded to propose TIT-FOR-TAT as a suitable paradigm for human cooperation across the board. In describing its virtues, he says:

> What accounts for TIT-FOR-TAT's robust success is its combination of being nice, retaliatory, forgiving and clear. Its niceness prevents it from getting into unnecessary trouble. Its retaliation discourages the other side from persisting whenever defection is tried. Its forgiveness helps restore mutual cooperation. And its clarity makes it intelligible to the other player, thereby eliciting long-term cooperation.

As a consequence of Axelrod's claims, a whole generation of social scientists has grown up believing that TIT-FOR-TAT embodies everything that they need to know about how reciprocity works.

But it turns out that TIT-FOR-TAT wasn't so very successful in Axelrod's simulation. The successful strategy was actually a mixture of six entries in which the probability of TIT-FOR-TAT was only a little more than one sixth. Nor is the limited success TIT-FOR-TAT does enjoy robust when the initial population of entries is varied. The unforgiving GRIM does extremely well when the initial population field of entries isn't biased in favor of TIT-FOR-TAT. Nor does evolution generate nice machines when some small fraction of suckers worth exploiting is allowed to flow continually into the system. Mean strategies like TAT-FOR-TIT then outperform TIT-FOR-TAT. As for clarity, it is only necessary for cooperation to evolve that a mutant be able to recognize a copy of itself.

All that is then left on Axelrod's list is the requirement that a successful strategy be retaliatory. This is perhaps the claim that has done most harm, because it applies only in *pairwise* interactions. For example, it is said that reciprocity can't explain the evolution of friendship. It is true that the offensive–defensive alliances of chimpanzees can't be explained with a tit-for-tat story. If Alice needs help because she is hurt or sick, her allies have no incentive to come to her aid, because she is now unlikely to be useful as an ally in the future. Any threat she makes to withdraw her cooperation will therefore be empty. But it needn't be the injured party who punishes a cheater in multiperson interactions. Others will be looking on if Bob abandons Alice to her fate, and they will punish his faithlessness by refusing to form alliances with him in the future. After all, who wants to make an alliance with someone with a reputation for abandoning friends when they are in trouble?

I think the enthusiasm for TIT-FOR-TAT survives for the same reason that people used to claim that it is rational to cooperate in the one-shot Prisoners' Dilemma. They want to believe that human beings are essentially nice. But the real lesson to be learned from Axelrod's Olympiad and many later evolutionary simulations is infinitely more reassuring. Although Axelrod's claims for TIT-FOR-TAT are overblown, his conclusion that evolution is likely to generate a cooperative outcome seems to be genuinely robust. We therefore don't need to pretend that we are all Dr. Jekylls in order to explain how we manage to get on with each other fairly well much of the time. Even a society of Mr. Hydes can eventually learn to coordinate on an efficient equilibrium in an indefinitely repeated game.

5.2 Folk Theorem

II:3.3

Playing TIT-FOR-TAT is just one of many ways that Alice and Bob can sustain cooperation as a Nash equilibrium in the infinitely repeated Prisoners' Dilemma. So what are the others? The folk theorem goes a long way towards answering this question by characterizing all possible Nash equilibrium outcomes for all infinitely repeated games.

The simple idea behind the folk theorem will be illustrated using both the Prisoners' Dilemma and the Ultimatum Minigame. The four payoff pairs from each of their payoff tables are shown in figure 13. If Alice and Bob were to bargain about how to play, they might agree on any of these four points, but they have many other options as possible agreements. For example, they might compromise by tossing a coin or agreeing to take turns to settle any dispute that may arise over which alternative should be adopted.

To take all such possibilities into account, it is necessary to expand Alice and

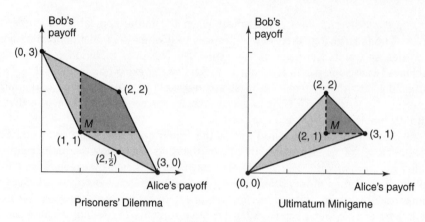

Figure 13: The folk theorem for infinitely repeated games.

Bob's set of feasible agreements to the lightly shaded region in each of the diagrams of figure 13. This is the smallest convex set that contains all four payoff pairs from the game's payoff table. For example, if Alice and Bob agree that she will always play *hawk* in the Prisoners' Dilemma and he will play *hawk* only every other day, then they will implement the payoff pair $(1, 1)$ one half of the time and the payoff pair $(3, 0)$ the other half of the time. Alice then expects 2 on average, and Bob expects $\frac{1}{2}$. But the point $(2, \frac{1}{2})$ lies halfway between $(1, 1)$ and $(3, 0)$, and is therefore in our lightly shaded set.

The problem with the bargaining story is that it won't work without some kind of external agency willing and able to enforce any contracts that Alice and Bob may write. Without such an external agency, any agreements that Alice and Bob make must be self-enforcing. That is to say, only equilibria are available as viable deals. In the one-shot Prisoners' Dilemma, the absence of external enforcement therefore spells disaster, since the only equilibrium is the inefficient outcome in which both Alice and Bob play *hawk*. But we lose nothing of any significance at all in the infinitely repeated Prisoners' Dilemma. Every outcome on which rational players might agree in the presence of external enforcement is also available *as an equilibrium* when we repeat the game.

The basic argument is so easy that it is no wonder it was discovered by pretty much everyone who gave repeated games any thought after Nash published his equilibrium idea in 1951. Pick a point P in the feasible set of the game to be repeated. We will make this an equilibrium outcome by punishing anyone who is seen to deviate from the strategy necessary for Alice and Bob to get P each time the game being repeated is played. It is easiest to use the kind of implacable punishment characteristic of the GRIM strategy, in which any deviation is punished forever in the most severe manner available.

In figure 13, the worst payoffs that each player can inflict on the other are indicated by the letter M. Any P in the darkly shaded set—in which both players get no less than their worst punishment payoffs—can therefore be sustained as an equilibrium outcome in the infinitely repeated game. Both players prefer to stay at P than to deviate, because the result of deviating is that they will end up with their payoff stuck at M.

In the Prisoner's Dilemma, the worst that a player can do to the opponent is to play *hawk* all the time, in which case the victim will respond by playing *hawk* to minimize the damage. Thus M is $(1, 1)$. In the Ultimatum Minigame, the worst that Alice can do to Bob is to play *low*, to which he will reply with *yes* to minimize the damage. The worst that Bob can do to Alice is to play *no*, to which she will reply *high* to minimize the damage. Thus M is $(2, 1)$.

Although it doesn't matter much, the worst punishment that can be inflicted on Alice is her *minimax* payoff, obtained when Bob seeks to miminize Alice's payoff in the knowledge that she will respond by making a maximal reply to his attempt at punishment. If we are in a context in which it makes sense to use mixed strategies, we can then appeal to Von Neumann's celebrated theorem of 1928, which says that Alice's minimax payoff is the same as her maximin payoff.[1] But you would never agree to a deal that paid off less than your maximin payoff, because you have a strategy that guarantees at least this much whatever the opposition may do. This observation allows us to round off what we need from the folk theorem:

> *Every* contract on which rational players might agree in the presence of external enforcement is available as an equilibrium outcome in an infinitely repeated game.

With the help of the folk theorem, we can reduce a social contract question to a bargaining problem like that illustrated in figure 1. The disagreement point D corresponds to the state of nature, which I identify with the equilibrium acting as the current social contract. The points in the feasible set correspond to all the equilibrium outcomes that are available as alternative social contracts.

What can go wrong?   Easy though it is to prove, I think the folk theorem embodies perhaps the most significant insight available to political philosophy. However, it has at least two limitations.

In the version presented, the payoffs must be measured in utils that add up in a sensible way. We used this fact in evaluating both lotteries and income streams in terms of their *average* payoffs. The latter is the more serious restriction, because it implies that the players are infinitely patient—that a dollar promised in a thousand years is worth no less than a dollar promised tomorrow.

We can relax this unrealistic assumption in two ways. Our *infinitely* repeated games can be replaced by *indefinitely* repeated games, in which there is always a

---

[1] Von Neumann's theorem implies that the players' maximin payoffs sum to zero in a two-person, zero-sum game. It is therefore a Nash equilibrium for both to use their maximin strategies, because neither can hope for more if the other player does the same.

very small probability that any given repetition will be the last. We can also assume that the players discount the future at some fixed rate of interest. An approximate version of the folk theorem then survives for the case when both the interest rate and the probability that any repetition is the last are small. In brief, for the folk theorem to hold, we need the players to care enough about the future that it is worth their while to value long-term relationships.

The second limitation is a great deal more troublesome. The version of the folk theorem presented assumes that any deviations from equilibrium will be observed by the other players. This is probably not a bad assumption in the case of the small bands of hunter-gatherers in which I believe fairness norms first arose. As in the small towns of today, presumably everybody knew everybody else's business. But this certainly isn't true of modern city life. In the anonymity of a big city, it isn't possible to sustain the tight social contracts of small societies, because it isn't possible to detect and punish deviants often enough to deter cheating. We do our best with policemen and tax inspectors, but nobody would want to claim that our efforts in this direction are anywhere near efficient.

I don't have to face up to the information problem in this book, because my focus is on how fairness norms evolved in the first place, but reformers can't escape the problem. However, they won't get a lot of help from game theorists, because we don't yet know very much about folk theorems in which the players can keep some of their information secret.

5.3 Punishment

The punishments that are used in proving the folk theorem are the worst punishments available, but one would only expect to see such punishments inflicted on outsiders in real life. If severe punishments for trivial offenses were inflicted on everyone, then insiders like ourselves and our loved ones would be put at unnecessary risk. The punishments prescribed for deviant insiders must therefore be expected to be minimal.

Napoleon's exile in Elba is an extreme example. After all, any ruler may be overthrown. On the other hand, we bourgeois folk don't ever expect to steal a pizza, and hence the Californian doctrine of three strikes and you're out.

As explained in chapter 1, very few of the punishments that sustain a social contract are administered through the legal system. Indeed, nearly all punishments are administered without either the punishers or the victim being aware that a punishment has taken place. No stick is commonly flourished. What happens most of the time is that the carrot is withdrawn a tiny bit. Shoulders are turned slightly away. Greetings are imperceptibly gruffer. Eyes wonder elsewhere. These are all warnings that your body ignores at its peril.

I was particularly delighted to find anthropological accounts describing higher stages of punishment observed among hunter-gatherer societies, because they mirror so accurately similar phenomena that the academic world uses to keep rogue thinkers in line. First there is laughter. If this doesn't work—and who likes being laughed at—the next stage is boycotting. Nobody talks to the offending party, or refers to his research. Only the final stage is maximal: a persistent offender is expelled from the group, or is unable to get his work published.

Once the subtle nature of the web of reciprocal rewards and punishments that sustains a social contract has been appreciated, it becomes easier to understand why it is so hard to reform corrupt societies in which criminality has become socially acceptable. As the case of Prohibition shows, imposing the type of draconian penalty in which rednecks delight on the criminals unlucky enough to be caught is unlikely to be effective. The resulting disincentives will be almost certainly be inadequate, since the probability of any individual being unlucky is necessarily small when nearly everybody is guilty.

The role of the emotions.   Emotions were once dismissed as irrational urges *II:3.5* left over from our evolutionary history. The socially aroused emotions associated with pride, envy, and anger are still counted among the seven deadly sins. But if these emotions are as self-destructive as tradition holds, how come evolution equipped us with them?

I share the now widely held view that tradition is plain wrong in seeing no useful social role for the emotions. I think they evolved to help police primeval social contracts, and they remain useful to us for this purpose.

For example, the prototypical scenario for the expression of anger arises when Adam treats Eve unfairly. In her anger at his unjust treatment, she is then likely to inflict some harm on Adam. Adam therefore takes care to keep his acquisitive urges under control lest he incur her ire.

In this way, it is possible to sustain efficient equilibria in repeated games without any of the players even being aware that they are playing a repeated game. How else would chimpanzees be capable of sustaining high levels of reciprocal altruism? How would humans be capable of the same feat if we always had to spend half an hour or more calculating what to do before taking any action? Some of our thinking in these situations must surely be hardwired, and perhaps getting into an emotional state is simply how it feels when our autopilot takes over the controls.

Revenge.   Suppose Eve risks damage to herself in launching an angry attack on Adam after he has treated her unfairly. Her behavior might then easily be dismissed as irrational by observers who fail to notice that she isn't necessarily acting wildly in a one-shot game, but may be carrying through her part of an equilibrium in an indefinitely repeated game.

Experiments on the Ultimatum Game currently provide a focus for this kind of confusion. Why doesn't the responder accept anything she is offered in one-shot versions of the Ultimatum Game played in the laboratory? A popular answer is that she gets angry and refuses out of spite. Analysis of the testosterone levels in the sputum of responders would seem to confirm that this explanation is right insofar as it goes.

But why should responders get angry? I think that they get angry because this is their habituated response to an unfair offer in the situations in which we encounter ultimata in real life. It is then almost never true that the game is one-shot. Even if it isn't a repeated game, there will normally be onlookers who need to be dissuaded from thinking of us as a soft touch.

For example, the folk theorem for the Ultimatum Minigame illustrated in figure 13 shows that the "fair" outcome $(2, 2)$ can just be supported as an equilibrium in an infinitely repeated version of the game—but only if Bob is prepared to punish any attempt by Alice to get more than her fair share.

Some instructive examples are provided in a recent cross-cultural study of behavior in the Ultimatum Game and other canonical games.[2] Aside from confirming that fairness norms vary markedly across cultures, the authors note the manner in which norms adapted to repeated situations are applied in unfamiliar one-shot laboratory environments. For example, "Orma experimental subjects quickly dubbed the public goods experiment a *harambee* game, referring to the widespread institution of village-level voluntary contributions for public goods projects such as schools or roads. Not surprisingly, they contributed generously."

Critics of the view that people become habituated to norms that are adapted to repeated games argue that subjects in experiments know perfectly well that they are playing a one-shot game, so why should they respond with behavior appropriate to a repeated game? But one might as well ask why a sailor keeps walking with a rolling gait when he comes ashore after a long voyage.

Are we then mere robots controlled through our emotions by our genetic heritage? The evidence suggests otherwise. People's behavior adapts to the one-shot games they play in the laboratory as they gain experience. In the one-shot Ultimatum Game their behavior adjusts much more slowly than in the one-shot Prisoners' Dilemma, but it adjusts nevertheless.

This view of things is disputed by economists from both ends of the political spectrum. Behavioral economists argue thatwe really do have a taste for reciprocity built into our preferences, and that the evidence that people adjust their behavior as they gain experience is either illusory or irrelevant. I think this theory of "strong reciprocity" can be maintained only by refusing to look beyond a small number of experiments that have been deliberately designed with a view to providing support for the theory.

Traditional economists are equally skeptical about the evidence for learning. They say that there is nothing for the responders to learn in the Ultimatum Game, since they already know that something is better than nothing. But what the responders' bodies have to learn is that there isn't any point in getting angry with a stranger you are never going to meet again. This is a hard lesson, as Smallville folk visiting Metropolis for the first time will readily confirm. But the harder the knocks, the quicker we are conditioned with emotional responses that fit the actual game we are playing.

---

[2] J. Henrich, R. Boyd, S. Bowles, E. Fehr, H. Gintis, and R. McElreath, "In search of Homo economicus: behavioral experiments in fifteen small-scale societies", *American Economic Review* 91 (2001), 73–78.

5.4 Quis custodiet ipsos custodes?

II:3.3.6

The gossamer threads of shared knowledge and experience that hold an equilibrium together seem but flimsy bonds when compared with the iron shackles of duty and obligation that traditionalists imagine chain a society down. As David Hume says:

> Nothing appears more surprising to those who consider human affairs with a philosophical eye, than the ease with which the many are governed by the few, and the implicit submission with which men resign their own sentiments and passions to those of their rulers. When we inquire by what means this wonder is effected, we shall find that, as Force is always on the side of the governed, the governors have nothing to support them but opinion. It is therefore on opinion only that government is founded, and this maxim extends to the most despotic and most military governments as well as to the most free and most popular.

In short, the authority of popes, presidents, kings, judges, policemen, and the like is just a matter of convention and habit. Adam obeys the king because such is the custom—and the custom survives because the king will order Eve to punish Adam if he fails to obey. But why does Eve obey the order to punish Adam? In brief, who guards the guardians?

Immanuel Kant naively thought that to answer this question is necessarily to initiate an infinite regress, but we can adapt the folk theorem to show that the chains of responsibility can be bent back on each other. This is done by showing that the theorem is true not only for Nash equilibria, but for *perfect* equilibria.

Recall that a perfect equilibrium is a strategy profile that calls for the play of a Nash equilibrium in all subgames of the original game—whether these are reached on the equilibrium path or not. Chapter 4 noted that perfect equilibria are no more rational than other Nash equilibria, but Reinhard Selten showed that the same ceases to be true if we change the game slightly by assuming that there is always a chance that players will make any mistake available to them with some small probability. Nash equilibria of this new game are then approximately perfect equilibria of the old game. Given the human propensity to error, treating social contracts as perfect equilibria therefore seems a useful first approximation.

If someone deviates and we go to one of the subgames off the equilibrium path, it remains optimal in a perfect equilibrium to stick to your original strategy provided everybody else does. In particular, if your strategy tells you to punish the deviant at some cost to yourself, it will be optimal for you to carry through on the punishment. If you deviate by trying to escape your duty to punish, you will take us to yet another subgame where it is optimal for some other player to punish you for your dereliction of duty. If he fails to discharge his duty, we go to yet another subgame—and so on forever. With only a finite number of players, these chainsof responsibility are necessarily closed in the manner that Kant failed to consider.

In the case of a social contract with a monarch, Eve obeys the king because she fears Ichabod will otherwise punish her. Ichabod would obey the order to punish Eve because he fears that Adam will otherwise punish him. Adam would obey the order to punish Ichabod because he fears that Eve will otherwise punish him.

At first sight, such a spiral of self-confirming beliefs seems too fragile to support anything solid. It is true that the beliefs go round in a circle, but the folk theorem shows that their fragility is an illusion, since the behavior generated by the beliefs holds together as a perfect equilibrium.

It is a bad mistake to allow the paraphernalia of the modern state—its constitution, its legal system, its moral code, its pomp and ceremony—to blind us to the insight that it all rests on nothing more than the self-confirming beliefs of its citizens. Laws and directives, even if written on tablets of stone, are simply devices that help us coordinate on an equilibrium in the game of life. The fact that a judge is supposedly an instrument of the Law no more excludes him from our social contract than the Great Seal of State that symbolizes supreme power excludes a king or a president.

In order that we coordinate efficiently, it is necessary that a modern social contract assign leading roles to certain individuals, but the power we lend to the mighty actually remains in our collective hands. Since the mighty can't be trusted not to abuse their privileges, a liberal social contract makes effective provision for this collective power to be brought quickly to bear when corruption threatens the integrity of the state. As Hume so aptly observes: "In constraining any system of government and fixing the several checks and controls of the constitution, every man ought to be supposed a knave and to have no other end in all his actions than private interest." In the jargon of economics, the roles the social contract assigns to officers of the state must be compatible with their incentives. Or, to return to Juvenal's dictum, the bigger the guardians, the more they need to be guarded.

5.5   Emergent Phenomena

II:3.4

One unfortunate result of the star billing achieved by TIT-FOR-TAT has been to persuade a generation of evolutionary thinkers that no other forms of reciprocating behavior are worthy of attention. It is taken for granted that TIT-FOR-TAT is adequate to serve as a paradigm for the whole class of reciprocating mechanisms covered by the folk theorem. But it is a bad mistake to think that a cheater must be disciplined by the person he injures. In a big society, the cheater can be disciplined by a third party. As a consequence, the range of social contracts that can be sustained as an equilibrium in a repeated game is much wider than commonly supposed.

Altruism and duty.   Anthropologists tell us that food is gathered and distributed in pure hunter-gatherer societies largely according to the Marxian principle that each contributes according to his ability, and benefits according to his need.

How can such a social contract survive? If only the tit-for-tat mechanism were available, nobody would ever offer food to powerless folk outside their immediate family. But the punishment for failing to share food needn't be administered by whoever is left to go hungry. In modern foraging bands, the whole group joins in punishing a deviant. Everyone is therefore a citizen within a social organization which resembles the Marxian utopia that supposedly follows the withering away of the state.

To see how this can work, imagine a world in which only a mother and a daughter are alive at any time. Each player lives for two periods. The first period is her youth, and the second her old age. In her youth, a player bakes two (large) loaves of bread. She then gives birth to a daughter, and immediately grows old. Old players are too feeble to work, and so producenothing.One equilibrium requires each player to consume both her loaves of bread in her youth. Everyone will then have to endure a miserable old age, but everyone will be optimizing given the choices of the others. All players would prefer to consume one loaf in their youth and one loaf in their old age. But this "fair" outcome can only be achieved if the daughters all give one of their two loaves to their mothers, because bread perishes if not consumed when baked.

Mothers can't retaliate if their daughters are selfish, but the fair outcome can nevertheless be sustained as an equilibrium. In this fair equilibrium, a conformist is a player who gives her mother a loaf if and only if her mother was a conformist in her youth. Conformists therefore reward other conformists, and punish nonconformists.

To see why a daughter gives her mother a loaf, suppose that Alice, Beatrice, and Carol are mother, daughter, and granddaughter. If Beatrice neglects Alice, she becomes a nonconformist. Carol therefore punishes Beatrice, toavoid becoming a nonconformist herself. If not, she will be punished by her daughter—and so on. If the first-born player is deemed to be a conformist, it is therefore a perfect equilibrium for everybody to be a conformist. However, the injured party is never the person who punishes an infringement of the social contract. Indeed, the injured party is dead at the time the infringement is punished!

The standard reaction to this kind of story is impatience that game theorists don't know that real daughters look after their aged mothers because they love them. But this reaction misses the point of the model, which teaches us that, even if all daughters were stonyhearted egoists, their aged mothers wouldn't necessarily be neglected—which is just as well for some very unpleasant old ladies of my acquaintance, whose daughters uncomplainingly bear the burden of their care only out of a sense of duty. Why do they feel a sense of duty? Ultimately, because they would be censured by their community if they were to fail to carry out the role assigned to them by the current social contract.

Reputation and trust. Alice delivers a service to Bob, trusting him to reciprocate by making a payment in return. But why should he pay up if nothing will happen to him if he doesn't? Sociologists model this hold-up problem using the toy game of figure 14 that I call the Trust Minigame. The one-shot game has a unique Nash equilibrium in which Alice doesn't deliver the service, because she predicts that Bob won't pay.

But people mostly do pay their bills. When asked why, they usually say that they have a duty to pay, and that they value their reputation for honesty. Game theorists agree that this is a good description of how our social contract works, but we want to know *why* it embodies such virtues. We therefore look at the infinitely repeated version of the Trust Minigame.

The folk theorem says that all points in the shaded region of figure 14 are equilibrium outcomes of the repeated game, including the payoff pair $(2, 2)$ that arises when Alice always delivers and Bob always pays. We explain this equilibrium in real life by saying that Bob can't afford to lose his reputation for honesty by cheating on Alice, because she will then refuse to provide any service to him in the future. In practice, Alice will usually be someone new, but the same equilibrium works just as well, because nobody will be any more ready than Alice to trade with someone with a reputation for not paying.

Nobody in ordinary commercial life needs to have this explained. I found the neatest summary of why traders trust each other in the *New York Times* of 29 August 1991. When asked whether he could rely on the honesty of the owner of the antique store that sold his finds on commission, a dealer replied: "Sure I trust him. You know the ones to trust in this business. The ones who betray you, bye-bye."

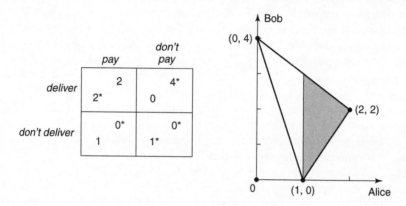

Figure 14: The Trust Minigame.

Leadership and authority. I think it highly significant that anthropologists report that modern foraging societies have no bosses. The existence of such leaderless societies implies that humans don't need bosses to live in societies. So why do we have them?

One popular argument holds that leaders are necessary because, like Uncle Joe Stalin, they know what is good for us better than we know ourselves. But whether leaders know what they are doing better than their followers or not, they can be very useful to a society as a coordinating device for solving the equilibrium selection problem in games for which the traditional methods are too slow or uncertain. On a sailing ship in a storm or in a nation at war, one can't afford to wait for due process to generate a compromise acceptable to all. Henry Ford told us that history is bunk, but at least it teaches us that the way to get a society moving together in a crisis is to delegate authority to a single leader.

The purest examples come from primitive societies—as when Rome made Cincinnatus into a temporary dictator, or the Native Americans of the great plains nominated a temporary war chief. What is the social mechanism that secured obedience to such leaders during their period of tenure, but not before or after?

Traditional theories of how authority works are remarkably threadbare. There is the divine right of kings—but who says God intended that guy to be king and not me? There is the Hobbesian social contract, in which citizens supposedly promise to obey a sovereign in return for security—but why should I keep such a hypothetical promise if I won't suffer from breaking my word? There is the Lockean social contract, in which citizens conditionally trade their natural rights in return for the advantages of living in a civil society—but I wasn't born clutching a little certificate granting me the right to anything at all. There is Rousseau's argument purporting to prove it rational to subordinate one's own desires to the General Will as perceived by those blessed with sublime wisdom—but it isn't rational to cooperate in the Prisoner's Dilemma. And so on.

The real reason that authority can work is that a leader's role is simply to point at a perfect equilibrium of the game being played. If the convention is to honor the leader's choice, then everyone will be optimizing when they do so. No individual will therefore have an incentive to deviate.

The fact that it is only deviations by individuals that are suboptimal is important here, because leaders are unseated by *coalitions* whose members act together in destabilizing a social contract. As James Madison explained, a leader who chooses an equilibrium too far from what a society considers fair therefore risks creating a focal point around which an opposition can coalesce. Rival leaders then appear who appeal to the sense of fairness of their prospective followers.

The small societies created by the pirate crews of the late seventeenth century provide an interesting example. Despite the bloodcurdling stories of popular romance, their social contracts were very democratic. They couldn't dispense with leaders, but pirate captains who failed to treat their crews very fairly would simply be voted out of office. This is one of a number of natural experiments in which small isolated communities have reverted to a social contract closely resembling those of our foraging ancestors.

5.6 Unpleasant Behavior

Utopians like to pretend that unpleasant behavior is necessarily irrational. We have already encountered several examples that show otherwise, and here are some more.

Cheating. Someone brought up in a Western democracy would find the social ambience of a modern hunter-gatherer band unbearably stifling. Our nearest approach is perhaps the teenage clan, whose members discipline each other's behavior so severely that one sometimes wonders whether they received their conformity training in the military. In both cases, the crucial feature that allows the dictatorship of the many to operate so successfully is the small size and closeness of the group, which ensure that a deviation by a member of the group is likely to become common knowledge very quickly. The coordination problem faced by the group in administering punishment is therefore easily solved.

Nevertheless, people living in hunter-gatherer societies still cheat on their social contracts when they think their cheating might not be detected. In some foraging societies, cheating is sufficiently close to the surface that food is shared via tolerated theft and aggressive begging. Cheatingin such a society differs from cheating in ours only in that hunter-gatherers find it harder to get away with it than us, because they live under the continuous public scrutiny of neighbors who are shamelessly inquisitive. My guess is that we therefore all devote a great deal more of our brain capacity to this activity than we realize. It is surely no accident that the psychologists Cosmides and Tooby find that people are very much better at solving logical problems when they arise in the course of tracking down cheaters in social contract problems than elsewhere.

I think it important that we finally put the rose-tinted spectacles of anthropologists like Margaret Mead back in their case. We need to get real about the supposedly noble savages who live in hunter-gatherer societies. Their human nature is no different from ours. The anonymity of a large industrial society creates informational problems for us that our invention of specialized police forces mitigates only to a limited extent. Crime and corruption are therefore rampant in our societies. But it isn't because life in the big city has made us wicked. Hunter-gatherers cheat and steal as well. They murder more often than we do. If their societies look idyllic from the outside, it is only because the equilibrium selection problem in their game of life is easier to solve than ours.

Punishing the innocent. A police force can serve to deter crimes that are traceable to a specific culprit, but what about the kind of antisocial act that it is very hard to pin on any particular individual? Although game theorists have had little success in general in extending the folk theorem to environments in which information is sparse, one punishment mechanism capable of precariously sustaining efficient outcomes has been studied enough to know that it can work. It is called by the aptly unpleasant name of contagion.

An old story gives the basic idea. Sir Walter Raleigh struck his son at a grand dinner for telling the story of a whore who refused to service the son on the grounds that she had lain with his father not an hour before. Some vestigial feelings of filial duty prevented his hitting his father back, and so the son struck an innocent bystander instead, crying, "Box about, 'twill come to my father anon!"

If members of a population are anonymously drawn at random to play the Prisoners' Dilemma over and over again, Raleigh Junior's strategy can be implemented if everyone always plays GRIM without taking into account that their opponent is always some new nameless stranger. If anyone ever cheats, defection will then spread through the whole community like a disease, as more and more innocents are punished for the crime of just one person. Eventually, cooperation will collapse altogether, and the actual criminal will suffer along with everyone else. If prospective deviants are sufficiently rational, they will predict this outcome and curb their impulse to cheat. As the saying goes: what goes around, comes around.

Although the policy of punishing the world for the sins of an individual quickly ceases to make sense when the population gets large, equilibria in which the innocent are punished can still be viable when the cheater can be identified as belonging to a small enough group. Instead of punishing the world when cheated, a player then only punishes the cheater's group. The arrangement works better if all the members of the group being punished are related so that the cheater's personal utility function actually takes into account the pain suffered when others in his group are punished. It works better still when the fact that a member of one clan has been cheated by the member of another clan can be communicated quickly by word of mouth so that the contagion spreads faster than the game can be played.

Examples of cases when such precarious equilibria are upset and the punishment schedule gets implemented are depressingly familiar. One famous case is the hillbilly feud between the Hatfields and the McCoys. Another provides thesetting for *Romeo and Juliet*. But sweeping generalizations from such cases to the inevitability of racism and war are inappropriate. It is just as irrational to punish everybody in a very large group for the misdeeds of its individuals as to punish the whole world.

Public lies. False claims about the world can be kept alive by a web of self-confirming beliefs in much the same way that the authority of kings is sustained. People keep their doubts to themselves for fear of being punished if they don't.

Hans Christian Andersen's story of the naked emperor is the classic example, but my personal favorite is Plato's *Republic*. How is it possible that a book which advocates a mirthless police state run by a racially pure class of natural rulers should be celebrated as a *liberal* masterpiece?[3] The answer is easy. Simply direct amused contempt at anyone who rocks the boat by suggesting otherwise.

Even contradictions can be sustained in this way. The same Council of the Catholic Church that invented Papal Infallibility also proclaimed the necessity of having faith that faith isn't necessary: "If any one say that it is not possible, by the natural light of human reason, to acquire a certain knowledge of the One and True God, let him be anathema." Here it is explicit that punishment is to be inflicted on skeptics, although burning doubters at the stake had gone out of fashion by the late nineteenth century.

The urge to laugh is strong, but how can one forget the millions upon millions of burnt and tortured bodies with which such bizarre memes have defended their existence throughout human history? People tell me that science will eventually triumph, but the immediate prospect seems anything but rosy. Even within the scientific community, the very folk that we trust to guard our standards of truth and objectivity routinely apply the age-old methods of social coercion to suppress ideas of which they disapprove. As in everything else, we need to develop better ways of guarding our guardians, but I don't see any sign of progress on this front.

---

[3] "And God proclaims as a first principle to the rulers, and above all else, that there is nothing we should so anxiously guard as the purity of the race"—Plato's *Republic*.

5.7   Free for All?

Game theory is a morally neutral tool of analysis. To challenge the optimizing assumptions on which it is based because they are thought to entail morally abhorrent conclusions is particularly silly in the context of the folk theorem. Far from implying that only selfish behavior can survive in equilibrium, the theorem shows that a caring attitude toward the weak and helpless can be a stable component of a social contract—even in a society of heartless Mr. Hydes.

But it also works the other way. The same mechanisms can be used to sustain behavior that most readers of this book would prefer were absent from our social contract. Consider, for example, the exclusion of the Ainu from regular Japanese society. Why is it stable to treat the Ainu as outsiders? Because those who don't are treated as outsiders themselves.

After listening to such conclusions, critics often react by saying that it's a waste of time to pay any attention at all to the folk theorem, because its conclusions simply echo the relativist folly that morality is a free-for-all, where anything goes. Let me therefore reiterate the reasons why this response is mistaken.

First, the folk theorem doesn't say that anything goes. For an equilibrium to hold together, the system of duties it embodies must be finely tuned to provide all players with the right incentive to do just the right thing at the right time. It is true that the folk theorem nevertheless leaves the field open for a vast range of different social contracts. But if this were false, the folk theorem would necessarily have failed to take account of something important in human nature. After all, what do we find in the history books if not a vast range of diverse social contracts?

Second, it is foolish to complain that moral judgments—whether absolute or relative—are absent from the statement of the folk theorem. The folk theorem is about what is *feasible*. It tells us the class of social contracts that can survive as equilibria. To say something about what is *optimal*, we need a theory of how social contracts are selected from the feasible set.

Chapter 6

Duty

Keep me always at it, and I'll keep you always at
it, you keep someone else always at it. There you are
with the Whole Duty of Man in a commercial country.

Mr. Pancks, from Dickens' *Little Dorrit*

6.1 The Good, the Right and the Seemly

Secular moral theories can be loosely categorized into theories of the Good, the Right,
and the Seemly. Those who lean to the left emphasize the Good. Philosophers call
them consequentialists. They maintain the existence of an *a priori* common good
whose advancement takes priority over our own selfish concerns. Utilitarians and
welfarists are the most vocal members of this lobby.

Conservatives prefer theories of the Right. Philosophers call such theories deontological, and see them as the natural opposition to the consequentialist theories
of the left. Deontologists maintain the existence of natural rights, which it is our
duty to respect regardless of the consequences. The right to private property is
particularly cherished.

Diogenes remarked that he had seen Plato's cups and table, but had yet to see
his Cupness or Tableness. I feel much the same about the Platonism of traditional
theories of the Good and the Right. To pretend that the good and the right are
anything other than products of human evolution is to abandon all hope of making
sense of human morality.

It is inadequate to say that talk of inalienable or imprescriptible natural rights
in documents like the 1789 Declaration of the Rights of Man is nonsense. In the
words of Jeremy Bentham: it is "nonsense upon stilts". I value my personal liberty
no less than the founders of the American Republic or the engineers of the Glorious
Revolution of 1688, but I don't see that anything but ephemeral advantage is to be
gained by asserting the obviously false proposition that we *can't* be stripped of our
liberties—especially when those claiming this "truth" to be self-evident turn out to
be slavers like John Locke or Thomas Jefferson.

Don't we imprison or execute criminals and therefore deprive them of their supposedly inalienable rights? The illusion that matters are otherwise is only maintained by pretending that those whose rights are alienated are not properly to be counted as citizens. The real and unwelcome truth is that we possess only those rights we are actually able to exercise—and history shows that we can be stripped of these very easily indeed.

We retain what rights we have only because enough of us keep sufficient power in our collective hands that authoritarians are unable to take them away. Any propaganda that conceals this harsh reality is a danger to those of us who don't wish to live under oppressive regimes. I believe that we would do better to abandon all the rhetoric about inalienable natural rights—however effective it may be in the short run—lest we succeed in convincing our children that the price of freedom isn't eternal vigilance.

Since naturalists like myself believe that the Good is no less a human invention than the Right, traditionalists imagine that we have nowhere left to stand. But our denial of the existence of the Good and the Right as moral absolutes doesn't imply that we are talking nonsense when we distinguish the good from the bad and the right from the wrong in our daily lives. Cupness and Tableness are no less human inventions than the Good and the Right, but cups and tables nevertheless exist.

I try to capture this down-to-earth attitude to morality by calling it a theory of the *seemly.* Although theories of the seemly aren't currently popular among moral philosophers, they have a long and respectable intellectual history. Aristotle, Epicurus, and Hume are perhaps the most famous western exponents of the approach, but if one could mention only one name it would have to be that of Confucius.

Within a theory of the seemly, things aren't good or right in themselves; they are good or right because they are generally held to be good or right in a particular society. For example, I believe that successful societies need to treat certain privileges as though they were inalienable, and certain duties as though they were obligatory. But we don't behave like this because we are gifted with some inborn notion of the Right, any more than baboons are guided by some Higher Morality when they decide whether it is their turn to groom or be groomed.

In seeking to put together a theory of the seemly, naturalists lay a heavy burden on their backs. For consequentialists and deontologists everything is simple. A few passes with a metaphysical wand, a puff or two of philosophical smoke, and here is yet another example of the one true Good or Right, bristling with jargon and looking round for rivals to define out of existence. But naturalists have to try and explain why their mundane concepts of the good and right evolved. How do they work? What is their evolutionary function?

6.2   Rights

II:3.2

I believe that human conceptions of the good derive from observing how real societies *select* equilibria in practice. We therefore won't be able to say anything much about the good until we finally get round to studying how fairness norms work in the coming chapters. But we can tackle the subject of rights and duties immediately, because I think that human conceptions of the right derive from observing how we *sustain* equilibria, as described in the previous two chapters.

Even this proposed division of labor between the good and the right is controversial, since it overturns the traditional view that a choice must be made between consequentialism and deontology. The way I see it, one might as well insist on a choice being made between optimality and feasibility. We can't say what social contracts are feasible without knowing how equilibria are sustained in the game of life. We can't say what social contracts to call optimal without knowing how equilibria are selected in the game of life.

It follows that the good and the right aren't rival concepts in a theory of the seemly. They are simply words we use to help describe aspects of a social contract. Something is morally right when an approved strategy has been followed in sustaining the current equilibrium. Something is morally good when an equilibrium has been selected in the manner approved by the current social contract.

Duties. To say it is right to do something will be taken to mean the same as saying that one has a duty to do it. The English language invites confusion here by allowing us to argue that it is right that we should care for our own parents when they grow old, but that we have a right to leave elderly strangers to the care of others. I believe this second usage is adequately captured by saying that we have a right to take an action if and only if we have no duty to avoid it.

In game theory terms, Adam's duty lies in not deviating from the rules that characterize the strategy or strategies specified for him by the social contract.

This isn't the same as saying that players have a duty to abide by the rules of the game of life. Players *can't* break the rules of the game. If it were within their power to break them, they wouldn't be the correct rules. But nothing physical prevents Adam from deviating from the strategy assigned to him by the current social contract. If he doesn't, then it is appropriate for us to congratulate him on doing his duty. If he does, then the strategies the social contract assigns to us require that we punish his deviation. Usually our duty in this regard will consist of no more than registering disapproval of his antisocial behavior, but it is a duty nevertheless, and we will be punished to some degree by others if we are thought to be shirking it.

It is right to do one's duty, but one has *a* right to take an action if and only if one doesn't have a duty to refrain from it. Most people are happy with this definition until they realize that it restricts the extent to which the rhetoric of rights can be applied in defending the welfare of the helpless. For example, the definition makes it empty to claim that a tree has a right not to be cut down, or that the generations to come have a right to be left a fair share of the world's resources.

A tree or an unborn human is powerless, and so can't be a player in the game of life. Animals, babies, the senile, and the mentally ill are only marginally less helpless, and hence equally unable to take on duties. They are therefore correspondingly unable to exercise any rights under the social contract. Critics take this to mean that those without power are to be thrown on the scrap heap, but nobody is saying anything of the kind. Looking out of the window right now, I can see my grandchildren playing against a background of ancient trees. Neither the trees nor my grandchildren have any power, but they don't need any power because I am here to look after them. If my parents were still alive, I would defend them equally stoutly, even if the whole world were to join Plato in asserting that those who can no longer work lose their right to live.

Nor is it necessary that the powerless suffer even when they are totally unloved. In the previous chapter, we saw an example of a stable social contract in which the elderly are helpless invalids unloved by anyone, but who nevertheless fare as well as their younger compatriots. They aren't helped because they have a right to be helped. They are helped because those who are still playing the game have a duty to care for their elders—a duty that is enforced by other players in the game.

I am not denying that it can often be very effective as a matter of practical politics to invent supposedly inalienable rights that would improve the lot of various underclasses if taken seriously. But such inventions wouldn't be effective in a rational world, because everyone would recognize that the rhetoric with which they are pressed is just so much hot air. Instead, people would urge a move to a social contract in which those with the power to help were duty bound to do so.

For those who wish to live in a caring society, I believe it to be a dangerous mistake to allow sentiment to blur this point. There isn't any point in talking about rights without simultaneously discussing their concurrent duties. One then can't evade the nub of the matter: how are these duties enforced?

6.3   Dressing Up

II:3.2.2

In simple cases, identifying a right action with an equilibrium action trivializes the notion of a right, since the set of actions from which a player is free to choose after fulfilling his obligations may then contain only one alternative.

Suppose, for example, that the game of life is the infinitely repeated Prisoners' Dilemma, and the social contract being operated calls for Adam and Eve to use the GRIM strategy, which requires that players always cooperate by playing *dove* as long as the opponent reciprocates, but switch permanently to *hawk* if the opponent ever cheats on the implicit deal. With the GRIM social contract, Adam has a duty to play *dove* unless Eve has previously deviated by playing *hawk*. In the latter case, Adam has a duty to punish Eve by always choosing *hawk*. After doing his duty, Adam is then left no room for any discretion in the exercise of his rights.

The idea of a right only becomes significant in games of life with more structure. Amartya Sen has popularized the case of the right to choose what clothes you wear.[1]

I:2.3.3

Should Adam have the right to decide whether he goes naked or wears a fig leaf?

One can graft this issue onto the regular repeated Prisoners' Dilemma without much difficulty. Before each repetition of the Prisoners' Dilemma, assume that a chance move determines whether Adam prefers to wear a fig leaf or go naked today. He remains free to dress according to his preferences or not, but if he acts

---

[1]Sen's paradox—that individual rights are incompatible with efficiency—evaporates with my definition of a right.

in accordance with his preferences, add a tiny amount to each of his payoffs in today's Prisoners' Dilemma. If he acts contrary to his preference, subtract a tiny amount from each of his payoffs. Eve always prefers that Adam cover his nakedness in public. To register this preference, add or subtract a tiny amount to her payoffs in today's Prisoners' Dilemma, depending on what Adam wears.

It is easy to write down two social contracts for this new game of life. In the first, both players use the GRIM strategy without any reference to the manner in which Adam is dressed. In the second social contract, Eve plans to administer the same grim punishment if Adam leaves off his fig leaf as she would apply if he were ever to play *hawk*. He reciprocates by planning to switch to *hawk* should he ever forget himself by appearing naked in public.

In the first social contract, Adam has a duty never to play *hawk* unless Eve does so first, but he has a right to dress as he chooses. In the second social contract, Adam has a duty never to play *hawk* nor to appear naked. When it come to the exercise of his rights in this second case, his choice therefore reduces to wearing a fig leaf or wearing a fig leaf.

6.4 Moral Responsibility

II:3.2.3

Traditional theories of distributional justice differ as to the criteria that should determine who gets what. We are variously told that Adam's share of the social cake should be depend on his need, his worth, his merit, or his work. In the case of work, for example, the Bible tells us that a laborer is worthy of his hire. Aesop has the story of the ant and the grasshopper. Plato's *Republic* tells us that someone who can no longer work loses the right to live.

It seems to me that all such traditional theories have something valuable to say about how rewards and punishments are determined by our current social contract. Each theory has its own domain of application. For example, social benefits are supposedly determined by need, and Nobel prizes by merit. But none of the theories is adequate as a universal explanation of how we currently assign blame or desert.

Nor is the claim that a utopian society would settle on one of the theories to the exclusion of the others often strongly pressed. I take this fact as a tacit acceptance of the need to look for a radically different type of theory—one that isn't anchored in the practices or prejudices of a particular society or subsociety at some particular period in its history, but that explicitly recognizes that blame and desert are relative concepts that often vary sharply as we move from one social contract to another.

My specific suggestion is that attributing blame to players in the game of life is operationally equivalent to identifying them as appropriate targets for punishment within a particular social contract. To attribute desert to players is to identify them as a suitable targets for reward. From this perspective, saying that Adam is to blame ceases to be regarded as an *explanation* of why he is punished; it becomes instead a *description* of a person who has deviated from the current social contract.

For example, when the GRIM social contract is employed in the infinitely repeated Prisoners' Dilemma, a player is deemed to be worthy of blame if he deviates from equilibrium play, and deserving of credit if he doesn't. His reward in the latter case is that his opponent continues to play *dove*. His punishment if he deviates consists in his opponent playing *hawk* at all later times.

My theory therefore treats the concepts of blame and desert as emergent phenomena. Neither concept appears as a primitive notion when we specify the equilibrium in the game of life that constitutes the current social contract, but they arise naturally when we try to describe how the strategies that sustain an efficient social contract operate in practice.

I:2.2.4   **Causal reversal.** Such an approach to blame and desert recalls a major fallacy that critics of modern utility theory seem unable to avoid. The modern theory doesn't say that Eve chooses a rather than b because the utility of a exceeds that of b. On the contrary, the utility of a is chosen to be greater than the utility of b because it has been observed that Eve always chooses a rather than b.

Similarly, according to my account of blame and desert, Eve is isn't punished *because* she is to blame. Eve is held to be to blame *because* the social contract being operated requires that she be punished.

In spite of the various aphorisms that recognize the need we feel to hate those whom we have injured, traditionalists find it hard to believe that anyone might be serious in proposing that the causal chain taken for granted by folk psychology needs to be reversed. How can it be possible to talk about just punishment in the absence of an *a priori* understanding of the nature of moral responsibility? What will happen to society if we cease to hold individuals responsible for their own actions?

The answer to the first question is that this is what happens already. Compare the horror with which Don Carlo expresses his love for his stepmother in Verdi's opera with the matter-of-fact assumption in old Tibet that the son of a widower had a right to sleep with his father's new wife. This is just one of many examples in which one society insists that we have a duty to avoid a piece of behavior that would be right in another society. As for just punishment, the following psychological experiment is surely food for thought.[2]

Subjects viewed live pictures of an innocent victim supposedly suffering painful electric shocks for some considerable time. When powerless to intervene, the subjects invent reasons in debriefing sessions why the victim is somehow unworthy, as compared with subjects who think they can diminish the shocks by pressing a button. The experimenters speculate that the subjects denigrate the victim in order to sustain the false belief that we live in a "just world"—that it is "fair" for victims who apparently suffer more to be treated so because they are less worthy. This seems a very reasonable interpretation to me, but the immediate point is that the subjects certainly aren't behaving according to the tenets of traditional thinking on the way blame and desert are assigned.

As for the second question, nobody is suggesting that we cease to hold people responsible for their own actions. On the contrary, identifying an efficient social contract with an equilibrium in a repeated game makes it necessary that people be punished for their deviations. However, when people ask the second question, they really mean to protest at the idea of blaming or rewarding people for things over

---

[2]Lerner and Simmons, *Journal of Personality and Social Psychology* 4 (1966), 203–210.

which they have no control. The inference is that only acts we commit of our own free will should be subject to punishment.

Free will. The orthodox view is that those who act immorally are to blame for their actions because they were free to choose otherwise. Since they are to blame, we are then entitled to punish them in proportion to their crime. But is a kid brought up in the ghetto really free to choose? Isn't he just a victim of his environment? *II:3.2.4*

A traditionalist sees this classic left–right dilemma as a problem about free will, and expects a naturalist to tackle it by proposing some mechanistic alternative to the personalized unmoved mover inside our heads that Kantians think is necessary to explain free choice. It is true that our language structures the problem in this way, but naturalists see no need to accept the way problems were structured by the folk wisdom of our ancestors.

This isn't to deny that what people say is often useful in explaining why they do things. Nor is it to suggest for one moment that anything but natural phenomena are involved when I consciously decide to twiddle my thumbs, and then my thumbs twiddle. The point is rather that a natural explanation of the notion of blame and desert doesn't hinge on how we explain free will.

A suitable analogy is to be found in the social mechanism traditionally used to control the outbreak of a dangerously infectious disease like scarlet fever. We recognize that being quarantined is unpleasant, but we don't ask whether people got infected by accident or through negligence before temporarily imprisoning them. We isolate them, because the alternative is that the disease will spread, and we don't want healthy people to catch it.

Traditionalists who reject this suggestion fail to notice that our current social contract *already* institutionalizes this practice. This isn't to say that the level of punishment we administer to defaulters is never determined by the extent they were in control of the events leading up their crimes. On the contrary, such cases are clearly the norm, because an efficient social contract won't call for penalties to be inflicted when the circumstances under which the crime was committed are such that inflicting the penalty won't deter similar deeds.[3]

If it can be demonstrated that Abel's death at the hand of Cain was accidental by pointing to the immediate cause of the crime, we don't need to follow the practice of our Saxon predecessors by holding Cain to blame, and demanding the payment of weregeld. But when the causal chain is uncertain, our social contract needs to be ruthless. All of us, for example, are held to be guilty until proved innocent when it comes to paying tax.

Some legal examples are even more blatant. Consider the doctrine that ignorance of the law is no excuse. It is clear why this doctrine is necessary. If the prosecution had to prove the accused knew each letter of the law in question, everybody would plead ignorance nearly all the time, and the legal system would collapse.

---

[3]But there are plenty of exceptions, as with the continuing execution of mentally ill criminals in Texas. The paranoid schizophrenic executed today subscribed to the same folk wisdom as his executioners: " I knew it was a mistake. I have no one to blame but myself."—*New York Times*, 26 March, 2003.

The doctrine that the seriousness of a crime is determined by the consequences to the victim also fits the same pattern, because the extent of the damage suffered by a victim is often largely outside the criminal's control. For example, a mugger may hit two victims equally hard, but he will only be tried for murder if one of them happens to have an unusually thin skull. Nearer to home, how many of us have escaped imprisonment and ruin as a consequence of negligent driving only because we happen not to have hurt anybody?

At the social level, we routinely inflict the most exquisite psychological tortures on those around us we find ugly, boring, clumsy, socially inept, or charmless. Those of us who think of ourselves as intellectuals are relentless in the humiliations we heap on the stupid and uneducated. In medieval times, those suffering from clinical depression were held to account for the sin of *accidie*. Within living memory, bastards were held in contempt. Skin color and sex still provide ammunition for those unable to come up with other reasons why they are entitled to inflict injury on others. It is particularly revealing that we commonly excuse ourselves from taking an interest in street people by calling them schizos.

Such examples refute the claim that the principle on which our social contract works is that legal or social punishments are determined according to some prior notion of moral responsibility. Presumably, people hang on to this idea because they believe that taking a more realistic attitude to the attribution of blame and desert will lead to the collapse of our moral institutions. But our prisons are *already* full of youngsters from deprived backgrounds whom everyone agrees "never had a chance". All that will change if we stop pretending they had the same free choice as youngsters from privileged backgrounds is that we will stop kidding ourselves.

The conclusion certainly won't be that criminals from the ghettos will be let off because "they couldn't help it". A social contract that doesn't discourage antisocial behavior won't survive, and so deviants have to be punished for the same reason that we quarantine those suffering from dangerous diseases.

Chapter 7

Kinship

Love, love, love.
It's easy.

John Lennon

7.1 Sympathy

My priorities for social contracts are stability, efficiency, and fairness. We have seen how stability can be modeled by requiring a social contract to be an equilibrium in the game of life. We have also seen how efficient social contracts can be sustained in repeated games by the reciprocity mechanism. The ground has therefore been cleared for a discussion of fairness norms, but we still have quite a lot of hoeing and ploughing to do before we can sow any seeds.

One of many problems in writing about fairness is that critics are impatient with the idea that it evolved as an equilibrium selection device. They prefer to explain our concern for justice by arguing that we just happen to have the kind of other-regarding preferences that make us care for the well-being of others.

Nobody denies the existence of other-regarding preferences. Mothers will sometimes sacrifice their own lives that their baby might live. Lovers commonly claim to be similarly devoted to their partners, and sometimes they are. In such cases, the relevant economic jargon is characteristically dismal. People are said to have a *sympathetic* utility function, with arguments that directly represent the welfare of others.

However, to recognize that we sometimes care a lot about the welfare of some other people isn't to concede that we always care a lot about everybody. The contrary view is sustained only by turning a blind eye to anything but the good relations that commonly hold within circles of close friends and the family. But the evidence that people feel little sympathy for the welfare of strangers is just as compelling as the evidence that they love their near and dear. Indeed, our history is an almost unbroken record of the misery, suffering, and cruelty that some human beings choose to inflict on others.

This chapter explains the evolutionary reasons why we should expect people to love their near and dear—and only their near and dear. For those who think that love is what makes the social world go round, this seems like a disastrous conclusion. But if love were the solution to all our social problems, why would Nature have needed to endow us with a sense of justice?

I think that folk wisdom fails to distinguish adequately between love and fairness because evolution is a tinkerer that seldoms invents a new mechanism if it can adapt an old mechanism to a new purpose. When endowing us with the *empathetic* preferences that we need as inputs to the original position when using a fairness norm to solve coordination games played with strangers, Nature therefore recycled the same structure that had evolved for the *sympathetic* preferences that operate within families. Naive utopians like John Lennon—who thought that love is all you really need—then fall into the trap of confusing an empathetic preference with a sympathetic preference. However, the reasons why I think this is such a bad mistake will have to wait until the next chapter.

7.2   Kin Selection

II:2.5.2

The animal kingdom overflows with examples of cooperation within the family. African hunting dogs regurgitate food to help out a hungry pack brother. Marmosets and tamarins help to care for their nephews and nieces in extended families. Male birds of some species do the same when the chances of their being able to reproduce in the current year are low enough. Some aphids will give up their lives defending their siblings from attack. Musk oxen similarly form a defensive ring around the weaker members of the family when attacked by wolves. Why is kinship so important in the animal kingdom?

Hamilton's rule.   William Hamilton's *Narrow Roads of Geneland* is an account of the life and work of an oddball genius, whose worth wasn't recognized until relatively late in his life. One of his achievements was to formulate the evolutionary explanation of cooperation within the family nowadays known as kin selection.

Animals related by blood share genes. A gene that modifies some piece of behavior will therefore be replicated more often if it takes into account, not only the extra reproductive opportunities that the modified behavior confers on a host who carries the gene, but also the extra reproductive opportunities it confers on those among the host's relatives who also carry the same gene.

The point was famously made in a semi-serious joke of J. B. S. Haldane. When asked whether he would give his life for another, he replied that the sacrifice would only be worthwhile if it saved two brothers or eight cousins!

Haldane's joke is only funny if you know that your degree of relationship to a full brother is one half, and your degree of relationship to a full cousin is one eighth. These numbers are the probabilities that a recently mutated gene in your body is also to be found in the body of the relative in question.

For example, your degree of relationship to a sibling is one half, because this is the probability that the parent who passed the mutant gene to you also passed it to a sibling. To see that your degree of relationship to a cousin is one eighth, imagine that your cousin is the daughter of your mother's sister. The probability that a mutant gene in your body came from your mother rather than your father is one half. If it came from your mother, the probability it is also in the body of your aunt is one half. If it is in the body of your aunt, the probability she passed it to your cousin is one half. Multiplying these three halves together, we get one eighth.

It is sometimes said that the degree of relationship can't really matter, because human beings share nearly all their genes anyway. But this is to miss the point that we are never concerned with genes that are *always* present in the human body, but only with a particular piece of behavior that will be modified or left alone according to whether a recently mutated gene is present or absent. In line with the selfish gene paradigm, it is from the point of view of such a mutant gene that fitness must be evaluated—not that of the individual host in whose body the gene is carried.

What counts in calculating the fitness of a gene is the average number of times it gets replicated in the next generation. But it doesn't matter which of two or more identical versions of a gene is copied. A copy made from a gene in my sister's body is just as good as a copy made from an identical gene in my own body. When we figure out the fitness of a gene in my body, we therefore have to take account, not only of the effect of my behavior on my own reproductive success, but of its effect on the reproductive success of my relatives. Hamilton called the outcome of such a calculation an *inclusive* fitness.

If my sister is my only relative, then a mutant gene in my body shouldn't simply count the extra number of children I will have on average as a consequence of its modifying my behavior. It should use Hamilton's rule, which requires adding in the extra number of children that my sister will have—weighted by one half, because this is the probability that the mutant gene is also in her body. For example, if I expect to have one child less as a consequence of changing my behavior, and my sister expects to have four children more, then Hamilton's rule says that the inclusive fitness of my new strategy is $-1 + \frac{1}{2} \times 4 = 1$. My personal loss is therefore outweighed by my sister's gain.

Figure 15 shows how our assessment of a social contract in terms of fitnesses needs to be changed from S to T when Alice and Bob cease to be unrelated strangers and become brother and sister.

Does Hamilton's rule work in practice? There is no shortage of anthropological evidence demonstrating the importance of kinship in primitive societies. For example, in societies whose social contract doesn't punish promiscuity, some of the functions undertaken by a father in our own society are taken on by a child's maternal uncle— the reason being that he knows his degree of relationship to the child is a quarter, whereas nobody knows who the real father may be.

Such anthropological data is suggestive, but it doesn't provide a numerical test of Hamilton's rule for humans. However, two studies carried out by a team of psychologists headed by Robin Dunbar and Henry Plotkin suggest that it may work surprisingly well.

The experimenters chose a relative from a list provided by each subject. This relative was paid according to the length of time that the subject was willing to persist in performing a demanding knee-bending exercise. When the degree of relationship

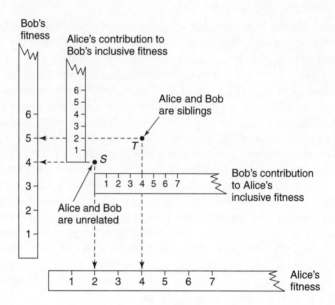

Figure 15: Assessing social contracts in terms of inclusive fitnesses.

was plotted against the logarithm of the time the exercise was endured, the data points clustered around a straight line—as predicted by Hamilton's rule.[1] Subjects were asked whether they liked or disliked the relatives on their list, but this variable turned out to have little or no predictive power.

Blood is thicker than water. It will now be obvious why evolutionary biologists expect to find sympathetic preferences holding among family members in proportion to the closeness of their family relationship. As the saying goes: blood is thicker than water.

We have already seen the implications for game theory in chapter 4, where we explored the consequences of replacing the players in the Prisoners' Dilemma by a pair of lovers. The concern that lovers show for each other has the obvious biological explanation that they are likely to raise children together, but the same principles apply whenever players sympathize with each other.

When relatives play a game, the payoffs need to be identified with their inclusive fitnesss rather than their individual fitnesses. Sometimes this will change the character of the game entirely, as when we replaced the players by lovers in chapter 4, and so converted the Prisoners' Dilemma into the Prisoners' Delight. More generally, we must expect that the equilibria of games played within the family will

---

[1] "A cross-cultural experimental study of altruism", R. Dunbar *et al*, Department of Psychology, University College London.

involve a great deal more cooperation than those played between strangers.

I think this is why one piece of folk wisdom is right on target: morality begins in the family. As Aristotle explained, it is within the household that we must first seek the "sources and springs of friendship, political organization, and justice".

7.3 Social Insects

In game theory, the unit of analysis is the individual rather than the group. Philosophers call this the principle of methodological individualism. The dangers in diverging from the principle are plain to see.

In biology, there is Wynne-Edwards' group selection fallacy. In social science, there are the many fallacies claiming that cooperation is rational in the Prisoners' Dilemma. In political philosophy, abstract entities like Labor and Capital were once treated as players in a mighty two-person game. This Marxian fancy is now out of date, but communitarian philosophers maintain the tradition by similarly personalizing the notion of Community.

Behind these and similar mistakes is the belief that we can rely on altruism or solidarity to persuade individuals to put the interests of their group before their own. Nobody denies that one can persuade some of the people to sacrifice themselves some of the time, but proponents of this line need to convince us that the same can be true for most of the people most of the time. Thomas Hobbes explained long ago why such aspirations are hopeless: "Certain living creatures, as Bees or Ants, live sociably one with another ... and therefore some man may perhaps desire to know why Mankind cannot do the same. To which I answer ... amongst these creatures, the common good differeth not from the private."

Is this really why the social insects are so different from us? I think the way biologists answer this question also teaches us something about ourselves.

Eusociality. A species is eusocial if it lives in colonies with overlapping genera-   *II:2.5.3*
tions in which one or a few individuals produce all the offspring, and the rest serve as sterile helpers.

Eusociality is rare except among the *Hymenoptera*—the order of insects that includes ants, bees, and wasps. It is thought that true eusociality has evolved independently at least twelve times in the *Hymenoptera*, but only twice elsewhere— the exceptional cases being the termites of the order *Isoptera* and the recently studied naked mole-rats of the order *Rodentia*.

Why did evolution generate casts of sterile workers? Why do they work tirelessly for the sake of others? Why is this phenomenon common among the *Hymenoptera* and rare elsewhere?

The sum is greater than its parts. At one level, the puzzle is easy to resolve. Groups working together are usually more productive than individuals acting separately. Economists say that the productive process then has increasing returns to scale. Up to some limit, each extra worker increases the amount produced by more than the worker before.

Adam Smith famously gave the example of a pin factory. If each worker had to make each pin all by himself, the total number of pins produced per day wouldn't be very large. But if the factory is organized so that each worker has a specialized task, like sharpening the pin or drawing out the wire, the output can be increased enormously. In the case studied by Adam Smith, this division of labor increased each worker's productivity by a factor of 240.

The same is true in a beehive or an anthill. Very large numbers of sterile workers specialize in protecting and caring for the young, while the queen specializes in being an egg-laying machine. As a consequence, the total number of young produced is immensely larger than if pairs of bees or ants brought up separate families by themselves.

It is clear why the queen benefits, but what's in it for the workers? They sacrifice the opportunity to bring up their own children in favor of bringing up the queen's children instead. Critics of methodological individualism see such puzzles as a vindication of their position, but true understanding comes from more methodological individualism rather than less. We need to remember that the real players in this game aren't the ants or bees we see scurrying around, but the genes they carry in their bodies.

Each fertile child the queen produces is related to the workers. They are the workers' brothers and sisters. A mutant gene that expresses itself in the body of a worker therefore has a lot of relatives to count when it computes its inclusive fitness. All the queen's fertile children—weighted by their degree of relationship to a worker—must be counted when calculating the benefit to a worker of striving hard in support of the queen. Since a pin factory has nothing on a beehive or an anthill when it comes to productivity, the balance therefore comes down very firmly on the side of eusociality.

All this would be equally true of the human species if we had a sterile worker cast, but we traditionally bring up our children in extended families rather than biological factories. So why didn't evolution take us down the same road as the *Hymenoptera?*

Sex.   The *Hymenoptera* are haplodiploid, which means that unfertilized eggs grow into haploid males and fertilized eggs grow into diploid females. In a haploid species, each locus on a chromosome hosts just one gene. Humans are diploid, with each locus hosting two genes, one from the mother and one from the father. This is why the degree of relationship between human sisters is one half, since a child gets one gene from each parent at every locus, and the gene it gets from each parent is equally likely to be either of the two genes the parent carries at that locus.

By contrast, Hamilton pointed out that the degree of relationship between sisters in the *Hymenoptera* is three fourths, because each locus on their chromosomes gets the *same* gene from their father, and a randomly chosen gene from the pair carried at that locus by their mother. The probability that any particular gene in the body of one of the sterile workers—who are genetically female—comes from one particular parent is one half. The probability that a paternal gene is the same in two sisters is one. The probability that a maternal gene is the same is one half. Putting all this information together we get a degree of relationship of three fourths by calculating $\frac{1}{2} \times 1 + \frac{1}{2} \times \frac{1}{2}$.

Robert Trivers took this further by observing that we mustn't forget that colonies reproduce through their male offspring as well as their female offspring. We therefore need to worry about the degree of relationship between the genetically female workers and their brothers, the drones. The calculation is then $\frac{1}{2} \times 0 + \frac{1}{2} \times \frac{1}{2}$, which is only one fourth.

Sex ratios. If the sex ratio among the *hymonoptera* were 50:50, as it is in a species with relatively simple genetics like our own, then the average degree of relationship between a sterile worker and a fertile sibling would only be the average of three fourths and one fourth, which is one half—the same as in our own species. But the sex ratio among the hymoneptera isn't 50:50. In many species, it is about 75:25 in favor of fertile females as opposed to fertile males. How come?

To answer this question we have to think about the mating game different species play. Our own mating game is rather like a multiplayer version of Matching Pennies, in which each player hopes for a mismatch. Assuming that the probability that a member of one sex gets to mate is proportional to the number of members of the other sex in the population as a whole, then a mutant that always produced only members of the sex in short supply would always be able to invade the population.

For an equilibrium, we therefore need the same number of fertile men and women in the population. If everybody uses the same strategy, it follows that the probability of a boy and a girl must always be the same at every birth. This isn't quite true in *Homo sapiens*, because baby boys used to die more frequently than baby girls before modern health care was available. The actual sex ratio at birth—about 100:105—was therefore just about right to equalize the numbers of girls and boys who survived to breeding age.

Among the *Hymenoptera*, it is the genes expressed in the workers that determine the sex ratio, because it is the workers who rear the young. The sex ratio must therefore make a worker indifferent between raising a fertile male or a fertile female infant. This happens only when the sex ratio is 75:25, because the payoff to a mutant gene expressed in the body of a worker is then $\frac{3}{4} \times \frac{1}{4}$ from producing a male and $\frac{1}{4} \times \frac{3}{4}$ from producing a female. Since these payoffs are equal, a mixed equilibrium can survive in which females are born with probability three fourths and males with probability one fourth.

With this sex ratio, the average degree of relationship a sterile worker has with a fertile brother or sister is $\frac{3}{4} \times \frac{3}{4} + \frac{1}{4} \times \frac{1}{4}$, which is five eighths. If the worker were human, the degree of relationship would be one half. Human workers would therefore have to work harder on behalf of a human queen in order to derive the same benefit as a worker in an anthill or a beehive.

Getting started? The fact that game theory allows evolutionary biologists to predict sex ratios in species where these aren't symmetric is one of the more convincing demonstrations that we must be doing something right, but we still don't have an explanation of how eusociality got started in the first place.

Presumably, all ants and bees were once fertile. The sex ratio would then have been $50:50$, just as in humans. Perhaps daughters pitched in to help their mothers raise their siblings to some extent, as with some primate and bird species. Now imagine the appearance of a mutant gene that changed the behavior of less fertile daughters so that they helped their mothers a little bit more in a manner biased towards raising *girls*.[2] Would such a gene be able to invade the population? Since the degree of relationship among sisters in the *Hymenoptera* is three fourths, conditions would be favorable if the change of behavior generated more than $1\frac{1}{3}$ extra sisters for each child of her own that a worker lost. For conditions to be favorable among humans, a worker would need more than 2 extra siblings for each lost child of her own.

Of course, many mysteries remain. Why are the *Hymenoptera* haplodiploid? How come only some species in the order are eusocial? What about colonies with multiple queens? What of Pachycondyla villosa, in which species *unrelated* queens apparently found colonies together? What of the many puzzles posed by termites?

Critics seize on such admissions of ignorance as an excuse to accuse sociobiologists of telling just-so stories, but I think their criticisms simply reveal a failure to understand how science works.

7.4   Modifying Hamilton's Rule?

Hamilton's rule predicts that Alice will make decisions on a utilitarian basis by maximizing the sum of her relatives' fitnesses after weighting them according to her degree of relationship with each relative. Biology therefore seems to have cast a vote in favor of Bentham and Mill, but Kantians needn't despair, since Hamilton's rule isn't the end of the story.

Hamilton's rule works fine when animals interact with the outside world. For example, should a worker bee commit suicide by stinging an intruder it finds in the hive? The answer is yes, because its inclusive fitness is thereby increased. But things aren't so simple when relatives play a game *with each other*. We are then led to a principle that isn't so distant from Kant's categorical imperative.

In chapter 4, we replaced the players in the Prisoners' Dilemma by two lovers who care twice as much for their partner as they do for themselves. The game then became the Prisoners' Delight of figure 7, in which it is a Nash equilibrium for both players to cooperate by playing *dove*.

If we do the same thing when the players are identical twins, we get a new version of the Prisoners' Delight shown in figure 16. Its only Nash equilibrium requires that both players choose *dove*—but the logic of Nash equilibrium isn't appropriate here. It makes sense only if Alice and Bob are separate players, who make their strategy choices *independently*. But if their choice of strategy is genetically determined, this won't be true of a pair of twins. Any gene present in the body of one player is

---

[2] Not boys, because a worker's degree of relationship to a brother is only one fourth.

then also present in the body of the other. Whatever one player does, the other will therefore do the same.

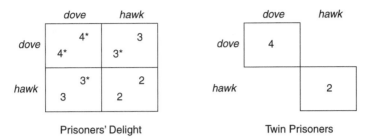

Figure 16: Playing with your twin.

It is therefore wrong to model the situation as the *two-player* game on the left of figure 16. The right model is the *one-player* game shown on the right, in which a single player chooses between (*dove, dove*) and (*hawk, hawk*), receiving $2 + 2$ in the first case and $1 + 1$ in the second case. Since 4 is bigger than 2, the solution to this one-player game is (*dove, dove*).

The reasoning is that of Kant's categorical imperative. When used to analyze a two-player game, it is therefore sometimes called the fallacy of the twins. But it isn't a fallacy here, because our Alice and Bob really are twins.

What happens if Alice and Bob aren't identical twins, but brother and sister? If we are talking about a dominant gene, the game being played is then shown on the left of figure 17.[3] Each payoff is half the corresponding payoff in the Prisoners' Dilemma plus half times twice the payoff a player would get if the opponent were to choose the same strategy. The halves in this calculation arise because the probability that human siblings share a recently mutated gene is one half. The second payoff is multiplied by two because this is the case in which Alice and Bob share the same gene, and hence are effectively twins.

Figure 17: Sibling rivalry

The starred payoffs show that cooperation continues to be an equilibrium when

---

[3] A more complicated calculation is necessary for a recessive gene.

Alice and Bob are brother and sister, but it will be obvious that this will cease to be true if we decrease their degree of relationship enough. In fact, making them cousins is enough to tip the balance so that defection again becomes the only equilibrium.

Utilitarian or Kantian?   Both utilitarians and Kantians argue for cooperation in the Prisoners' Dilemma; the former because the sum of utilities is then maximized, the latter because the categorical imperative says so. In the absence of external enforcement, neither position is acceptable to a game theorist, because both ignore the fact that individuals have an incentive to deviate from the proposed solution.

Matters change when we consider games played within the family. Hobbes wasn't quite right in saying that the common good among ants and bees differeth not from the private good, but he was near enough. Genetically programmed relatives often have their goals sufficiently closely aligned that a game which would be the Prisoners' Dilemma if played by strangers becomes a game in which only cooperation survives as an equilibrium.

I think this result casts light on where both utilitarians and Kantians get their intuition from. They would get the kind of outcomes they want for the kind of reasons they give if the world were merely a larger edition of the comfortable homes in which most bourgeois liberals were lucky enough to be raised. We would then all be one big family, and so the Prisoners' Dilemma would never be played by strangers. But this isn't the way that Nature made us.

7.5   Learning to Play an Equilibrium

The previous section explains how Hamilton's rule needs to be modified when relatives who are genetically programmed with a strategy play each other in a game. The modification is evidently necessary when studying plants and insects, which have ony a limited capacity for learning. But what of birds or mammals?

Clearly the strategies played by higher animals in some games are genetically determined—as in the game over bodily resources played between a mother and her fetus, or the similar game played between fledglings in the nest. But humans aren't genetically programmed with strategies for most of the social games we play.

We mostly find our way to an equilibrium by trial-and-error learning, or by imitating the behavior of more successful players—who may themselves be passing on a tradition established over many generations. Sometimes we even think things out a little, or gain some insight from reading a book. Even more rarely, we may consciously choose an equilibrium after a rational discussion of the options. But none of these ways of arriving at an equilibrium is biological. They are all examples of different kinds of social or cultural evolution.

The assumption that players must *learn* how to play a game makes a significant difference to how we analyze a game played between relatives. If twins have to learn how to play a game, then Alice can no longer count on Bob's playing the same strategy as herself, even though he is her twin. He will play the strategy he has learned to play whatever she may do. Hamilton's rule still applies, and so we must modify the payoffs of the Prisoners' Dilemma to obtain the version of the

Prisoners' Delight shown on the left of figure 16, but now it is correct to take the Nash equilibrium of this modified game as our solution to the problem.

Similarly, if Alice and Bob are brother and sister, then assuming that they have to learn how to play means that we have to replace the game on the left of figure 17 by the game on the right, in which cooperation only just survives as an equilibrium. Any lesser degree of relationship yields a game in which only defection is an equilibrium.

The simplifying paradigm I am proposing for the study of games played by humans therefore has both a biological and a cultural component. Biological considerations determine the payoffs of the game according to Hamilton's rule. Where relevant, we write inclusive fitnesses into the payoff table instead of individual fitnesses. The fact that people have to learn how to play is the cultural aspect of the model. We operationalize this large assumption by simply computing the Nash equilibria of the new game—ignoring the fact that we would need to do something more sophisticated if play were genetically determined.

7.6   Extending the Family

The experimental study on Hamilton's rule in humans mentioned earlier also found that best friends get treated pretty much like brothers or sisters. This is perhaps not so surprising, since the ceremony of sealing friendship with blood to make two men as brothers has independently arisen in several cultures. As for women, the fact that they band together like sisters seems to be taken for granted.

To understand this behavior, I think we need to ask how people know who their relatives are. Can we somehow taste or smell the genetic differences between our relatives and strangers? Women asked to sniff sweaty tee-shirts apparently express a preference for owners whose DNA is remote from their own, but other evidence suggests that their knowledge of what smells to count as exotic has to be learned. For example, children brought up together in communal nurseries on old-style kibbutzim almost never show a sexual interest in each other at a later stage, no matter how distant their genes. It therefore looks as though we have to deduce our degree of relationship to others from the extent to which we find ourselves thrown into their company. Thus Eve deduces that Adam is her brother from the fact that he is always hanging around at mealtimes competing for attention with her mother.

If this conjecture is correct, it has important consequences for the evolution of ethics. It means that the mechanisms that promote altruism within the family may also be triggered within a sufficiently close-knit group of unrelated individuals, as in an army platoon under combat conditions or a teenage street gang. In the clan games played by such groups, my guess is that the brotherhood of man becomes more than an empty metaphor, and actually describes quite closely how members of small insider-groups relate to each other.

How big can such an extended family get? Robin Dunbar suggests that a physical limit is imposed by the inability of our neocortex to handle the enormous volume of information necessary to keep track of the social relationships operating between large numbers of individuals. He offers a variety of anecdotal evidence which suggests that the maximum size for a surrogate family of the type under discussion is something under 150 individuals or so—which is about the right size for a hunter-gatherer community or an army platoon.

7.7 Warm Glow

John Lennon told us that love is easy, but it isn't. Fairness wouldn't be so important to us if we had the capacity to treat everybody like brothers or sisters. Utopians continue to claim that laboratory experiments show otherwise, but we have already seen that such claims don't survive close scrutiny in the case of experiments on games like the Prisoners' Dilemma. It has been repeatedly demonstrated that, as the subjects gain experience, the incidence of cooperation declines until nearly everyone is defecting.

However, although the experimental evidence confirms that our potential for altruism is severely limited, it also refutes the pessimists in the economics profession who claim that people are entirely selfish. We may not be capable of treating all men as brothers, but most of us are capable of treating almost anybody as a relative of some kind. An explanation of this phenomenon isn't hard to find; we evolved in groups of hunter-gatherers in which pretty much everybody was in fact some kind of relative.

This is perhaps why we find ourselves feeling curiously obligated to old school friends or office colleagues, whom we may actively dislike at the conscious level. Our bodies are telling us that this pushy individual demanding an inconvenient favor must be a cousin or an aunt. Even establishing eye contact with a beggar in the street somehow creates enough inner discomfort at neglecting a potential relative that we are sometimes moved to hand over our small change with no prospect of any recompense.

But let me insist one last time that the warm glow we feel when treating strangers like distant relatives isn't enough to change a game like the Tragedy of the Commons into a game in which cooperation emerges as an equilibrium. Matters are different in the games we play with the friends and neighbors in our extended family, but we aren't programmed to treat strangers like members of the family, and only disaster can be expected from utopian projects that proceed as though we were.

Chapter 8

Empathy

O wad some pow'r the giftie gae us
To see oursels as others see us.

Robert Burns

8.1 Empathetic Preferences

When Adam and Eve use the original position to make a fairness judgment, they imagine themselves behind a veil of ignorance that conceals their identities while they bargain over the equilibrium on which to coordinate. While bargaining, both players think it equally likely that they will turn out to be Adam or Eve when they emerge from behind the veil of ignorance.

To evaluate the options available to them in the original position, the players need to compare how it would be to be Adam or Eve in a whole variety of situations. For example, one of the players might prefer to be Adam wearing a fig leaf than Eve eating an apple. Such preferences are called *empathetic*.

It is important to distinguish such empathetic preferences from our personal preferences. I think we have both kinds of preference at once. We reveal our personal preferences whenever we make a rational choice. To buy chocolate ice cream rather than strawberry ice cream when they are equally priced is to reveal a preference for the taste of chocolate to that of strawberries. To plug your ears with wax when Wagnerian music is played is to reveal a preference for silence over noise.

All the transactions considered in orthodox economics are therefore explicable in terms of personal preferences alone. So why are all socially integrated human beings able to express empathetic preferences? What are empathetic preferences for? Nobody can ever *choose* to be Adam wearing a fig leaf rather than Eve eating an apple. We are all stuck with being who we are, whether we like it or not. The situation envisaged in the original position is entirely hypothetical; it can only happen in our imaginations—never in the real world.

I think we have empathetic preferences as well as personal preferences, because we need them as inputs when using the original position to find fair solutions to

113

coordination problems. If I am right in the bold conjecture that we don't use empathetic preferences for anything else, it is a measure of how important fairness must have been to the evolution of our species that Nature should have equipped us with the expensive mental machinery we need to process them.[1]

In any case, it is clear that we need to understand empathetic preferences before we can start trying to figure out what Adam and Eve would agree on if they were to bargain behind the veil of ignorance.

8.2 Empathetic Identification

Adam empathizes with Eve when he puts himself in her shoes to see things from her point of view. Humans can certainly do this. Chimpanzees also seem to be able empathize with each other. Monkeys are said not to be able to do it at all. How do we manage this trick that separates us from most other animals?

We all have an internal model of ourselves that we run when we need to predict how we would feel under different contingencies that our actions might bring about. The phantom limbs experienced by some amputees make this manifest. When Adam empathizes with Eve, his brain presumably runs this model of himself, but substituting her personal parameters for his own.

Autism. We normally empathize with those around us so effortlessly that we don't notice what a remarkable gift evolution has put in our hands. It is only when one interacts with autistic people that it is possible to appreciate how hard it would be to get by in society without being able to empathize with other people.

In a famous experiment, an autistic child looks on while Bob hides a toy. When Bob is out of the room, the toy is hidden elsewhere. The autistic child is now asked where Bob will look for the toy on his return. The answer is that he will look in the new hiding place rather than the old. The child thereby reveals his difficulty in seeing things from Bob's point of view.

Oliver Sachs' *Anthroplogist from Mars* gives a related account of a highly intelligent autistic woman who explains how going out on a date is a torment for her, because she isn't gifted with the ability to put herself in her escort's position, and so understand what the signals he is sending her mean.

It isn't perhaps surprising that we take our empathetic capacity for granted, since neuroscientific studies suggest that we have a module in our brains that automatically does the work for us that autistic people must painfully attempt using their general cognitive ability.[2] But once the intrinsic difficulty of empathizing has been

---

[1] In evaluating the claim that we make effective use of our empathetic preferences *only* as inputs to the original position, it is necessary to bear in mind that the capacity to hold an empathetic preference requires more of human beings than that they are able to empathize with their fellows. The latter capacity is obviously useful in predicting what other players are going to do.

[2] I know that evolutionary psychologists have overplayed the module game by claiming that we have special modules for all kinds of skills without being able to point to anything very solid in the way of evidence, but the evidence for some modular structure in the brain is overwhelming. Face recognition is a good example that is relevant in this context.

appreciated by putting ourselves in the shoes of someone suffering from autism, it becomes apparent that our capacity for empathetic identification lies at the heart of human social organization. Without the ability to empathize, we wouldn't be able to operate decentralized social contracts that rely on our coordinating on an equilibrium without subordinating ourselves to the direction of a dominant individual.

Empathy and sympathy. It is a curious quirk of intellectual history that the recognition of the importance of empathetic identification to human sociality was delayed until the Scottish Enlightenment—and then immediately forgotten in the dark age of moral philsosophy initiated by Immanuel Kant that followed. However, neither David Hume nor Adam Smith properly appreciated the distinction that modern psychologists make between empathy and sympathy. *I:1.2.6*

Adam Smith defined sympathy to be something close to what we would nowadays call empathy, but later forgot his definition and used the idea of sympathy as though it meant much the same as in this book. I think it very important to avoid this particular confusion.

A conman might well *empathize* very successfully with an old lady by finding the right kind of story to persuade her to part with her life savings. But in tricking her out of her money, he won't *sympathize* with her in the least. To sympathize with her would be to feel concern for her welfare—to feel her future distress in some part as though it were his own. But a professional conman feels no such distress. He can imagine how it would feel to be a vulnerable old lady, but he doesn't confuse these hypothetical feelings with his own urges and desires. He puts himself in her shoes to see things from her point of view only to exploit her weakness. He therefore empathizes with her without feeling any sympathy for her at all.

I think we must learn to do the same if we are to keep our ideas straight. I don't mean by this that we should all set about conning old ladies out of their pensions. Aside from other considerations, there aren't enough credulous old ladies to go round. I mean that we must learn to recognize that we can empathize with others without simultaneously seeking to enhance their welfare. Nobody need feel antisocial about engaging in such a cold-hearted enterprise, since Agatha Christie's entirely proper Miss Marple observes that she does this all the time when figuring out why whoever did it dunnit.

Empathetic and sympathetic preferences. It isn't true that the ability to empathize implies that a person must be able to express empathetic preferences. The latter ability is an evolutionary extra we acquired along with the capacity to adjudicate coordination problems using fairness norms. However, just as empathy isn't the same thing as sympathy, so it is important to recognize that an empathetic preference isn't the same thing as a sympathetic preference.

A sympathetic preference is part of an individual's personal preferences. Just as Alice may be willing to pay some money to buy an ice cream, so she may be willing to endure a cost to obtain a benefit for one or more of her near and dear. Hamilton's rule tells us how large the benefit would have to be to justify the cost in the case of animals programmed to care only about fitness questions.

Since an empathetic preference isn't part of an individual's personal preferences and a sympathetic preference is, it follows that empathetic and sympathetic preferences aren't even the same kind of entity. But anyone might be forgiven for confusing them, since it turns out that they share a similar structure—as will become evident once the connection between empathetic preferences and interpersonal comparison of utility has been established.

8.3   Utility

I:4.1

Before presenting a potted version of John Harsanyi's theory of interpersonal comparison of utility, it is necessary to clear the air by challenging some shibboleths that the economics profession traditionally holds dear.

Comparing possessions?   Traditional economists suffer from a severe case of schizophrenia on the subject of the interpersonal comparison of utility. In classes on welfare economics, the idea that we can compare how much utility different people are getting is so taken for granted that nobody feels the need to explain how this is possible. But in the class next door, students of microeconomics are simultaneously being taught that interpersonal comparison of utility is so obviously a laughable impossibility that nobody need give the reasons why.

If interpersonal comparison of utility were really impossible, welfare comparisons that took account of anything more than efficiency considerations would have to be made in terms of physical commodities like money. In the most popular theory of this kind—taught to some undergraduate students as though it were gospel—social welfare is said to be the value in dollars of the "economic surplus" that a policy creates. Why economic surplus and not one of the infinite number of alternatives? Because maximizing economic surplus is what happens when a perfectly competitive market operates without constraint!

This dishonest argument makes the operation of the market seem socially optimal only by slipping in the assumption that each extra dollar is equally valuable no matter to whom it is assigned. But most of us would rather have our tax dollars spent on relieving the suffering of the poor and needy rather than providing tax breaks for the rich and powerful. How silly we are is the response! Don't we know that such inequities are necessary to generate an efficient outcome? I certainly know no such thing. On the contrary, I think that fairness norms evolved to select among the efficient equilibria of the repeated game of life, and so the idea that some trade-off between equity and efficiency is necessary makes no sense at all.

These arguments have been mentioned here only to deny that the criterion for judging a standard of interpersonal comparison should be whether or not it seems to support using markets for everything. However, there is another line of reasoning that is a lot more respectable. It is argued that an assignment of goods should be deemed to be fair if nobody envies the bundle of commodities assigned to someone else. That is to say, nobody thinks they would gain by swapping what they have with what someone else has.

The unsatisfactory nature of this no-envy criterion illustrates why there is no escaping the need to compare *utilities*. For Eve to envy Adam, it isn't enough for her to imagine having his possessions. She needs to empathize with him. When she compares her lot with his, she needs to imagine herself *in his shoes* with his possessions. Even if she is poor and he is rich, Eve won't envy Adam if he is suffering from incurable clinical depression. She literally wouldn't swap places with him for a million dollars.

Revealed preference. In the early nineteenth century, Jeremy Bentham and John Stuart Mill used the word *utility* to signify some notional measure of happiness. But even if someone were to invent a scientific measure of happiness derived perhaps from counting how many times appropriate neurons are firing, would this really tell us anything genuinely significant about the relative intensity of Adam and Eve's subjective experiences?

The historical answer to this question is *no*. Indeed, whole academic careers have consisted of little more than ridiculing the idea that the answer might be *yes*. However, the satirists soon forgot that their somewhat shaky arguments applied only to utility-as-pleasure-or-pain, and blithely extended their strictures to any concept of utility at all. Fortunately, John Von Neumann didn't know or care that the economists of his time thought that measuring utility was a ridiculous endeavor. So he went ahead and spent an afternoon inventing the theory of utility on which much of modern economics is now firmly based.

More than sixty years later, critics still quote satirists like Lionel Robbins to the effect that measuring utility is impossible, apparently unaware that it is a very long time since the economics profession abandoned the naive psychological approach of Bentham and Mill. However, far from maintaining that our brains are little machines for generating utility, the modern theory of utility makes a virtue of assuming *nothing whatever* about what causes our behavior.

This doesn't mean that economists believe that our thought processes have nothing to do with our behavior. We know perfectly well that human beings are motivated by all kinds of considerations. Some people are clever, and others are stupid. Some care only about money. Others just want to stay out of jail. There are even saintly people who would sell the shirt off their back rather than see a baby cry. We accept that people are infinitely various, but we succeed in accommodating their infinite variety within a single theory by denying ourselves the luxury of speculating about what is going on inside their heads. Instead, we pay attention only to what we see them doing.

The modern theory of utility therefore abandons any attempt to explain *why* Adam or Eve behave as they do. Instead of an explanatory theory, we have to be content with a descriptive theory, which can do no more than say that Adam or Eve will be acting inconsistently if they did such-and-such in the past, but now plan to do so-and-so in the future. The way this works is illustrated in chapter 4 with an analysis of the Prisoners' Dilemma in which the payoffs are assumed to be determined in accordance with this theory of "revealed preference".

I:4.2.2   **Rationality as consistency.** Oskar Morgenstern turned up at Von Neumann's house one day complaining that they didn't have a proper basis for the payoffs in the book on game theory they were writing together. So Von Neumann invented a theory on the spot that measures how much a rational person wants something by the size of the risk he is willing to take to get it. Critics sometimes complain that a person's attitude to taking risks is irrelevant to what is fair, but as it says in the Book of Proverbs: it is the lot that causeth contentions to cease.

Von Neumann's rationality assumptions simply require that people make decisions in a consistent way, but his conclusion is surprisingly strong. Anyone who chooses consistently in risky situations will look to an observer as though he or she were trying to maximize the expected value of something. As explained in chapter 4, this abstract "something" is what we call *utility* in this book. To maximize its expected value is simply to take whatever action will make it largest on average.

Philosophers sometimes claim that some utility functions are more rational than others, but economists follow David Hume in treating reason as the "slave of the passions". There can then be nothing irrational about consistently pursuing any end whatever. As Hume extravagantly observed, it wouldn't be *irrational* for him to prefer the destruction of the entire universe to scratching his thumb, because rationality is about means rather than ends.

Is it reasonable to assume that the players in our games make choices consistently? The evidence from psychological laboratories isn't very encouraging. Behavioral economists have therefore sought to modify Von Neumann and Morgenstern's theory to make it fit the data better, but without much success. One might summarize the results of a great deal of effort on this front by saying that the original theory doesn't fit the laboratory data all that well, but it fits better overall than any of the rival theories that have been proposed. However, in proceeding on the orthodox assumption that players always choose consistently, I am motivated more by the consideration that genes or memes that consistently promote their own replication are more likely to survive than those that don't.

Measuring in utils. It is easy to find Adam's utility function if we have enough data on the choices he makes between risky prospects. Pick two outcomes, W and L, that are respectively better and worse than any outcome that we need to discuss. (One can think of W and L as winning or losing everything there is to be won or lost.) These outcomes will correspond to the boiling and freezing points used to calibrate a thermometer, in that the utility scale to be constructed will assign 0 utils to L, and 100 utils to W.

Suppose we now want to find Adam's utility for getting a fig leaf. For this purpose, consider a bunch of (free) lottery tickets in which the prizes are either W or L. As we offer Adam lottery tickets with higher and higher probabilities of getting W as an alternative to the fig leaf, he will eventually switch from saying no to saying yes. If the probability of W on the lottery ticket that makes him switch is 75%, then Von Neumann and Morgenstern's theory says that his fig leaf is worth 75 utils. Each extra percentage point added to the indifference probability therefore corresponds to one extra util.

As with measuring temperature, it will be obvious that we are free to choose the zero and the unit on the utility scale we construct however we like. We could, for example, have assigned 32 utils to $\mathcal{L}$, and 212 utils to $\mathcal{W}$. One then finds how many utils a fig leaf is worth on this new scale in the same way that one converts degrees Celsius into degrees Fahrenheit. So a fig leaf worth 75 utils on the old scale is worth 167 utils on the new scale.

A person's utility needn't correspond to anything physical, but life is a lot simpler if it does. If Eve consistently seeks to make as much money as she can on average, then we can choose a utility scale in which one util corresponds to one dollar. If an animal has evolved to maximize its expected fitness, then we can chooose a utility scale in which one util corresponds to one extra child in the next generation.

Sharing food.   The outcomes in the Meeting Game of chapter 2 were assessed in utils without any explanation of what a util is. The following example addresses this deficiency by working out the Nash bargaining solution for a case in which the focus is on what the player's utilities mean.

Alice and Bob are desperately hungry, but all there is to eat is one small rabbit, which has been donated by a kindly hunter on condition that they agree on how to share it. How will the rabbit get divided if the players bargain face-to-face without paying any attention to fairness?

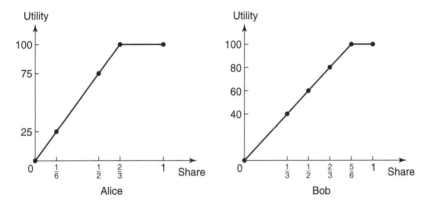

Figure 18: Von Neumann and Morgenstern utilities. Alice and Bob's respective needs are measured in terms of the risk each will endure rather than give up a claim to some share of the rabbit. The risk is assessed by finding when the player becomes indifferent between the share in question and a lottery in which he or she either ends up with nothing or the whole rabbit. The probability with which the player gets the whole rabbit in this lottery is then plotted as the utility of the share.

Figure 18 shows how many utils Alice and Bob assign to each possible share that they may receive. For example, Alice's graph shows that if she were offered two thirds of the rabbit, she wouldn't be prepared to take any risk at all of ending up with nothing in order to get a chance at the whole rabbit. On the other hand, Bob is willing to swap a sure two thirds of the rabbit for a gamble in which he gets the whole rabbit 80% of the time and nothing the rest of the time. The same is also true if the whole rabbit is replaced by five sixths of the rabbit in the gamble, because Bob isn't prepared to take any risk at all of ending up with nothing to improve on a share of five sixths.

We use the Nash bargaining solution of chapter 2 to solve Alice and Bob's bargaining problem. The disagreement point D is the payoff pair in which both players get nothing. The set X of feasible payoff pairs is shown on the left in figure 19. For example, the players could agree that Alice should get one third of the rabbit and Bob should get two thirds. Alice gets 50 utils from this deal. Bob gets 80 utils. So the payoff pair $(50, 80)$ is a point in the feasible set.

The Nash bargaining solution of this problem occurs at the outcome in the feasible set at which the product of Alice and Bob's utilities is largest. A little arithmetic conforms that this happens at the outcome to which Alice assigns 75 utils and Bob assigns 60 utils. In this overly simple case, they get these payoffs by splitting the rabbit evenly between them.

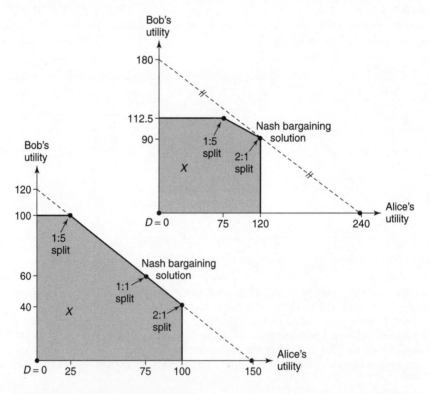

Figure 19: Using the Nash bargaining solution to solve some food-sharing problems.

The diagram on the right of figure 19 shows how the set of feasible payoffs must be altered if Alice and Bob are siblings.[3] The Nash bargaining solution now awards 120 utils to Alice and 90 utils to Bob. The fact that Alice and Bob are siblings therefore shifts the agreement from an even division of the rabbit to a split in which Alice's share is twice as large as Bob's.

8.4 Interpersonal Comparison of Utility

Because the zero and the unit on a utility scale are arbitrary, it is commonly said that comparing Von Neumann and Morgenstern utilities across individuals is impossible. This is obviously wrong, because nothing prevents our fixing on one utility scale for Adam and another for Eve, and then observing, for example, that Adam would get 75 utils on his scale if we awarded a fig leaf to him, and Eve would get 167 utils on her scale if we awarded the fig leaf to her. We would then have a criterion which said that Eve would benefit slightly more than twice as much as Adam. *II:2.3.1*

So the problem isn't at all that making interpersonal comparisons is impossible. On the contrary, there are an infinite number of ways this can be done. For example, if two people both seek to make as much money as they can on average, we could assign them both utility scales in which one extra util corresponds to one extra dollar. But what would be the point of saying that giving an extra dollar to each is the same if one is a billionaire and the other is a beggar? The problem therefore isn't to find *some* way of comparing Adam and Eve's utils, but to characterize a way that people find meaningful. Otherwise, as Jeremy Bentham wisely observed, we shall find ourselves adding so many apples to so many pears.

One half of this problem solves itself. In any bargaining problem, the status quo will always provide one of the two anchoring points that we need to establish a meaningful joint utility scale for the players. There isn't therefore going to be a problem about comparing Adam and Eve's utility *levels* in a bargaining context. But how are we to compare the *units* on their utility scales?

Getting into your head. The time has come to follow Harsanyi in applying orthodox utility theory to empathetic preferences.[4] These are revealed whenever players use a fairness criterion to solve an equilibrium selection problem.

Harsanyi's contribution was to show that expressing a consistent set of empathetic preferences about Adam and Eve is the same thing as determining a rate at which Adam's utils are to be traded against Eve's. Although Pandora may not realize it, her empathetic preferences therefore implicitly determine a standard for making interpersonal comparisons of utility.

As with much else in this book, Harsanyi's argument is embarrassingly simple. The argument depends on two assumptions about Pandora's empathetic preferences. The first assumption is that they are consistent. It then follows from Von Neumann and Morgenstern's theory that we can describe her empathetic preferences

---

[3] The payoffs must now correspond to fitnesses, since Hamilton's rule is to be applied.

[4] Empathetic preferences were first studied by the philosopher Patrick Suppes, who called them extended sympathy preferences.

by assigning an appropriate number of utils to each event that she might have to evaluate—for example, that Adam gets a fig leaf, or that Eve gets an apple.

Pandora's empathetic utility function implicitly attributes preferences to Adam and Eve. For example, if Pandora assigns more utils to Eve's getting a fig leaf than an apple, she implies that wearing a fig leaf is better for Eve then eating an apple. But Eve may not agree. If so, then Pandora has failed in her attempt at empathizing with Eve. She tried to put herself in Eve's shoes to see things from her point of view, but allowed her own thinking on what is good for people to intrude on her judgment of what Eve thinks is good for herself.

The following paraphrase of a conversation reported by Longinus makes Alexander the Great an unexpected authority on this point:

> Parmenio: If I were Alexander, I would accept this treaty.
> Alexander: If I were Parmenio, so would I!

Alexander points out that Parmenio fails to identify with Alexander adequately in considering whether to accept a Persian peace proposal. Parmenio puts himself in Alexander's shoes, but retains his own preferences. But if Parmenio were Alexander, he would have Alexander's preferences!

Harsanyi's second assumption is that when Pandora puts herself in Eve's position to see things from her point of view, she doesn't make Parmenio's mistake. She accepts that if she were Eve, she would have Eve's preferences. We therefore assume that Pandora is very good at empathizing; she really does know what Eve wants. We also assume that Pandora isn't the kind of do-gooder who thinks she knows better what is good for people than people do for themselves.

The latter assumption conflicts with the approach of old-style utilitarians like John Stuart Mill, and with modern paternalists like Amartya Sen. But remember that we are trying to put together a theory of how fairness evolved to solve equilibrium selection problems—and there isn't any point in inventing a theory that solves a coordination game different from the game the players think they are playing.

It is therefore the other assumption—that people fully understand each other—at which criticism deserves to be directed. Since it is probably failures on this front that are responsible for most coordination breakdowns, the assumption is only excusable because building in something more realistic would create a model that would be too difficult to analyze.

Trading-off utils. Once we have made Harsanyi's assumptions, his conclusion follows from the fact that two utility scales for the same preferences are connected in the same way that degrees Celsius are connected to degrees Fahrenheit. The utility scale that Pandora attributes to Adam must therefore be related in this way to whatever utility scale he is using for himself. The same goes for the utility scale that Pandora attributes to Eve.

Figure 20 illustrates the conclusion. In the original position, Pandora has to consider various social contracts represented by points like S. We can read off Adam's personal utility for the social contract S on his personal utility scale. We can similarly read off Eve's personal utility for S on her personal scale. Pandora has two empathetic scales, one of which records her utility for S if she were Adam, and another which records her utility for S if she were Eve. If she thinks that she is equally likely to turn out to be Adam or Eve in the social contract S, then her overall assessment of S is the average of these two empathetic utilities.

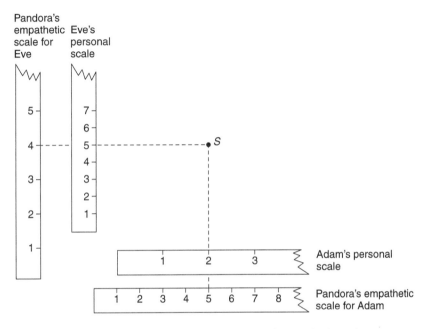

Figure 20: Translating between personal and empathetic scales.

In figure 20, the units on Adam's personal scale are twice as big as those on Pandora's empathetic scale for Adam. One extra unit on Adam's scale therefore counts the same as two extra units on Pandora's scale. Pandora therefore weights Adam's personal utils by multiplying them by a factor of 2. The units on Eve's personal scale are half as big as those on Pandora's empathetic scale for Eve. Pandora therefore weights Eve's personal utils by multiplying them by a factor of $\frac{1}{2}$. She then makes decisions in the original position as though seeking to maximize the sum of these two weighted personal utilities.[5] That is to say, she makes decisions as though she were a utilitarian who trades off Adam's personal utils against Eve's at a rate equal to the ratio of her two weights. In figure 20, this ratio is 4, which means that she counts each of Adam's utils as being worth the same as four of Eve's utils. Or to say the same thing another way, Pandora's social index for Eve is

---

[5]Her full empathetic utility function is actually obtained by dividing this sum by 2 and adding a constant. But we can forget the constant here, as it is the same for each social contract S.

four times as large as her social index for Adam.

Suppose, for example, that Adam and Eve consistently act to maximize their own expected monetary gain. We might then choose a utility scale for Adam in which each util corresponds to ten dollars, and a utility scale for Eve in which each util corresponds to a dime. Having fixed these utility scales, we now examine Pandora's empathetic preferences to find the rate at which she trades Adam's utils off against Eve's utils. Perhaps it turns out that she regards each of Adam's utils as being worth the same as ten of Eve's. This evaluation may take into account a whole raft of considerations. Who is rich or poor? Old or young? Male or female? Sick or well? Clever or stupid? Strong or weak? Insiders or outsiders? Who invested how much in any surplus to be divided? How much effort was needed? What is our degree of relationship?

The list of factors that may be relevant is obviously endless, but everything that Pandora thinks is relevant can be summarized in a single trade-off rate. Of course, just as we would have to change our estimate of how much warmer it is inside the house than outside if we switch from measuring the outside temperature in degrees Fahrenheit to degrees Celsius, so we must change the trade-off rate from 10 to 20 if we stop measuring Eve's utils in dimes and start measuring them in nickels.

Unequal chances.   This is perhaps the place to comment on the fact that nothing much hinges on the assumption that Pandora thinks it equally likely that she will turn out to be Adam or Eve in the original position. We can reduce the case in which she thinks that her chances of turning out to be Adam or Eve are unequal to the case studied in the text simply by multiplying her weights by suitable factors. For example, if Pandora thinks it twice as likely that she will be Adam, then we just carry on as before after multiplying the weight she assigns to Adam's personal utility by two.

Comparison with Hamilton's rule.   We have seen that Pandora makes decisions in the original position like a utilitarian. I don't think it an accident that we also found that Hamilton's rule takes a utilitarian form. The only difference is that biological fitness replaces personal utility in Hamilton's version, and the weights are determined by Adam and Eve's degree of relationship.

I think this is a significant finding, because it provides a possible evolutionary route to the emergence of empathetic preferences that allows us to treat Nature as a tinkerer who adapts existing structures incrementally, rather than producing hopeful monsters, like rabbits out of a magician's hat.

When Eve uses the original position to make a fairness judgment, she puts herself in the position of a hypothetical individual we have been calling Pandora, who doesn't know whether she is Adam or Eve. To evaluate the options available to her in this situation, she appeals to her empathetic preferences. But in doing so, we now know that she behaves *as though* Adam were a relative.

Assuming that Nature had already taught our ancestors to evaluate kinfolk according to Hamilton's rule, she therefore only had to teach them to treat strangers as though they were kin for the purposes of the original position. That is to say, evolution had only to tinker with an existing mechanism.

This still leaves us with the need to explain the appearance of the device of the original position itself without treating it as a hopeful monster, but this is an issue for the next chapter.

8.5 The Evolution of Empathetic Preferences

A major problem has been passed over in presenting Harsanyi's theory of interpersonal comparison of utility. With Harsanyi's assumptions, Alice's empathetic utility function determines a rate at which Adam's utils are to be traded off against Eve's. But what if Bob's empathetic utility function trades them off at a different rate?

Rawls and Harsanyi both claim that there is actually a strong consensus in our own social contract on how interpersonal comparisons should be made. This is my impression too, although I can't point to any hard evidence. Philosophers who invent some kind of Ideal Observer to whom interpersonal comparisons are implicitly to be delegated presumably have the same intuition—although they never seem to ask themselves why philosophers who live in different times and places invent Ideal Observers different from their own. Even Adam Smith's Impartial Spectator would be regarded as rather partial nowadays.

Why should such a consensus exist? If there is a consensus, how does it come about that people jointly fix on one standard of interpersonal comparison rather than one of the infinite number of other possibilities?

Social evolution. I think that standards of interpersonal comparison are similar in many ways to language. Just as it is part of our genetic heritage that we should speak some language, so we are wired up to operate some standard of interpersonal comparison. But the particular language we speak and the standard of interpersonal comparison we use are artifacts of our culture. Like languages, our standards of interpersonal comparison therefore vary according to the context in which they are used. Like languages, they also visibly change over time in response to the pressures of social evolution.

As children mature, they are assimilated to the culture in which they grow up largely as a consequence of their natural disposition to imitate those around them. The role of empathy in this evolutionary process is as important here as it is elsewhere. For human children to use acquired pieces of behavior as effectively as they do, evolution must have equipped them with an innate ability to understand the purpose behind the actions they copy. This ability has been extensively observed in the great apes, but not among monkeys. It is therefore encouraging for the theory that field studies have found that monkeys show little or none of the imitative capacity traditionally attributed to them. "Monkey see, monkey do" is apparently just one more urban myth.

Evolutionary psychologists say that animals like chimpanzees and dolphins who are able to understand why others do things are gifted with a theory of mind. In the case of humans, an economist would argue that children develop an internal theory of revealed preference and belief that not only allows them to predict what others are likely to do in the future, but to understand the motives for their actions in the present. Consciously or unconsciously, a child can then reason that if she sees a successful individual doing such and such, then she may also be successful if she copies him on those occasions in the future when her preferences and beliefs resemble those she attributes to him now.

One of the social phenomena that children observe is the use of the device of the original position in achieving fair compromises. They are, of course, no more likely to recognize the device of the original position for what it is than Adam and Eve when they use it in deciding who should wash how many dishes. Instead, they simply copy the relevant behavior patterns. In doing so, they acquire both a set of empathetic preferences, and the habit of appealing to them when selecting equilibria in coordination games.

II:2.5.4   **Empathy equilibrium.** I treat empathetic preferences as memes propogated largely by imitation. When Adam and Eve use fairness to solve a coordination problem, it will be assumed that their empathetic preferences are common knowledge. Everybody can then see the payoff to having one set of empathetic preferences rather than another.

If people sometimes change their empathetic preferences in favor of alternatives that generate higher payoffs, we are looking at an evolutionary process that will only stop working when it reaches a Nash equilibrium of the underlying evolutionary game. In this case, the players' strategies in the underlying game correspond to their (largely involuntary) choices of different standards of interpersonal comparison. An *empathy equilibrium* arises when we reach a Nash equilibrium of this evolutionary game. Nobody will then have an incentive to switch from their current standard to one they see being operated by others.

One can think of an empathy equilibrium as encapsulating the cultural history of a society that led people to adopt one standard of interpersonal comparison rather than another. It is true that this history will be shaped by the way in which power is distributed in the society under study, but this is the kind of bullet we have had to bite a great deal already.

The reward for biting the bullet is that we can then give stylized answers to two questions on which orthodox moral philosophy has nothing substantive to say:

Question: What standards of interpersonal comparison should we study?
Answer: Those that appear as strategies in an empathy equilibrium.

Question: When can we rely on there being a consensus on a standard?
Answer: When the relevant empathy equilibrium is symmetric.

There are various ways in which we could operationalize the notion of an empathy equilibrium. It turns out that we get the same answers independently of whether we use a crude form or a refined form. I give the latter version, since it is harder to analyze, and critics find it less provocative.

> To test whether a profile of empathetic preferences is an empathy equilibrium, ask each player the following question:
>
> > Suppose you could deceive everybody into believing your empathetic preferences are whatever you find it expedient to claim them to be. Would such an act of deceit seem worthwhile to you *in the original position* relative to the empathetic preferences *you actually hold?*
>
> The right answer for an empathy equilibrium is *no.*

The crude version substitutes "personal preferences" for "empathetic preferences" in the second sentence, and omits the italicized phrases. Which version makes sense depends on how an onlooker evaluates who gets how much in a fairness transaction.

Suppose that Alice looks on while Eve settles a coordination problem with Adam using the device of the original position. In doing so, Eve empathizes with a hypothetical Pandora, who has Eve's empathetic preferences, but thinks it equally likely she will be Adam or Eve when she emerges from behind the veil of ignorance. With whom does Alice empathize? If we assume that she always empathizes with Eve without following the empathetic chain on to Pandora, then the memes with which we are concerned will propogate according to the *personal* preferences of the players. The crude version of an empathy equilibrium then applies. If Alice always follows the chain on to Pandora without being brought up short by the reflection that Pandora exists only hypothetically, then the memes will propogate according to the *empathetic* preferences of the players. In this case, the refined version applies.

My guess is that there is always some confusion between these possibilities, and so both personal and empathetic preferences matter in a manner that would be very hard to figure out. It is therefore fortunate that both the crude and the refined version of an empathy equilibrium lead to the same conclusion.

Symmetry.   If empathetic preferences are acquired in a society in which everybody plays the same coordination games and everybody sees everybody else as a potential locus for emulation, then only the symmetric empathy equilibria of the underlying evolutionary game make sense as possible end-products of the evolutionary process. Any asymmetric empathy equilibria can be discarded as irrelevant to the discussion.

But what of the case when societies are split into castes or factions? For example, traditional societies assign different roles to men and women. Aristotle's society distinguished between citizens and slaves. Feudal societies distinguished between the gently born and everybody else. In our own society, teenage kids and old folk sometimes seem to represent different species.

In such heterogeneous societies, one must expect cultural evolution to operate separately in different groups, so that asymmetric empathy equilibria may arise. It is then significant if we find that only symmetric equilibria can exist, since such a finding implies that the same standard of interpersonal comparison is shared by all the different groups.

But it doesn't then follow that people from different groups will be regarded as equally worthy. All that follows is that everyone agrees on the criteria for worthiness. In an aristocratic society, even the lower orders commonly accept that it is right and proper that they be regarded as unworthy.

Chapter 9

The Golden Rule

> It is a simple thing, this Golden Rule, and all that is required. Political economy and the survival of the fittest can go hang if they say otherwise.
>
> Jack London, *People of the Abyss*

9.1 Sages down the Ages

Why does the device of the original position strike a chord with most of us the first time we hear about it? I think it's because we recognize the deep structure of the fairness norms that we routinely use in resolving everyday coordination problems. Since this deep structure seems a human universal, I suspect it is built into our genes. What support is there for this conjecture?

The obvious place to begin is with the observation that the original position is just an elaboration of the ubiquitous Golden Rule:

> Do as you would be done by

that responds to the objection:

> Don't do unto others what you would have them do
> unto you—they may not have the same tastes as you.

Adam likes being shaken awake before dawn for a cold shower and a ten-mile run. Eve prefers a gentle awakening at a late hour with a cup of coffee and a newspaper. Adam therefore doesn't want Eve to do to him what she would like him to do for her. Eve would like it even less if Adam were to do to her what he would like her to do for him.[1]

We all prefer that others do to us what they would like done to them—but only if they had our preferences rather than their own. With this interpretation, the Golden Rule becomes:

---

[1] The sexual innuendo was unintended, but perhaps it makes the point even better.

129

> Do as you would be done by—if you were the
> person to whom something is to be done.

which is the principle operationalized by the device of the original position.

Who endorses the Golden Rule? A full list would be endless. It certainly includes King Alfred, Aristotle, Darwin, Epictetus, Hobbes, Locke, Mill, and Spinoza. My mother had her own version, and I dare say yours did as well. But here are some quotes from the superstars:

> **Zoroaster:** That nature alone is good that refrains from doing to another what is not good for itself.
>
> **Buddha:** Hurt not others in ways that you yourself would find hurtful.
>
> **Confucius:** Do not unto others what you would not have them do unto you.
>
> **Hillel:** Do not to others that which you would not have others do to you.
>
> **Jesus:** Do to others whatever you would have them do to you.

What other principles garner such universal support? In the moral arena, the anwer seems to be: none at all.

9.2   Hunters and Gatherers

Westermarck was an early anthropologist famous for his moral relativism, but even he reports that the Golden Rule is almost universally endorsed in primitive societies. Modern work on pure hunter-gatherer societies is equally striking in the strong parallels it has uncovered between the social contracts of geographically distant groups living in starkly different environments.

II:4.5   There is no shortage of cultural differences between Kalarahi bushmen, African pygmies, Andaman islanders, Greenland eskimos, Australian aborigines, Paraguayan Indians, and Siberian nomads, but the consensus is strong among modern anthropologists that these and other pure hunter-gatherer societies all operate societies without bosses or social distinctions that share food—especially meat—on a relatively equal basis.

These societies aren't pastoral idylls, inhabited by noble savages filled with sweetness and light. Infanticide and murder are common. So is selfishness. Citizens of foraging societies don't honor their social contract because they like giving up food when they are hungry. They will therefore cheat on the social contract by secretly hoarding food if they think they can get away with it. The reason they comply with the norm most of the time is because their fellows will punish them if they don't.

Nor is there necessarily anything very nice about the way that food and other possessions are shared. In some societies, a fair allocation is achieved through "tolerated stealing". Eve may grab some of Adam's food because she thinks he has more than his fair share. If the rest of the group agree, Adam is helpless to resist. Even when possessions are voluntarily surrendered to others, the giver will sometimes explain that he or she is only complying with the norm to avoid being the object of the envy that precedes more serious sanctions. Indeed, we would find it unbearably stifling to live in some foraging societies because of the continual envious monitoring of who has what.

There is therefore squabbling and pettiness aplenty in foraging communities, but there is also laughter and good fellowship. In brief, human nature seems much the same in foraging societies as in our own. So if their nature includes an instinctive bias to structure sharing in a particular way, isn't it likely that ours does too?

Prehistory. Our nearest relatives are the chimpanzees and bonobos. Our common ancestor lived several million years ago. Nobody knows why our evolutionary path took a different direction from theirs, although many theories have been proposed. Is our tool-making ability a cause or an effect? What of fire and the ability to cook otherwise inedible roots? What of our unusual sex arrangements in which men contribute to bringing up their children? What of our comparative longevity? What of our ability to pass on our culture?

I don't plan to survey the many answers that have been offered to such questions about the origins of *Homo sapiens*. I want to focus instead on some of the issues that have been neglected, but on which game theory can perhaps shed some light.

When our ancestors began to be recognizably human, the consensus is that they lived in groups who survived by hunting and gathering. We lived like this for perhaps a million years before the bulk of the population turned to animal husbandry and agriculture. The standard theory is that farming appeared only over the last 10,000 years or so in response to local population crises, that may or may not have been associated with dramatic climatic changes.

As with the social insects, greater productivity requires more efficient organization. This is perhaps Karl Marx's only genuine insight: that the social contract of a society is inextricably linked to its economic means of production. There are certain social contracts that can't work if a society is insufficently productive. There are certain productive systems that can't operate if the current social contract doesn't provide adequate incentives.

Modern societies are very hierarchical indeed. We have bosses up to our ears. But it wasn't always so. As the means of economic production becomes more sophisticated, anthropological reports record fairness only gradually being displaced by leadership as the standard coordinating device. And it isn't hard to see why leadership became necessary.

We need entrepreneurs to innovate and to organize the division of labor that generates increasing returns to scale from cooperation in farming and industry. Chiefs are necessary to organize the warbands that protect the stored surplus of your own society, and seek to steal the surplus of neighboring societies. We invest authority in the captain of a ship for the same reason. Who wants a debate about which crew member should do what in the middle of a storm?

A nice example on the emergence of private property comes from the much studied Ache of Paraguay, who recently turned to serious cultivation. In accordance with their traditional customs they tried tilling the land in common. But it didn't work, because it was too easy for some to shirk the labor while still claiming a "fair" share of the product. So they quickly adopted a new social contract in which the land is split into privately owned plots. By contrast, the historical economic stagnation of the Navajo of the American south west is sometimes attributed to their clinging to a social contract that disincentified entrepreneurs by requiring them to share their profits.

Most evolutionary biologists think that 10,000 years is too short a period for the ground rules of the social contracts that allow greater economic production to have been written into our genes. If they are right, then cultural evolution rather than biological evolution must be responsible for our success once we ceased to hunt and gather. Our genes remain as they were when we followed a foraging life. We are predisposed toward the kind of social behavior appropriate to a hunter-gatherer society, but these behavioral predispositions have been overwritten by cultural imperatives without which we couldn't be so productive.

Maryanski and Turner's *Social Cage* is one of a number of books that attribute our malaise at living in a modern industrial society to this phenomonen. They argue that we are victims of a dissonance that arises from our genes finding themselves at odds with the memes with which they have been overlaid. Our hearts pull one way and our heads the other, so that contentment is held beyond our reach.

In summary, cultural evolution has taken different societies in many different directions, but there remain universals which register that we all belong to the same species. The respect accorded to the Golden Rule would seem to be one of these universals, but where should we look if we want to know more?

An obvious answer is that we should look at the social contracts of the hunter-gatherer communities that existed 10,000 or so years ago, before cultural evolution set off on the helter-skelter ride that got us into our current mess. But social contracts don't leave any fossils. The best we can do is to look at the social contracts of those foraging societies that survived into modern times—both human and chimpanzee.

Chimpanzee communities.   We share all but a tiny fraction of our genes with chimpanzees, so it isn't surprising that we resemble them so closely. But in talking about fairness, I think we step across the narrow chasm that separates us from them. Chimpanzees seem to have both the evolutionary motivation and the necessary biological equipment to have developed fairness as an equilibrium selection device, but nevertheless lack anything analogous. Like language, a sense of fairness would seem to be unique to *Homo sapiens*. But perhaps studying chimpanzee societies can tell us something about the conditions that prevailed in prehuman societies at the time that our sense of fairness evolved.[2]

Chimpanzees live in social groupings in which kinship is an important factor. Males stay with the group into which they were born, but females usually move to

---

[2]For some expert views, see *Tree of Origin*, edited by de Waal, Harvard University Press (2001).

a neighboring group. When in estrus, females typically mate with all males of their group. It is thought that this is an evolutionary response to the risk of infanticide by males programmed to care only about the welfare of their own offspring. But the same anonymity that deters males from infanticide also provides no incentive for them to assist in bringing up children who are unlikely to be their own. This is a major difference between chimpanzees and humans.[3]

Among both males and females, social dominance matters a great deal. Female chimpanzees are subordinate to males, but the reverse applies with bonobos. Maintaining a place in the hierarchy depends not only on a chimpanzee's personal strength and character, but also on a shifting pattern of alliances between different chimpanzees. Grooming is an important factor in signaling social relationships. As Robin Dunbar observes, grooming seems to fulfill the same function in chimpanzees as gossip does for us. There seems no doubt that chimpanzees are able to empathize with each other, and actively use their empathetic skills in an attempt to improve their social standing.

It was once thought that chimpanzees were almost exclusively vegetarian, but it turns out they hunt and eat monkeys on a much larger scale than was previously understood. Willliam McGrew reports that they may eat up to 65 grams of meat a day in some seasons, and that meat-eating correlates with reproductive success.

When a group of male chimpanzees hunt together, their bag is greater than it would have been if each chimpanzee were to hunt alone. As with the social insects, their cooperation therefore enjoys increasing returns to scale. However, the catch is commonly shared—although not in a manner that humans would regard as fair—on a sufficiently wide basis that it provokes selfish-gene questions that also apply to cooperative hunting in human foraging communities. Cooperative hunting clearly makes the group as a whole better off, but what's in it for each individual hunter?

Human foraging communities.   A prehistoric food crisis caused by overpopulation may have spelled the end of foraging as the normal productive mode among humans, but it didn't wipe out hunter-gatherers altogether. Foragers continue to survive in marginal habitats on the fringes of deserts or the polar icecap or the heart of tropical jungles, where growing crops or herding animals is difficult or impossible. Indeed, the fact that such habitats were colonized is one piece of evidence that favors the overpopulation theory.

There are probably no *pure* foraging societies left at all. That is to say, societies whose economic means of production consists exclusively of hunting and gathering, with no division of labor beyond that dictated by sex or age, seem to be extinct. However, enough foraging societies did survive into the twentieth century for there to be extensive records of their way of life. It is these societies to which we have to turn when making guesses about the social contracts of 10,000 years ago.

Two features are universal. The first is that pure foraging societies have no bosses or chiefs. Some individuals get more respect than others when offering

---

[3]Although DNA evidence apparently shows that husbands in our own society who claim to be the father of one of their wife's children may only have four chances in five of being right. For the first-born child, the odds are much worse!

advice. Sometimes such individuals have a title. But they are never able to exercise any personal authority, and are usually careful not to give the impression that they think they can.

The reason they tread softly isn't because the urge to dominate doesn't burn as deeply within their breasts as it does within our own. Biologically, they are the same as us. Like us, they presumably inherited the same instinct for hierarchy that we still see in chimpanzees or bonobos. But the instinct to dominate is held in check by another mechanism of later origin.

This anti-dominance mechanism demands that folk who shows signs of throwing their weight around be restrained by the threat of escalating punishment from the rest of the group. The first step calls for the would-be leader to be mocked. If he persists, the second step calls for him to be boycotted. If he still persists, especially if his attempts at establishing dominance are violent, then he is expelled from the group altogether.

I think it no accident that these three steps are equally familiar in our own society. The mockery stage is particularly interesting. There is nothing overtly damaging about being laughed at, so why do we dislike it so much? Presumably because our genes interpret mockery as a signal that genuinely damaging punishment will follow if we don't mend our ways.

How is cooperation possible in societies without leaders responsible for determining who gets how much of any surplus generated? I think our sense of fairness evolved alongside the anti-dominance mechanism in response to this problem. A social species that doesn't have leaders to nominate an equilibrium in a society's game of life must use some other equilibrium selection device. In the case of our own species, the device that evolved was fairness.

Sharing food in human foraging societies is commonplace, but only with meat does the sharing rule seem to be universally fair. How important is this phenomenon to the hunter-gatherer societies in which it is practiced? It is necessary to ask this question because the paradigm of "man the mighty hunter" has been debunked a good deal in recent years. The debunking is appropriate to the extent that the survival of foraging societies obviously depends just as much on the female role in gathering and child care as on the male role in hunting, but claims that hunting can be treated as an optional extra in food provision don't survive close examination.

It is true that successful hunters are more attractive to women, and so get to reproduce themselves more often, but hunting is more than an arena for young men to send costly signals of their prowess to young women. Recent research by Kaplan and others on the food budgets of modern foraging societies surprisingly shows that men actually supply 97% of the calories consumed by children, and all their protein.[4] Without hunting, the group couldn't survive in the occasional bad years in which evolution distinguishes between the fit and the unfit. It is therefore of major significance that meat is universally shared fairly.

Some anthropologists see a mystery here. If hunting is organized on the principle that each contributes according to his ability and each benefits according to his need, why aren't we in a Prisoners' Dilemma? If a man gets less meat for his family by

---

[4]See *Moral Sentiments and Material Interests*, edited by Gintis *et al*, MIT Press, forthcoming.

cooperating with others in a hunt for big game than he would by foraging for small game by himself, why participate in the hunt at all, given that there is no authority to punish him if he doesn't?

Jean-Jacques Rousseau asked much the same question in his story of a stag hunt in which a hunter has to choose between abandoning a cooperative enterprise that might yield a share of a large stag if successful, and bagging a small hare for sure that will be his alone. But since his answer reduces to the claim that it is rational to cooperate in games like the Prisoners' Dilemma, it doesn't help us much. *I:2.3.2*

However, I don't see that there is much of a mystery, provided that one remembers that the group selection fallacy doesn't apply when each group is operating an *equilibrium* in the game its members play with each other. It is then only necessary to make two points:

- Societies in which men hunt cooperatively are more successful than societies in which they don't, because they produce more food overall.

- Cooperative hunting can be sustained as an equilibrium by punishing men who don't pull their weight. Young men have an especially strong incentive to learn the necessary hunting skills, since young women in foraging societies apparently find their mighty hunters no less attractive than the popstars and athletes who capture the hearts of our own teenyboppers.

9.3 Mechanism Design

Knauft is an anthropologist who draws a U-shaped curve that represents the postulated level of dominance in hominid social contracts as a function of evolutionary time. It begins high on the assumption that our prehuman ancestors operated social contracts with a strong social dominance structure like that of modern chimpanzees and bonobos. It then declines to a low level on the assumption that the anarchic structure of modern foraging societies mirrors the organization of the ancient foraging societies of 10,000 years or so ago. It then rises to a high level again to reflect the increasingly complex social hierarchies that have emerged since that time in agricultural and industrial societies.

If this story is right, then a sequence of genetic mutations presumably suppressed our instinct to organize hierarchically by overlaying it with an imperative to gang up against potential leaders. But why should the resulting anarchic societies represent an evolutionary improvement?

Decentralized organization. This question provides an excuse for an aside on the subject of mechanism design. This branch of game theory is perceived as one of its big successes because of its widespread use in raising billions of dollars for governments in telecom auctions. As a result, journalists no longer treat game theorists as just another breed of ineffectual social scientists. Now we are dangerous Machiavellian meddlers! For my part in designing a telecom auction that raised the enormous sum of $35 billion, *Newsweek* magazine described me as a "ruthless, Poker-playing economist", which I guess translates into the proposition that fat cats don't like the methods they use to extract money from the public being used to extract money from them for the benefit of the community as a whole.

The discipline of mechanism design is based on the obvious principle that decision-making should be decentralized to the people who have the necessary knowledge and expertise. Everybody knows the frustration of being ordered to do stupid things by an ignorant or incompetent boss. The inefficiencies that can then result may be enormous, as with the hugely dysfunctional command economy that eventually failed so spectacularly in the Soviet Union. But the problem with decentralizing power is that power breeds corruption. As we all know, the Jacks-in-office to whom we delegate power eventually learn to make decisions that benefit themselves rather than the community they supposedly serve.

The selling of public assets like telecom licenses provides an instructive case study. Western governments traditionally made the Soviet mistake of allowing public officials to determine the selling prices, rather than delegating this decision to the only people who know what they are really worth—namely the potential buyers themselves. Perhaps they had read David Hume on this subject: "In constraining any system of government and fixing the several checks and controls of the constitution, every man ought to be supposed a knave and to have no other end in all his actions than private interest." It would certainly be very naive to suppose that a telecom magnate would tell the truth if a public official asked him to say how much a license was worth to him!

But we don't need to restrict our attention to naive ways of persuading people to act in the public interest. Mechanism design takes up Hume's challenge by designing games in which the knaves to whom power is delegated are treated as players. The checks in the constitution are the rules of the game. These are used to prevent a player going off the rails in situations that the designer can effectively monitor and evaluate. However, it is the controls that are more important, since these apply to decisions that the designer can't monitor, or doesn't know how to evaluate. To get the players to act in accordance with the designer's aims rather than their own in such situations, it is necessary that the payoffs of the game be carefully chosen to provide the right *incentives*.

For example, one can incentify the bidders in a telecom auction to reveal what they think a license is worth by using a Vickrey auction, in which the winners pay only the bid of the highest loser.[5] There is then no point in bidding more than your valuation, because if this is what is necessary to win a license, it is because the highest loser has bid more than you want to pay. Nor is there any point in bidding less than your valuation, because this can only reduce your chances of winning a license, without changing how much you have to pay if you win.

In a Vickrey auction, all the licenses are sold at the amount they are valued by the highest loser. Under appropriate conditions, it can be proved that this is the *most* that a seller who is ignorant of the valuations of the bidders can expect to

---

[5]William Vickrey was another eccentric genius like Nash and Harsanyi, who spent his professional life crying unheard in the wilderness. Aside from the achievements for which he is now known, he also deserves to be credited alongside Harsanyi and Rawls as an inventor of the original position. He died three days after eventually being awarded a Nobel prize.

get. A Vickrey auction is therefore optimal in such a second-best world (although not uniquely so).

The design gives the bidders the right incentives to reveal their true valuations, but the cost of extracting this information is that the seller has to be satisfied with a lot less than the winners would actually be willing to pay. In a first-best world, the seller would know the winners' valuations in advance, and offer each of them a take-it-or-leave-it offer only slightly smaller than they are willing to pay.

This is only the simplest of a number of cases in which we can quantify how much is lost as a consequence of our being a second-best species that lies and cheats when we think we can get away with it. As in the case of selling telecom licenses, the losses can be enormous. But there isn't any point in crying over such spilt milk. Instead, mechanism design accepts our second-best status and seeks to prevent our ending up with the kind of third-rate outcome with which we are usually saddled.

Blind watchmaker. The point of the preceding aside on mechanism design, is that one can think of the social contract of a hunter-gatherer society as the product of an exercise in mechanism design, with Nature in the role of a "blind watchmaker" who metaphorically fits appropriate social cogs and springs together into a harmonious whole.[6]

In planning her design, Nature knows that genes are knaves who can't be trusted to act for the good of the species, and so she takes for granted that they will optimize their own fitness. Only equilibria of the game of life are therefore available as possible social contracts. This creates no problem for cooperative hunting, which we have seen can be sustained aspart of an equilibrium. But what kind of cooperative hunting is optimal, in the sense that it maximizes the net benefit to the group?

The relevance of the decentralizing principle of mechanism design now becomes obvious. Each individual hunter is then free to use his own intelligence and expertise to the best advantage in cooperation with the rest of the group. The control is that meat gets shared according to a fixed rule. Each hunter then maximizes the amount of meat his own family will get by maximizing the total amount of meat available to the group as a whole. Of course, there are also costs as well as benefits. The risk that each hunter is willing to take in hunting big game isn't controlled by the sharing rule, but it is presumably no accident that brave young men are sexier than cowards.

Wouldn't things sometimes be better if someone were to coordinate the hunt by assigning different roles to different individuals? The answer is obviously yes, provided that such a leader has no punishment powers to abuse. Experienced hunters do in fact take on such a coordinating role in modern foraging societies, although they are careful when offering advice not to appear to be giving orders. However, our focus isn't on modern foraging societies, but on the foraging societies that existed before language had evolved very far. Some planning ahead was still

---

[6]As with "selfish genes" or "invisible hands", nothing teleological is intended when speaking of "blind watchmakers". Such metaphors merely signal an appeal to the claim that evolution leads to the same equilibria that rational players would choose (section 1.4). The only difference here is that an implicit appeal is being made to the type of group selection defended in section 1.5.

doubtless possible, but it seems unlikely to have been very sophisticated. Presumably, different individuals got into the habit of occupying different roles as they gained experience of hunting together. Chimpanzees manage to do this quite effectively, so why not humans?

In summary, cooperating hunting may have been more productive in leader-less societies—especially before the emergence of language—because the lack of a leader able to punish disobedience allows decision-making to be decentralized to the efficient level.

Memes or genes?   I hope I've made it plausible that there are good reasons why evolution might have suppressed the instinct for social dominance that we presumably once shared with chimpanzees. But couldn't it have been cultural evolution that played this trick? After all, it is cultural evolution that is said to be responsible for our later adaptation to a farming lifestyle.

There are several reasons why I think the transition to fair social contracts with no bosses was probably genetically engineered. The most important reason is the universality of the deep structure of modern hunter-gatherer societies, even though these are dispersed in geographically distant and diverse environments. I have heard it argued by social anthropologists that this phenomenon can be attributed to parallel cultural evolution, but their arguments seem to be more motivated by an urge to hang on to the blank-slate paradigm of the human mind than by any serious consideration of the scientific plausibility of the hypothesis.

Some supplementary evidence comes from a small number of natural experiments in which a society previously operating a modern social contract has been forced to revert to a pure foraging economy. Jared Diamond's *Guns, Germs, and Steel* records the fate of the Moriori, a Polynesian people who found their way to the remote Chatham Islands, which are too far south for Polynesian crops to flourish. The social contract of the foraging society that resulted replicated the universal features of such societies—as one would expect if these features are genetically determined. Titular chiefs persisted, but lost all authority. But their new social contract left them helpless when invaded in 1835 by a smaller number of Maoris from New Zealand, who doubtless reenacted an oft-played scene when they ruthlessly wiped the Moriori from the face of the earth.

There is also the neuroscience work of John Allman and his colleagues. They have located a structure involving some 100,000 very large "spindle" neurons, found only in humans and other African apes. Allman believes that the kind of social activity required by the kind of deep fairness structure I am postulating is controlled by this remarkable collection of cells.

Finally, there is our own psychology. Why are we so resentful when subjected to the authority of bosses who treat us unfairly? At an astonishingly early age, my children were already expressing their outrage at being bossed around by saying "It isn't fair!" in circumstances that often fit the bill uncomfortably well. And what are the countries in which people are happiest and most productive? They are the countries with constitutions that protect their citizens from tyranny, and guarantee the fair adminstration of justice.[7] I don't think any of this is accidental or coincidental. I think evolution wrote a yearning for freedom and justice into our nature that no amount of social conditioning by the Stalins and Hitlers of this world will ever be able to eradicate.

9.4 An Origin for the Golden Rule?

Recognition of the Golden Rule seems to be universal in human societies. Is there any reason why evolution should have written such a principle into our genes? Some equilibrium selection devices are obviously necessary for social life to be possible, but why should something like the Golden Rule have evolved?

If the Golden Rule is understood as a simplified version of the device of the original position, I think an answer to this question can be found by asking why social animals evolved in the first place. This is generally thought to have been because food-sharing has survival value.

Insurance contracts. The vampire bats mentioned in chapter 1 provide an example. Unless a vampire bat can feed every sixty hours or so, it is likely to die. The advantages of sharing food among vampire bats are therefore strong—so strong that evolution has taught even unrelated bats to share blood on a reciprocal basis.

II:2.5.4

By sharing food, the bats are essentially *insuring* each other against hunger. Animals can't write insurance contracts in the human manner, and even if they could, they would have no legal system to which to appeal if one animal were to hold up on his or her contractual obligation to the other. But the folk theorem tells us that evolution can get round the problem of external enforcement if the animals interact together on a *repeated* basis.

By coordinating on a suitable equilibrium in their repeated game of life, two animals who are able to monitor each other's behavior sufficiently closely can achieve whatever could be achieved by negotiating a legally binding insurance contract. It will be easier for evolution to find its way to such an equilibrium if the animals are related, but the case of vampire bats shows that kinship isn't necessary if the evolutionary pressures are sufficiently strong.

From uncertainty to ignorance. What considerations would Adam and Eve need to take into account when negotiating a mutual insurance pact?

Imagine a time before cooperative hunting had evolved, in which Adam and Eve foraged separately for food. Like vampire bats, they would sometimes come home lucky and sometimes unlucky. An insurance pact between them would specify how to share the available food on days when one was lucky and the other unlucky.

If Adam and Eve were rational players negotiating an insurance contract, they wouldn't know in advance who was going to be lucky and who unlucky on any given

---

[7]The original constitution of United States of America sometimes reads like a textbook exercise in the application of the principles of mechanism design. I wonder to what extent its authors were aware of the debt they owed to David Hume.

day on which the contract would be invoked. To keep things simple, suppose that both possibilities are equally likely.[8] Adam and Eve can then be seen as bargaining behind a *veil of uncertainty* that conceals who is going to turn out to be Ms. Lucky or Mr. Unlucky. Both players then bargain on the assumption that they are as likely to end up holding the share assigned to Mr. Unlucky as they are to end up holding the share assigned to Ms. Lucky.

I think the obvious parallel between bargaining over such mutual insurance pacts and bargaining in the original position is no accident. To nail the similarity down completely, we need only give Adam and Eve new names when they take their places behind Rawls' veil of ignorance. In the same spirit that led the utilitarian philosopher Hare to call his Ideal Observer an Archangel, Adam and Eve will be called John and Oskar (on the grounds that the inventors of game theory reasoned like angels while they were still among us).

Instead of Adam and Eve being uncertain about whether they will turn out to be Ms. Lucky or Mr. Unlucky, the new setup requires that John and Oskar pretend to be ignorant about whether they will turn out to be Adam or Eve. It then becomes clear that a move to the device of the original position requires only that the players imagine themselves in the shoes of somebody else—either Adam or Eve—rather than in the shoes of one of their own possible future selves.

If Nature wired us up to solve the simple insurance problems that arise in food-sharing, she therefore also simultaneously provided much of the wiring necessary to operate the original position.

Of course, in an insurance contract, the parties to the agreement don't have to *pretend* that they might end in somebody else's shoes. On the contrary, it is the reality of the prospect that they might turn out to be Ms. Lucky or Mr. Unlucky that motivates their writing a contract in the first place. But when the device of the original position is used to adjudicate fairness questions, then John knows perfectly well that he is actually Adam, and that it is physically impossible that he could become Eve. To use the device in the manner recommended by Rawls and Harsanyi, he therefore has to indulge in a counterfactual act of imagination. He can't become Eve, but he must pretend that he could. How is this gap between reality and pretense to be bridged without violating the Linnaean dictum: *Natura non facit saltus?*

II:2.5   **Expanding the circle.**   As argued earlier, I think that human ethics arose from Nature's attempt to solve certain equilibrium selection problems. But Nature doesn't jump from the simple to the complex in a single bound. She tinkers with existing structures rather than creating hopeful monsters. To make a naturalistic origin for the device of the original position plausible, it is therefore necessary to give some account of what tinkering she might have done.

In Peter Singer's *Expanding Circle,* the circle that expands is the domain within which moral rules are understood to apply. For example, Jesus sought to expand the domain of the principle that you should love your neighbor by redefining a neighbor

---

[8]There isn't any point in agonizing about what happens if they aren't equally likely, since unequal probabilities can always be absorbed into the players' social indices (section 8.4).

to be anyone at all. How might evolution expand the domain within which a moral rule operates?

My guess is that the domain of a moral rule sometimes expands when players misread signals from their environment, and so mistakenly apply a piece of behavior or a way of thinking that has evolved for use within some inner circle to a larger set of people, or to a new game. When such a mistake is made, the players attempt to play their part in sustaining an equilibrium in the inner-circle game without fully appreciating that the outer-circle game has different rules. For example, Adam might treat Eve as a sibling even though they are unrelated. Or he might treat a one-shot game as though it were going to be repeated indefinitely often.

A strategy profile that is an equilibrium for an inner-circle game won't normally be an equilibrium for an outer-circle game. A rule that selects an equilibrium strategy in an inner-circle game will therefore normally be selected against if used in an outer-circle game. But there will be exceptions. When playing an outer-circle game as though it were an inner-circle game, the players will sometimes happen to coordinate on an equilibrium of the outer-circle game. The group will then have stumbled upon an equilibrium selection device for the outer-circle game. This device consists of the players behaving *as though* they were constrained by the rules of the inner-circle game, when the rules by which they are actually constrained are those of the outer-circle game.

No hopeful monsters. Chapter 7 argues that the origins of moral behavior are to be found in the family, because the equilibrium selection problem is easier for evolution to solve in such games. This chapter makes the additional point that the games on which we should focus are those in which the efficient equilibria correspond to long-term understandings between the players to share food so as to insure each other against hunger. Solving the equilibrium selection problem in such games would require providing neural wiring for a primitive version of the device of the original position.

The circle was then ready to be expanded by including strangers in the game by treating them as honorary or fictive kinfolk, starting with outsiders adopted into the clan by marriage or cooption. Indeed, if you only interact on a regular basis with kinfolk, what other template for behavior would be available?

The sympathetic preferences provided by Nature to assess the comparative welfare of relatives wouldn't apply to a stranger, but it isn't a big step to suppose that a social consensus would emerge about what kind of relative a particular stranger should be taken to be.

The next step requires combining these two developments so that the original position gets to be used not just in situations in which Adam and Eve might turn out to be themselves in the role of Ms. Lucky or Mr. Unlucky, but in which they proceed as though it were possible for each of them to turn out to occupy the role of the other person. To accept that I may be unlucky may seem a long way from contemplating the possibility that I might become another person in another body, but is the difference really so great? After all, there is a sense in which none of us are the same person when comfortable and well fed as when tired and hungry. In

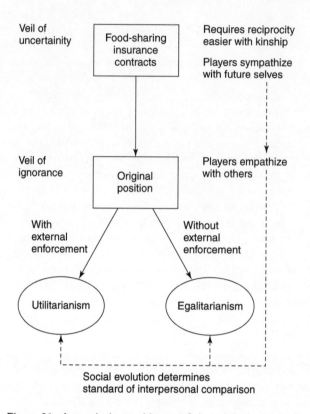

Figure 21: An evolutionary history of the original position?

different circumstances, we reveal different personalities and want different things.

To pursue this point, consider what is involved when rational players consider the various contingencies that may arise when planning ahead. To assess these, players compute their expected utility as a weighted average of the payoffs of all the future people—lucky or unlucky—that they might turn out to be after the dice has ceased to roll. When choosing a strategy in a family game, players similarly take their payoffs to be a weighted average of the fitnesses of everybody in their family. In order to convert our ability to negotiate insurance contracts into a capacity for using fairness as a more general coordinating device in the game of life, all that is then needed is for us to hybridize these two processes by allowing players to replace one of the future persons that a roll of the dice might reveal them to be, by a person in another body. The empathetic preferences that are needed to assess this possibility require nothing more than that they treat this person in another body in much the same way that they treat their sisters, cousins, or aunts.

Figure 21 illustrates the evolutionary history of the original position in the story told so far. It also draws attention to two problems. The first concerns the standard of interpersonal comparison built into the empathetic preferences with which Adam and Eve enter the original position.

The weights we use when discounting the fitnesses of our partners in a family game are somehow obtained by estimating our degree of relationship to our kinfolk from the general dynamics of the family and our place in it. But where do we get the weights to discount Adam and Eve's personal utils when constructing an empathetic utility function? My answer is that these weights are determined by the action of social evolution. In the coming chapters, the notion of an empathy equilibrium introduced in chapter 8 is used as a crude means of saying something about the implications of this assumption.

The second problem is that of enforcement. As figure 21 indicates, this makes all the difference between whether the use of the original position leads to utilitarian or egalitarian conclusions. Chapter 10 shows that if we follow Harsanyi in assuming that the hypothetical deal reached in the original position is enforced by some outside agency, then the outcome will be utilitarian. Chapter 11 shows that if we assume no external enforcement at all, then the outcome is egalitarian.

How social contracts are policed is therefore a big deal, and so it is important not to close this chapter without reviewing how enforcement works in modern hunter-gatherer societies, and how it might have worked in prehistoric societies.

9.5 Enforcement

It is sometimes easy to forget that biological evolution didn't stop working on chimpanzees when we split off to go our own way. In fact, bonobos branched off after we did. Even more important is the thought that cultural evolution was also busy in human foraging societies all the time that it was shaping our farming and industrial societies. It is therefore risky to treat modern foraging societies as fossilized replicas of the prehistoric societies within which evolution added the final touches to human nature. I think we need to be particularly careful about the question of policing in a social contract.

Modern foraging societies. The pure foraging societies that survived into modern times were pushed into marginal habitats with little or no opportunity for emigration. I can think of at least two reasons why being banished to such tough environments would have led to their adopting more disciplined social contracts than would otherwise be necessary.

II:4.5

The first reason is the need of egalitarian societies to prevent the population size from getting out of hand. The harshness of their environment when times are bad doubtless does much of this for them, but they also use "natural" methods of birth control—like the delayed weaning of children, or straighforward infanticide. There are also sometimes reports of old people acquiescing in being abandoned when nomadic groups move on.

A second reason is that leaders with bright ideas are dangerous for folk living near the edge of survival, and so the evolutionary pressure for effective anti-dominance mechanisms will be that much stronger. Sahlins has pointed out that the lean years when food is scarce are rare, but they are the years that determine whether the group's social contract will survive. If the crisis in a lean year is sufficiently severe, some members of the band may die, and the rest seek refuge with neighboring bands. In the fat years that intervene between such crises, memories of the privations of the last lean year fade. The band is then at risk of being seduced by a charismatic entrepreneur into coordinating on a social contract that does better at exploiting the surpluses available in fat years. Disaster then ensues if this new social contract is being operated when a lean year comes along.

In brief, the social mechanisms that inhibit the appearance of such leaders serve as a kind of collective unconscious that preserves a folk memory of disasters narrowly avoided in the past. The stubborn conservatism of supposedly stupid peasants occupied in subsistence farming doubtless has a similar explanation.

We therefore have at least two reasons why we should anticipate that cultural evolution would have generated social contracts with more effective policing whenever possible. In particular, the potential for the behavior of small numbers of individuals to be policed by public opinion in the group as a whole would presumably be exploited to the full. Why does a Kalahari bushman pass on an especially nice tool after keeping it for only a few days? Because he will start to be punished by the group as a whole if he incurs envy by keeping it too long.

This consideration implies that the social contracts of smallish subgroups needn't satisfy the same equilibrium requirements as the social contract of the group as a whole. There is nobody to act as an external enforcement agency for the whole group, and so its social contract must be entirely self-policing, but a small enough subgroup does have a potential external enforcement agency:namely the coalition of everybody not in the subgroup.

The game of life of the subgroup therefore differs from that of the group as a whole, because its rules must take account of the policing behavior of people outside the subgroup. If the device of the original position continues to be used in modern foraging societies, one might therefore perhaps see transactions between pairs of individuals being carried out on a utilitarian basis, while sharing in the group as a whole is carried out on an egalitarian basis.

Prehistoric societies. The social contracts of our hominid ancestors were presumably less disciplined than those of modern foraging societies. Not only did cultural evolution have the opportunity to shape the latter over a period of 10,000 years or more, but they were also subjected to extra pressures in favor of more internal discipline.

One obvious point is that there is nowhere for rebels to escape discipline in a modern foraging group, except to a neighboring group with a similar social contract. However, matters would have been very different for our hominid ancestors, with a whole world to expand into. Without barriers to emigration, their social organization must have been anarchic to an extent that would make modern hunter-gatherer societies look positively paternalistic. How could it have been otherwise when a dissident group always had the Lockean option of breaking away at relatively low cost to set up shop in pastures new? Neither public opinion nor personal authority can act as Big Brother when punishment can be evaded simply by walking off.

I believe that the distress we all feel at the exercise of arbitrary authority derives from attitudes that were hardwired into our heads under such circumstances. As Nietzsche's Zaruthustra put it: "My brethren, will ye suffocate in the fumes of their maws and appetites? Better break the windows and jump into the open air! ... Empty still are many sites around which floateth the odor of tranquil seas. Open still remaineth a free life for great souls." In 1888, there were indeed still wild and free places in America, but the tragedy of today is that nowhere is left to which we can escape. In this respect, our own overpopulation crisis is a perhaps a replay of the prehistoric crisis that brought authoritarianism back into our social world.

However, the main point I want to make about the social contract of our hominid ancestors is that public opinion in the group as a whole wouldn't have controlled transactions between pairs of individuals as in modern foraging societies. Sharing for insurance reasons between pairs of individuals could therefore have got going in much the same way that it got going in vampire bats. Once a sharing rule was established, it would then be profitable for production as well as consumption to become cooperative. Since there are substantial returns to scale in hunting, the way was then open for the circle to expand from small groups to larger groups.

Chapter 10

Utilitarianism

> This addibility of happiness, however when considered rigorously it may appear fictitious, is a postulatum without the allowance of which all political reasonings are at a stand.
>
> Jeremy Bentham

10.1 John Harsanyi

The stuffed and mounted corpse of Jeremy Bentham is kept on public display in a glass case in the foyer of my college in London. As a macabre jest, he left instructions that it was to preside over meetings of the governing board after his death. I know that Jeremy's remains do in fact sometimes preside at meetings of the college's Bentham Society, since I once sat beside them. In contrast to many dinner companions, I think he would have been more jolly when alive.

Bentham is the founder of utilitarianism.[1] He was as cranky as they come, but his work overflows with creative insight. John Stuart Mill supposedly provided a intellectually sound foundation for his ideas, but on this subject at least he strikes me as no more than an amiable fudger. In particular, Mill's much cited "proof" of utilitarianism just consists of a chapter devoted to the claim that what people desire is happiness. But what we want to know is whether happiness is really something that can be sharply defined. How do we measure it? How do we add it up? Why substitute the sum of everybody's happiness for our own?

To get straight answers to such questions, the world had to wait for John Harsanyi. His life was by no means easy. As a Jew in Hungary, he escaped disaster by the skin of his teeth not once, but twice. Having evaded the death camps of the Nazis, he was then forced to cross illegally into Austria with his wife to escape persecution by the Communists who followed. And once in the West, he had to build his career again from scratch, beginning with a factory job in Australia.

---

[1] Bentham credits Helvetius. Mill says that the idea goes back at least as far as Epicurus, but I don't think Epicurus would have been pleased to be classified as an early Benthamite!

Although he finally won a Nobel prize, the economics profession has yet to accord his ethical work the recognition it deserves. As with David Hume, to accept his common-sense insights requires junking centuries of earnest scholarship as worthless—and which of us is ready to dump our own books first? One would have thought that philosophers would be more open to his ideas, but his use of elementary mathematics seems to have closed that door to whole-hearted recognition also.

This praise of John Harsanyi's genius doesn't imply that I agree with everything he says. On the contrary, I disagree very much with his attempt to defend utilitarianism as a Kantian system of personal morality, but I nevertheless plan to borrow the tools he created for this purpose to explain why we should expect fairness norms operated in the presence of an omnipotent and omniscient policeman to have a utilitarian structure.

This chapter is therefore concerned with the left-hand branch of figure 21. If people bargain behind the veil of ignorance in the presence of an external enforcement agency, why will the outcome be utilitarian? And how will the necessary standard of interpersonal comparison be determined?

One possible application is to the behavior of small groups within a modern foraging society. Another is to modern welfare economics: how should an all-powerful but benevolent government formulate policy? Of course, while discussing such matters, we mustn't forget that there can be no external enforcement agency when society is considered as a whole. Readers who are impatient to see why I think that this case leads to an egalitarian conclusion, as indicated by the right-hand branch of figure 21, may therefore wish to skip forward to the next chapter.

10.2   Skyhooks?

I have been fiercely critical of the skyhooks that various thinkers have dreamed up to explain why they should be allowed to proceed as though an external enforcement agency exists when no such entity is anywhere to be found. It is particularly distressing to find economists who write on constitutional design making this mistake by applying the methods of mechanism design when nothing compels the citizens of a state to honor the rules built into their invented constitutions.

Even Jeremy Bentham was unwilling to look kindly on the species of skyhook that models a government as a body of omnipotent and omniscient officials who are somehow immune to the corrupting personal incentives of the citizens whose activities they direct. As he repeatedly explains, the law needs to protect us at least as much from the officers of the state who govern us as from our fellow citizens.[2] This is why chapter 1 insists that a social contract for a whole society be modeled as an *equilibrium* in whatever game of life is being played.

I have made this case so strongly, that it is necessary to insist that I am not

---

[2] Just as Rawls' assumptions should have made him a utilitarian, one can therefore argue that Bentham's assumptions should have made him an egalitarian! But perhaps he wouldn't have been as displeased as we imagine, since he frequently claims that his "greatest happiness" principle will tend to promote equality in cases where modern utilitarians would argue for the sacrifice of a few for the sake of the many.

claiming that it *never* makes sense to assume the existence of an external enforcement agency. On the contrary, when looking at the organization of a subsidiary grouping within a society, or at some special activity of a whole society, it ceases to be true that we are necessarily attaching a hook to the sky when postulating external enforcement. For example, when considering what tax regimes are fair, one may separate the fiscal role of a government from its policing role. When considering the constitution of a trade union or the wording of a commercial contract, one can appeal to the state's legal system if enforcement becomes necessary.

If our arena is less than the whole activity of a whole society, it is therefore often sensible to build an external enforcement agency into the rules of the game of life to be studied. The set of available social contracts will then be *larger* than it would have been without the agency.[3] For example, if the game of life were the one-shot Prisoners' Dilemma, then an agreement that both players will play *dove* becomes an equilibrium outcome if everyone knows that anyone cheating on the deal will be punished severely by some powerful onlooker.

Since the analysis in this chapter and the next works for all games of life, I don't need to come down one way or another on what it is reasonable to assume in a given context about enforcement mechanisms that are explicitly built into the rules of the game of life. What separates the two chapters is whether a deal hypothetically reached *in the original position* is to be regarded as binding or not.

When such deals are taken to be binding, I think it vital that we be offered a mundane explanation of how and why they are binding. For example, in the case of a modern foraging band, the way that two neighbors settle a fairness dispute between them may well be policed by everybody else in their band, but this couldn't have been the case in the ancient foraging bands in which fairness first evolved as an equilibrium selection device.

10.3 Summum Bonum?

A utilitarian needs to answer three questions: *II:2.2.3*

- What constitutes utility?
- Why should individual utilities be added?
- Why should I maximize the sum of utilities rather than my own?

Harsanyi answers the first of these three questions by abandoning Bentham and Mill's attempt to quantify happiness in favor of the theory of Von Neumann and Morgenstern, so that the players' utilities simply serve to describe the preferences revealed by their choice behavior.

Some confusion has been engendered by the fact that Harsanyi offered two entirely distinct answers to the second question. The first answer requires postulating   *II:Appendix B* a set of axioms that encapsulate the intuitions we supposedly share concerning an absolute Good, conceived of as some Platonic form existing independently of our evolutionary history. But such an approach has no place in a book that denies such

---

[3]My guess is that Rousseau and Kant were saying no more than this when advocating submission to the skyhook of a General Will.

supernatural concepts.[4] His second answer is more interesting, since it calls upon the device of the original position, which Harsanyi invented independently of Rawls. I describe a reinterpreted version of this approach in the next section.

However, Harsanyi has nothing substantive to say in reply to the third of the three questions. The existence of a moral Good whose advancement somehow takes priority over our own individual concerns is simply taken for granted.

I think it a major error for utilitarians to fudge the third question. What needs to be decided is whether utilitarianism is a moral system to be employed by *individuals* in regulating their interactions with others, or a set of tenets to be followed by an *organization* that has the power to enforce its decrees. It is understandable that utilitarians are reluctant to argue that their doctrine should be forced down the throats of people who find it hard to swallow. They prefer to imagine a world in which their thoughts are embraced with open arms by all the citizens of a utilitarian state. As with Marxists, there is sometimes talk of the state withering away when the word has finally reached every heart. On the other hand, most utilitarians see the practical necessity of compulsion. As Mill puts it: "For such actions as are prejudicial to the interests of others, the individual is accountable, and may be subjected to social or legal punishment."

My own view is that utilitarians would be wise to settle for the public policy or social welfare option, a modest version of which I defend in the rest of the chapter using an argument inspired by Harsanyi's theory of the original position.[5]

II:2.2.6

10.4   Political Legitimacy

The political legitimacy of a government is nowadays almost universally held to derive from a mandate of the people. That is to say, the people somehow determine or endorse the policies that their government enforces. But there is nothing sacred about the periodic elections that are thought adequate to deliver a mandate to the government of a representative democracy. On the contrary, there are often complaints that the process is unfair—particularly in its treatment of minorities in countries with a history of factional unrest. So one can ask what would happen if we used the device of the original position to determine a government's mandate. But how would such a consensus be enforced?

Harsanyi and Rawls answer this question by inventing very similar skyhooks. In Harsanyi's case, the social contract agreed in the original position is supposedly policed by the "moral commitments" of the players. In Rawls' case, it is policed by the players' sense of "natural duty". However, we don't need to believe in such skyhooks to find their arguments worthy of attention. If correct, they apply whenever there is a real source of external enforcement.

---

[4] John Broome's *Weighing Goods* provides an admirably clear exposition.

[5] I think that taking this view provides an incidental resolution of a long-standing dispute between act utilitarians and rule utilitarians. It seems to me that only rule utilitarianism makes sense with a public policy interpretation, whereas only act utilitarianism makes sense with a personal morality interpretation.

Harsanyi's argument. Harsanyi's own analysis is easy to describe. Behind his thick version of the veil of ignorance, Adam and Eve forget everything about themselves that there is to be forgotten. This includes their own empathetic preferences as well as their own personal preferences.

But nobody can bargain in the original position without empathetic utility functions to assess the various alternatives. Harsanyi therefore assumes that Adam and Eve will construct new empathetic preferences appropriate to the informational vacuum in which they find themselves. He then appeals to a principle that has affectionately become known as the Harsanyi doctrine: that rational people in precisely the same situation will choose in precisely the same way. If so, then Adam and Eve will construct precisely the *same* empathetic preferences behind Harsanyi's veil of ignorance.

Adam and Eve's bargaining problem is then trivial. They will be unanimous in wanting to implement whatever social contract is optimal relative to their commonly held empathetic preferences. However, we know from chapter 8 that maximizing an empathetic utility function is the same as maximizing a weighted sum of Adam and Eve's personal utilities. But this is precisely what utilitarians say we should do.

Rawls' argument. Rawls simply assumes the problem of why Adam and Eve have the same empathetic preferences away. They subscribe to the same standard of interpersonal comparison, because they are somehow endowed with the same index of what he calls "primary goods".

So why doesn't Rawls get the same utilitarian answer as Harsanyi, albeit expressed in a somewhat different way? The answer is that Rawls denies orthodox decision theory. He argues that after Adam and Eve have agreed on securing certain basic rights and liberties, they will apply the maximin principle to distributional issues. However, we saw in chapter 5 that this principle only makes sense in a zero-sum game in which the opponent is your bitter enemy. But why should Adam and Eve assume that the universe manipulates how dice will roll with the sole aim of damaging them as much as possible?

In brief, Rawls escapes a utilitarian conclusion only by an iconoclastic evasion of the logic of the decision problem he creates for Adam and Eve behind the veil of ignorance. Philosophers sometimes defend his position on this front, but I think they seldom appreciate the enormity of the heresy they are endorsing. If orthodox decision theory were wrong in a simple situation like the original position, then it would always be wrong. I'm all in favor of bringing down the temple on the heads of the Philistines, but Samson was at least aware that this is what he was doing!

Rawls' analysis is therefore faulty, but I think his intuition is nevertheless sound. Basically, he argues that the use of the original position will generate a social contract like that of our foraging ancestors. But we won't get to this conclusion by analyzing the original position on the assumption that "natural duty" provides an external enforcement agency. This skyhook leads to utilitarianism! For a different conclusion, we need to take what Rawls says later in his *Theory of Justice* about the "strains of commitment" much more seriously. When we do so in the next chapter, we shall find that the kind of egalitarian solution he was seeking comes rolling out.

10.5   Bargaining in the Original Position

Harsanyi argues that there is an ideally rational set of empathetic preferences, but how would we poor mortals ever find out what they are? One might try adopting the pose of Rodin's thinker in an imagined Kantian limbo, but I don't suppose anyone thinks that this would help very much. This section therefore begins an attempt to provide a naturalistic reinterpretation of Harsanyi's approach.

I think that the "rational" social indices of Harsanyi's utilitarian utopia are just another skyhook. They are no more to be found than the "natural" language an Egyptian pharoah sought to discover by having children brought up without social contact with adults. The social indices that describe an actual standard of interpersonal comparison are *culturally* determined. So how could we possibly figure out what they are by divesting ourselves of all cultural influences?

In my naturalistic reinterpretation, Eve enters the original position to resolve an everyday fairness problem with her *own* empathetic preferences—not some abstract or ideal set of empathetic preferences invented by a moral philosopher. She acquired her empathetic preferences from her culture, and so this is where we must look if we want to know what they are like.

Harsanyi and Rawls are doubtless right to observe that there is normally a strong consensus in a society on the appropriate standard of interpersonal comparison, but I don't think this is just an interesting curiosity to be mentioned in passing. On the contrary, it seems to me that understanding how and why social evolution might generate such a consensus is part and parcel of understanding how and why the social indices a society employs are what they come to be.

The next step in naturalizing Harsanyi's argument is therefore to study what happens when Adam and Eve enter the original position with *different* empathetic preferences. They will then no longer be unanimous about what social contract to adopt, and so their bargaining problem will cease to be entirely trivial. Having worked out what happens when there is no consensus on a standard of interpersonal comparison, the final step is to ask why these outcomes are less stable than those in which there is a consensus.

All this will have to be done again in the next chapter without the assumption that there is an external enforcement agency, but the simpler analysis offered here will hopefully allow us to take some of the bargaining questions for granted, so that attention can be focused on the equilibrium issues.

II:2.6

A marriage contract.   The analysis of bargaining in the original position will be dramatized by making the players Adam and Eve in the Garden of Eden, which comes equipped with God as the ultimate enforcement agency. Adam and Eve plan a Californian-style marriage contract that specifies how the benefits and costs of their relationship will be shared. (Think Jane Austen rather than Charlotte Brontë.)

We shall work at a level of abstraction that makes it unnecessary to assume very much about the rules of Adam and Eve's game of life. If you find it helpful to think of a particular game in this role, the Nash Demand Game of chapter 4 will do fine. The important thing is that we have a set X like that shown in figure 1 to represent Adam and Eve's set of feasible marriage contracts.

We also need a point D to represent the default social contract—the social contract that Adam and Eve are currently operating while still unmarried. In bargaining theory, this outcome is variously called the disagreement point or the status quo. In my theory, it substitutes for what Hobbes famously called the state of nature, but although I guess single folk are solitary by definition, I don't want to suggest that they are necessarily also nasty, brutish, or short.[6]

We now have the the minimum amount of structure necessary to define a bargaining problem. Adam and Eve can agree on any social contract in the set X. If they fail to agree, they continue with the social contract D.

If Adam and Eve were bargaining face-to-face, each trying to squeeze as much from the other as possible, our prediction of the agreed marriage contract would be the Nash bargaining solution marked as N in figure 1. But the aim here is to figure out what Adam and Eve will regard as fair.

Remember that the notion of fairness we are working with isn't in the least sentimental. In modern times, it substitutes for face-to-face bargaining when there isn't time for conversation, or there are too many people for everyone to say their piece. Instead of bargaining for real, people unconsciously predict what deal *would* be reached if they *were* to bargain in the original position.

We therefore need to apply the Nash bargaining solution to the bargaining problem Adam and Eve face behind the veil of ignorance in their new roles as John and Oskar (Section 9.4). The first step is to tie down this bargaining problem. What is the set Z of feasible deals in the original position? What is the status quo Q?

Modeling the original position. It is easiest to start with the status quo. How will John evaluate the prospect of a failure to agree?

Although Adam puts this out of his mind when mentally entering the original position, John is actually Adam with Adam's empathetic utility function, which he uses to evaluate the prospect of a disagreement on the assumption that he has half a chance of turning out to be Adam and half a chance of turning out to be Eve.

As we learned in chapter 9, John computes his empathetic utility for the event that he turns out to be Adam in the default social contract D simply by rescaling Adam's personal utility for this event in much the same way that one would convert a temperature given in degrees Celsius to degrees Fahrenheit. He similarly computes his empathetic utility for the event that he turns out to be Eve by rescaling Eve's personal utility for this event. With these rescalings, John now has two empathetic utilities for the disagreement possibility that reflect the standard of interpersonal comparison between Adam and Eve with which he entered the original position. His overall assessment of the default social contract is then obtained simply by averaging these two empathetic utilities.

The point D_{AE} in figure 22 is the pair of empathetic utilities that John and Oskar assign to the event that they end up as Adam and Eve respectively in the

---

[6]Game theorists may ask why I don't use Nash's variable threats theory to determine the status quo in the original position. The state of nature would then be very Hobbesian. My answer is that it is unrealistic to postulate an external agency that somehow enforces threats that wouldn't actually be implemented in a bargaining session that doesn't really take place.

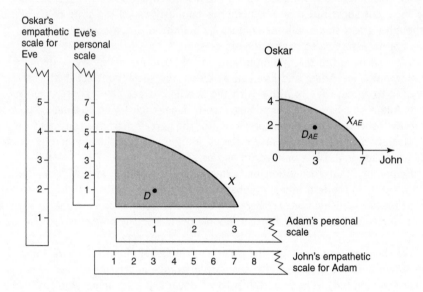

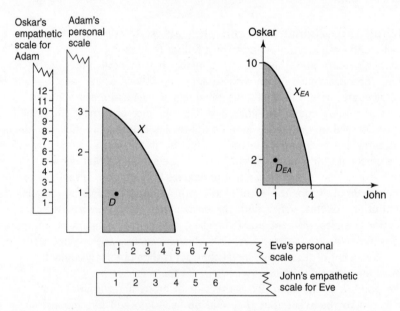

Figure 22: Finding John and Oskar's empathetic utilities.

default social contract D. The point D_{EA} is the pair of empathetic utilities that John and Oskar assign to the event that they end up as Eve and Adam respectively in the default social contract. The status quo Q for the bargaining problem in the original position is found by averaging John and Oskar's utilities in D_{AE} and D_{EA}. It is therefore located halfway between these two points in figure 23.

The points J and K in figure 23 are possible social contracts. One possible agreement in the original position is to implement J if John turns out to be Adam and Oskar turns out to be Eve, and to implement K if John turns out to be Eve and Oskar turns out to be Adam. John and Oskar identify this deal with the point L, which is halfway between J and K. The set Z of all such points is the feasible set of the bargaining problem in the original position.

Agreement in the original position. John and Oskar bargain over which point in the feasible set Z to agree on, given that the result of a disagreement will be Q. The Nash bargaining solution for this problem is marked as P in figure 23.

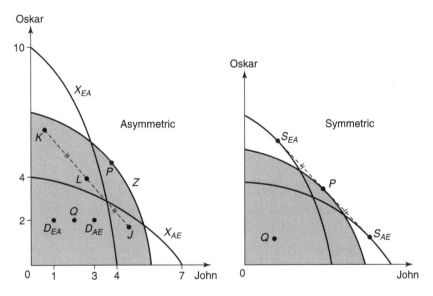

Figure 23: The bargaining problem in the original position.

The diagram on the right of figure 23 shows a symmetric version of the problem in which Adam and Eve enter the original position with the *same* empathetic preferences. The Nash bargaining solution P is then also symmetric; it assigns John and Oskar the same empathetic payoff. What does this imply about the social contract that Adam and Eve then actually implement when they emerge from behind the veil of ignorance?

In the symmetric case, two conclusions can be read off from figure 23. The first is that the *same* social contract S will be operated no matter who turns out to be

Adam or Eve. This social contract is likely to favor one player over the other, in the sense that the less favored player would prefer to return to the original position to have the phantom coin that determines who will be who tossed again.

But we have God as an external enforcement agency in this chapter to enforce the deal reached in the original position. His attitude is that Adam and Eve would have agreed in the original position to honor the toss of the phantom coin, and He will now use His power to prevent any attempt by one or the other to wriggle out of the hypothetical deal. So the phantom coin that determines who gets the gravy gets tossed once and once only—and those who don't like it must lump it.

It is somewhat surprising to find Rawls joining Harsanyi in endorsing this conclusion, but he is quite explicit. In my version of his argument, a slaveholder seeks to justify the institution of slavery to a slave: "If you had been asked to agree to a structure for society without knowing who you would be in that society, then you would have agreed to a slaveholding society because the prospective benefits of being a slaveholder would have outweighed in your mind the prospective costs of being a slave. Finding yourself a slave, you therefore have no just cause for complaint." Rawls denies that a slaveholding society would be agreed in the original position, but insists that if it were agreed, slaves would indeed have a "natural duty" to submit to their masters.

The second conclusion to be read off from the symmetric version of figure 23, is that P happens to be the utilitarian solution of the bargaining problem in the original position. It occurs where the sum of John and Oskar's unweighted empathetic utilities is largest. What is the implication for the social contract S to be operated in Adam and Eve's game of life?

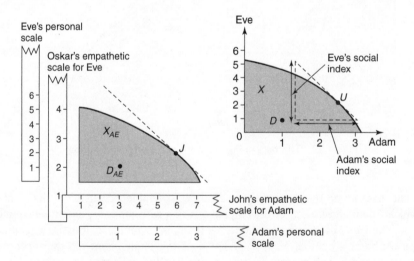

Figure 24: Returning from empathetic utilities to personal utilities.

To answer this question, we have to reverse the rescaling that took us from the bargaining problem with which we started (with everything expressed in personal utilities) to the bargaining problem in the original position (with everything expressed in empathetic utilities). Figure 24 shows that when our conclusion is expressed in terms of Adam and Eve's personal utilities, we recover Harsanyi's utilitarian claim that S is the social contract at which the sum of Adam and Eve' personal utilities is maximized after they have been suitably weighted.

10.6   Social Evolution

The preceding section ends with the conclusion that if Adam and Eve enter the original position with the *same* empathetic preferences, then they will agree on a utilitarian outcome. But the section began as an exploration of what happens when they enter the original position with *different* empathetic preferences. We now return to this latter question with the intention of determining how cultural evolution determines the utilitarian social indices taken for granted in Harsanyi's approach. I am anxious not to pretend that what I have to say on this subject is anything but a crude first stab at a naturalistic theory of interpersonal comparison of utility, but someone has to make a start somewhere.

To keep things simple, I distinguish three different time periods: *II:2.5.5*

- The *short run* corresponds to economic time—the time it takes for a market to adjust to an unanticipated piece of news. I think of the short run being measured in minutes or hours.

- The *medium run* corresponds to social time—the time it takes for cultural norms or social conventions to adjust to a change in the underlying environment. I think of the medium run being measured in months or years.

- One may regard the *long run* primarily as biological time—the time one has to wait for a gene pool to adjust to a new challenge. I think of it being measured in generations.

The modeling technique to be employed in adopting these distinctions is borrowed from the economic theory of the firm. Economic, social, and biological processes actually proceed simultaneously, but models which reflect this reality would be prohibitively difficult to handle. One therefore attempts to approximate the way the world actually works by assuming that short-run processes are infinitely faster than medium-run processes, and medium-run processes are, in turn, infinitely faster than long-run processes.

When studying short-run dynamic processes, one treats medium-run and long-run variables as fixed. The values of these medium-run and long-run variables then serve as parameters that determine the equilibrium to which the short-run process converges. In studying medium-run dynamic processes, one treats the long-run variables as fixed, but sets the short-run variables to their values at the economic equilibrium calculated in the short-run analysis. The long-run variables then serve as parameters that determine the social equilibrium to which the medium-run process converges. The same principle also applies to long-run equilibria, but I won't have much to say about long-run dynamic processes in this book.

My use of this modeling technique requires some heroic simplifying assumptions. All the decisions a player makes are short-run phenomena. The players' personal preferences and empathetic preferences are therefore fixed in the short run. In the medium run, the players' personal preferences remain fixed, but their empathetic preferences adjust until an empathetic equilibrium is reached. In the long run, the players' personal preferences may evolve as well.

What happens at an empathy equilibrium? I shall just state the result

II:2.6.2

baldly. After social evolution has moved Adam and Eve's empathetic preferences to an empathy equilibrium, the resulting social contract is the Nash bargaining solution of their underlying problem. That is to say, they end up with the same personal utilities as if they had bargained face-to-face with no holds barred.

My excuse for not offering a geometric proof of this result is that there is a sense in which it is obvious that this must happen. Of course social evolution will leach out all the moral content of the original position in the medium run! The only surprise is that this holds true with the weak definition of an empathy equilibrium offered in chapter 8, as well as with stronger forms in which the tendency to drift toward self-interest is more immediately apparent.

The next chapter shows that empathy equilibria are necessarily symmetric in the absence of external enforcement, but that isn't true here. There are multiple empathy equilibria, of which only one is symmetric. Chapter 8 explains that we therefore have a good answer to the consensus problem in the case of external enforcement only in the case when the population is sufficiently integrated that everybody treats everybody else as a potential role model.

Teenage fashion is a useful analogy. It is amazing how uniformly adolescents can dress when left to choose for themselves. Social evolution operates within the group to generate a symmetric equilibrium. But different groups may coordinate on different uniforms. For my model to generate a uniform standard of interpersonal comparison, we need the whole population to act like a single teenage group.

I make this unwelcome assumption throughout the rest of this chapter, but I think it important to register again that it is unnecessary in the next chapter.

10.7   How Utilitarian Justice Works

If social evolution leaches out all the moral content of a fairness norm in the medium run, why bother with fairness at all? What use is morality if all this talk of justice

II:2.7

merely conceals the iron fist in a velvet glove?

One answer was given in chapter 2, which considers the consequences of applying the same fairness norm simultaneously to a variety of different versions of the Meeting Game, but I want to concentrate in this chapter on the more important issues of timing that were barely mentioned in chapter 2. For this purpose, I shall stick with the simplifying assumption that the fairness norm is applied to only one coordination problem at a time.

If couples from a sufficiently cohesive society continually face the same coordination problem, then my theory says that they will use the utilitarian bargaining solution to solve it when there is adequate external enforcement. In the medium run, cultural evolution will then adjust the social indices in the utilitarian solution so that they can be computed as follows:

(1) Find the Nash bargaining solution N of the coordination problem.

(2) Choose social indices to make the utilitarian solution U coincide with N.

So why bother with the utilitarian solution at all? The answer is that the type of morality with which we are concerned has its bite in the short run—and the moral content of a fairness norm is eroded only in the medium run.

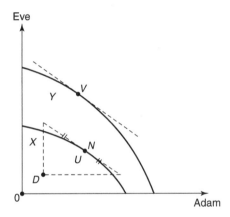

Figure 25: Justice in the short run.

To pursue this point, imagine that a new event or innovation unexpectedly results in the set of available social contracts expanding from the set X to the set Y, as illustrated in figure 25. It is in such situations that the fairness norm has a chance to fulfill the function for which it originally evolved—to shift its minisociety to a new, efficient social contract V without damaging internal conflict. In the short run, the utilitarian social indices that are adapted to X remain fixed, and so the new social contract V is located as shown in figure 25. In brief:

(3) In a new coordination problem created by expanding the feasible set, the fair social contract V is the utilitarian solution with social indices adapted to the old feasible set.

In this highly idealized situation, the shape of the set X represents the historical power structure in the Garden of Eden. Cultural evolution working in the medium run eventually succeeds in impressing the realities of power onto Adam and Eve's social indices. They will still use the rhetoric of fairness in discussing the equilibrium in X on which it is their custom to coordinate, but they would get the same result by bargaining directly. It is only when they apply their traditional fairness norm to a new coordination problem that it has any genuine moral content.

Traditionalists will complain that a norm isn't "really" fair if the social indices that characterize it are merely artifacts of the balance of power embodied in past social contracts, but I think that the scientific question is whether the social indices we actually observe in real life are consistent with my explanation or not.

Of course, if the representative problem faced by Adam and Eve continues to be characterized by Y for long enough, then the standard for making interpersonal comparisons will adjust to the new situation and so the moral content of the social contract will again be eroded away. But cultural evolution will often be too slow to keep up with the rate at which new coordination problems present themselves.

10.8   A Food-Sharing Example

Alice and Bob have a rabbit to divide. In the past, their bargaining problem has been characterized by the feasible set X and the disagreement point D of figure 26. But they now have to resolve a new bargaining problem with the same disagreement point D but a new feasible set Y.

If Alice and Bob belong to a modern hunter-gatherer society, then I have argued that the group as a whole may act as an effective enforcement agency in respect of their bilateral relations. If so, then the theory says that Alice and Bob will operate a utilitarian fairness norm when interacting together. To find the appropriate social indices, there are three steps to follow.

We already carried through the first step in chapter 8. The Nash bargaining solution of the old problem is $(75, 60)$, as illustrated in figure 19. The second step is to choose social indices for Alice and Bob that make the utilitarian bargaining solution U coincide with $(75, 60)$. As figure 26 shows, we can make this happen by choosing Alice's social index to be 5 and Bob's to be 4. The third step is to find the utilitarian solution V of the new problem using these social indices. This is the point $(80, 200)$.

It may help to expand on the tale that goes with these calculations. When Alice and Bob have had a rabbit to divide in the past, their preferences over different shares have been as shown in figure 19. Social evolution has therefore led them to the point U, which corresponds to splitting the rabbit evenly. But the new situation is different in two ways. The animal is now a suckling pig, and each player has the preferences normally held by the other. Applying the utilitarian solution with the traditional social indices, we find that the pig will be divided so that Bob gets twice as large a share as Alice.[7]

---

[7]We can tell a similar story for the case when Alice and Bob have historically been equally likely to be the more desperate. Because the underlying situation is then symmetric, social evolution will generate the same social index for them both. However, a fair division of the pig will still award Bob twice Alice's share. To get a different outcome, we need history to endow Bob with a social index that is substantially larger than Alice's. The pig will then be divided so that Alice gets five times Bob's share.

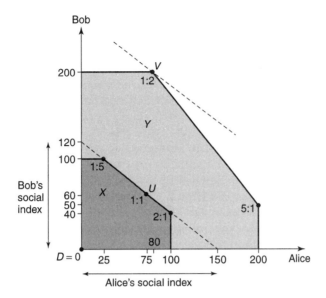

Figure 26: A food-sharing example.

10.9 Relativity

In our analysis of the original position, the set X of feasible social contracts should really be understood as a representative of a whole class of coordination problems to which Adam and Eve apply the same fairness norm. But what if Adam and Eve do distinguish between different sets X, because they arise in different contexts? In the medium run, different standards of interpersonal comparison will then evolve for these different contexts.

The same players may therefore employ different standards of fairness in different contexts. As Epicurus observed: "There is no such thing as justice in the abstract, it is merely a compact among men ... [It] is the same for all, a thing found useful by men in their relations with each other; but it does not follow that it is the same for all in each individual place and circumstance." I think that what is the same for all is the deep structure of fairness that I model as the original position, but there is a great deal else that may vary with the place and circumstance under which a fairness norm is invoked.

Among the contextual parameters that are likely to matter are the availability of external enforcement, the social standing of different members of the group, their relative needs and abilities, their blood relationships, and the effort that each has exerted in providing a surplus to share. As a result, it may often be quite difficult to evaluate the fairness of a particular sharing rule observed in the field. For example, kinship considerations alone can have a major influence on who gets how much when food is shared on a fair basis in a hunter-gatherer society.

II:4.5.4   **Modern hunter-gatherers.** I think the original position evolved from social contracts that provided some insurance against starvation. The food-sharing example of the preceding section tries to capture the essence of such situations. But the sharing of food in foraging societies is complicated by the fact that much of the sharing take place between relatives. How will this affect how fairness operates?[8]

Table 2 shows who gets what share of the pig when family relationships are taken into account. The listed social indices are those that must be used in the utilitarian solution to get these shares. Notice how these differ from the social indices 4 and 5 that we would use all the time if we mistakenly worked with Alice and Bob's individual fitnesses instead of their inclusive fitnesses.

The degree of relationship between siblings is a half. The same would be true between parents and children, but if a son has survived until puberty and his mother is no longer nubile, then we must alter their degrees of relationship to take account of their different chances of reproducing their genes. In this example, I consider the extreme case when the effective degree of relationship of the child to the parent is zero, but the degree of relationship of the parent to the child remains a half.

Alice	Bob	Alice's share	Bob's share	Alice's index	Bob's index
unrelated	unrelated	$\frac{1}{2}$	$\frac{1}{2}$	4	5
cousin	cousin	$\frac{6}{11}$	$\frac{5}{11}$	3	4
brother	sister	$\frac{2}{3}$	$\frac{1}{3}$	1	2
daughter	father	$\frac{2}{3}$	$\frac{1}{3}$	3	10
mother	son	$\frac{1}{6}$	$\frac{5}{6}$	4	3

Table 2: Sharing in a modern foraging band.

Except when Alice is Bob's mother, the closer the relationship between Alice and Bob, the more her greater need is recognized. When she interacts with her father or brother, her needs are met in full. Such recognition of Alice's need is also evident in the standards of interpersonal comparison that operate in the different cases. For example, when Alice and Bob are siblings, one of Alice's utils is deemed to be worth only half of one of Bob's. When they are cousins, her utils are worth three quarters of his. In the exceptional case when Alice is Bob's mother, her unreciprocated concern for his welfare results in his needs taking total precedence over hers. His utils are then deemed to be worth three quarters of hers.

Although no simple formula connects who gets what with how they are related, kinship is clearly relevant to the question of why the needy receive special treatment in modern hunter-gatherer societies. The phenomenon is only strengthened if we take account of the fact that inbreeding will increase the degrees of relationship.

---

[8] The reference to modern hunter-gatherer societies allows me to assume that pairs of individuals share on a utilitarian basis policed by the rest of the band.

10.10 Why Not Utilitarianism?

II:2.8

I now briefly doff my descriptive hat, and don a prescriptive hat instead to talk about utilitarianism from the same perspective as Harsanyi or Rawls. My basic point is that critics who reject utilitarianism because it is a second-best creed fall prey to the treason of making the right decision for the wrong reason. They are wrong to reject utilitarianism as second-best because Harsanyi's arguments, whether taken straight or adapted as in this chapter, provide good reasons why utilitarianism should be regarded as the first-best creed. But it is precisely because it is a first-best creed rather than a second-best creed that it should be rejected.

To make sense of this apparent paradox, it is necessary to understand how economists use the terms *first-best* and *second-best*.

A first-best solution to a mechanism design problem is one that would be engineered by an omnipotent and omniscient God, acting as an external enforcement agency. A second-best solution is the best that can be engineered by a designer who accepts that his ability to police is limited, and that human beings will eventually learn to exploit any system he may create to their own advantage. Utopians aim at first-best solutions that inevitably fail, leaving us with a third-best solution or worse. Economists think it wiser to settle for second-best by taking it for granted that only *equilibria* of the games they create for people to play are genuinely viable.

As a simple example, consider how things would be if eyes could be transferred from sighted people to blind people, but eyes from dead people were useless. The utilitarian expedient of running a fair lottery to decide who should be forced to give up an eye to a blind person would then seem first-best. If assured of adequate external enforcement, I would certainly agree to this in the original position, because my chances of turning out to be blind would be equal to my chances of turning out to be a sighted person who has to give up an eye—but it is worse to be blind than one-eyed.

However, we find such proposals repugnant, and so philosophers invent high-flown moral reasons why they shouldn't be imposed. But the real reason for rejecting the proposal is that the prospect of having an eye surgically removed is so horrific that we would be only too ready to join with our like-minded fellows to force a second-best solution on society—no matter what suffering we thereby inflicted on the blind.

Chapter 11

Egalitarianism

> What is just . . . is what is proportional.
>
> Aristotle

11.1 Original Sin

The previous chapter set the tale of Adam and Eve's marriage contract in a time before their expulsion from the Garden of Eden, but we now move to a world in which the apple has been eaten. As Milton says:

> Bad Fruit of Knowledge, if this be to know,
> Which leaves us naked thus, of Honour void.

Without God or Honor to enforce their agreements, neither Adam nor Eve will observe the terms of any social contract, unless it is in his or her interest to do so. Any marriage contract on which they agree will therefore need to be self-policing—an equilibrium in whatever game they are playing.

Recognizing that we are a second-best species whose members can't be relied upon to honor principles that conflict with their underlying incentives does nothing for our self-esteem, but is the form of egalitarianism to which one is then led so repugnant? I think not, because it is the creed that actually governs our fairness transactions in everyday life.

11.2 Equity

II:4.4

What do ordinary people think is fair? No knock-down conclusions have emerged from laboratory experiments that seek to answer this question. Part of the reason is that psychologists have had no theory to help them decide how to control their experiments, while behavioral economists have backed themselves into a blind alley by fitting personal utility functions to the data on the naive assumption that people play fair because playing fair just happens to be one of the things that people like doing. I would be discouraged that each new experiment seems to require subjects to have a brand new utility function, but behavioralists are made of sterner stuff!

The equity law. Although the overall picture is one of confusion and disarray, there is a solid core of experimental evidence that favors what some psychologists call the "law of equity". The law says that problems of fair social exchange will be resolved by equalizing the ratio of each person's gain to their worth. It only seems to work in certain environments, but then it seems to work rather well.

But how are gains to be measured? Where is the zero to be located on whatever scale is chosen? How is worthiness to be construed? Psychologists seem agreed that the coefficients which measure worthiness in the equity law are highly dependent on the social context in which a fairness judgment is made, but what are the relevant factors? Experimental work has focused on effort or investment, but what about social status, merit, or need? Why do people honor the equity law at all? Why does it go wrong in certain environments?

II:4.3.2   **Egalitarian solution.** The first step in trying to answer some of these questions is to draw attention to the remarkable parallel between the equity law and the egalitarian bargaining solution introduced in chapter 2. To make the parallel exact, we need to make two identifications. The base point from which gains are measured in the equity law must be identified with the disagreement point in a bargaining problem. More controversially, the worthiness coefficients of the equity law must be identified with the social indices of figure 3. I hope that the use of the neutral term *social index* as a substitute for *worthiness coefficient* will help prevent our prejudging how these numbers should be interpreted in differing contexts.

Drawing this parallel already advances matters a little, because the egalitarian bargaining solution has a solid theoretical backing. Almost any set of axioms that one might propose for a fair bargaining solution that incorporates *full* interpersonal comparison of utility turns out to characterize the egalitarian bargaining solution.[1]

But such an axiomatic approach leaves open the question of how the standard of interpersonal comparison is determined in the first place. It can therefore say nothing about how the social context may influence the worthiness coefficients in the equity law. Although I appreciate that my current approach is very crude, I hope that it will eventually offer a handle on this important problem.

11.3   Rawls' Difference Principle

John Rawls claimed that rational bargaining in the original position will yield a social contract in which certain basic rights and liberties are first safeguarded, and then the remaining distributional issues are settled using his difference principle. However, I think that Rawls is entitled to neither of his two conclusions.

---

[1]The utilitarian bargaining solution only compares utility units. The egalitarian solution compares both units and levels.

The first conclusion can't possibly follow from the circumstances of the original position alone. You would have to know a great deal about Adam and Eve's game of life before you were entitled to draw any conclusions at all about what rights and liberties they would wish to write into their social contract. For example, if your game of life consists of an eternal war against an implacable enemy, then your continued survival would probably take priority over your personal liberty. A Hobbesian social contract—in which the citizens acquiesce in accepting the direction of an absolute ruler—would then seem preferable to a constitution in which each citizen is free to do his own thing.

Even when the game of life is sufficiently close to our own to justify Rawls' first conclusion, the previous chapter shows that distributional issues would be settled along utilitarian lines—provided that we follow Rawls in assuming that "natural duty" can serve as an adequate substitute for an external enforcement agency. But Rawls intended his *Theory of Justice* as a counterblast to the utilitarianism that held sway among the political philosophers of his time.

Rawlsian scholars sometimes bridle at such criticism, and respond with quotations from the *Theory of Justice* intended to show that I don't understand the theory, but Rawls himself was more open minded. He knew that his analysis of the original position needed fixing, and wrote me several long letters in beautiful copperplate handwriting encouraging me to persist with my project when I showed signs of flagging. Those who doubt that Rawls had second thoughts need only compare the *Theory of Justice* with his later *Political Liberalism*.

In offering a reinterpretation of Rawls' ideas, I therefore don't feel that I am departing from the spirit of his work. This isn't by any means to claim that Rawls was converted to moral naturalism in later life, but nor was he willing to rule out the possibility that there might be something to be learned from such an approach.

Modifying Rawls. My first point merely strengthens what Rawls says at length on the "strains of commitment", since I take what he says on this subject to its logical extreme. There is no internal substitute for an external enforcement agency. Natural duty won't do the trick, and nor will anything else. This applies whether we are discussing constitutional issues that embrace a whole society, or picayune matters like how unsupervised folk pass each other in narrow corridors.

Without external enforcement, viable social contracts must police themselves. They must therefore be equilibria in whatever game is being played. An important consequence is that the folk theorem of repeated game theory then tells us that the set X of feasible social contracts will be convex.

II:4.6.5

My second point is that Rawls' insistence that certain rights and liberties be maintained in a fair society shouldn't be seen as a consequence of bargaining in the original position, but as a prerequisite for fairness to act instead of authority or leadership as the operative equilibrium selection device. The most extreme examples are the prehistoric hunter-gatherer societies that apparently got by with no authority structure at all.

My third and final point is that Rawls' difference principle can be interpreted as the egalitarian solution of an appropriate bargaining problem. Recall that the difference principle is essentially the maximin criterion. This says that the best social contract makes the least advantaged player (or class) as well off as possible. But if we measure Adam and Eve's payoffs with empathetic scales whose zero points are located at the current status quo and the feasible set X is convex, then the maximin criterion just picks the egalitarian bargaining solution.[2] The difference principle is therefore equitable because it equates Adam and Eve's empathetic payoffs.

11.4   The Phantom Coin

II:4.6.4

The next section offers a new defense of Rawls' ideas by showing that bargaining in the original position without external enforcement generates the egalitarian solution.

But how is a maximin rabbit to be extracted from an expected utility hat? Unless we follow Rawls in throwing orthodox decision theory out of the window, we have to agree with Harsanyi that a player behind the veil of ignorance will assess the available social contracts like a good little utilitarian. He prefers whichever social contract maximizes a weighted sum of Adam and Eve's personal utilities. But if John and Oskar both have such utilitarian preferences, why would they agree to an egalitarian outcome?

The answer is to be found by focusing on the hypothetical toss of a coin that John and Oskar pretend determines who will be Adam and who will be Eve when they leave the original position. When is this phantom coin tossed? Why do they feel obliged to honor an agreement based on the way it falls? How do they know which way it falls?

God made them high or lowly?   Alice and Bob both need a heart transplant, but only one heart is available. If the lives of both are regarded as equally valuable, then a utilitarian will be indifferent between giving the heart to Alice or Bob. But Alice would regard it as grossly unfair if the heart were then given to Bob on the grounds that he is a man—or because he is white or rich. Nor would she be at all mollified if told that she had an equal chance of being a man when the egg from which she grew was fertilized in her mother's womb.

Alice therefore cares a lot about *when* the phantom coin is tossed. If such a random event is to be used to determine who gets the heart, she will argue that a real coin should be tossed right now.

Bob, of course, will argue to the contrary. He likes the idea that it is fair to abide by the toss of a phantom coin that has already fallen in his favor. Like all conservatives, he is only too happy to sing the hymn that goes:

> The rich man in his castle,
> The poor man at his gate,
> God made them high or lowly,
> And ordered their estate.

---

[2]At any other point on the boundary of X, the disadvantaged player remains the same when we move the point slightly to improve his empathetic payoff.

This piece of propaganda is meant to torpedo the subversive argument that it isn't fair that peasants should labor in the fields while the gentry take their ease. It combines an appeal to God as the ultimate external enforcement agency with the suggestion that any new appeal to justice will merely confirm serfs like ourselves in our servitude—since the only right and proper model of the hypothetical coin toss that determines who will occupy what role in society is the original Act of God that condemned us to serfdom in the first place.

This is an attractive argument for the gentry, but it is hard to imagine that any peasants were ever convinced by such an appeal to their intuitions on how fairness norms work. One might as well ask a gambler to play roulette knowing that the wheel is fixed to ensure that he loses!

Early contractarians like Grotius and Pufendorf replaced God in this story by some ancient folk gathering at which a consensus was reached that somehow binds all those living today, but Hume's devastating criticisms of such theories of an "original contract" remain unanswerable. I wish Hume were alive today to comment on the even more fantastic conceptions of the original position proposed by Harsanyi and Rawls. Their idea is that we are somehow obligated to honor a hypothetical agreement negotiated in some Kantian limbo outside space and time, where a phantom coin is eternally frozen in the act of falling heads. Even the mad hatter's tea party makes better sense than this!

In any case, such metaphysical fancies have no place in a naturalistic theory of fairness. Both the putative evolutionary origin of the original position, and our own experience of how real fairness norms work make it clear that an appeal to fairness requires that any coin that is tossed to determine who enjoys an advantage must be a real coin tossed right now.

If at first you don't succeed. With external enforcement, any appeal to fairness may be over-ruled by a previous fairness adjudication. For example, when two soccer captains toss a coin to decide who chooses which end of the pitch to defend in the first half, the loser might complain that it isn't fair that his team must play with the sun in their eyes. It may be true that he called tails, and a coin lying on the grass is showing heads, but so what? He feels unfairly treated, and so demands a new adjudication.

The reason that this doesn't often happen in real life is that the rest of the world won't allow a captain to demand that the coin be tossed and tossed again until he wins. In the unthinkable event that a captain tried this trick, he would be pilloried unmercifully in the press. But what if there is no external enforcement, and the issue is one of life and death—as with Alice's heart transplant?

This consideration highlights the fundamental difference between naturalistic and metaphysical conceptions of fairness. Naturalists think that fairness evolved as a device for balancing power, whereas metaphysicians think of fairness as an alternative to the exercise of power. Since I am developing the naturalistic line, we must face up to the fact that Alice doesn't lose whatever power she has to influence the outcome because a coin falls one way rather than another. She will therefore exercise whatever power she has if she loses the toss, since anything is better for her than creeping away to die. She may therefore break a promise to honor the fall of the coin, but as the saying goes: all's fair in love and war.

Two obvious objections can be made. The first is that it is immoral to break promises—even imaginary promises made in the hypothetical circumstances of the original position. But this objection overlooks the point that we are supposedly using the original position to *decide* what is moral. Or to paraphrase David Hume, we need a better reason for not breaking our word than simply that we've given our word to keep it.

The second objection is that if Alice is always free to repudiate a fall of a coin that she dislikes, then nothing will be achieved by appealing to the original position. But this is wrong. Coordinating agreements in which the players are assigned roles between which they are indifferent remain possible.

Why be egalitarian?   The last point makes it clear why egalitarianism emerges from the original position in the absence of external enforcement. Players behind the veil of ignorance will only be indifferent about how the phantom coin falls if it assigns them *equal* empathetic utilities—as in the egalitarian bargaining solution.

As with many game-theoretic resolutions of philosophical paradoxes, critics sometimes become apoplectic at being fobbed off with such a trivial answer. Can the difference between egalitarianism and utilitarianism really hinge on what can be settled by tossing a coin? Surely such a deep and difficult question must have a deep and difficult answer, but I'm not to blame if the answer is easy. Usually it is Von Neumann who deserves the brickbats for making things simple, but here all the blame should be heaped on Harsanyi and Rawls for solving the deep and difficult problem of finding a good way to ask the question.

11.5   Fair Social Contracts

II:4.6.1

This section retells the story of the original position for a society in which there is no external enforcement, so that everything that happens must be self-policing. There are no strains of commitment, because commitments that are not explicitly modeled as moves within the game of life are impossible. Everyone is free to respond to their incentives, given the choices of the other players.

Under these conditions, my theory offers a vindication of Rawls' intuition:

> In the absence of external enforcement, a new coordination problem will be solved using the egalitarian bargaining solution with social indices that are determined by the past history of the society.

There is a lot to say in setting up the model that leads to this conclusion, but I think it important not to let all the verbiage obscure the trivial insight that lies at the heart of the egalitarian outcome that emerges—namely that people will only honor the toss of a coin that falls to their disadvantage if the alternative is worse.

Morality games. I have argued that fairness norms evolved because they allow groups who employ them to coordinate quickly on more efficient equilibria as they become available, and hence to outperform groups that remain stuck at the old equilibrium. The metaphor of the expanding circle was borrowed from Peter Singer to describe the mechanism envisaged. Players sometimes learn how to coordinate on equilibria in a new circle of games by playing these games as though they were games from a familiar class. Occasionally, they thereby succeed in coordinating on an equilibrium in games from the wider circle. If this behavior becomes established, they will then have discovered an equilibrium selection device for some games that works by the players pretending to be bound by the rules of more restrictive games.

The latter class of games might be called *morality games* when the way they select equilibria in the game of life permits a fairness interpretation, but morally neutral equilibrium selection devices frequently operate in much the same way. For example, if all players proceed as though it were impossible to break the law by choosing *left* in the Driving Game, then they will succeed in coordinating on the equilibrium in which everyone chooses *right*. Chapter 5 describes a less trivial example in which entirely selfish daughters are induced to share the product of their labor with their powerless mothers. The rules of the morality game acccompanying this social contract will specify that caring for elderly parents is a moral duty which Edmund Burke tells us that children are "bound indispensibly to perform".

It is anything but original to observe that the rules of the game of life are physically binding while the rules of a morality game bind only by convention, like the rules of Chess. The *physis* versus *nomos* controversy dates from the fifth century before Christ! In the words of the ancient sophist, Antiphon: "The rules of law are adventitious, while the rules of nature are inevitable; and the rules of law are created by covenant and not produced by nature." But this simple truth somehow became obscured during the transition from papyrus to paper. Modern scholars nowadays routinely confuse the issue by referring to the rules of morality games as "natural laws". However, if this misleading terminology is to be used, it seems to me necessary either to follow Hobbes and Hume in making it clear that so-called "natural laws" are actually unnatural and don't compel obedience—or else to follow Spinoza in arguing that we have a natural right to do anything that Nature has put within our power.

The game of morals. I consider only one morality game, which I call *the* game of morals. My guess is that the notion of a game of life and a morality game being played simultaneously has substantial descriptive validity for the way *Homo sapiens* runs his societies, but it would be absurd to claim that any simply characterized morality game could come close to encompassing the full richness of human moral interaction. The rules of the particular game of morals I propose come to grips only with fairness phenomena.

The *game of morals* is a twin to the game of life except that it offers the players additional moves that are not available in the real world. Between each and every round of the repeated game of life, the rules of the game of morals specify that any player has the opportunity to appeal to the device of the original position—whether or not such appeals to justice have been made in the past. When an appeal is made, the players disappear behind a veil of ignorance where they negotiate in ignorance of their current and future identities about what equilibrium in the game of morals should be operated in the future. A chance move then reshuffles their places in society so that each player has an equal chance of ending up either as Adam or Eve.

A *fair social contract* is then taken to be an equilibrium in the game of life that calls for the use of strategies which, if used in the game of morals, would never leave a player with an incentive to exercise his right of appeal to the device of the original position. So a fair social contract is an equilibrium in the game of morals, but it must never be forgotten that it is also an equilibrium in the game of life; otherwise evolution will sweep it away. Indeed, the game of morals is nothing more than a coordination device for selecting one of the equilibria in the game of life.

People *can* cheat in the game of morals, just as they can move a bishop like a knight when playing chess. But they have no incentive to do so in a fair social contract, because playing the game of morals as though its rules were binding leads to an equilibrium in the game of life. So nobody can gain by deviating, unless someone else acts against their own best interest by deviating first.

The bargaining problem. Without external enforcement, we have to rely on reciprocity to sustain social contracts incorporating high levels of cooperation. But reciprocity can only operate when the players interact repeatedly. It is therefore important that the game of life is modeled as an indefinitely repeated game, whose equilibria are the only stable social contracts.

The folk theorem of chapter 5 tells us that the set of all equilibrium outcomes is a convex set X like that of figure 1, where each point in X is a pair of payoffs that represent the average utility flow a player receives in equilibrium.

The default social contract D is identified with whatever social contract is currently being operated. Those critics who attack Harsanyi and Rawls for proceeding as though a society were free to discard its history, and plan its future as though newly born can therefore rest easy. History isn't neglected in my theory. It is built into the culture that informs the current social contract.

II:4.6.3   **Modeling the original position.** As in chapter 10, we have to determine the bargaining problem faced by John and Oskar behind the veil of ignorance.

If John and Oskar could be counted on to honor the fall of the phantom coin, their feasible set Z would be the average of the sets X_{AE} and X_{EA}, as in figure 23. But they are without honor in this chapter. The only agreements that are viable are therefore those in which John and Oskar get the *same* payoff whichever way the phantom coin falls. To be precise, if John and Oskar agree to implement one payoff pair J should John turn out to be Adam and Oskar turn out to be Eve, and another payoff pair K should John turn out to be Eve and Oskar turn out to be Adam, then J must be the same point as K.

John and Oskar's feasible set Z is therefore the intersection of the two sets X_{AE} and X_{EA}. This means that Z is the set of all payoff pairs that lie in *both* the sets X_{AE} and X_{EA} simultaneously. However, the status quo Q for John and Oskar's bargaining problem remains the average of D_{AE} and D_{EA}. But even here things are simpler than in the case with external enforcement, because D_{AE} must be the same point as D_{EA} for the scenario to make sense.

That is to say, John and Oskar mustn't care who they turn out to be if the current social contract is continued by default because they are unable to agree in the original position. Otherwise they wouldn't even be able to agree to disagree. Adam and Eve's empathetic utility scales must therefore assign the *same* utility level to the current social contract.

The current equilibrium is therefore always deemed to be fair—but this doesn't mean that whatever anybody happens to be doing currently is fair. Anyone straying from the current equilibrium path will be behaving unfairly, and so liable for punishment. What is being said is that when everyone is behaving fairly according to current standards, everyone will be deemed to be getting the right payoff for their level of worthiness. Someone looking in from the outside or back from the future may not agree, but who are they to insist that their standards should take precedence over those of the society they are criticizing?

Agreement in the original position. Figure 27 is a reprise of figure 23 that incorporates the changes necessary to take account of the absence of external enforcement. John and Oskar's bargaining problem is to find an agreement in the feasible set Z, given that the result of a disagreement will be Q. The Nash bargaining solution for this problem is marked as P. If the situation isn't too asymmetric, it occurs where Z has a corner.

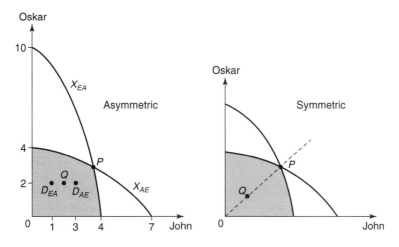

Figure 27: The bargaining problem in the original position.

The diagram on the right of figure 27 shows a symmetric version of the problem in which Adam and Eve enter the original position with the same empathetic preferences. The Nash bargaining solution P is then also symmetric in that it assigns

John and Oskar the same empathetic payoff. What does this imply about the social contract that Adam and Eve then actually implement when they emerge from
behind the veil of ignorance?

As in the utilitarian case, two conclusions can be read off from the symmetric
version of figure 27. The first is that the *same* social contract S will be operated
no matter who turns out to be Adam or Eve. But this social contract is quite unlike
its utilitarian cousin in that neither player would prefer to return to the original
position to have the phantom coin that determines who will be who tossed again.
The external enforcement agency that prevented any such return in chapter 10 is
therefore unnecessary here.

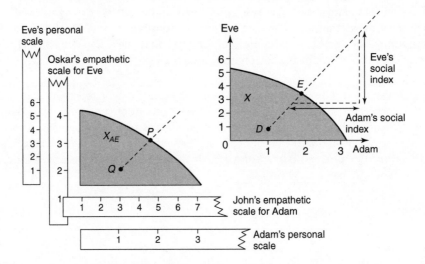

Figure 28: Returning from empathetic utilities to personal utilities.

The second conclusion is that P happens to be the egalitarian solution of the
bargaining problem in the original position. It occurs where John and Oskar's
unweighted empathetic utilities are equal. What is the implication for the social
contract S to be operated in Adam and Eve's game of life?

To answer this question, we have to reverse the rescaling that took us from the
bargaining problem with which we started (with everything expressed in personal
utilities) to the bargaining problem in the original position (with everything expressed
in empathetic utilities). Figure 28 then shows that the social contract S simply
equates Adam and Eve's personal utilities after they have been suitably rescaled.
That is to say, we have a vindication of Rawls' intuition that rational bargaining in
the original position will generate the egalitarian bargaining solution.

11.6   How Egalitarian Justice Works

We studied how a naturalized version of utilitarian justice works in the previous chapter. This section runs through an abbreviated version of the same argument, pointing out the differences as they arise.

What happens when social evolution moves Adam and Eve's empathetic preferences to an empathy equilibrium? As in the case with external enforcement, they end up with the same personal utilities as if they had bargained face-to-face with no holds barred. That is to say, the resulting social contract is the Nash bargaining solution of their underlying problem. So all the moral content of their fairness norm will have been leached away.

II:4.6.6

A major difference from the case with external enforcement is that the empathy equilibrium which Adam and Eve reach in the medium run is necessarily symmetric. We therefore have reason to believe that social evolution will *automatically* create a consensus on a standard of interpersonal comparison. If a group continually faces the same coordination problem in the absence of external enforcement, my theory therefore says that it will eventually end up using the egalitarian bargaining solution because everybody will enter the original position with the same standard of interpersonal comparison.

In the medium run, social evolution will adjust the social indices in the egalitarian solution so that they can be computed as follows:

(1) Find the Nash bargaining solution N of the coordination problem.

(2) Choose social indices to make the egalitarian solution E coincide with N.

When a new event or innovation results in the set of available social contracts expanding from the set X to the set Y, as illustrated in figure 29, the fairness norm now has a chance to fulfill the function for which it originally evolved—to shift its society to a new, efficient social contract F without damaging internal conflict. In the short run, the egalitarian weights that are adapted to X remain fixed, and so the new social contract F is located as shown in figure 29:

(3) In a new coordination problem created by expanding the feasible set, the fair social contract F is the egalitarian solution whose social indices are adapted to the old problem.

Of course, if the representative problem faced by Adam and Eve continues to be characterized by Y for long enough, then the standard for making interpersonal comparisons will adjust to the new situation and so the moral content of the social contract will again be eroded away.

11.7   Trustless Transactions

II:1.6

How does a society move from one social contract to a more efficient alternative? The Stag Hunt Game of chapter 4 shows that this isn't just a matter of rational

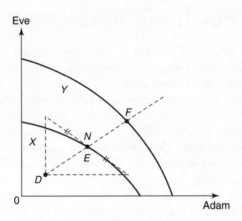

Figure 29: Justice in the short run.

players agreeing to move to an equilibrium of the game of life that they all prefer, and then simply getting on with it. If people don't have good reason to trust each other, they will rightly fear that opportunists will hijack the reform process with a view to reaping an extra advantage for themselves. So how is the transition from one equilibrium to another to be managed?

Sometimes the switch can be managed overnight, as when Sweden switched from driving on the left to driving on the right. After the fall of the Soviet Empire, some East European countries attempted a similar quick shift from a centrally planned, command economy to a Western-style market economy, with varying degrees of success. Such attempts to move fast are sometimes criticized as rash and brutal, especially when things go wrong. However, critics seldom recognize that moving fast can minimize the risk of a regime being destabilized altogether while the system is in an out-of-equilibrium transitional phase.

The alternative is to move gradually from the original state to the planned improvement through a long sequence of neighboring equilibria. This is the route to reform that one would expect to see employed by a rational society, since it removes the possibility of control being lost while the reforms are being implemented. Gorbachev's attempt to reform the Soviet Union along these lines is admittedly not a good advertisement for such a cautious approach. On the other hand, China seems to be managing a similar step-by-step shift without yet sliding into chaos.

The Centipede Game of chapter 4 explains how rational players can manage a trustless transaction by arrranging a continuous flow of the goods to be exchanged from one party to the other. However, this example takes for granted that the terms of trade can't be renegotiated during the play of the game. But what if they can?

II:1.6.2   **Renegotiation.**   Imagine a game that is repeated every day between the workers and the management of a firm. Each point in the set X of feasible social contracts in the diagram on the left of figure 30 corresponds to a pair of payoff flows that

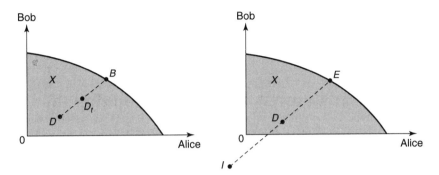

Figure 30: Bargaining without trust.

results from the players coordinating on one of the many equilibria of the repeated game they play together. They are currently operating the inefficient equilibrium corresponding to the point D. Meanwhile they are bargaining about how to share the surplus that would result if agreement could be reached on a move to a more efficient equilibrium. Thus D is the status quo for a bargaining problem.

Suppose the solution to their bargaining problem is B. For the purposes of this discussion, it doesn't matter whether B is the Nash bargaining solution, the egalitarian bargaining solution, or the utilitarian bargaining solution. Everything that is said applies equally well to all three alternatives.

Is it possible for the firm to get from D to B when the two sides don't trust each other? Such a move will involve the gradual surrender of entrenched privileges and practises by both management and workers. Once surrendered, these won't necessarily be recoverable in their old form. If the move to B is broken off before it is completed as a consequence of one side or the other insisting on a renegotiation, the firm will lapse into a *new* equilibrium. The point D_t of figure 30 corresponds to such an equilibrium. If there is a call for a renegotiation at time t, then D_t will serve as the new status quo during the negotiations that follow.

For the original agreement to be viable, we need that any call for renegotiation during the transition period should be pointless, because the bargaining that then takes place will just reproduce the original agreement. This happy conclusion is easily engineered simply by ensuring that each temporary status quo D_t during the transition period lies on the straight line joining D and B. That is to say, the way to get from the social contract D to the social contract B, is to move through the set of intermediary social contracts that lie on the straight line joining D and B.[3]

---

[3]I therefore made no fuss about the possible relocation of the status quo when discussing how justice works in the short run. Nothing changes if the status quo is moved to any point on the straight line joining D and F in figure 29. In particular, things remain the same if the status quo is moved from D to E. The argument also provides a subsidiary explanation of why John and Oskar must assign equal empathetic utilities to the status quo in the original position. If they didn't, the party disadvantaged by the fall of the phantom coin would demand a renegotiation as soon as the agreed reforms started to shift the social contract.

Making the punishment fit the crime. In Gilbert and Sullivan's *Mikado*, the emperor of Japan is deeply interested in the administration of justice:

> My object all sublime
> I shall achieve in time—
> To let the punishment fit the crime—
> The punishment fit the crime.

Pool hustlers are condemned to play on a cloth untrue, with a twisted cue, and elliptic billiard balls. Chatterers whom lectures bore are sent to sermons by mystical Germans, who preach from ten till four.

Why do we take such satisfaction in seeing the biter bit? In hoisting him by his own petard? In returning a tit for a tat? In taking an eye for an eye, and a tooth for a tooth? In brief, why is justice only poetic when the punishment fits the crime?

I believe the reason we think punishments should be fair is quite simple. When punishing a deviant insider or compensating an injured party, the actions we take shouldn't just make the deviant action unprofitable; they should also move the status quo to a point from which an appeal to fairness will reproduce the social contract that was operating before the deviation.

Investment. Psychological experiments on the law of equity have been most successful in simulations of economic problems in which subjects have to say what is fair when strangers from similar backgrounds have each invested a sum of money in a joint enterprise, and the question is now how they should share the resulting profit. The standard answer is that investors should each receive a share proportional to the size of their investments.

I suspect that the reason this type of experiment does well is that it finesses most of the difficulties that a general test of the equity law would encounter. The status quo is that both players gain nothing. A util can be identified with a dollar. Moreover, the investments the players have made provide data on their social indices.

To see why, consider the diagram on the right of figure 30. The point D is the original status quo, when Alice and Bob had invested nothing. The fair, final outcome is E. The slope of the straight line joining D and E then tells us what Alice and Bob's relative social indices are in this context. But to get to E from D, Alice and Bob have to begin by making themselves temporarily worse off by each sinking an investment. This moves the status quo from D to I. But it will now be optimal for one of the players to make a new appeal to the device of the original position after the investments have been sunk—unless I lies on the same straight line that passes through D and E.

We should therefore expect that the investments Alice and Bob make in a fair deal to be proportional to their social indices. That is to say, the size of the investment is a proxy for a player's social index.

11.8 Social Indices and the Context

II:4.7

The psychological law of equity says that a fair outcome is one in which players are rewarded in proportion to their worthiness. Psychologists who defend the law insist that a player's worthiness depends heavily on the context in which the fairness judgment is being made.

Instead of the worthiness coefficients of the psychologists, we have the social indices that weight the players' personal utilities in both the egalitarian and utilitarian bargaining solutions, but it remains true that the context matters enormously in determining their values. This section asks how we should expect a player's social index to vary as we change the context by altering such parameters as need, effort, ability or status.

Since the shape of X determines a player's social index in the medium run, the way to answer this question is to examine how the set X of feasible social contracts varies as we alter the contextual parameters.

What matters about the context?   Although I am no admirer of Karl Marx, it has to be admitted that he put his finger on all the characteristics of a person that seem to be of interest in studying how a society identifies the worthy. Recall that, after the revolution, workers were to be rewarded according to their labor. The Marxist labor theory of value is certainly no jewel in the crown of economic thought, but it is nevertheless true that the relative levels of *effort* Adam and Eve need to exert in creating a source of surplus must be one of the major parameters requiring attention in determining their worthiness when it comes to splitting the surplus they have jointly created.

Of course, according to Marx, labor was to provide only a stopgap measure of worthiness. In the socialist utopia that would ensue after the state had eventually withered away, the rule was to be: to each according to his needs—from each according to his abilities. Human nature being what it is, such an incentive scheme seems designed to convert the able of a large society into the needy overnight. Nevertheless, both *ability* and *need* are parameters that must be taken into account when evaluating worthiness.

Finally, we need to add *status* to effort, ability, and need. For Marx, social standing was a feudal survival to be swept away along with all of history's other failed experiments in human organization, but a realistic social contract theory cannot ignore the fact that the power structures of today evolved from the power structures of the past. A person's status, as measured by the role assigned to him in the social contract currently serving as a society's status quo, is therefore highly relevant to how his worthiness is assessed by those around him.

Power is fundamental.   In discussing slippery concepts like need or status, it II:4.7.1 is important not to lose sight of the fact that the set X of feasible social contracts is determined by the underlying power structure of a society. Not only must we accept that fairness norms exist to find a new balance of power when things change, we must also accept that the social indices that characterize a fairness norm will reflect the historical accidents frozen into the power structure of the social contract currently being operated.

Stating this unwelcome truth often generates a good deal of hostility from those who take it to mean that I am endorsing the Thrasymachian doctrine that worthiness is to be equated with brute force. But I hope that the examples of chapter 5 show that power in a large society playing a repeated game of life is likely to be exercised in much more subtle ways. How else would the hand that rocks the cradle so often rule the world as well?

In any case, I hope for some suspension of disbelief while I demonstrate that the manner in which contextual parameters are filtered through the power structure is much more in line with ordinary thinking than anything Thrasymachus would have been likely to suggest.

II:4.7.3   **To each according to his need?**   Our language for discussing moral issues is so suffused with mistaken assumptions from folk psychology that it's a wonder we ever manage to say anything coherent at all. The idea of need is particularly fuzzy.

In colloquial English, to say that Alice is needy always means that she is in want. But it also suggests that she is powerless to alleviate her want, whether acting alone or collectively with others in the same boat. Nor does her plight raise sufficient sympathy in the breasts of others that those with the power to help are willing to exert themselves on her behalf. I separate this sense of helplessness from my definition of need, because it conflates Alice's personal tastes with the social circumstances operating in her society. A powerless person is certainly likely to be in need, but a person in need isn't necessarily powerless.

Our need for water is a good example. It is essential to our survival both when we are enjoying a beer in a local bar and when we are gasping our last breath in the desert. The only difference is that we can satisfy our need in the former situation but not in the latter.

Once Alice's need has been identified with how much she wants something, we can measure it by the size of the risk she is willing to take to get it. The problem of determining how need affects Alice's social index then becomes trivial, because the Nash bargaining solution punishes players who are more averse to taking risks by awarding them a smaller share of whatever is being divided. The intuition is simple. People in need get more because their desperation leads them to bargain harder.

To see the implications of this result, imagine two Alices with whom Bob might interact: a needy Alice and a comfortable Alice. In the medium run, who gets how much will be determined by the Nash bargaining solution. If we determine the zero and the unit for the personal utility scales of both Alices in the same way, the needy Alice will therefore get at least as large a payoff as the comfortable Alice.[4] In the medium run, social evolution will therefore assign needy folk a larger social index than their comfortable counterparts.

---

[4]The needy Alice doesn't necessarily get *strictly* more than the comfortable Alice. As we make Alice less needy in the food-sharing example of chapter 8 by reducing the minimal share she will accept rather than taking any risk, she continues to get half the rabbit until her minimal acceptable share is less than one half.

A laborer is worthy of his hire?   The surplus that players have to divide   *4.7.4*
doesn't usually appear from nowhere, like manna from heaven. The players commonly work together to produce it, so that there are both costs and benefits to be
shared. However, in the coming example, it will be Alice's effort alone that produces
a surplus. But she can enjoy some fraction of the fruits of her labor only with the
consent of Bob, who therefore fills the role of a traditional robber baron. But in
spite of being a peasant, Alice isn't entirely powerless. If mutual agreement on a
social contract can't be achieved, she will produce nothing at all.

This is the old story of Capital versus Labor. In prehistoric times, the capital
was the strength invested in male bodies by Nature. In the time of Adam Smith,
the relevant capital consisted of the state-enforced property rights of rentiers, which
allowed them to expropriate a sizable fraction of an agricultural surplus to whose
production they contributed nothing whatever. In modern times, very rich people
commonly contrive to pay no taxes at all, while simultaneously enjoying public
goods provided from taxes subtracted directly from the paychecks of the poor.
Performances of grand opera subsidized in this way are a particularly blatant example.

Figure 31 illustrates how things change when a surplus for division ceases to be
manna from heaven and is produced instead by Alice exerting an effort. Each point
in the old set X of feasible social contracts is displaced a fixed distance to the left
to obtain the new set Y of feasible social contracts. The displacement represents
how many utils Alice thinks her effort is worth.

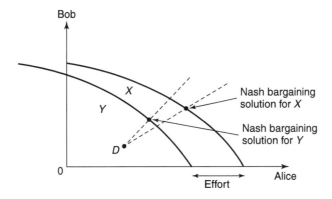

Figure 31: Effort and social indices.

As in figure 31, the Nash bargaining solution of the new bargaining problem
is always on a line through the disagreement point D that is at least as steep as
the corresponding line to the Nash bargaining solution of the old problem. In the
medium run, social evolution will therefore assign Alice a smaller social index if she
must exert an effort to create the surplus than if the surplus comes for free.

If this conclusion seems counterintuitive, it's because we don't nowadays commonly encounter situations in which an individual has Bob's power to reduce all
of Alice's effort to naught. Under more normal circumstances, Bob must perforce

concede the lion's share of the surplus to Alice lest she opt out of their relationship. Even a prehistoric gatherer didn't have to bring home all of her product. Her outside option was to feed herself and her children wherever the fruits of the field were gathered. Similarly, a modern worker has the outside option of taking another job, or going on the dole. Bob will only perceive Alice as being unworthy because she earns their bread by the sweat of her brow, if she has no option but to submit to his power. She is then effectively a serf.

Nobody is a serf in a modern democracy, but it doesn't follow that the feudal memes that made forced labor a source of unworthiness are dead. In the neofeudal social contracts operated by modern Western democracies, contemporary robber barons no longer hire troops of mercenaries to extract tribute from those powerless to resist. Instead, they use the apparatus of the state as an intermediary in funneling money from our pockets to theirs. We peasants don't have the option of avoiding taxation legally. So we are perceived as unworthy *even by ourselves* when compared with fat cats powerful enough to get their tax evasion schemes legalized.

II:4.7.5   **From each according to his ability?**   An able person is someone who can produce the same output as a less able rival without exerting as much effort. The problem of studying the effect of changes in ability on worthiness is therefore trivial. The more able we make Adam, the less effort he will need to exert in order to create a given level of surplus. Since effort decreases his social index, ability will therefore increase it.

One might summarize the preceding results on effort and ability by saying that, other things being equal, egalitarianism favors talented aristocrats over retarded serfs. But utilitarians should hesitate before congratulating themselves on reversing this bias. We no longer live in a stagnant feudal economy, and even utopians need to consider the impact of their system on the dynamics of incentives and innovation.

II:4.7.6   **Noblesse oblige?**   If Aristotle's concept of nobility is identified with social status, it becomes apparent why temperance is regarded as a noble virtue in fair societies. Other things being equal, a person's social index *declines* with social status. The high and mighty therefore take a smaller share of a new surplus than their lowly brethren. Perhaps this explains why people feel paradoxically resentful when dinner companions insist on paying the whole bill rather than sharing the cost. In doing so, the bill grabber is claiming superior social status. But once you realize that his behavior signals that he isn't too sure of how you view his social standing, it becomes possible actually to enjoy being patronized in this way.

A crude measure of Alice's social status is the payoff she receives at the current status quo. If we increase her social status by moving the disagreement point D to the right, then Alice's payoff at the Nash bargaining solution for the problem will also increase. Improving Alice's social status therefore makes her better off. But what happens to her social index? This may increase or decrease, since her total payoff consists of the sum of her payoff at the status quo and her share of the surplus to be divided.

The question is easily resolved by recycling the argument used to show that effort reduces worthiness. Moving the status quo point to the right is equivalent to first displacing X the same distance to the left and then shifting the whole configuration the same distance to the right. Increasing Alice's social status in the current status quo therefore reduces her social index.

An obvious application is to the question of progressive taxation. Its critics argue that each taxpayer should be required to pay the same percentage of their income, but my theory predicts that people will regard it as fairer if rich people pay a larger percentage of their income than poor people.

11.9   The Market

II:4.8

One often hears from the intellectual right that fairness is out of date because the market is now available as a more successful means of getting society to an efficient outcome. As when the laws of supply and demand finally overthrew the medieval concept of a fair price, hasn't the time come to admit that our intuitions about a just society have been superseded by a new paradigm? Once the market meme has replaced the fairness meme altogether, so the story goes, it will become irrelevant whether the market is unfair in the traditional sense.

This section argues against such a dramatic scenario. I agree that evolution is eventually likely to generate social contracts that sometimes operate like markets— but not because the market mechanism embodies a set of striking new values that trump a bunch of outdated fairness norms, which survive only as fossil memories of social contracts operated in prehistoric times. On the contrary, insofar as the market is fated to triumph when the circumstances are favorable, I think it is because the market is precisely what one should expect to see in the long run as a result of people's personal preferences adapting over time to the use of the device of the original position as a fairness norm.

We know what happens when allocations are made using the device of the original position after *empathetic* preferences have been allowed to adjust in the medium run. Although Adam and Eve may continue to describe their social contract as fair, they will actually agree on the Nash bargaining solution to their bargaining problem. All moral content in the fairness procedure they employ will then have been eroded away, since the compromise they reach is the same as if they had negotiated face-to-face using whatever bargaining power lay at their disposal.

This medium-run argument takes for granted that the players' personal preferences remain fixed while their empathetic preferences vary. But the classification of time spans introduced in chapter 10 maintains this assumption only in the short and medium run. In the long run, *personal* preferences may also adapt to whatever allocation mechanism is in use. We then need to ask what personal preferences Adam and Eve would choose to reveal if both were seeking to maximize their fitness on the assumption that the preferences they reveal will serve only as inputs to the Nash bargaining solution. If neither player would wish to misrepresent his or her personal preferences in a situation that can be modeled in market terms, then it turns out that the use of the Nash bargaining solution generates the the same outcome that

II:4.8.2

would result from operating a perfectly competitive market.

The market is therefore the final step in a process that first leaches out the moral content of a culture and then erodes the autonomy of its citizens by shaping their personal preferences. We may congratulate ourselves on the fact that a perfectly competitive market mechanism is hard to corrupt, but the reasons offered in my story are not particularly comforting. Just as a rock that has fallen into a pit cannot easily be induced to fall any further, so a market cannot easily be corrupted because evolution has corrupted its institutions already.

However, although nobody has any grounds for delighting in the fact that the moral values of a culture operating in a fixed game of life will be eroded away in the long run, neither is there cause for despair. One certainly isn't entitled to the conclusion that morality has no role to play in a developed society. Our short-run and medium-run conclusions remain valid whatever may happen in the long run. A short-run modification of the game of life, perhaps caused by a technological or environmental change, will therefore provoke the same demands for a fair distribution of the surplus in an advanced economy as in a band of hunter-gatherers.

The down-home example of the market for shovels after a snowfall captures the realities of the phenomenon very neatly. When the snow falls, the demand for shovels increases. If supply is to be equated with demand and shovels are in fixed supply, then the price of shovels must rise. But consumers then react by condemning the rise in price as unfair, since they see no reason why the snowfall should change anybody's social index. They therefore punish the retailers for cheating on the perceived social contract by refusing to buy.

Conservative politicians who ignore such out-of-equilibrium phenomena put the social contracts entrusted to their care in peril. They make the classic mistake of assuming that everything is always in equilibrium. But all social systems take time to find their way to an equilibrium. To find their way to a long-run equilibrium, they need a *long* time. But fairness evolved to provide *short-run* resolutions to the equilibrium selection problem.

Chapter 12

Planned Decentralization

Sir, I perceive that you are a vile Whig.

Samuel Johnson

12.1 A Third Way?

I:1.1

Once upon a time, politics seemed a simple choice between left and right, but the fall of the Soviet empire has discredited socialism without ushering in a corresponding triumph for the free marketeers of the libertarian right. One hears talk of a third way in which social justice isn't abandoned in an anarchic scramble for individual power and status. But is this third way merely another utopian chimera that serves only to divert attention from urgently needed bread-and-butter reform, or is there really some means of planning a fair society that doesn't stifle individual enterprise by placing too much power in the hands of faceless bureaucrats?

I think the ideas presented in this book provide grounds for optimism. We don't need to tie ourselves into an authoritarian straitjacket to create a fair social contract. Nor does the preservation of individual freedom entail allowing fat cats to rip us off whenever the opportunity arises. Our species evolved to operate in foraging societies that were simultaneously free and fair. We were forced to adopt other social contracts by the need to become more productive, but we are now moving into a postindustrial era that will perhaps allow us to return to a type of social contract more suited to our genetic inheritance.

The social contracts that I believe fit our nature best are egalitarian in character, but my mundane reasons for advocating such egalitarian social contracts are so different from those of moden egalitarian philosophers that I prefer to say that I am defending the kind of *whiggery* that motivated the authors of the Glorious Revolution of 1688 and the Declaration of Independence of 1776. I know that calling oneself a whig sounds somewhat quaint in modern times, but at least it has the advantage that nobody speaking up for the cause of whiggery is likely to be mistaken for a preacher.

185

Preaching would in any case be entirely misplaced in a chapter that consists largely of pointing out numerous gaps and inadequacies, not only in my own theory of fairness, but in the way game theorists in general attack social problems. It is as though one were seeking to envisage how a cobweb will look before a spider has strung more than a few foundational strands. But I persist with this chapter nevertheless, since the first step in filling in the holes is to be aware of the fact that there is a structure whose holes are worth filling.

12.2   Whiggery

II:4.10.1

There is sometimes much to be learned from how an intellectual or political position is misrepresented by its critics. For example, American politicians who resent tax dollars being spent on helping out the needy reveal a great deal about themselves when they choose the word *liberal* to insult their enemies.

The following piece of doggerel by the poet Yeats is equally instructive about the attitudes of an earlier set of reactionaries:

> What is Whiggery?
> A levelling, rancorous, rational sort of mind
> That never looked out of the eye of a saint
> Or out of a drunkard's eye.

Yeats is right to say that whigs respect rationality. Whigs believe that the way to a better society lies in appealing to the rational self-interest of all concerned. Yeats is also right that whigs are levelers, and so their demands for a fairer society naturally seem rancorous to an unreconstructed Tory like Yeats.

Yeats also tells us that whigs aren't saints. He is right about this also. Not only are whigs not saints, they don't think that people have the capacity to become saints, as the more naive thinkers of the left would have us suppose. People can temporarily be persuaded to put the interests of the community as a whole ahead of their own private concerns, but a community based on the assumptionthat its citizens can be relied upon to behave unselfishly most of the time toward those outside their own extended family simply won't work.

Finally, Yeats is right that whigs see no reason to behave like drunkards, lurching from crisis to crisis. Planning and reform needn't be dirty words. They don't require the existence of some mythical "common good". We can plan instead to institutionalize "common understandings". Nobody need make great sacrifices in the process, once it is understood that it isn't in the self-interest of the strong to let the weak fall by the wayside. We can go from the old to the new *by mutual consent*. We don't need to set up stultifying and inefficient bureaucracies along the way. Nothing prevents our planning to use markets wherever markets are appropriate, but a society that relies only on markets is leaving much of its potential unfulfilled.

History.   The Whigs were originally a British political party that arose in opposition to the Tories of the seventeenth century. The modern Conservative party is a direct descendant of the Tories. The Whigs were eventually outflanked by the modern Labour party, and squeezed into insignificance. Their remnants survived as the Liberal party, which now continues in a revived form as the Liberal Democratic party. However, in recent years, Labour has perhaps become even more whiggish than the Liberal Democrats.

What did the Tories and the Whigs represent? Etymology doesn't help, since a Tory was originally an Irish bogtrotter, and a Whig a Scottish covenanter. Nor does it assist to observe that Edmund Burke was the Whig credited with being the founder of modern conservatism; nor that David Hume, whose ideas are the inspiration for my own brand of whiggery, was held to be a Tory by his contemporaries, since he famously confessed himself able to shed a tear for the beheaded Charles I. It is more informative to observe that the Whigs are traditionally associated with the Glorious Revolution of 1688, in which the Catholic and authoritarian James II was expelled in favor of the Protestant and constitutionally minded William III.

American history also boasts a Whig party, broadly similar in character to its British counterpart. It was vocal in its opposition to Andrew Jackson's authoritarian innovations in the use of the presidential veto. Before joining the newly emergent Republican party, Abraham Lincoln was a Whig. But the true flowering of whiggery in America came earlier with the founding of the Republic, which whigs see as a triumphant continuation of an ongoing war for justice and liberty in which the English Civil War and the Glorious Revolution were earlier battles.

Like James Madison, modern whigs believe that "justice has ever been and ever will be pursued until it is obtained, or liberty lost in the pursuit." A mature free society must therefore necessarily be a fair society. But the world has moved on from the times of the founding fathers. Their great experiment in constitutional design was a huge success, but like all social constructs it needs to be constantly overhauled in the face of newly emerging challenges to justice and liberty. Our task today is therefore to rethink the thoughts of the founding fathers of the American Republic as they would be urging us to rethink them if they were alive today.

Classifying political attitudes. The big issues for a society are liberty and justice. It is therefore natural to propose a two-dimensional classification of political theories that takes these ideas as basic. It is surely no accident that the psychologist Eysenck found that the data he used in matching personality types with political attitudes fits much more comfortably into such a scheme than the classical one-dimensional political spectrum between left and right.

II:4.10.2

Figure 32 uses freedom and fairness axes to distinguish four regions that I could untendentiously have labeled unplanned centralization, unplanned decentralization, planned decentralization, and planned centralization. But the language of economics is so dismally dull that I have translated these terms into neofeudalism, libertarianism, whiggery, and utilitarianism. In terms of the traditional left–right political spectrum, utilitarianism sits out on the socialist left and libertarianism sits out on the capitalist right. The same dichotomy appears in moral philosophy as a split between the consequentialist followers of the Good and the deontological followers of the Right.

However, far from seeing our problems of political organization as a battle be-

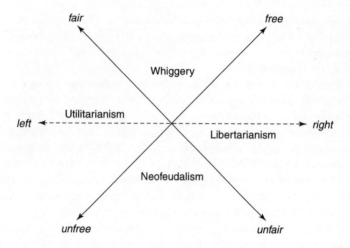

Figure 32: Classifying political attitudes.

tween the ideals of the left and right, I see utilitarianism and libertarianism as the Scylla and Charybdis between which reformers must steer a course if we are to escape our feudal past. Utilitarianism provides no safe port of call, because nothing can prevent the bosses in an authoritarian society from becoming acquisitive. Libertarianism is similarly unsafe, because possessions cannot be held securely in an anarchic society. Those who advocate abandoning all social mechanisms other than the market simply fail to see that they would thereby be throwing away the foundations on which the market mechanism is based.

The unworkable utopias of both utilitarians and libertarians therefore have no more relevance to genuine human concerns than the metaphysical disputes on the properties of Absolute Morality that divide those who worship the Good from those who honor the Right. Just as we have to assimilate the issues that trouble consequentialists and deontologists into a single theory of the seemly before we can say anything compatible with what evolution has made of human nature, so we have to separate the feasible from the infeasible in the aspirations of utilitarians and libertarians before abandoning the possibility that they may have some common ground on which to stand.

The opposition that I think should supersede the sterile and outdated dispute between left and right contrasts free societies in which fairness is used to coordinate collective decisions with societies that delegate such decisions to individuals or elites. I use the term *neofeudal* to describe the latter kind of social contract. In brief, we need to cease thinking outdated thoughts about where we would like to locate society on a left–right spectrum. Choosing between utilitarianism and libertarianism makes as much sense as debating whether griffins make better pets than unicorns. We need to start thinking instead about how to move in the orthogonal direction that leads from neofeudalism to whiggery.

12.3 Why Decentralize?

Three levels of priority for a social contract appear in chapter 1: stability, efficiency, and fairness. Utilitarianism won't work because it fails to recognize the first priority.

A benign philosopher-king may command this or that, but his organization will eventually unravel unless it calls for his subjects to coordinate on an equilibrium of the game of life. Even if the philosopher-king recognizes the need to take account of the individual incentives of his subjects by operating a constrained form of utilitarianism in which only equilibria are included in the feasible set from which a social contract is chosen, he will still be in trouble at the next level of priority.

To achieve efficiency, he will need to decentralize decision-making to the level at which the necessary knowledge and expertise resides. That is to say, an efficient social contract will necessarily grant a substantial amount of freedom to a wide variety of individuals at all levels of the production process. It is particularly stupid to restrict the autonomy of potential entrepreneurs, without whose activities we would never find out that we were doing things inefficiently in the first place.

The fall of the Soviet empire makes it unecessary to press this point further. Even erstwhile Marxists now agree that command economies are hopelessly inefficient. Not only are people happier when they aren't bossed around all the time, they can be immensely more productive. This would seem to be one of the few clear lessons that history has to teach. Some measure of individual freedom is a necessary condition for an innovative society.

This doesn't imply that an innovative society need be fully democratic. Classical Athens was a slave-holding society. Republics were rare in renaissance Italy. Suffrage was severely restricted during the industrial revolution in England. Women didn't have the vote when the American Republic rose to be a world power. Nazi Germany maintained a highly productive and innovative economic sector. Nor is democracy a sufficient condition for economic success, as the British experiment with socialism after the Second World War shows only too well.

Finally, a utilitarian will be in difficulty at the third level of priority. A philosopher-king who recognizes that an efficient social contract will necessarily allow a considerable measure of freedom to at least some of its citizens, will also have to face up to the fact that they will have their own ideas on how to coordinate their behavior. For example, a factory boss who reorganizes the production process with a view to improving efficiency should appreciate that she is really only changing the rules of the minigame of life the workers play within the factory. She may wish that they would operate her preferred equilibrium in that game, but they will use their own view of what counts as fair in solving the equilibrium selection problem she creates for them.

12.4 Why Plan?

Wholehearted libertarians are opposed to any kind of central planning at all. They think that everything should just be left to the market. Von Hayek even quoted Gödel's theorem in an attempt to demonstrate that efficient planning is *impossible—*

failing to notice that if he were right, markets wouldn't be able to work efficiently either, because the whole of society can be thought of as a kind of gargantuan computing machine.

I share the libertarian distaste for authority, but it seems to me that we have to recognize that some measure of regulation must be built into the social contract of a modern state if only to secure the property rights of the entrepreneurs on whom we rely for the creation of wealth.

Moderate libertarians accept that we need a social contract to maintain law and order and to protect property rights, but not for anything else. Followers of Ronald Coase are particularly keen on the idea that all social problems can be solved by assigning property rights to everything. The Coase "theorem" then supposedly guarantees that rational bargaining among the owners will result in an efficient outcome, provided that transaction costs are negligible. Coasians usually have a first-best concept of efficiency in mind when they quote the Coase theorem, but one of the more remarkable results of game theory shows they are then a long way off target. All profitable deals would indeed be realized if everybody could always be relied upon to tell the truth, but who begins a negotiation by putting all their cards on the table? Rational bargainers will try to convince their opponent that they are stronger than they really are. In a manner reminiscent of the Prisoners' Dilemma, negotiations will therefore often break down when there are feasible agreements that would make both bargainers better off.

Consider, for example, a buyer and seller whose valuations for a fancy house might be anywhere between $1 million and $5 million. Half the time, the buyer's valuation will exceed the seller's valuation, and so they could both profit by agreeing on a price between these two numbers. But they will only succeed in agreeing when the buyer's valuation exceeds the seller's valuation by at least $1 million—even though they bargain rationally in the absence of transaction costs using a bargaining protocol that maximizes the expected surplus from such encounters.

Nor does it help to move to a second-best concept of efficiency when the players have private information, since all bargaining models then have many equilibria, most of which are inefficient. Coasians sometimes gloss over this fatal flaw in their approach by arguing that the possession of secrets by one party or the other should be counted as a transaction cost, but all that they gain by this maneuver is to restrict their theory to cases that seldom occur in the real world.

Nor is it true that markets are necessarily efficient. Libertarian economists certainly know that the conditions under which a market is perfectly competitive, and therefore efficient, are very restrictive. Their rhetoric to the contrary is therefore deliberately misleading. To name only one of numerous sources of inefficiency, many industries can support only a small number of producers, who naturally exploit the market power that the consequent lack of competition affords them whenever they aren't restrained by govenment regulation. I guess that libertarians gloss over the failings of real markets because they think that even the most imperfect market is likely to be more efficient at matching supply and demand than any centralized bureaucracy. So why not just say so, rather than inventing the dangerous myth than we can dispense with authority and regulation altogether in a modern society?

It is true that govenment regulation is often inexcusably bad. Government officials seldom feel the need to take advantage of modern expertise in mechanism design. Nor do they perceive any need to test a new regulatory system in the laboratory to iron out any wrinkles. No wonder their naive efforts result in disasters like the California Power Exchange!

I think this kind of negligence should be regarded as a species of institutionalized corruption. Advances in game theory mean that we now know how to design regulated markets for some industries that would be immensely more efficient than those that currently operate, and it is frustrating that we have to wait so long to see this new knowledge put into practice.

But efficiency isn't the only issue. Fairness also matters. Libertarian economists evade this issue in various ways. The most blatant is the attempt to define the fairness issue out of existence by saying that *any* efficient outcome is "socially optimal". That is to say, society can never be made better off by moving from one efficient outcome to another. Underpinning this claim is the unsound dogma that interpersonal comparisons of utility are intrinsically meaningless.

A second line of defense is less dishonest, since it is indeed a valid objection to fairness concepts that violate the principle that efficiency should take priority over fairness. It is said that there is an unavoidable trade-off between efficiency and equity—that trying to be fair hinders productivity. It is true that squabbles over who should get how much of a cake often result in a smaller cake becoming available for division, but this kind of collective irrationality can't occur when the principle that efficiency should take priority over fairness is honored. One then first identifies all the efficient outcomes of which a society is capable, and only then applies fairness criteria in making a selection among them.

A final line of defense is the claim that perfectly competitive markets are in fact fair, because they maximize economic surplus. It is true that economic surplus is maximized at a competitive equilibrium, but why should it be thought fair to maximize expected surplus? Who thinks it fair that every dollar should be regarded as equally well spent, whether allocated to a hungry child or a bloated plutocrat?

An economic example. Perhaps a simple example will help to explain how I think one should reply to the economic arguments of the intellectual right.

Imagine that some ancient king granted a salt monopoly to a court favorite. The current heir would then be onto a really good thing if the intervening evolution of the social contract left the family's property rights intact.

If the heir sold each grain of salt at the same price, like a textbook monopolist, then his profit-maximizing output would be inefficient. However, if he were clever enough to find a way of exploiting his market power so as to make everyone pay the amount at which they value each extra grain of salt they buy, then *all* the surplus would go to the monopolist. Nobody could then be made better off without making him worse off and so the outcome would be efficient, but it would be grotesque to say that such an exploitive arrangement is socially optimal.

What could be done about such an unfair but efficient outcome? One answer is that the government could regulate the salt industry by forcing the monopolist to sell each grain of salt at the price it costs the monopolist to produce the final grain that anyone wants to buy at that price. The result will then be efficient—and a great deal fairer. But it is just as hard for a government to find out how much it costs a company to produce something as it is to find out how much income tax you or I ought to be paying. You can ask us to fill in forms reporting our income, but only saints are entirely truthful in such matters. This is one of the reasons that old-style command economies don't work well. An overall central plan can't be efficient if the planner has no effective way of extracting vital economic information from the people she bosses around.

Another alternative would be to abolish the salt monopoly. After all, why should we band together to protect the property rights of someone who uses the protection we provide him to make himself unfairly rich at our expense? After the reform, salt could then be produced and sold by a large number of small firms, thus creating a perfectly competitive market that would generate the same efficient outcome as the regulated market considered in the previous paragraph—but without any bureaucrat needing to know anything about the salt production process.

Like a lover who can find no fault in his sweetheart, libertarians are so enamored by this discovery of Adam Smith that they refuse to look any further. But there are always *many* efficient ways of organizing an industry. Even when operating an unregulated market is one of these—as in our salt industry example—there is no particular reason why the manner in which it redistributes wealth among the citizens of a society should be fair.

None of this criticism of the libertarian position is meant to detract from the value of the market as an instrument of good social contract design. When properly regulated and operated alongside an enlightened taxation policy, markets would play a major role in any whiggish program of reform. But the idea that the way to solve our social problems is simply to "leave it to the market" is impossibly naive.

12.5   Designing a Social Mechanism

The nearest game theory comes to providing a recipe for the planning of social contracts is the subject of mechanism design.

The framework outlined in chapter 9 is appropriate only in the case when an external enforcement agency is available to police the rules that the designer invents. But even when the environment is simplified in this way, designing an optimal mechanism is seldom plain sailing. The review of the steps involved in constructing a mechanism given below draws attention to some of the difficulties, but its chief purpose is to present the principles on which the design process is based, since the same principles also apply to the even more difficult problem of designing a social contract or a constitution.

Step 1: Objective.   Textbooks say that the objective in designing an optimal mechanism is to maximize the value of a welfare criterion that fully quantifies the relative importance of all the competing desiderata.

I have done a good deal of work applying the principles of mechanism design to practical problems for various governments and commercial enterprises, but I have never been so fortunate as to be given such a welfare criterion. It is often hard even to persuade one's principal that determining the trade-offs between competing desiderata is a political rather than a technical issue.

I therefore think that one of the aspects of practical mechanism design that needs development is helping principals to determine their priorities. Just as we determine individual utility functions by observing what choices people make (or would make) under various contingencies, so we should offer a principal a variety of scenarios to rank. The ranking can then be used to determine the principal's implicit priorities.

But who would pay for all the hard work and research that would be necessary to generate a sufficiently wide range of scenarios in which all relevant parameters were quantified realistically? My own experience is that clients expect a fully worked out design by next Tuesday. The idea that one might expend the same kind of money and effort on designing a social mechanism as on designing a building or a bridge would strike them as absurd.

Step 2: Regulation.   To achieve an efficient outcome, it is necessary to decentralize decision-making, but the agents to whom decisions are decentralized won't usually share the objectives the designer is seeking to achieve. Some of them will want to embezzle the funds entrusted to their care. Others will appoint their nephews and nieces to positions of authority in preference to better qualified candidates. Entrepreneurs will wish to get together to fix their prices to the detriment of the consumer. And so on.

To some extent, the agents' behavior can be controlled by straightforward regulation that forbids certain practices, and makes others mandatory. But only behavior that can be effectively monitored can be controlled in this way. Deviants can then be detected and punished by the external enforcement agency whose existence is taken for granted in classical mechanism design. It is pointless, however, to forbid or mandate behavior that can't or won't be monitored.

Probably the disgrace of the American auditing industry that followed the fall of the energy company Enron when its corrupt accounting practices were exposed will be forgotten by the time this book is published. But it is a textbook case of what to expect from trusting even apparently respectable pillars of the community to carry out their public duties without adequate supervision. They mostly don't set out intending to stray from the strait and narrow path, but it is easy to tell oneself little stories that justify deviating from the rule-book a little more each time, once it has become plain that others are getting away with it without being caught.

Step 3: Incentives.   A major mistake in most attempts at reform is the failure to recognize that people will adapt their behavior to the new system. The reform is therefore put together on the assumption that people will continue to behave as before. But the hard lesson that economists are always in trouble for pushing is that it is in the nature of the human animal to respond to its incentives. In planning a reform, it is therefore necessary to look ahead to what the incentives of the agents will be *after* the reform is in place.

It is for this reason that the current enthusiasm for behavioral economics is potentially dangerous. Its advocates explicitly urge that the laws of behavior they think they have discovered should be applied in public policy. But they fail to recognize that the regularities in behavior that they describe by attributing a taste for fairness or reciprocity to laboratory subjects aren't stable over time—as the enormous volume of data in games like the one-shot Prisoners' Dilemma amply demonstrates. People are habituated to behaving *as though* they have a taste for fairness or reciprocity, because this is necessary to sustain the equilibria to which they are accustomed. But when we change the game they are playing, their behavior will gradually adjust to a new equilibrium, after which they will behave as though they have new tastes for fairness or reciprocity.

It is in the planning of the incentives that players will experience after the reform that the ingenuity of the designer is mostly required. I think it important to recognize that money incentives are only part of the story. People certainly care about money, but only because it allows them to satisfy more fundamental drives. In particular, we are social animals who care deeply about our relative position in society. The contempt of our peers for a poorly done job is therefore usually a much more effective punishment than the loss of a monetary bonus.

Step 4: Equilibrium. Game theory is needed in mechanism design to predict what will happen after the players have responded to their new incentives. The prediction is obtained by finding an appropriate equilibrium of the game created by the design.

In the current state of the art, the problem of equilibrium selection usually gets little attention. The implicit assumption is that the designer can successfully act as a coordinating device by pointing to the equilibrium she would prefer to be played. But bosses in real factories don't find things so easy! The boss may point to a more productive equilibrium, but will her workers acquiesce in coordinating on this new equilibrium if they don't think it fair?

As anyone who has worked in a factory knows, the boss has only limited control over what goes on in her factory. She can alter some of the rules of the indefinitely repeated game the workers play with each other, but she can't alter their local social contract by fiat, because she has no way of preventing workers who try to follow her lead from being mocked or ostracized by their fellows. However, the problem isn't hopeless, as Japanese car manufacturers have shown by persuading foreign workers in overseas factories to adopt Japanese working practices.

Step 5: Optimization. In simple situations, it is sometimes possible to use game theory to compute the optimal mechanism from scratch. In spite of the billions of dollars involved, selling telecom licenses counts as such a simple situation—and hence our success in tailoring auctions to the market conditions under which the sale takes place.

In more complicated situations, working out an optimal mechanism from first principles can be prohibitively difficult. Introducing reforms then becomes as much of an art as a science—but this is no excuse for abandoning science altogether. One can write models that are admittedly too simple to be realistic, and test the principles on which a reform is based by seeing whether they would improve matters if used in such a simplified world. One can write computer simulations to the same end. One can run laboratory experiments or field trials with real people to see whether they actually learn to behave as assumed in the reform. If such research is negative, then one can begin again at step 2.

However, bureaucrats seldom see any need for research. Not only is it expensive in time and money, but it will also clearly involve the necessity of producing data that nobody has bothered to gather. Reforms that affect the health and welfare of millions of people are therefore routinely put into place without any serious preliminary testing at all. Mrs Thatcher's introduction of so-called "internal markets" into the British Health Service is a particularly outrageous example. The only testing consisted of two role-playing exercises whose outcomes were officially summarized by saying that "chaos was narrowly avoided".

Libertarians are certainly right when they argue that no planning at all is better than this kind of dogma-driven, irresponsible meddling. But the rational alternative to bad planning isn't not to plan at all. It is to plan well.

12.6   Reforming a Social Contract?

I don't suppose any of us would want to live in one of the classical utopias like More's *New Atlantis* or Plato's *Republic*. I don't even think that the idea of a utopia is coherent, since it implies some absolute standard against which different social contracts are to be measured. But one doesn't need to be a utopian to join with others in seeking reform. Perhaps the citizens of other societies in other places and other times may not agree that the reforms we seek are improvements, but we are children of our culture and not of theirs.

Nor do I think there is much point in contemplating massive overhauls of our current society. History would seem to confirm that revolutions seldom go where the initiating revolutionaries intended. Whigs like myself believe that we do better by actively reforming in a small way all the time if only to prevent revolutionary sentiment getting a grip on people's minds.

But what principles should inform our reforming zeal? I don't pretend to know the answer. The best I can do is to go through the steps involved in designing a mechanism again, pointing out where social contract design differs.

Step 1: Objective. A group of potential reformers whose fingers are close enough to the levers of power to have some hope of being effective wouldn't have got together in the first place unless their individual aspirations for society were aligned to some extent. But they face the standard leadership problem. If they seek to recoordinate expectations on a social contract that is perceived as unfair, then they risk creating an opposing coalition that uses fairness as its rallying call.

There is therefore a social dynamic that is likely to foster the success of political parties or pressure groups whose proposals for reform don't stray too far from what is currently regarded as fair. If you think that any equilibrium selection device is better than none, it follows that you have a pragmatic reason for promoting reforms that will be regarded as fair.

Step 2: Regulation.   It remains true that to achieve an efficient outcome, it is necessary to decentralize decision-making. An efficient society must therefore be a free society to some extent, but it can't avoid bosses altogether. Nor can it avoid controlling behavior through the use of impersonal laws and conventions.

It is here that a schism opens between mechanism design and the planning of constitutions or social contracts. In mechanism design, it is assumed that one big boss who sits outside the system can monitor the regulations she decrees, and punish any defaulters sufficiently severely that nobody will wish to default. In planning a social contract, nobody sits outside the system. We therefore can't treat the problem as that of creating a game for the citizens to play. We have to take the underlying game of life as given. Our problem is to describe a new equilibrium in this game of life, and a feasible means of changing expectations to get us there from where we are now.

Instead of regulations enforced by an external agency as in mechanism design, we therefore have to think of duties as defined in chapter 6. Because of the monitoring problem, it will often be necessary to create internal enforcement agencies—like the police force or the tax inspectorate—that specialize in detecting failures by individuals to carry out particular duties assigned to them by the social contract. Sometimes it will be possible to rely on agencies that organize themselves spontaneously—as with the informal association of neighbors who bluntly threatened my family with social exclusion on the day we moved into a new house if we didn't mow our lawn regularly. But formally constituted agencies won't be avoidable altogether.

In institutionalizing enforcement agencies, the lesson that free societies seem to find hardest to learn is that guardians always need to be guarded if the system is to survive as an equilibrium. Who guards the guardians? The answer is that they must be organized to guard each other—as in totalitarian states in which the secret police spy on each other.

There is no place for secret police in a free society, but we do need to recognize that the price of freedom is indeed internal vigilance when the enemy is the kind of creeping corruption that finally results in institutions being operated for the convenience of their officers rather than the purpose for which they were founded. As usual, David Hume was here first: "When there offers, therefore, to our censure and examination, any plan of government, real or imaginary, where the power is distributed among several courts, and several orders of men, we should always consider the separate interest of each court, and each order; and, if we find that, by the skilful division of power, the interest must necessarily, in its operation, concur with the public, we may pronounce that government to be wise and happy."

Step 3: Incentives.   Planning a social contract is immensely more difficult than designing a mechanism, but the subject of incentives is at least one area in which things are conceptually simpler in the social contract arena. The focus in orthodox mechanism design is on tangible incentives like money, but we all know that we care at least as much about the pervasive social pressures with which those around us influence our behavior.

One can try and build such intangibles into a mechanism design framework by postulating that people care directly about such issues as honesty or loyalty, but such an approach is bound to be unacceptably *ad hoc* until we learn to model such emergent phenomena in terms of equilibria within a social contract framework.

Step 4: Equilibrium. All that needs to be said under this heading is that the fact that fairness is already in use as an informal equilibrium selection device is clearly a major asset for a planner aiming to institutionalize a fair social contract. We don't need to change a society's perception of what counts as fair if our criterion for selecting among equlibria is what society currently regards as fair.

Step 5: Optimization. What would a whiggish "utopia" look like? I suspect it would be a lot more like the social contract of the early years of the American Republic than anything we see around us today. The industrial revolution ran off with that particular ray of sunshine, but perhaps the postindustrial world of the future will allow a return to something closer to the social contracts of the hunter-gathering folk for whose way of life our genes are predisposed.

12.7   Unfinished Business

The science of fairness has hardly been born, but here am I writing a chapter about using it to engineer improvements in modern social contracts. To underline my presumption, I shall end by drawing attention to some major failings of my theory that would need to be overcome before it could be put to such a purpose.

Coalitions. From Von Neumann onward, game theorists have proposed many *II:4.9.1* models that are intended to explain coalition formation among rational players, but none can be said to have succeeded in capturing everything that matters. I have therefore only studied the case in which current theory is adequate—that of a two-person society containing only Adam and Eve. The opportunities for applying the theory directly are therefore limited to those rare situations in which Adam and Eve can realistically be seen as representatives of monolithic blocs. I think this restriction is a major obstacle in applying the theory to the social contracts of large societies, because the character of a modern democracy is largely defined by the manner in which its coalitional patterns shift in response to stresses and strains.

A large society consists of a complex system of interlocking organizational hierarchies that coordinate behavior at many different levels. Even in chimpanzee and baboon societies, the evidence supporting the importance of coalition formation and social networking is overwhelming. An attempt to describe the current *status quo* that takes no account of this reality would clearly be futile, as would any similar attempt to describe the potential social contracts to which the society might aspire.

Not only do the subsocieties into which society as a whole is split exist, they are essential to its efficient operation.

The existence of subsocieties necessarily requires that distinctions be made between insiders and outsiders. This isn't to argue that the irrational dehumanizing criteria currently used to blackball various classes of unfortunates are inevitable or "legitimate". It is simply to accept, as a matter of practical necessity, that we can't all be insiders in everything. Nor need outsiders be seen as opponents. Indeed, two individuals may well be fellow insiders in one subsociety while simultaneously belonging to rival organizations on orthogonal issues.

One can imagine the device of the original position being used to resolve coordination problems between several such subsocieties with fully briefed delegates serving as representatives of each subsociety. The brief of each such delegate would in turn be decided by a similar use of the original position in resolving coordination problems within each separate subsociety—which will itself typically be split into factions and splinter groups. However, it is inevitable that different standards of interpersonal comparison would arise at different levels and in different contexts. In consequence, a person might well regard one deal as fair when interacting with a fellow insider, and something quite different as fair when interacting with an outsider. However, such complexities are beyond my grasp.

II:4.9.2 **Incomplete information.** All the models in this book implicitly assume that Adam and Eve's preferences are common knowledge among the players. Under this hypothesis, it is reasonable to assume that they will bargain to an efficient outcome. But what if Adam and Eve's preferences aren't common knowledge?

I think that this problem is largely technical in character. Aside from his work on ethics, John Harsanyi invented a theory of "games of incomplete information" to which one can appeal. When this theory is applied to bargaining problems, the models typically generate large numbers of equilibria among which it is difficult to make a selection. But the circumstances of the original position ease this equilibrium selection problem to a degree that I think allows progress to be made.

However, there seems little point in pursuing the theory in this direction when so many more pressing issues rermain to be resolved.

II:4.9.3 **A changing game of life.** The mainspring of human sociality is to be found in the reciprocity mechanism. Since this can't be captured in one-shot games, this book turned to the theory of indefinitely repeated games for the simplest possible model of the game of life that allows the reciprocity mechanism to operate in a reasonably realistic manner. But the decision to work with repeated games makes it necessary to be unrealistic about another important matter.

I believe that fairness norms evolved to make it possible for communities to exploit new sources of surplus without destabilizing internal strife. But we can't model the appearance of a new source of surplus without stepping outside the framework of a repeated game, in which each new day presents the players with exactly the same problem as the day before. I finesse this modeling difficulty by imagining that the players never anticipate the possibility that a new source of surplus may become available. They suddenly wake up one morning to find that their feasible set X has expanded to Y, but never take into account the possibility that the same might happen again at some future time. Still less do they contemplate the uncomfortable possibility that they might wake up one morning to find that their feasible set has shrunk overnight, leaving less to go round than there was before.

Such a crude modeling approach is excusable only as the first step toward a more sophisticated theory in which the game of life is modeled as what game theorists misleadingly call a *stochastic game*. This terminology makes it seem as though a stochastic game is merely a repeated game in which a chance move determines which of a number of one-shot games is to be played in the next period. Such stochastic games certainly are of interest, but when questions are asked about the extent to which the current generation is entitled to consume exhaustible resources or to pollute the environment at the expense of future generations, it becomes necessary to consider stochastic games in which the strategies chosen by today's players can influence not only their own payoffs, but also the game played by tomorrow's players.

Stochastic games in which players can make possibly irreversible strategic choices about the games to be played in the future are obviously much harder to analyze than repeated games. As things stand, we don't even know the class of stochastic games in which some recognizable analogue of the folk theorem holds. Probably no such analogue exists if the players are able to restrict the options available in future games sufficiently quickly. If this is the nature of the modern game of life, then the prospects of our being able to sustain a civilized social contract seem more than a little gloomy. But we may perhaps hope that technological advances will open up new options faster than they they allow us to close others down.

12.8   A Perfect Commonwealth?

David Hume wouldn't have approved of this chapter very much. Talk of planning a whole society would have seemed like hubris to him. It is true that he wrote an essay called *On the Idea of a Perfect Commonwealth*, but his tongue was firmly in his cheek in giving such a title to a bunch of proposals for small reforms that he thought would improve matters here and there. The social and biological sciences have advanced a great deal since the time of the Scottish Enlightenment, but it remains true that we can only say anything practical about the kind of small reforms that David Hume was willing to contemplate.

So what do the ideas presented in this book have to teach us about the way to organize our thoughts when planning such small reforms? Perhaps the most important consideration is the necessity of separating the question of what is feasible from what is optimal. To make a decision sensibly, first decide what alternatives will work, and then choose whichever of the workable alternatives you like most.

The chief problem in practice is that reformers want to neglect the feasibility constraint. Rather than ask what new equilibrium will be played in the game of life after the reform, optimists prefer to assume that people will ignore their new incentives and either play as they have in the past, or else turn into selfless paragons for whom incentives have no relevance. This is where game theory comes in. Even when it can't be used directly because the problem is too difficult to be solved analytically, it provides guidance in designing the computer simulations, field trials, or laboratory experiments that are otherwise necessary to test that a proposed reform is likely to work as predicted.

Optimality is conceptually much more difficult. The pundits and gurus who claim to know the uniquely Good or Right way to do things are just windbags and blowhards; the reality is that we have only our own likes and dislikes to guide us. But reformers who are unwilling to compromise with the likes and dislikes of others are unlikely to be able to build the kind of coalition that is necessary to get even small reforms implemented. I argue that one can sensibly view the problem of building such a coalition as a complicated coordination game with many equilibria. Fairness is the social tool washed up on the human beach by the tide of evolution for solving such coordination problems—so why don't we use it?

If David Hume were alive today, he would be delighted to explain that we can no more provide a Rational Justification for using fairness as a coordination device in this way than we can justify using inductive reasoning. But the fact that Hume thought it impossible to justify inductive reasoning didn't stop him using inductive reasoning in formulating his program of whiggish reform. So why should we allow the fact that we can't find an absolute justification for the fairness norms that circulate in our society to prevent our using them to improve our way of life?

Bibliography

[1] J. Alcock. *The Triumph of Sociobiology.* Oxford University Press, New York, 2001.

[2] R. Alexander. *The Biology of Moral Systems.* Aldine de Gruyter, Hawthorne, New York, 1987.

[3] Aristotle. *Nicomachean Ethics.* Hackett, Indianapolis, 1985. (Translated by T. Irwin).

[4] R. Aumann and M. Maschler. *Repeated Games with Incomplete Information.* MIT Press, Cambridge, MA, 1995.

[5] R. Axelrod. *The Evolution of Cooperation.* Basic Books, New York, 1984.

[6] K. Binmore. *Fun and Games: A Text on Game Theory.* Heath, Lexington, MA, 1992.

[7] K. Binmore. *Playing Fair: Game Theory and the Social Contract I.* MIT Press, Cambridge, MA, 1994.

[8] K. Binmore. *Just Playing: Game Theory and the Social Contract II.* MIT Press, Cambridge, MA, 1998.

[9] R. Boyd and P. Richerson. *Culture and the Evolutionary Process.* University of Chicago Press, Chicago, 1985.

[10] J. Broome. *Weighing Goods.* Blackwell, Oxford, 1991.

[11] L. Cavelli-Sforza and M. Feldman. *Cultural Transmission and Evolution.* Princeton University Press, Princeton, 1981.

[12] M. Cohen. *The Food Crisis in Prehistory: Overpopulation and the Origins of Agriculture.* Yale University Press, New Haven, 1977.

[13] A. Damasio. *Descartes' Error: Emotion, Reason, and the Human Brain.* Grosset-Putnam, New York, 1994.

[14] C. Darwin. *The Descent of Man and Selection in Relation to Sex.* Murray, London, 1871.

[15] C. Darwin. *The Expression of the Emotions in Man and Animals.* University of Chicago Press, Chicago, 1965.

[16] R. Dawkins. *The Selfish Gene.* Oxford University Press, Oxford, 1976.

[17] R. Dawkins. *The Blind Watchmaker.* Penguin, London, 1986.

[18] D. Dennett. *Darwin's Dangerous Idea: Evolution and the Meanings of Life.* Allen Lane, London, 1995.

[19] J. Diamond. *Guns, Germs, and Steel.* Norton, New York, 1997.

[20] F. Dostoyevsky. *House of the Dead.* Penguin, London, 1985.

[21] R. Dunbar. *Grooming, Gossip, and the Evolution of Language.* Faber, London, 1996.

[22] J. Elster. *Local Justice: How Institutions Allocate Scarce Goods and Necessary Burdens.* Russell Sage Foundation, New York, 1992.

[23] H. Eysenck. *Sense and Nonsense in Psychology.* Pelican Books, Harmondsworth, UK, 1957.

[24] P. Farber. *The Temptations of Evolutionary Ethics.* University of California Press, Berkeley, 1994.

[25] C. Furer-Haimendorf. *Morals and Merit.* Weidenfeld and Nicolson, London, 1967.

[26] D. Gauthier. *Morals by Agreement.* Clarendon Press, Oxford, 1986.

[27] H. Gintis *et al* editors. *Moral Sentiments and Material Interests.* MIT Press, Cambridge, MA, 2004.

[28] R. Goodin. *Utilitarianism as a Public Philosophy.* Cambridge University Press, Cambridge, 1995.

[29] J. W. Gough. *The Social Contract.* Clarendon Press, Oxford, 1938.

[30] A. Hamilton, J. Jay, and J. Madison. *The Federalist.* Everyman, London, 1992. (Edited by W. Brock. First published 1787–1788).

[31] W. Hamilton. *Narrow Roads of Geneland: Collected Papers of W. D. Hamilton, Volume 1: Evolution of Social Behaviour.* Freeman, Oxford, 1996.

[32] W. Hamilton. *Narrow Roads of Geneland: Collected Papers of W. D. Hamilton, Volume 2: Evolution of Sex.* Oxford University Press, Oxford, 2001.

[33] J. Harsanyi. *Rational Behavior and Bargaining Equilibrium in Games and Social Situations.* Cambridge University Press, Cambridge, 1977.

[34] J. Henrich, R. Boyd, S.Bowles, E. Fehr, H. Gintis, and R. McElreath. *Foundations of Human Sociality: Economic Experiments and Ethnographic Evidence from Fifteen Small-Scale Societies.* Oxford University Press, Oxford, 2004.

[35] T. Hobbes. *Leviathan.* Penguin Classics, London, 1986. (Edited by C. B. Macpherson. First published 1651).

[36] G. Homans and C. Curtis. *An Introduction to Pareto: His Sociology.* Knopf, New York, 1934.

[37] D. Hume. *A Treatise of Human Nature (Second Edition).* Clarendon Press, Oxford, 1978. (Edited by L. A. Selby-Bigge. Revised by P. Nidditch. First published 1739).

[38] I. Kant. *Groundwork of the Metaphysic of Morals.* Harper Torchbooks, New York, 1964. (Translated and analyzed by H. Paton. First published 1785).

[39] I. Kant. *Critique of Practical Reason.* Macmillan, New York, 1989. (Translated by L. Beck. First published 1788).

[40] M. Lerner. *The Belief in a Just World.* Plenum, New York, 1980.

[41] N. Levy. *Moral Relativism: A Short Introduction.* Oneworld Publications, Oxford, 2002.

[42] J. Mackie. *Ethics, Inventing Right and Wrong.* Penguin, London, 1977.

[43] J. Mackie. *Hume's Moral Theory.* Routledge and Kegan Paul, London, 1980.

[44] B. de Mandeville. *The Fable of the Bees—or Private Vices, Publick Benefits.* Liberty Classics, Indianapolis, 1988. (Edited by F. Kaye. First published 1714).

[45] A. Maryanski and J. Turner. *The Social Cage: Human Nature and the Evolution of Society*. Stanford University Press, Stanford, 1992.

[46] J. Maynard Smith. *Evolution and the Theory of Games*. Cambridge University Press, Cambridge, 1982.

[47] G. E. Moore. *Principia Ethica*. Prometheus Books, Buffalo, N.Y., 1988. (First published 1902).

[48] S. Pinker. *The Language Instinct: The New Science of Language and Mind*. Penguin, London, 1994.

[49] K. Popper. *The Open Society and its Enemies*. Routledge, London, 1945.

[50] M. Power. *The Egalitarians: Human and Chimpanzee*. Cambridge University Press, Cambridge, 1991.

[51] J. Rawls. *A Theory of Justice*. Oxford University Press, Oxford, 1972.

[52] J. Rawls. *Political Liberalism*. Columbia University Press, New York, 1993.

[53] O. Sachs. *An Anthropologist on Mars*. Knopf, New York, 1994.

[54] P. Singer. *The Expanding Circle: Ethics and Sociobiology*. Farrar, Strauss and Giroux, New York, 1980.

[55] P. Singer. *How Are We to Live: Ethics in an Age of Self-Interest*. Opus: Oxford University Press, Oxford, 1997.

[56] B. Skyrms. *Evolution of the Social Contract*. Cambridge University Press, Cambridge, 1996.

[57] B. Skyrms. *The Stag Hunt and the Evolution of Social Structure*. Cambridge University Press, Cambridge, 2003.

[58] A. Smith. *The Theory of Moral Sentiments*. Clarendon Press, Oxford, 1975. (Edited by D. Raphael and A. Macfie. First published 1759).

[59] A. Smith. *The Wealth of Nations*. Liberty Classics, Indianopolis, 1976. (First published 1776).

[60] R. Sugden. *The Economics of Rights, Cooperation and Welfare*. Blackwell, Oxford, 1986.

[61] R. Trivers. *Social Evolution*. Benjamin Cummings, Menlo Park, CA, 1985.

[62] E. Ulmann-Margalit. *The Emergence of Norms*. Oxford University Press, New York, 1977.

[63] J. Von Neumann and O. Morgenstern. *The Theory of Games and Economic Behavior*. Princeton University Press, Princeton, 1944.

[64] F. de Waal. *Good Natured: The Origins of Right and Wrong in Humans and Other Animals*. Harvard University Press, Cambridge, MA, 1996.

[65] G. Wagstaff. *Making Sense of Justice: On the Psychology of Equity and Desert*. Meller, Liverpool, 1998.

[66] E. Westermarck. *The Origin and Development of Moral Ideas, I and II*. MacMillan, London, 1906.

[67] A. Whitten. *Natural Theories of the Mind: Evolution, Development and Simulation of Everyday Mindreading*. Blackwell, Oxford, 1991.

[68] E. Wilson. *Sociobiology: The New Synthesis*. MIT Press, Cambridge, MA, 1975.

[69] V. Wynne-Edwards. *Animal Dispersion in Relation to Social Behavior*. Oliver and Boyd, Edinburgh, 1962.

[70] P. Young. *Equity*. Princeton University Press, Princeton, 1994.

Index

The Wondrous World
of Seedless Plants

The Wondrous World
of Seedless Plants

WILLIAM C. GRIMM and

M. JEAN CRAIG

illustrated by William C. Grimm

THE BOBBS-MERRILL COMPANY, INC.

Indianapolis   New York

To my nephew, Jim
W.C.G.

We wish to thank Dr. Clark T. Rogerson, Senior Curator of Cryptogamic Botany at the New York Botanical Garden, for critically reading the manuscript and for his helpful suggestions. Thanks are also due Ruth Curtis Grimm for her help with the preparation of the senior author's manuscript and other details; and to Miriam Chaikin, editor of Books for Young People at the Bobbs-Merrill Company, for her interest which has made this book possible.

W.C.G.

THE BOBBS-MERRILL COMPANY, INC.
PUBLISHERS INDIANAPOLIS   NEW YORK
Text copyright © 1973 by Bobbs-Merrill
Illustrations copyright © 1973 by William C. Grimm
Design by Jack Jaget
Printed in the United States of America
ISBN 0-672-51709-4
Library of Congress catalog card number: 73-1757
0 9 8 7 6 5 4 3 2 1

Contents

Prologue

BEFORE we enter the world of seedless plants, let us first understand what a seed is. A seed is a reproductive body made up of a large number of cells. It contains an embryo or tiny plant and also, usually, a supply of food to give this little plant a start in life.

Today the most familiar of the earth's plants are seed plants. Yet a few hundred million years ago there were no plants which produced seeds. There were also no plants with flowers. There were no grasses or lilies, no roses, no sunflowers or daisies. There were no flowering trees such as birches, willows, cherries, maples, or magnolias.

Even now at least a third of the known kinds of living plants do not grow from seeds or have flowers. About a quarter of today's plants do not have roots or stems or leaves. And quite a large number of them have no chlorophyll (KLOR-o-fill), the remarkable green substance which makes it possible for plants to manufacture food from carbon dioxide, water, and the energy of the sun, a process known as photosynthesis (foto-SIN-thi-sis).

A wondrous world of these seedless plants grows all around us. The purpose of this book is to describe some of them and the strange and interesting ways in which they live. We may think we do not know these plants, but we really do. Some of them, such as the bacteria and the yeasts and molds, are all about us. A number of these seedless plants may grow in our own dooryards. Many more may be found on even a short ramble through the countryside—in fields and forests, ponds and flowing streams—if we look for them. Often we have passed them by without even noticing that they were there.

Plants?—or Animals?

LET US consider briefly some tiny bits of life that might well be represented by a big question mark. Are they plants? Or are they animals? Even the scientists who have studied them do not agree.

The Flagellates

During the summer and fall a bright green, velvety film often covers the surface of wayside pools. To our unaided eyes it doesn't look like much. But let us put a bit of it on a glass slide and examine it through a microscope.

What a surprise! We see a host of tiny living things scurrying about. Each one is a single cell, more or less spindle-shaped. At one end there is a long hairlike whip, or flagellum (fla-JELL-um), which lashes about furiously, propelling the minute cell through the water. This tiny living thing is called the *Euglena* (yew-GLEE-na). But is it a plant? Or is it an animal?

Euglenas are green because they contain chlorophyll. And

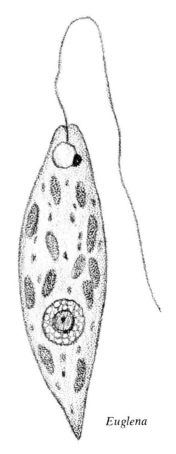

Euglena

9

the presence of chlorophyll indicates that they are plants. Thus botanists, the scientists who study plant life, claim that they are single-celled green algae.

On the other hand, *Euglenas* do not have cell walls composed of cellulose (SELL-yew-lohs), such as plants ordinarily have. In addition, they move about very much the way animals do. For these and other reasons, zoologists, the scientists who study animal life, insist that they are protozoans (pro-toe-ZO-unz), or one-celled animals. Perhaps we could call them plant-animals or animal-plants.

Euglena is only one of a large group of one-celled living things called the flagellates (FLAJ-i-lates). Flagellates are common in the waters of the world, even in temporary rain-water pools. Not all of them are green like *Euglena,* though; sometimes their green chlorophyll is masked by other pigments. One flagellate often colors the snow red in arctic regions. Another causes what is called "red rain." And some are much more like animals than is *Euglena.*

If you examine a drop of pond water through a microscope, you may see what appear to be tiny green spheres. Sometimes they are large enough to be seen by the naked eye as tiny green dots. Often they are so abundant that the water itself seems to be colored green. These little dots are colonies of *Volvox* (VOL-vox). Each colony is a hollow jellylike ball containing hundreds of minute green flagellates. The lashing of their flagella keeps the little spheres turning over and over as they move slowly through the water.

Flagellates usually reproduce very simply. The cell just divides into two parts, each of which goes on its way as an independent flagellate. Sometimes, however, one of the members of a *Volvox* colony will slip into the interior of the sphere. There it divides over and over again until another miniature ball-like colony is formed. Sooner or later this will escape

10

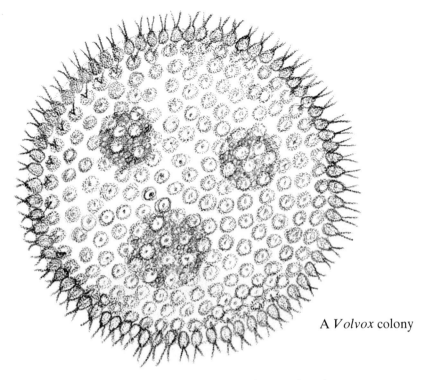

A *Volvox* colony

through the wall of the mother colony and go swimming away as a free and independent *Volvox* colony.

Most flagellates are innocent and even very useful members of the living community. They are particularly abundant in the sea, where they make up a large part of the free-floating mass of minute living things known as plankton. Plankton has often been called the "grass of the sea." It provides food for all the animals of the sea, from the tiniest of water fleas to fishes and giant whales.

The strange and often spectacular luminescence of the sea, which has fascinated mankind for ages, is caused by certain luminous flagellates, no larger than pinpoints, which abound in its waters. Whenever they are even slightly disturbed they give off light, causing the water and everything in it to glow at night. During the fall, particularly, they light up the water in

11

flashing sheets. The ancient mariners have told many weird tales about such "fiery seas."

There are, however, "black sheep" among the flagellates. One of them is *Gymnodinium breve* (jim-no-DIN-i-um BREV-ee), more popularly known as "Jim Breve." It is very familiar to people who live along Florida's Gulf coast. Usually there are only a thousand or so of these flagellates in a quart of sea water, and they go unnoticed. But sometimes a population explosion occurs, and their numbers soar to fifty million or more in each quart of water. When this happens, the water turns reddish and may become sirupy. Fish die and pile up along the beaches, and the resulting stench is unbearable. People sneeze, and their throats become sore. Nobody ever welcomes what Floridians call the "red tide."

In the waters along the Pacific coast a close relative of "Jim Breve" grows very abundant during the summer months. Mussels and clams feed upon the flagellates with no apparent harm, but people who make the mistake of eating the mussels and clams during the summer season become ill. Some have even been fatally poisoned.

Slime Molds

Not all of the borderline living things are confined to the water. On a ramble through a woodland you may notice a slimy, jellylike substance on a decaying log. It looks very much like the white of an egg, and it may be several inches across. Although it doesn't seem like anything living, even as you look at it, it seems to move, very slowly. It is indeed alive, for it happens to be one of the slime molds.

If you wait long enough, you will see a marvelous change take place in this slimy mass of protoplasm. It stops moving,

12

and then, after a while, it begins to pile up into many upright extensions. These slowly evolve into structures that produce spores. Spores, like seeds, are reproductive bodies. But, unlike seeds, spores are very simple. Usually they consist of only a single cell.

There are many different kinds of slime molds. Each one builds its own style of spore-bearing structures. Sometimes these structures resemble miniature puffballs, or little balls perched atop slender stalks. Others have spore-bearing heads which are latticelike, with a network of delicate threads. They may be white, yellow, orange, red, or brown in color. If you examine them through a hand lens, you will find that they are often extremely beautiful.

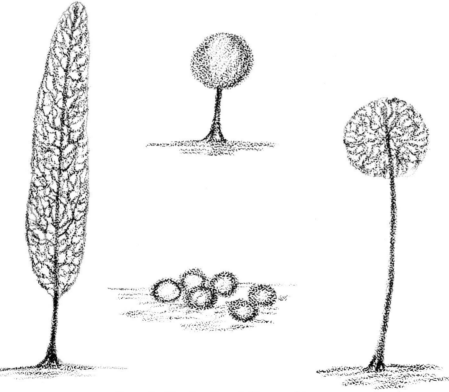

Some fruiting bodies of slime molds

Puffs of the microscopic slime-mold spores are carried away on every breeze. Those which do not land in a favorable spot, such as the damp surface of some decaying wood, soon perish. But those which do will germinate. Out of each spore comes a tiny bit of protoplasm. It creeps about very much like the one-celled animal known as the *Amoeba* (a-ME-ba) and quickly seeks the cool, damp darkness in the interior of the rotting wood. It is far too small to be seen with the naked eye. It soon begins to divide into two cells. Over and over again the new cells divide, grow to full size, and then divide again. In a day's time the bit of protoplasm that emerged from a single spore may have a hundred or more descendants, all of them creeping about as free-living individuals.

Sooner or later the amoebalike cells are attracted to one another and begin to crawl about as a slimy mass. Others join them, and the creeping mass keeps growing in size. All of this happens in darkness, within a decaying log or tree stump or beneath the damp mat of rotting leaves on the woodland floor. But eventually a time comes when the whole slimy mass will creep into the daylight again, and the cycle will be repeated.

Just what are these primitive living things which we call slime molds? During a part of their life cycle they both look and behave like some of the simple one-celled animals. At another stage, they definitely resemble plants. Botanists consider them as being among the fungi (FUN-jy)—and fungi are plants. Zoologists, on the other hand, classify them among the protozoa, claiming that they are animals. Plants or animals? Which?

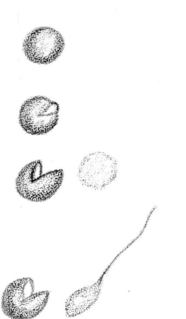

A slime mold emerges from a spore.

14

The Algae

FOR A VERY long time all life was confined to the waters of the sea. After who knows how long, the seaside rocks washed by the waves began to turn green. The green, mere specks of color, were single-celled plants called algae (AL-gee).

Algae were not only the first plants, they are also the most primitive plants which exist today. Most kinds never got into the mainstream of progress and are much the same now as they were ages ago. Many still have only a single cell, and even the many-celled algae have no roots, no stems, and no leaves, but just a simple plant body called a thallus (THALL-us).

The Humble Blue-Green Algae, Lowliest of the Low

Blue-green algae are the lowliest of all the algae. Their single cell has no well-defined nucleus (NEW-klee-us), as do the cells of other algae and of all of the higher plants. In the blue-green algae the chlorophyll seems simply to be dissolved in the outer portion of the protoplasm, and it is mixed with a blue pigment which tends to give these algae their bluish-green color. Some-

15

times, however, there are other pigments too, and then the blue-green algae look red, orange, yellow, purple, or even black.

Blue-green algae may occur any place where there is moisture. Most kinds are found in fresh waters, but some live in the sea. One kind gives the Red Sea its characteristic red color. Some kinds are able to live in waters which are really hot, with temperatures above 150 degrees Fahrenheit. Most of the brilliant colors seen in the hot springs of Yellowstone National Park are due to the presence of blue-green algae.

Blue-green algae often turn moist earth a deep-greenish to black color. And a few kinds live within the roots of some of the higher plants.

The single cell of a blue-green alga is too small to be seen without a microscope, but these algae often live together in colonies, where they can be seen. Sometimes the colonies are enclosed in a gelatinlike mass, and sometimes the cells arrange themselves into threads, or filaments, so that they look like many-celled plants.

The reproduction of blue-green algae is very simple: the single cell just divides into two cells, each of which becomes a new plant.

Most of us have seen blue-green algae, whether we knew what they were or not.

Gleocapsa (glee-o-KAP-sa), for instance, lives in jellylike masses, and often makes a slippery coating on rocks in streams.

The clumps of brownish "jelly" we sometimes find near the bottom of water plants, or on stones in rapids, are really colonies of *Rivularia* (riv-u-LAIR-i-a).

And the little lumps of green "gelatin" found on the bottoms of ponds, and sometimes in damp earth, contain tiny chains of *Nostoc* (NOSS-tock).

Oscillatoria (oss-sill-a-TOR-ia) is one of the blue-green algae which forms colonies of threads or filaments, and it is a rather remarkable one. Its filaments are constantly in motion, swaying back and forth, twisting and turning, coiling and un-

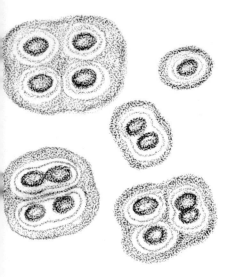

Colonies of *Gleocapsa*

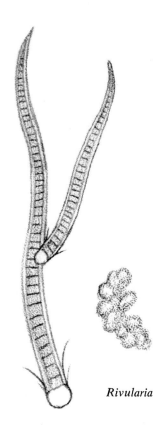

Rivularia

16

coiling. Pieces of the filaments often come loose and float on the surface of the water. *Oscillatoria* is dark blue-green, or nearly black, and is found in water or in almost any damp place. It lines the inside walls of watering troughs; it grows on the bottoms of lakes and ponds; it clings to the rocks in streams and even to the backs of turtles. Some kinds prefer damp soil and form the so-called "moss" on flowerpots in greenhouses.

Blue-green algae sometimes cause a condition called a "water bloom." During the heat of midsummer, the water of a lake or a pond may become cloudy. It may even begin to look like pea soup, with a frothy scum on its surface. As this scum decays it gives off an extremely unpleasant smell, and then people say that the pond is "working," or "blooming." The cause of this change is an excessive growth of the blue-green algae in the water.

Water blooms are common in still waters all over the world, and most of them are quite harmless. But during the first week of September 1948, a water bloom occurred on a small lake in Minnesota. Within a week, seventy-nine hogs, two horses, and an uncounted number of chickens, ducks, geese, cats, and dogs on the farms about the lake died from drinking the poisoned water. Also, the remains of many gray squirrels, muskrats, wild ducks, shore birds, sparrows, and fish were found along the shoreline. Toxic water blooms such as this one usually occur when a certain species of *Anabaena* (an-a-BEE-na) happens to be one kind of blue-green algae in the water.

From man's standpoint, blue-green algae have both good and bad effects. Many of them, including the free-floating chains of *Anabaena,* provide tiny water animals with food. These animals are eaten by aquatic insects and by the tiniest fishes, which, in their turn, become food for larger fishes. Certain of the blue-green algae enrich the soil they live in by changing the free nitrogen in the air into forms which other plants are then able to use. On the other hand, many blue-green algae give water

The chains of *Nostoc*

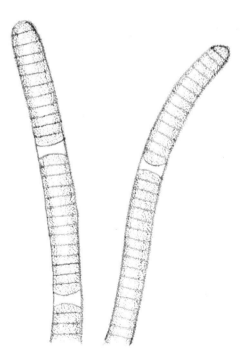

Threads of *Oscillatoria*

Anabaena

an unpleasant odor and a bad taste. They are not at all welcome residents of our reservoirs or other sources of drinking water.

Jewels of the Earth's Waters

The earth's waters are full of marvels. A drop of water taken from a pond may seem to have nothing in it at all, but when we look at it through a microscope we find it full of tiny wonderful living things.

Some of these minute bits of life are animals. Others may well be single-celled green algae so exquisitely beautiful that they look like tiny jewels. They are called "desmids."

Desmids are found in most fresh waters that do not contain too much lime. They often swarm in the acid water of peat bogs and the brown-stained water of swamps. They usually occur in still water, where they float about like miniature submarines, but sometimes they form a green film on the stones of swiftly flowing streams. They are, however, strictly fresh-water plants; there are no desmids in the sea.

Desmids are very beautiful indeed. They are always bright green in color but show an amazing variety of form and pattern. Some are shaped like rods, or ovals, or triangles, or even stars. Some, like *Closterium* (klos-TEER-i-um), look like crescents or archer's bows.

Whatever their shape, each desmid cell is made up of two identical halves. The cell has a clear band or often a constriction in the middle, within which lies the nucleus of the cell. Unlike the cells of the primitive blue-green algae, the single cells of the green algae, such as the desmids, do have a well-defined nucleus, and their chlorophyll is contained in bodies called plastids.

Desmids reproduce in two ways. Most often the cell simply

18

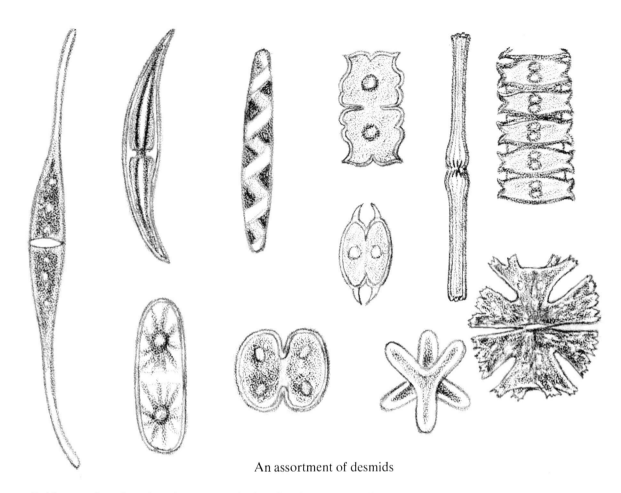

An assortment of desmids

divides at the clear band or constriction in the center. Each
half of the old cell receives a part of the nucleus and then just
develops into a new desmid plant. But at other times the contents of two desmid cells will unite to form a thick-walled
spore. After a period of rest, this spore germinates and produces two or more new desmid plants. This is really the most
primitive form of sexual reproduction, known as conjugation
(con-jew-GAY-shun).

Diatoms are jewel-like, also. But although they too, like
desmids, are a kind of one-celled green alga, they are rarely
green in color, because the green of their chlorophyll is masked

19

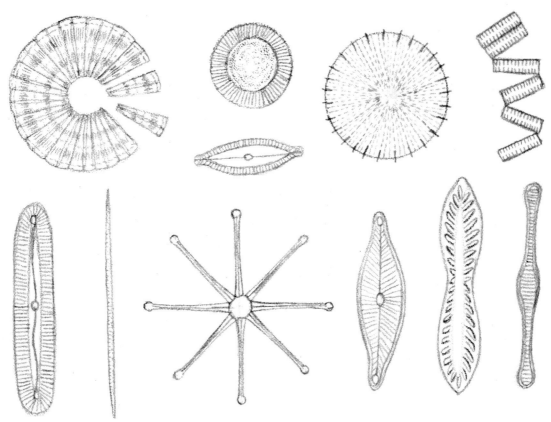

An assortment of diatoms

by a yellow pigment. Great masses of them sometimes tint stream beds a golden brown, and they sometimes form a slimy yellowish-brown coating on the stems and leaves of water plants, or cling to the hairs of aquatic insects. Some diatoms attach themselves to objects in the water by gelatinlike stalks, and others are held together by gelatinous bonds to form threads, ribbons, or branching colonies. Far more often, however, diatoms float about freely in the water. Unlike the desmids, diatoms do live in salt water—the sea is full of them.

The cell walls of diatoms are most unusual. They contain so much silica that they seem to be made of glass. Also, each cell wall has two separate halves. One half fits over the other like the lid of a box. Some diatoms look just like miniature pillboxes, but diatoms are found in many, many different boxlike shapes. Their silica shells often seem to be ornately sculptured with fine lines, dots, or grooves, and they, like the desmids, are extremely beautiful.

Like other single-celled algae, diatoms divide into two parts to reproduce, each part forming a new cell. But the two new diatom cells are not exactly the same, since one of them receives the old lid and the other the box. In both cases, the old part always becomes a lid for the new diatom and a new box is made to fit it. One of the new diatoms—the one made from the old box—is then, of course, smaller than its parent was. This could result in half of the diatom population becoming smaller and smaller with each division, but this doesn't happen, because the contents of two small diatom cells often escape their cell walls and unite to form a spore, which then develops into a full-sized diatom again.

Microscopic diatoms are among the most abundant of living things in the waters of the world. Much of the plankton of fresh-water lakes and ponds is made up of diatoms, and diatoms form at least six tenths of the plankton in the great "pastures" of the sea. And although diatoms are eaten in tremendous quantities by tiny aquatic animals, their number never seems to diminish. This is because of their remarkable ability to multiply rapidly. Biologists estimate that if the descendants of a single diatom all lived, there would be a hundred million of them at the end of one month!

The colorless silica shells of diatoms are just about indestructible. They are found abundantly, for instance, in the deposits of guano formed in the colonies of sea birds. The tiny diatoms were first eaten by minute sea animals, which were in turn eaten by the smallest fishes. The small fish were devoured by bigger fish, which were then eaten by the birds. After passing through such a series of stomachs, the diatom shells, unbelievable as it may seem, often still show their distinctive forms and markings.

Diatom shells continuously fall like fine snow to the bottoms of lakes, ponds, and the sea. They have been doing so for at least three to four hundred million years, and their accumulation on the floor of the sea is called diatomaceous (dy-a-tuh-MAY-shuss) ooze. Ages ago, many present-day land areas were covered by the sea, and in such places there are often thick beds of diatom shells known as diatomaceous earth. One large deposit is in California; it extends for hundreds of acres and is up to 1,400 feet deep. A single cubic inch of such diatomaceous earth may contain forty to fifty million diatom shells. Even though they are many millions of years old, their lovely, delicate sculpturing may still be seen under a microscope.

Today we put the shells of these ancient diatoms to many uses. Diatomaceous earth is used in the refining of sugar and in the purifying of antibiotics. It makes an excellent insulating material. And it goes into a variety of other products ranging from dynamite to paints, polishes, and scouring powders.

The real food makers of the world are not the land plants. Only certain cells in their leaves, and sometimes their stems, contain chlorophyll. The real food makers are the tiny diatoms and other microscopic algae of the plankton in the sea. Every cell of these plants is a chlorophyll-bearing, food-producing unit. Since they are distributed so uniformly in the sunlit water, they miss little of the sun's energy. Few land plants use as much as two percent of this energy; it has been estimated, in fact, that a field of corn uses only two thirds of one percent. But single-celled algae may utilize as much as twenty-five percent of the light energy that falls upon them to manufacture food.

The sea covers almost three quarters of the earth's surface; therefore about the same proportion of the solar energy that reaches the earth falls upon the sea. Further, the sea may well contain more than three quarters of the plant life of the world. Thus the sea offers a much greater opportunity for food production than do the land areas of the earth. Scientists have

22

estimated that land vegetation produces about forty billion tons of carbohydrates each year, by the process of photosynthesis. But diatoms and the other miscroscopic algae of the sea produce between three and four times as much. And since oxygen is a by-product of photosynthesis, they are also largely responsible for maintaining the oxygen content of our atmosphere.

Green Paint and Green Threads

During periods of cool wet weather, the trunks of trees, fence posts, the sides of unpainted buildings, stones, and even brick walls often suddenly turn a vivid green. No army of impish leprechauns has gone about the countryside with buckets of green paint and brushes. The redecorating has been done by one of the single-celled green algae known as *Pleurococcus* (plur-o-COCK-us).

When we scrape a bit of this bright green "paint" off and look at it through a microscope, it turns out to be a collection of plant cells. Many of them are quite round; others, like tiny green biscuits crowded together in a pan, are flattened where their sides touch.

Other green algae grow in water. But *Pleurococcus* is one of the plant pioneers, for all it needs is a little moisture in order to live and reproduce. Its cells have thick walls, which withstand a lot of drying. When the weather is dry they become dull in color and simply rest, and we do not even notice that they are there. Wet weather, though, stirs them into action, and they suddenly become a bright green and divide very rapidly to form many new cells. Algae very much like *Pleurococcus* may have colored the rocks green when life first ventured from the sea onto the land.

Some of the other one-celled green algae live in stranger

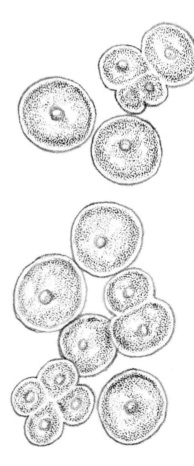

Pleurococcus

Part of a *Spirogyra* thread

places, such as the insides of animals. One of the hydras commonly found in our lakes and ponds is green in color because minute green algae live within its body cells. And some sea anemones, close relatives of the fresh-water hydras, look like many-petaled green flowers for the same reason. Some fresh-water sponges, too, owe their bright green color to the presence of algae.

Early in the spring, dense green mats of algae appear in pools and around the shores of ponds. Some people refer to them as "pond scum" or "frog spittle." They may be formed by several different species of threadlike green algae, but the most common ones are of the genus *Spirogyra* (spy-ro-JY-ra). Its filaments look like fine green hair or silk threads, so *Spirogyra* is sometimes called "pond silk" or "green silk." When we try to pick up the threads they slither between our fingers, because the thin, slimy, jellylike coating on each one makes them very slippery.

Next to a single cell, the simplest imaginable plant body is one in which cells are placed end to end to form a thread. And that is exactly what the plant body, or thallus, of *Spirogyra* and most other green algae is like. Through a microscope we can see that the *Spirogyra* thread is made up of many cells that resemble tall tin cans stacked end to end, with one or more chloroplasts in each cell. The chloroplasts look like spirally wound springs, and it is from them that the *Spirogyra* gets its name.

Sometimes, when two of the *Spirogyra* threads lie side by side and very close together, little bulges appear along the sides of the threads facing each other. The bulges grow until their tips meet, and then they form tubes connecting the cells of the two threads. Through these bridgelike tubes, the protoplasm of the cells of one of the *Spirogyra* plants moves across into the cells of the plant next to it. The protoplasm of the two joined cells unites, and thick-walled spores are then formed. In the end there will be a spore in practically every cell of one plant,

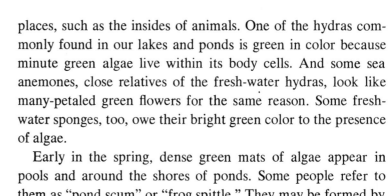

Germinating spore of *Spirogyra*

24

which is considered to be the female parent. The other one, the so-called male parent, ends up as nothing but a string of empty cells. But by this time, in any case, both of the parents are dead.

The spores, however, may live over winter in the mucky bottom of the pond, and when spring comes again each one may grow into a new *Spirogyra* thread. If the pond goes dry, they can wait until the rains come again. Then they will germinate and form the familiar green threads.

Like all green plants, *Spirogyra* makes food for itself—sugars and starches—during the hours of daylight. On sunny days the green mats of *Spirogyra* tend to float near the surface of the water, buoyed up by a multitude of bubbles caught in the tangled threads. These are bubbles of oxygen, a waste product of the food-making process. After sunset, when food-making stops, no more bubbles of oxygen appear, and the mats of *Spirogyra* sink lower in the water.

Each *Spirogyra* mat is a little community in itself. It is a splendid feeding ground and hiding place for tadpoles and small fishes, snails, and aquatic insects. These can all be seen, but there are also desmids and diatoms and a host of animals too small to see without a microscope. The oxygen given off by the green plants is used by the animals in breathing. And the animals give off carbon dioxide, a raw material the plants need to make food.

Another alga which may form floating masses of "pond scum" is called *Oedogonium* (ee-doe-GO-nee-um). Various kinds of *Oedogonium* are common in the quiet waters of ponds and ditches, and some of the larger species have threads like those of *Spirogyra,* except that they are usually coarser and much less slippery. Some species are so small that they appear as a fuzzy coating on objects submerged in the water.

Oedogonium plants have two methods of reproduction, one quite simple, the other rather complex.

Sometimes a large spore, with a halolike ring of short hairs or cilia (SILL-i-a) around one end, will form in the cells of the

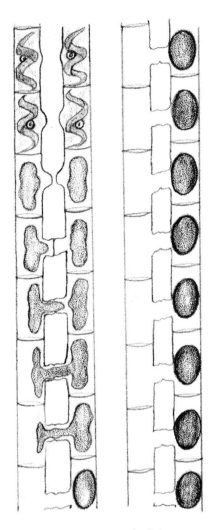

Formation of spores in *Spirogyra*

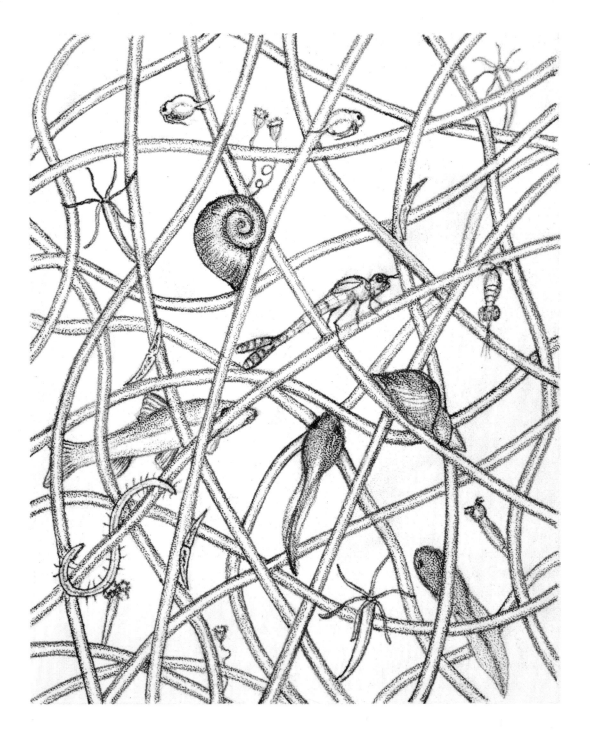

Many plants and animals live among the *Spirogyra* threads.

Oedogonium threads. After escaping and swimming about for a while, these spores settle down and grow into new threads. Since the spores have come from a single parent, this is not considered to be sexual reproduction.

But *Oedogonium* also reproduces sexually, in a more advanced manner than does *Spirogyra*. In some of the cells a solitary large body called an *egg* is produced. Other cells, in the same plant or in different plants, produce pairs of smaller bodies called *sperms,* which have rings of cilia and are active little swimmers. In some species of *Oedogonium* there is a great difference in size between the female plants which produce the eggs and the male plants which produce the sperms. The male plants are mere dwarfs and often seem to be only little branches on the much larger female plants.

Eventually one of the swimming sperms finds its way through an opening in the wall of the cell containing the egg, and the contents of the two cells combine. Such a union between a male and a female germ cell, or egg and sperm, is called *fertilization*. In the case of *Oedogonium* it results in the formation of a thick-walled spore.

The spore resulting from fertilization of the egg does not grow directly into a new *Oedogonium* thread. Instead, its contents divide into four smaller spores, each with a ring of cilia around one end. For a time these spores swim about actively, but eventually they settle down, lose their cilia, and grow into new *Oedogonium* plants.

Vaucheria (vaw-KAIR-i-a) is another of the green algae often found in ponds or wayside ditches. Its branching threads frequently form very dense patches on mud flats. One kind can be found in greenhouses, where it forms the "green felt" noticed on flowerpots and damp benches.

Vaucheria is very different from any of the other algae with threadlike thalli, such as *Spirogyra* or *Oedogonium*. If we examine its threads under a microscope, we see why. Its crooked, branched threads are like tubes, because there are no cross

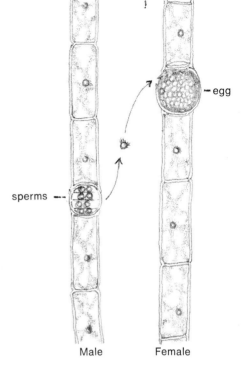

egg

sperms

Male   Female

Sexual reproduction in *Oedogonium*

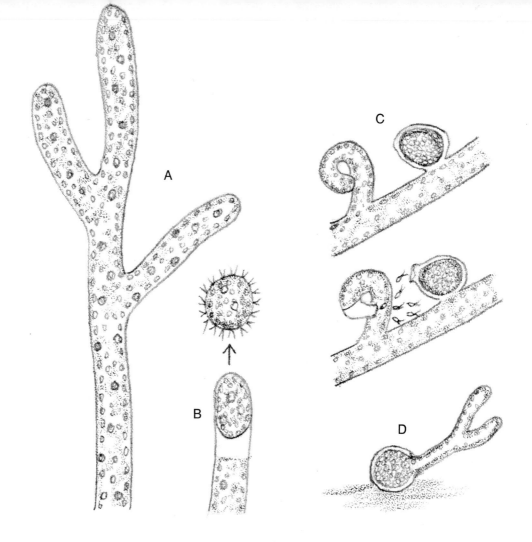

Vaucheria

A. Portion of a filament. B. Formation of asexual spore at the tip of a branch. C. Organs for sexual reproduction. D. Spore resulting from fertilized egg begins to grow into a new filament.

walls separating the cells. The cell protoplasm contains many nuclei and also a large number of little chloroplast disks.

Sometimes a wall cuts off the tips of *Vaucheria* branches. Within the space formed, a large round or oval spore is made, intensely green in color. These spores are just a bit of the parent plant, with many nuclei and chloroplasts in their pro-

28

toplasm and as many pairs of tiny cilia on the outside as the number of nuclei within. Eventually they break through the tips of the branches of the parent plant and go swimming away. After a time, they settle down and grow into new *Vaucheria* plants.

Vaucheria, however, can also reproduce sexually. When it does, little jug-shaped structures appear on some very short branches, and in each one there is a single large egg. Other short branches, either on the same plant or on different plants, have special organs which produce a large number of tiny sperms. After the egg is fertilized by one of the swimming sperms, it develops into a spore. The spore rests a while and then grows into a new *Vaucheria* plant.

Green algae are such essential food makers that without them no aquatic animals, including the fish, could exist. It is possible, however, to have too much of a good thing. Today our lakes and streams are threatened with death, and this situation involves the algae.

Nitrates and phosphates are highly essential plant nutrients, and they are as necessary for the growth of algae as for that of any other plants. They have always been present in natural waters in small amounts, but now man has vastly increased these amounts through pollution. Fertilizers washed away from cultivated fields account for some of the increase, and a great deal more is added by sewage, full of the phosphates used in detergents, and by other wastes which we dump into the waters. This extra material has been a feast for the algae, and as a result their growth has been excessive and unnatural.

When we are told that many of our lakes, and Lake Erie in particular, are suffering from eutrophication (yew-troff-i-KAY-shun), this means that the natural balance of life in their waters has been upset by overnourished algae. The algae have become so well fed that they grow abnormally fast; they populate the waters so densely that sunlight cannot penetrate to the plants in the deeper layers, and these plants then die and decay. Decay uses up oxygen. When the water is robbed of its oxygen, it cannot support animal life, including, of course, the fish.

Unfortunately, this is just the beginning of a sad story. Ponds and lakes are only temporary features of the landscape. They eventually fill up with sediment carried into them by streams and with the remains of plants growing in or invading the water. They then become swamps or bogs and finally a part of the land. Like most natural processes, this transition is a very slow one, requiring many thousands, or even hundreds of thousands, of years to complete. But now, through pollution, we are hastening the aging of many lakes, including even the Great Lakes. We are shortening the time it will take for them to become swamps.

The Seaweeds: Green, Brown, and Red

On the land most of the larger plants are seed plants, but there are no seed plants in the sea. In the sea all of the larger plants—the seaweeds—are seedless. They are the largest and most complex of all the algae. They belong to groups of green algae, brown algae, and red algae.

Aside from the tiny one-celled flagellates and diatoms, very few of the salt-water algae are green algae. *Ulva*—the sea lettuce—is perhaps the most familiar of the larger green algae found in the sea. Its cells do not form threads, as do the cells of the fresh-water green algae, but thin sheets, a few inches wide and several inches long. *Ulva* plants usually grow attached to rocks and pilings close to the shore. When they are torn loose by the waves and tossed up on the beach, they look very much like pieces of lettuce leaves. In Japan this sea lettuce is often gathered and used for food, and along our Atlantic coast it is an important part of the diet of wintering flocks of wild waterfowl.

All of the brown algae live in the sea. They are olive green to dark brown in color because they have a brown pigment which masks the green of their chlorophyll.

Kelps are among the best known of the brown algae. They grow attached to rocks by what seem to be roots but are actually massive holdfasts. And they have what seems to be a long slender stem which expands into a sort of blade that seems to be a leaf. This fairly complicated plant body is, however, merely a thallus, for algae do not have real roots, or stems, or leaves. At high tide the leaflike blade floats on the surface of the water, buoyed up by air in the hollow "stem" or in well-developed air bladders.

Some of the kelps are only a few feet long, but there are giants among them which are as long as trees are tall. However, these huge plants are mostly water, for when one of them is dried it weighs only a few pounds. Kelp plants are harvested by man, dried, and then burned to obtain potash and iodine from their ashes. A ton of air-dried kelp yields about five hundred pounds of potash salts and approximately three pounds of iodine. Farmers have often used the ground kelp plants as fertilizer, and, more recently, ground kelp called "seaweed meal" has been added to livestock fodder.

Anyone who has been to the seashore has seen the *Fucus* (FEW-kus), or Rockweed. This brown alga grows abundantly on rocks between the high- and low-tide lines, clinging to the rocks with holdfasts. When the tide comes in and covers the rocks, the plants float. When the tide goes out and they are exposed to the hot sun and the drying winds, they hang limply over the rocks. With the next high tide they will float again on the water, as good as they ever were.

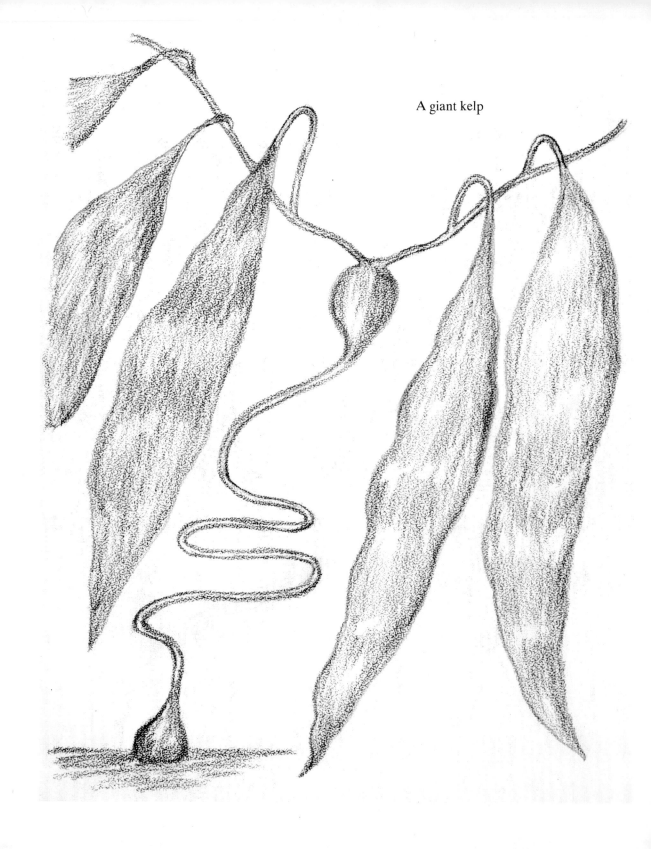

A giant kelp

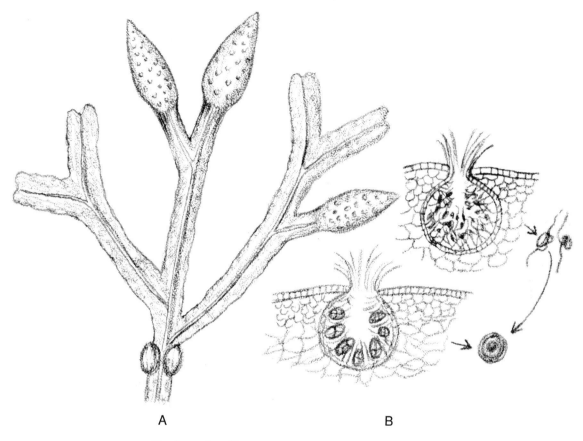

Rockweed or *Fucus*
A. Plant. B. Details of reproductive organs.

The thallus of *Fucus* is ribbonlike, flattened, and forking. Along it there are usually several swollen oval bladders filled with air. Its branches often have egg-shaped tips, in which there are numerous little pits. Within these pits are quite complex sex organs.

Another well-known brown alga is the *Sargassum* (sar-GAS-sum), or Gulfweed. Sometimes it, too, grows attached to rocks, but more often it floats freely in the water. It might be taken for a land plant with branches bearing leaves and berries, but the "branches" and "leaves" are merely parts of a thallus, and the "berries" are actually spore-bearing structures.

Sargassum

North of the West Indies there is a great eddy in the ocean where the water is covered, for hundreds of square miles, with a dense floating mass of *Sargassum*. This is the legendary Sargasso Sea. Within it dwell many strange aquatic animals, such as the Sargassum fish and the Sargassum crab. And it is here that female eels come, from both North America and Europe, to lay their eggs and then die.

The red algae have a red pigment masking their green chlorophyll. A few of the red algae live in fresh waters, but most of them live in the sea. They are abundant in cool waters, but they reach the peak of their development in the warm waters of the tropics, especially in places where they are

34

never exposed by the tides. Many even thrive at depths barely penetrated by sunlight, where most of the red end of the light spectrum has already been absorbed in the waters above. The red pigment in their cells makes it possible for them to make use of even the faint rays of light filtering down to their place of abode.

One of the best known of the red algae is a seaweed called Irish moss, which forms great beds along the rocky coasts of the North Atlantic. It is not especially nutritious, but for a long time people have used it for making soups, and when it is boiled with milk and sugar it makes a sort of jelly which is quite an acceptable dessert. Carrageenin often appears in the list of ingredients in cottage cheese and other foods. It, too, is derived from Irish moss.

Some other very useful products are derived from seaweeds. One of them is agar-agar, or simply agar, a gelatinlike substance obtained from certain red algae growing in the warmer waters of the Pacific. Agar is an important ingredient in the culture media used to grow bacteria and other fungi in laboratories, and it is also used medicinally. Oriental cooks put agar into soups and jellies, and it is sometimes used in making gumdrops and similar candies. Algin, obtained from a variety of seaweeds, including the kelps, is used to size and finish fabrics, as a stabilizer in ice cream and chocolate milk, and sometimes in making candies, jelly, cake frostings, and pastries.

The seaweeds are not only the largest but structurally the most complex of all the algae. They also have very advanced means of reproduction. Yet it was not the more developed seaweed but the simple small green algae of the fresh waters that evolved into higher forms of seedless plants and, eventually, into true seed plants. The seaweeds followed what has turned out to be a dead-end road. No higher plant developed from them.

Irish moss

The Fungi

LIKE ALGAE, the fungi are thallus plants. They have neither roots, nor stems, nor leaves. Botanists believe that they developed from some kinds of algae, for fungi and algae are alike in many ways.

Some time in the past, the plants which became fungi lost their green chlorophyll. A plant without chlorophyll cannot make food for itself. It must therefore get its living much as animals do: it must depend, directly or indirectly, on green plants for its food.

Some fungi are parasites (PAR-a-sites) and grow on or within other living things. They obtain their nourishment at the expense of their host and give nothing in return; in fact they very often kill their host. Other fungi are saprophytes (SAP-ro-fytes) and live upon the dead remains of other plants or animals. In some cases fungi have formed partnerships with other living things. Such a relationship between two living things, which is beneficial to both fungi and host, is known as symbiosis (sim-be-O-sis).

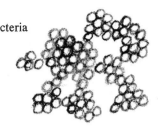

The Tiny Bacteria, Smallest of the Small

Bacteria are not only the tiniest of the fungi, they are the smallest of all known living things. The largest of them measure about 1/250 of an inch. The smallest are only about a thousandth as big and cannot be seen without a very powerful microscope. Thousands of them can occupy a single drop of water without being crowded for space, and many millions may be present in a teaspoonful of sour milk.

Each bacterium is only a single cell. Some bacteria are shaped like tiny rods, or minute balls. Others are curved, or twisted, or coiled something like a corkscrew. Some have cilia to help them move about.

Most bacteria are colorless, but some have purplish, reddish, or even greenish pigments—but not, of course, chlorophyll.

Bacteria resemble the blue-green algae in several ways, and may well have evolved from them. Like the blue-green algae, they have no well-defined nuclei in their cells. They too reproduce by a very simple cell division. When conditions are favorable, a bacterium may divide every half-hour or so. If the division took place only once an hour and if all of the new bacteria lived, a single bacterium would have nearly seventeen million descendants at the end of twenty-four hours. By the end of another twenty-four hours their number would total about 281 billion!

It is difficult to find a place where there are no bacteria. They are present in the air, in water, and in the soil—and even inside of us. Bacteria will thrive wherever there is food, adequate moisture, and an optimum temperature, all of which vary from species to species. Of course there are places which are not very favorable for the growth of bacteria, and in these places their numbers do not increase. Objects which are sterilized are free of living bacteria—until they are exposed again to sources of contamination.

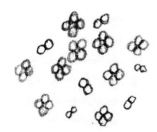

Cocci

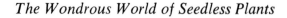

When conditions for growth become unfavorable, bacteria sometimes form thick-walled spores. Such spores are able to endure conditions which would quickly kill bacteria cells in their ordinary form. Spores can often withstand prolonged exposure to disinfecting chemicals, extreme dryness, and very low or very high temperatures. Some of these spores have survived as much as sixteen hours of constant boiling. When conditions for growth become favorable again, they discard their heavy cell walls and once more become active bacteria.

Most people think of bacteria as being invisible little demons that lurk in filthy places and cause diseases, and some of them do. It is bacteria that give us pneumonia, tuberculosis, diphtheria, scarlet fever, tetanus, and many other diseases. Bacteria also make us suffer from sore throats, boils, and cavities in our teeth. They can spoil food and even give us food poisoning. Fortunately, not very many of the bacteria which cause diseases form very resistant spores.

Bacteria also cause diseases of animals other than man. And although most plant diseases are caused by the higher fungi, bacteria are responsible for some of the plant ailments. The destructive "fire blight" of apple, pear, and quince trees, for example, is a bacterial disease. Another is the bacterial wilt of cucumbers, squashes, and melons.

Bacteria have also played a role in the much publicized "mercury problem." In recent years, high concentrations of mercury have been found in both fresh- and salt-water fish, and it has led to the banning of commercial and sport fishing in many lakes and rivers. Ninety percent of the swordfish and between five and ten percent of the tuna were found to have mercury levels far above the permissible level in food fish. All of a sudden the mercury problem alarmed ecologists and the general public throughout the world, for in most forms, mercury is poisonous. Like DDT it tends to become concentrated in the bodies of animals, and in humans it accumulates in the brain and destroys its tissues.

How do bacteria come into this problem? In 1967, scientists

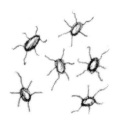

Bacilli

discovered that certain bacteria were able to convert inorganic mercury into an organic compound which is highly toxic. The bacteria are eaten by tiny aquatic organisms which form the food of small fish. The small fish in turn are eaten by larger fish. Predators such as pike and bass in fresh waters, and swordfish and tuna in the sea, are at the end of a long food chain and tend to have high concentrations of these persistent poisons.

Not all bacteria, however, are our enemies. Some are mankind's most useful servants.

Our caveman ancestors discovered that meat became tenderer and tasted better if an animal carcass was allowed to hang for a while before it was eaten. They had no idea why this was so, but we know now that bacteria break down the muscle fibers as the meat ages, and so we let our steaks age, too, before we eat them.

And bacteria assist us in many other ways. We need their services when we make cheese, vinegar, and sauerkraut, when we get the fibers out of flax plants to make linen, and when we produce leather from the hides of animals. They give butter its color and flavor and cause milk to sour, making possible such products as buttermilk, cottage cheese, and yogurt. Some of the bacteria which live in our intestinal tracts even help us to digest our food. Certain bacteria bring about the decay of organic matter. Often we think of them as foes, and in some cases they may be. But such bacteria help us to get rid of sewage and other wastes, and they play a most important role in the ecology of the world. In fact, without them we could not exist at all.

Think for a moment what the earth would be like if the dead remains of plants and animals did *not* decay. We would not even be here, for ages ago the surface of the earth would have become choked with this debris. Life on earth would have ceased to exist, not only for lack of room, but because the nutrients necessary to sustain life would have become locked up in the undecayed remains.

Spirilla

Bacteria and other organisms which feed upon dead organic matter and bring about its decay have prevented this from happening. They are constantly breaking down such matter and changing it into simpler chemical substances which are then returned to the soil and to the air. These elements are used over and over again by new living things, and it is only through such continuous recycling of nutrients that life has been able to continue on our planet.

Nitrogen is an absolutely essential nutrient; green plants must have it in order to live and grow. Nitrogen is needed to make proteins, which are essential building blocks in all living protoplasm. Yet, although about four-fifths of the earth's atmosphere is composed of gaseous nitrogen, plants are unable to use it as a gas. It has to be combined with other elements into chemical compounds called nitrates, which dissolve in the soil water and can then be absorbed by plant roots.

Certain bacteria are able to take nitrogen gas from the air surrounding particles of soil and change it into nitrates. They are called nitrogen-fixing bacteria. Some are free in the soil, but others live within little lumps or nodules on the roots of plants of the pea family, such as clovers, vetches, locust trees, peas, and beans. The bacteria are housed and nourished by the plants, but the plants get a great deal in return—the all-important usable nitrates. Farmers often plant legumes, or plants of the pea family, and plow them under to help enrich the soil.

Other bacteria present in the soil reverse this process. They break down nitrogen compounds and return free nitrogen to the atmosphere. Thus the supply of gaseous nitrogen in the earth's atmosphere is constantly being renewed. Scientists tell us that if this important part of the nitrogen cycle were to be broken, the supply of nitrogen in the air would eventually be depleted. It would probably be replaced by poisonous, suffocating ammonia gas.

The widespread use of chemical poisons to control insect

Plant of garden pea with nodules containing bacteria on its roots

The nitrogen cycle

A. Green plants. B. Plant-eating animals. C. Flesh-eating animals. D. Organic material decayed by bacteria. E. Nitrifying bacteria. F. Denitrifying bacteria release free nitrogen into the air. G. Nitrogen-fixing bacteria in soil and in nodules on roots of legumes. H. Free nitrogen of the air is combined with oxygen by lightning and carried to the soil by rain and snow.

pests is causing much concern, since they endanger other living things too, including man himself. DDT and other persistent chemical pesticides tend to build up in the bodies of animals. By now they have contaminated the environment in even the remotest parts of the world. Even the safest of such poisons are not very selective, for they kill insect friends and foes alike. For this reason, conservationists and other concerned people are urging a greater emphasis on biological controls, that is, the use of natural enemies to control harmful insects. One of such natural enemies is bacterial diseases.

The bacteria which cause diseases in insects are usually highly selective, attacking only certain species of insects. For instance, one of these bacterial diseases destroys only the larvae of the Japanese beetle. It is called the "milky disease," because when the grubs are infected by the bacteria their blood has a milky appearance. When the grubs die, bacteria from their bodies remain in the soil, infecting other Japanese beetle grubs and spreading the disease. This disease does control the Japanese beetle, but it does not harm other beneficial insects, other animals, or man.

Scientists are working on other biological controls, which they hope will someday replace our extremely dangerous pesticides. Already a bacterial preparation has been found which is effective in helping to control the gypsy moth, and others will no doubt be found in the near future.

Bacteria may shortly be helping us to solve another environmental problem, that of cleaning up the oil spills that all too frequently plague the earth's waters. Certain kinds of bacteria have been found which are oil eaters. Now scientists are planning to mass-produce these bacteria and freeze-dry them. When an oil spill occurs, they will be sprayed over the area by a helicopter or airplane. When their oily food supply is depleted, the bacteria will either die off or be eaten by other organisms. The nicest part about this procedure is that these bacteria are absolutely harmless to man and other animal life.

Yeasts and Molds: Little Enemies, Little Servants

Long ago man discovered that fruit juices, if left exposed to the air, made an intoxicating drink. The ancient Greeks believed that the wine they made from grape juice was a gift from their god Dionysus. The early Romans thought that their wine was a gift from their wine god Bacchus. All one had to do was to leave fruit juices exposed to the air and the gods would make them ferment and produce alcohol.

What really brought about this change remained a mystery for a long time. It was not until 1857 that Louis Pasteur finally convinced the scientific world that fermentation is caused by yeast, tiny unseen plants which are constantly floating about in the air.

We can see these minute yeast plants through a microscope. Each one is just a single oval or roundish cell. Often the cells have knobs of various sizes on them, which are called buds. As the buds grow larger, they break away from the parent cell to form new yeast plants. When they have sufficient warmth, moisture, and food, yeast plants multiply rapidly. When conditions are not so favorable they form resting spores.

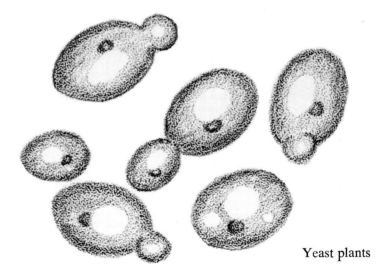

Yeast plants

Yeast plants may cause fruits and poorly sealed jars of preserves to spoil, but they are our servants in many ways. They feed upon sugar, changing it into alcohol and the gas carbon dioxide. Bubbles of carbon dioxide gas cause fruit juices to fizz as they ferment.

When yeast plants get into sweet apple juice, or cider, they cause it to ferment. The sugar is changed into alcohol and carbon dioxide, and we say that the cider becomes "hard." At this stage certain bacteria take over, feeding on the alcohol and changing it into acetic (a-SEE-tick) acid. Then we no longer have apple juice or hard cider either. What we have is vinegar.

We use yeast to make bread because the bubbles of carbon dioxide become trapped in the dough and cause it to rise. The alcohol produced in bread by fermenting yeast is driven off during baking and accounts for much of the delicious aroma about a bakery. Yeast plants are also used in the production of medicinal and industrial alcohol from grains, or from sugar derived from wood through a process known as hydrolysis (hy-DROLL-i-sis).

Mankind has long regarded molds as being among his foes. Molds do, indeed, attack anything of animal or vegetable origin. Some form greenish-blue patches on fruits like oranges and lemons. Some appear on cured meats, such as bacon and ham. Sometimes cloth, paper, or leather become moldy, and we are angry when things we are fond of are spoiled by mold. Molds or their spores can also cause diseases of the respiratory tract in birds, cattle, and man.

There are molds in our waters, too, which sometimes cause a cottony white growth on the fins and tails of living fish. When the molds get into the gills of the fish, the fish die. But the water molds also feed on the remains of dead insects and other water animals, helping to break them down, and in this respect the water molds are useful.

Molds, in fact, are not always our enemies. Some molds give

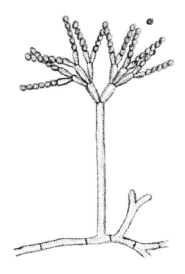

A blue mold: *Penicillium*

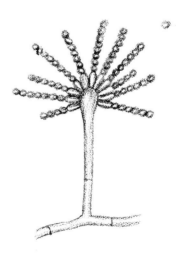

A green mold: *Aspergillus*

45

different kinds of cheeses their special flavors. One mold changes sugar into citric acid, a very useful chemical. Molds are the source of antibiotics, such as penicillin, which have helped to conquer many of the diseases of mankind and his domestic animals.

To see what molds are really like, suppose we examine a bit of moldy bread through a microscope. The cobwebby white mass on the bread turns out to be a tangle of separate threads or filaments. They look very much like the threads of some of the green algae, but they have no chlorophyll. These threads make up the plant body of the mold—as well as that of most

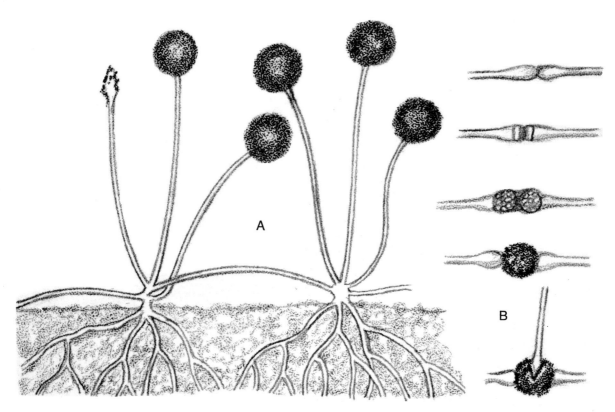

The bread mold
A. Plant producing spores. B. Formation of sexual spores.

other kinds of fungi. They are collectively called the mycelium (my-SEEL-i-um). The mycelium of the bread mold has branches which grow throughout the piece of bread, feeding upon its sugars and starches.

In time greenish or blackish patches appear on the bread. Through the microscope we see that they are made up of little stalks, each one bearing a ball at the top. The balls are spore cases, and they are full of exceedingly tiny dark-colored spores. When the walls of the spore cases break, the spores are released and go floating away on the air. Sometimes the tips of short branches of the mold threads meet, and then the contents of the end cells unite to form another kind of spore. This is a sexual spore similar to those formed by conjugation in *Spirogyra*.

Molds are very much like some of the green algae, both in structure and in their manner of reproducing. As a matter of fact, botanists believe that molds evolved from green algae. At some long-ago point in time, the algae lost their green chlorophyll and became dependent upon other living things for their food.

Mushrooms and "Toadstools"

Mushrooms are familiar to all of us. We find these fungi springing up from the lawn and in pasture fields. We see them among the fallen leaves on the forest floor and on decaying logs and stumps. They even grow on living trees. They seem, sometimes, to appear overnight, and then, often, within a few days they are gone. But where do they come from? And where do they go?

Actually, the mushrooms we see are only a part of the mushroom plant; they are only the fruiting structures which produce

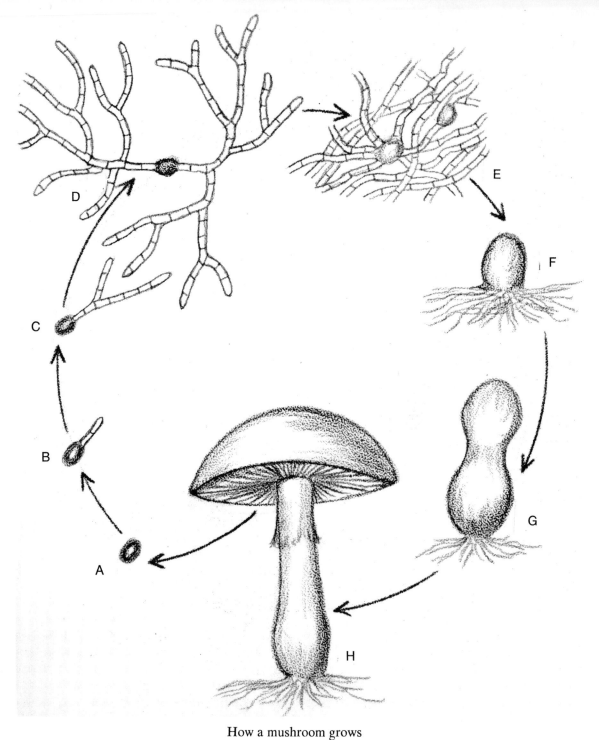

How a mushroom grows

A. A spore. B. The spore germinates. C & D. Growth of the mycelium. E. Formation of mushrooms. F. The "button" forms. G. Mushroom as it first appears above ground. H. Mature mushroom ready to shed spores.

spores. The rest of these plants are hidden from our view, among decaying matter in the ground, within the rotting wood of logs and stumps, or in the wood of the living tree. Turn over a sodden mass of fallen leaves, or tear apart a decaying log, and you will see them. They are cobwebby or often cordlike masses of extremely fine and usually whitish threads. These mycelium threads are made up of cells placed end to end. The mycelia are not very impressive, but they are the real mushroom plants.

Little lumps the size of pinheads may be seen on the mycelia. They grow larger and larger, and will finally appear as "button" mushrooms. Mushrooms do not really grow overnight, as some people think. Most of their growth takes place where it cannot be seen—beneath the ground or within decaying wood. It is true, however, that once mushrooms appear in the open they increase in size rapidly, the buttons expanding into full-sized mushrooms in a very short time. This is largely due to their intake of water, which is why mushrooms appear so quickly after a soaking rain.

Mushrooms are very fragile, but as they grow they can exert amazing pressure. They sometimes lift up stones, and they have even been known to break asphalt or concrete paving. Occasionally, the cellar floor of a new house is laid on top of mushroom mycelia which are buried in the ground. When this happens the homeowner may be astonished to see mushrooms coming up through the floor.

Many familiar mushrooms are shaped like open umbrellas. They have a stalk topped with an expanded portion called a cap. Hanging from the underside of the cap, and radiating about the stalk like the spokes of a wheel, many mushrooms have gills. These are thin, delicate plates covered with a layer of microscopic club-shaped filaments, each of which usually has four spores at its tip.

Instead of gills, some mushrooms have pores. Such mush-

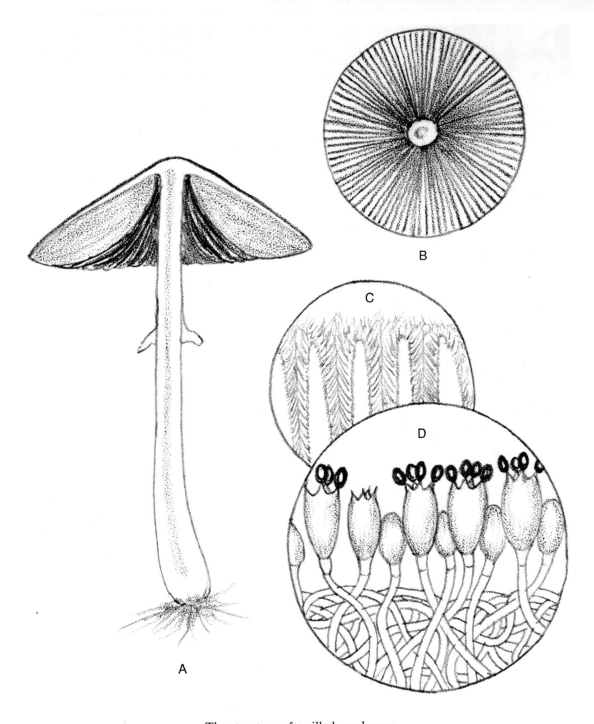

The structure of a gilled mushroom
A. Cross section showing gills. B. Bottom view of gills. C. Magnified cross section
of a few of the gills. D. Highly magnified portion of a gill showing stalks bearing
spores.

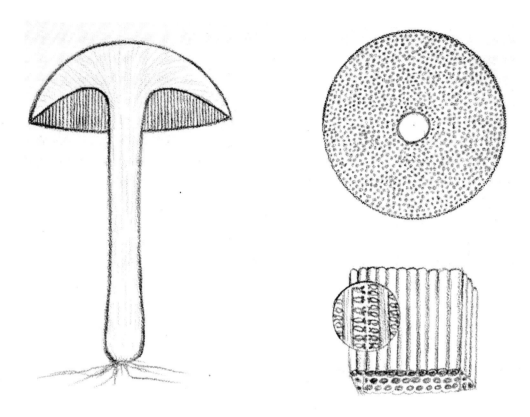

Structure of a pore fungus

rooms are called pore fungi. Their caps are made up of a great many very fine tubes, the open ends of which look like pores on the underside of the cap. Their spores are produced in groups of fours on tiny clubs which line the insides of the tubes.

The spores of mushrooms may be pink, brown, purple, black, or even white. They are so minute that it would take a great many of them laid side by side to equal the width of a human hair. However, a mass of them can be seen with the naked eye and can be used to make what is called a spore print.

If you would like to make a spore print, simply cut the cap off a fully grown gilled mushroom, place it bottom side down on a piece of unglazed white paper, and cover it with a tumbler or bowl. After several hours, carefully remove the tumbler and

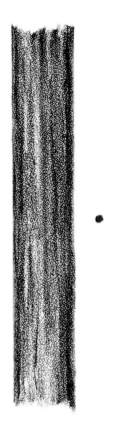

Comparison between a magnified human hair (left) and a magnified mushroom spore (right)

lift up the mushroom cap. If the mushroom has dark-colored spores, you will have a spore print on the paper. (If the mushroom has white or very pale spores, you will have to use a piece of dark or black paper.) If you wish to keep the spore print, spray it carefully with the kind of fixative artists use to protect pencil or charcoal drawings. Mycologists (my-KOLL-o-jists), the people who make a serious study of fungi, find that spore prints are very useful in identifying many kinds of mushrooms.

Is there a difference between a mushroom and a "toadstool"? Is it true that mushrooms are good to eat and that "toadstools" are poisonous? Mycologists make no such distinction, for they call them all mushrooms. But many are safe and quite edible. Others are rather unpalatable or unwholesome. A few are deadly poisonous.

Caution, those who like mushrooms and intend to gather some for dinner: make sure that you have learned how to identify the various kinds of mushrooms and that what you are gathering is safe to eat. The best way, of course, is to go afield with an expert. If you cannot do this, the next best thing is to get a good book on the identification of mushrooms and study it. With a little effort you should be able to recognize most of the commoner safe ones and avoid the unwholesome ones and the killers. Be careful, though; only mature mushrooms—not those in the button stage—can be used for certain identification.

Never rely on the so-called "tests" that many claim will distinguish a mushroom from a "toadstool." There is no truth in the belief that only poisonous mushrooms will blacken a silver coin or spoon. Neither is there a bit of truth in the notion that a mushroom is safe to eat if its cap can be peeled. Actually the caps of some of the most poisonous ones are as easy to peel as those of the best edible mushrooms. Poisonous mushrooms may smell just as good as the non-poisonous ones.

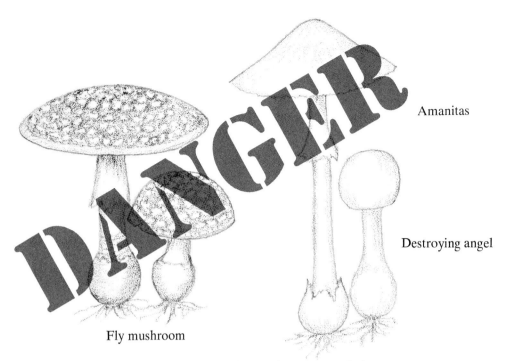

Amanitas

Destroying angel

Fly mushroom

Color is not a reliable guide either, for some of the most highly colored mushrooms are safe to eat. And don't think that mushrooms are safe for your dinner just because insects or other animals have been eating them.

The most deadly poisonous mushrooms are found among the *Amanitas* (am-an-EYE-tus), and the worst of it is that they look very attractive! They are tall mushrooms with a ragged-edged veil on the upper part of the stem and a pronounced swelling or cuplike structure—the "death cup"—at the base. One very common one is often called the fly mushroom. It has a big cap, yellow and often orange-red in the center and thickly sprinkled with whitish, warty scales. Another, called the destroying angel, is pure white, and its cap resembles the hats worn by Chinese coolies. Virtually all of the deaths from mushroom poisoning are caused by *Amanitas,* and the destroying angel rates as the most deadly of them all. They are mushrooms that every mushroom hunter should know and avoid.

One of the commonest of the edible mushrooms and one of the easiest to recognize is the meadow mushroom. It grows

Meadow mushroom

Two of the common puffballs

on our lawns and in pasture fields, but never in the woods. It is a squat little mushroom with a whitish to brownish cap and pink gills, which eventually become a dark chocolate brown. There is no noticeable swelling at the base of its short stem, and merely a little ring above. The meadow mushroom is a favorite of mushroom hunters. It is very much like the species of mushroom which is grown commercially in specially constructed mushroom houses, and which we buy fresh or canned at the store.

If you would like to try growing your own mushrooms, you can buy "mushroom spawn" from many seed houses. This spawn is really just a mass of mushroom mycelia, along with some of the organic matter upon which it grows. To grow mushrooms successfully, you need a well-ventilated place with a temperature between 50 and 65 degrees, and a relative humidity of about 80. Darkness is not absolutely essential, but it is desirable.

Puffballs are certainly among the easiest of all the mushrooms to recognize, and as long as they are firm inside and as white as cottage cheese, they are all good to eat. As a puffball ages, its flesh becomes yellowish, and it ends up as a brownish, dry, dusty mass of threads and spores. Perhaps you have stepped on dried puffballs to see them puff into "smoke." The "smoke," of course, is really spores, literally billions of them.

The champion of the puffballs is the giant puffball, ten to twenty or more inches across, and looking for all the world like an old-fashioned round loaf of bread. One of them may contain as many as seven trillion spores! Very few, however, of each million or more spores are successful in producing new puffball plants, since most of them are not fortunate enough to alight in places suitable for their growth.

Earthstars and bird's nest fungi are interesting relatives of the puffballs. When young, an earthstar looks like one of the smaller kinds of puffballs, except that it is usually pointed at its top. Later its thick outer covering splits from top to base into five or more pointed segments, which spread open to form the star. In the center is a roundish body like a little puffball, with a small hole at the top through which the spores escape. When the weather is wet, the points of the star are spread widely apart. When it is dry, they close up around the little round body in the center. You can look for earthstars in sandy open woods during the summer months.

Bird's nest fungi look very much like miniature bird nests, complete with a set of tiny eggs. Some are shaped like cups; others have stalks and resemble tiny sherbet glasses or goblets not more than half an inch tall. The small "eggs" within them are really like miniature puffballs and are full of spores. Colonies of these curious fungi may appear on the ground or on rotting wood between early spring and late fall.

Earthstars (open and closed)   Bird's-nest fungi

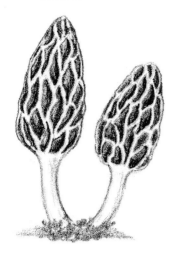

Common morel

In early spring, and sometimes in the late fall, you may come across a very strange-looking mushroom in some old apple orchard or in open woodland where the ground is carpeted with grass. It has a dingy yellow or tawny cap so deeply pitted that it looks like a sponge growing on a stalk. This mushroom is bound to be a morel (mo-RELL). The morels belong to a group known as the sac-fungi, because their spores are produced within club-shaped sacs instead of on club-shaped stalks. The irregular pits in the caps of the morels are lined with these sacs. Anyone who really knows mushrooms will tell you that morels are among the most delicious of all to eat.

Morels are not particularly beautiful, but if you take a stroll through the woods you may come across fungi which are quite spectacular. On decaying logs you may find growths only a few inches tall, with an intricate maze of upright branches of white, pinkish, lavender, or yellow. These are the coral mushrooms, and they are truly lovely.

Some late summer or fall, if you are fortunate, you may see masses of bear's-head hydnum (HID-num) growing on the

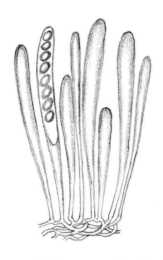

Sacs containing spores line the pits
in the caps of morels.

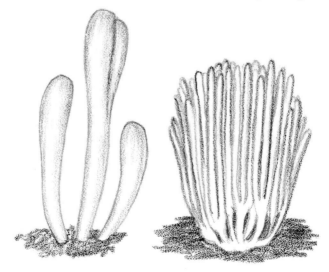

Two types of coral fungi

Bear's-head hydnum

side of a moss-covered log. At a distance it might almost be a patch of snow, but at arm's length it looks just like a miniature frozen waterfall, with tier upon tier of delicate, drooping, milky-white icicles.

For ages man has been fascinated by the rings of mushrooms which appear in grassy places. Some people once believed that the mushrooms marked the places where fairies had danced in circles. The early scientists, of course, discounted such a foolish and superstitious explanation. *They* thought that the rings appeared where bolts of lightning had struck the ground, or else they were due to whirlwinds, or perhaps the activities of ants or moles, or even the presence of haystacks. It was not until the latter part of the eighteenth century that an English botanist discovered that the rings were really caused by fungi growing in the ground.

A "fairy ring" begins when a mushroom plant starts to grow. As its mycelium uses up the nutrients in the soil, it steadily spreads outward and thus forms a ring. Each year, as

The fairy-ring mushroom

the mycelium continues to spread, the diameter of the circle of visible mushrooms becomes a little larger. The grass close to the fungus is stimulated by nitrogenous materials released by the fungus and becomes lush and dark green. This is followed by a zone so packed with the mycelium that the soil barely takes up water and the grass wilts in dry weather and often dies. A number of species of mushrooms are known to form fairy rings, but most often they are caused by the familiar little fairy-ring mushroom.

If, some summer night when you are camping out, you happen to see an old rotting stump glowing with an eerie, greenish-white light, don't become alarmed. The cold, ghostly light is what countryfolk and woodsmen have long known as "fox fire." It is given off by the mycelia of fungi growing in the decaying wood. Several kinds of mushrooms or their mycelia are capable of producing this luminescence, or cold light. One of the best known is the jack-o'-lantern, a large and bright yellow or orange mushroom, which grows in clusters about old stumps. Even by day it is quite a striking mushroom. At night it glows with a soft, pale, ghostly light. It is extremely poisonous.

The jack-o'-lantern

58

The Fungi

Most mushrooms are fleeting things, disintegrating soon after their spores are shed. But the ink-caps don't even wait for the wind to carry their spores away. As the spores ripen, the gills simply dissolve, ending up as a dripping, inky-black fluid—with millions of spores in the fluid. An ink-cap may be an attractive and quite edible mushroom today. Tomorrow it will be just a shapeless black mass.

On the other hand, the spore-bearing structures of some of the pore fungi persist for a long time, even for years. Some of them form the big punky shelves or brackets often seen on the trunks of trees. Children sometimes break these off and scratch pictures or write on their smooth, whitish lower surfaces. Other pore fungi frequently form extensive patches of smaller leathery fans, which may virtually cover decaying logs and stumps.

Tonguelike shelves of the beefsteak mushroom often grow from decaying crevices in oak or chestnut trees, and in mid-summer they are avidly sought by mushroom enthusiasts. This pore fungus is very easy to recognize. It is blood red above and creamy pink below, and the skin on its upper surface can be moved about like the skin on the back of your open hand. Here is a fungus which has an international reputation for its edibility.

Late in the nineteenth century a German scientist discovered an interesting relationship between various mushrooms and some higher plants. He found that the mycelia of mushrooms often form mantles of fine hairs, or "mushroom roots," on the roots of host plants. The relationship, however, is not a case of parasitism but is a symbiotic one that benefits both of the plants concerned. While the fungus receives nourishment from its host, its threadlike mycelia serve the host as root hairs, helping it to absorb water and mineral nutrients from the soil. This scientist called the "mushroom roots" mycorrhizas (my-ko-RYE-zuz), a name derived from two ancient Greek words meaning "fungus" and "root."

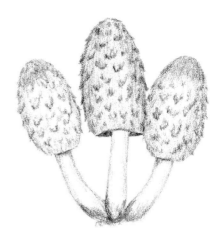

The shaggy mane, one of the common inkcaps

Two pore fungi which grow on wood

The beefsteak mushroom

59

It is now known that many kinds of plants, ranging from ferns and orchids to rhododendrons, pines, beeches, and oaks, benefit from an association of fungi with their roots and can grow much better if the right kinds of mushrooms are present. Most, if not all, of the shrubs which grow in acid bogs, for example, appear to be dependent on mycorrhizas, and some plants are apparently not able to grow at all if mushrooms are absent. It is quite possible that there are a great many other plants which depend on mycorrhizas, besides the ones we already know about.

Fungi and Plant Diseases

Plants have diseases just as animals do. Many plant diseases are caused by bacteria and viruses, but most of them are caused by the higher and more complicated fungi. It is the fungi that are responsible for the wide range of blights, rots, wilts, leaf spots, smuts, rusts, and mildews that afflict plants. Virtually all of our cultivated plants are affected by some of them, and the loss due to plant diseases in the United States alone amounts to three billion dollars or more every year.

Mildews are moldlike fungi which attack a great many kinds of plants.

Powdery mildews form a whitish or grayish coating on the leaves and stems of phlox, zinnias, asters, snapdragons, roses, peas, beans, squash, and many other garden plants. The mycelia of powdery mildews grow chiefly on the surface, but they send many suckers into the tissues of the host plant to obtain nourishment. Tiny erect branches produce chains of spores; these spread the fungus growth to other parts of the plant and to neighboring plants. Plants attacked by powdery

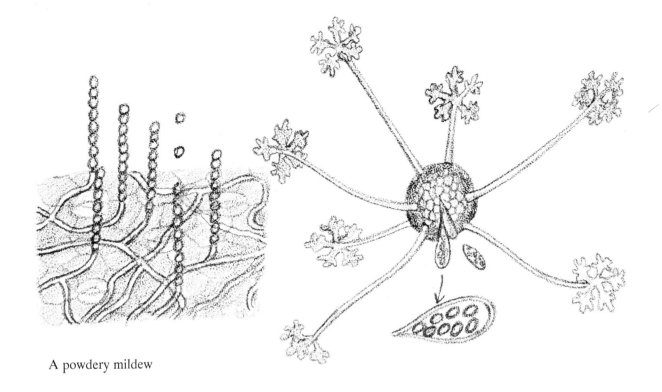

A powdery mildew

mildews commonly lose their leaves and become sickly in appearance—and often die.

Downy mildews flourish especially during long periods of cool, wet weather and attack such plants as cucumbers, melons, squash, and lima beans. Their mycelia grow within the tissues of the host. The spores which spread the disease are produced in downy patches that appear on the surfaces of the leaves or stems. Other thick-walled spores are also produced within the tissues of the host, and when spring comes they germinate and infect a new generation of host plants.

One downy mildew causes the destructive late blight of the potato, and was responsible for a devastating famine in Ireland in the middle of the nineteenth century. Between 1845 and 1860, most of the potato crop was lost, and a million people in Ireland died from starvation or from diseases resulting from malnutrition. Another million and a half left Ireland, most of them coming to the United States.

Rust fungi have destroyed man's crops of grains since ancient times. The early Romans thought the mysterious disease was a sign of the displeasure of the gods. They called it *robigo* because of its red color, and their god Robigus, the defender of their grainfields, was named for the rust. The festival of Robigalia was held each year on the twenty-fifth of April. After a grand procession, a dog was sacrificed to Robigus, in the hope that he would protect their fields from the destructive rust. Centuries later, in the year 1767, an Italian scientist finally discovered that the dreaded rust was caused by a fungus.

Some of the rust fungi must have two different kinds of plants, called alternate hosts, in order to complete their life cycles. These life cycles are complicated, with several separate stages.

In the case of the wheat stem rust, the alternate hosts are wheat, or certain other grasses, and the common barberry plant. In the spring, bright orange spots appear on the barberry leaves. From these spots, millions of spores float away into the air. If they land on wheat plants they begin to grow. By early summer, small specks appear on the leaves or stems of the wheat, and soon *they* produce little yellow or orange masses of "summer spores." These "summer spores" quickly spread the rust disease throughout the field of grain.

Then toward the end of the growing season, black streaks appear on the stems of the infected wheat plants, which in turn produce masses of thick-walled black "winter spores." Many are left on the stubble when the wheat is harvested; others fall to the ground; all of them wait for the following spring.

When spring comes, the black "winter spores" of the rust germinate and grow into microscopic fungus plants. These plants live only a very short time but nevertheless manage to produce, in *their* turn, millions of spores, which are carried far and wide through the air. These spores cannot infect wheat

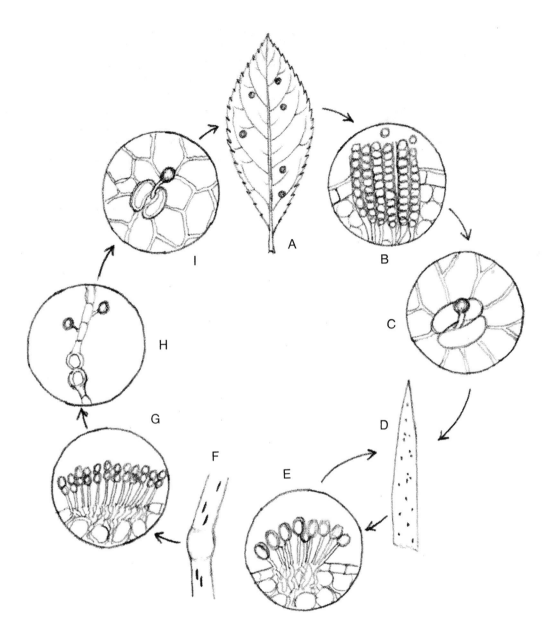

Life cycle of the wheat stem rust

A. Small orange dots appear on barberry leaves. B. These dots produce spores carried by the wind. C. These spores germinate on the leaves of wheat plants. D. Eventually small reddish spots appear on the wheat leaves. E. These spots produce spores which infect other wheat plants. F. Later black streaks appear on the wheat stems. G. They produce spores which will live over the winter. H. In spring these spores germinate and grow into tiny fungus plants which produce spores. I. These spores can grow only on the leaves of barberry plants.

plants. But if they settle on the young leaves of barberry bushes, they begin to grow, and then little orange spots appear once more on the barberry leaves, and the life cycle of the wheat stem rust begins all over again.

Another of the rust fungi shuttles back and forth between apple or crabapple trees and red cedars or junipers. It causes galls to form on the junipers, from which, in the spring, gelatinlike orange horns protrude and produce spores. These spores are carried by the wind to apple trees, where the growing fungi soon cause yellow spots on the leaves and fruits. The apple crop is often greatly reduced, and what fruits do develop are misshapen. The spores made by these fungi are carried during the summer back again to the junipers, the only place where the fungi can pass the winter.

White pine trees are often severely damaged and even killed by the white pine blister rust. Spores produced by the fungi growing on the white pines cannot infect other pine trees; they need alternate hosts. In this case, the alternate hosts are currant or gooseberry bushes. During the summer the fungus produces clusters of tiny blisters on their leaves. From the blisters come spores which infect other currant or gooseberry bushes—but not the pines. Then, in the late summer, *other* spores are produced. These spores cannot infect currants or gooseberries. But if they are carried by the wind to the needles of the pines, the pine trees become infected with the disease.

It is not so hard to control a fungus which has to have two hosts to complete its life cycle. All that is necessary is to eliminate the less valuable host plant. Wheat growers get rid of any barberry bushes near their grainfields; apple growers remove any junipers found near their orchards; foresters try to eradicate all currant and gooseberry bushes from places close to white pines.

Anyone who has ever grown corn is sure to be acquainted with corn smut. The first visible sign of its presence is the appearance of tumorlike swellings on the stalks, tassels, or ears. At first these swellings are covered with a thin, greenish-white skin. When the skin ruptures, a sooty black mass of spores appears. But long before the tumorlike growths put in their appearance, mycelia of the smut fungi have been growing unseen in the tissues of the corn plant.

The spores of corn smut live through the winter in old corn stalks, in the manure of animals which have eaten them, and even in the soil. They can lie in the soil for several years and still be able to infect corn plants again, but not directly. When the spores do germinate, they grow into microscopic fungus plants, each just a short filament made up of a few cells. But each cell produces one or more spores, and it is these spores which infect the corn and cause the smut.

Sometimes grains in the heads of rye, barley, and some kinds of wheat are replaced by hard black bodies a bit longer

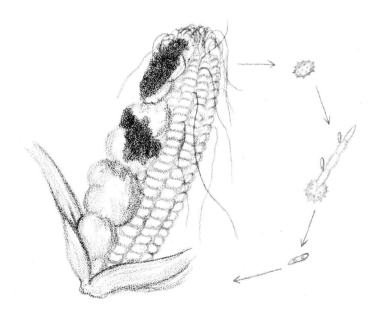

Life cycle of corn smut

than the grain would be, so that they protrude from the chaff. These bodies are called sclerotia (skler-O-sha), and they represent the resting stage of a fungus which causes the ergot disease of grains.

Ergot sclerotia contain substances which are poisonous to man and to his domestic animals. Even small amounts in the grain fed to cattle may result in serious losses of these animals. During the Middle Ages, when rye was the chief cereal of many European people, epidemics of ergotism cost thousands of lives. After the cause of the sickness became known, and ergot sclerotia were eliminated from the grain ground into flour, ergotism in human beings became rare.

But rye ergot also has a definite medicinal value. It contains substances which can contract the fine blood vessels or capillaries, and thus control bleeding, among other things. Ergot is produced commercially in several regions where the climate favors it, and sometimes rye fields are infected artificially to obtain a supply of the drug.

A few decades ago rice growers in Japan were faced with a serious and strange problem: the stems of their plants grew so fast that they became spindly and fell down. Japanese scientists investigated and discovered that the cause was a species of *Gibberella* (jib-ber-ELL-a), one of a group of fungi responsible for a variety of diseases in grain crops. But this fungus also produced chemicals which acted as a powerful growth stimulator. The scientists called the chemicals gibberellins (jib-ber-ELL-inz) and began to produce them themselves in laboratories by growing the fungi on nutrient cultures.

Experiments showed that different kinds of plants reacted to the gibberellins in various ways. Some biennial plants, which normally require two growing seasons to flower, bloomed within a few weeks after they were treated. Early flowering took place in some woody plants, such as hydrangeas. Many plants responded by making very rapid stem growth and shooting up to several times their usual size. In some cases, fruits were produced without seeds, and dormant plants often started growing immediately after the chemical was applied.

Growth regulators containing these gibberellins are available on the market, if you would like to try some experiments of your own.

We realize how devastating fungus disease of plants can be when we consider what happened to the American chestnut. This tree flourished in our eastern forests early in the present century and was one of our most valuable timber trees, aside from producing quantities of delicious nuts. Today, except for some sprout growth, the chestnut has vanished from our forests. These large trees were killed by a fungus accidentally introduced into our country from abroad. Its spores were carried from tree to tree by the winds, and the disease spread through the forests like wildfire, with deadly results.

Much more recently, another imported fungus disease has resulted in serious losses of elm trees. But unlike the wind-borne spores of the chestnut-bark disease, those of the Dutch elm disease are carried from diseased elms to healthy trees by bark beetles. It is thought that the fungus often overwinters in the bodies of the beetles; if we can eliminate the beetles which carry the fungus, this disease may eventually be controlled.

If shelves, brackets, or mushrooms of any kind appear on the trunks or branches of treasured shade trees, it is a warning sign that the mycelia of fungi are growing unseen in the wood of the tree and causing decay. In time a cavity will result, and the tree may even be lost. A competent professional tree surgeon can often save the tree. Every bit of diseased wood containing the mycelia of the fungus must be removed. The sound wood which is then exposed must be treated to prevent reinfection by wind-borne spores. If the cavity is a large one, it will probably require a filling, just as a tooth does.

The oyster mushroom, a destroyer of trees

67

Lichens, the "Two-in-Ones"

YOU WILL often see, thickly covering the trunks of trees or spreading across rocks, flat grayish-green patches of different sizes. These pretty rosettes are formed by *Parmelia* (par-ME-li-a), one of the most abundant of the lichens (LY-kinz).

Lichens are able to grow in barren and seemingly impossible places where no other plants can exist. They are found on bleak mountain peaks and in the burning desert, in tropical jungles and on the tundra beyond the Arctic Circle. They passively endure drought, heat, and extreme cold; then, when conditions become more favorable, they revive and grow again.

Lichens are usually the first plants to become established on the surface of a bare rock. There they anchor themselves so securely that they can be neither blown nor washed away. Weak acids which they secrete gradually dissolve mineral matter out of the rock. Bit by tiny bit they slowly "eat away" the rock surface, causing it to crumble into minute particles. The rock particles become mixed with fragments of dead lichens to form a thin film of soil, and in time there may be enough soil for other plants, such as mosses and ferns, to get a toehold on the rock.

Although botanists give lichens classifications and names as they do other plants, a lichen is not really a single plant, but

Lichens, the "Two-In-Ones"

what we could call a "two-in-one." It actually represents a partnership between one of the single-celled green or blue-green algae and a fungus. The fungus is usually one of the group known as the sac-fungi.

Both alga and fungus benefit from their odd partnership. The fungus, unable to make food for itself, depends entirely upon the alga for its nourishment. But the fungus absorbs water, at times even from fog or moist air, and passes it along to the alga. The fungus also anchors the lichen firmly to whatever it is growing on by means of tiny rootlike holdfasts.

The greater part of a lichen is made up of the fungus, with the algae plants completely wrapped up in its slender threadlike mycelia, and in some cases the mycelia actually penetrate the algae cells. The mutual benefit society thus formed makes it possible for lichens to grow where, often, neither of the two members could exist alone.

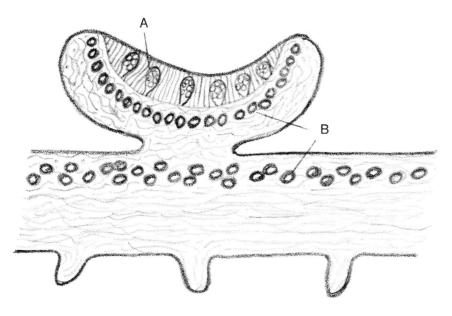

The inside of a lichen (cross section highly magnified)
A. Spores of the fungus. B. Algae enmeshed in the fungus threads.

Bodies which produce spores often appear on the surfaces of lichens. These are spores of the fungus. (The algae in the lichen also reproduce themselves, but by simple cell division.) The fungus spores are scattered by the winds, and if by chance they happen to come in contact with the right kind of free-living algae cells, then a new lichen may result. Spores not lucky enough to find an algal partner may germinate, but usually the fungus plants that grow from them soon starve to death.

There would be few new lichens if their formation had to depend on the chance meeting of a fungus with its proper algal partner, so lichens have other and much more reliable ways of reproducing. Sometimes pieces simply break off of a lichen and grow into new lichens, but most lichens form special reproductive bodies. These consist of masses of the fungus threads containing embedded algal cells, which break away to grow in a different place.

Scientists have separated the algae and fungi of various lichens, and then have recombined them. Some of the lichens thus artificially formed and grown in laboratories have been like the ones found in nature, but others have been altogether different from natural lichens.

All lichens are of three general types.

Some lichens are rather crusty and look like drops or daubs of paint found on the surface of a rock, on the soil, or on the trunks of trees. The colors of the "paint" can be yellow, orange, red, brown, blue, green, or even black.

The body of a second type of lichen is more or less flattened and leaflike. If you examine one of the rosettes of *Parmelia*, you will find that it is made of little lobed particles, loose at the edges. In dry weather these "leaves" are brittle and easily broken. During damp weather they absorb moisture and become pliable and brighter in color and much more noticeable.

The third type of lichen is often beautifully branched, like a minute bush. One of these is the so-called reindeer moss—

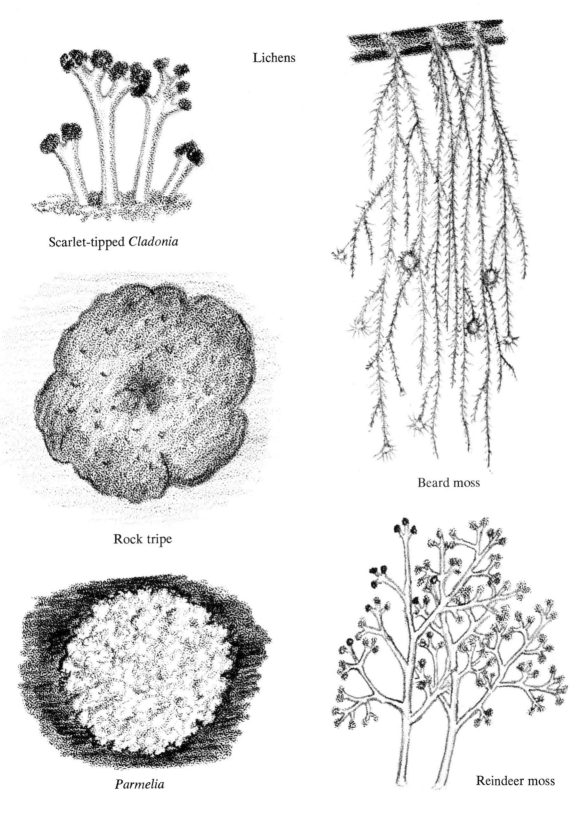

Lichens

Scarlet-tipped *Cladonia*

Rock tripe

Parmelia

Beard moss

Reindeer moss

which is *not* a moss. The reindeer moss grows abundantly on the tundras of the Far North and provides forage for the herds of reindeer, caribou, and musk oxen, but relatives of the reindeer moss can be found much nearer home. One called the scarlet-tipped *Cladonia* (kla-DOAN-i-a) has gray-green branches which end in bright scarlet knobs. It is known to many as "British soldiers," and is one of the most attractive of all the lichens. Be sure to watch for it when you walk through fields or woods.

Another of the bushy-branched lichens is the so-called beard moss (which is not a moss either), or old man's beard. This lichen hangs from the branches of trees in cool, moist forests, but it may sometimes be found in old apple orchards. The swaying grayish-green streamers of the beard moss lichen look very much like the Spanish moss which festoons trees in the warm, damp coastal regions of the Southeast. (This is not a moss either! Nor is it harmful to the trees. It is a seed plant belonging to the pineapple family which takes its nutrients from the air.) Beard moss and Spanish moss must appear very much alike to parula warblers, for these little birds make their nests in either of them.

Aside from their role as soil makers, lichens are the principal food of wood lice, mites, and numerous other insects. They are also eaten by snails, slugs, and other small animals. They have been used to some extent as food by man. In Iceland and the Scandinavian countries a lichen commonly known as Iceland moss (one more non-moss) is ground into a powder, treated to remove its bitter taste, and then used to make soups, bread, and other food, and medicine as well. In the deserts of northern Africa and western Asia another lichen known as "Bread from Heaven" is mixed with meal to make bread. Some people think this lichen is the manna which nourished the Israelites during the Exodus from Egypt.

In our northern and mountainous regions, rather large,

blackish, leathery-looking patches of another lichen, commonly called rock tripe, are found attached to rocks. When dry, this lichen is crisp and tends to curl up, but in wet weather it expands and becomes pliable and rubbery. Northern Indians and woodsmen have been known to eat rock tripe as an emergency food to stave off starvation. But nobody has ever claimed that it is a delicacy.

Dyes of various colors can be obtained from lichens. The most familiar of them, litmus dye, is obtained by grinding up a certain species of *Roccella* (rok-SEL-la) and extracting the coloring matter. In a neutral medium, litmus dye is a purplish color. A drop of acid, such as vinegar or lemon juice, will turn the litmus dye red; an alkali, such as household ammonia or baking soda, will turn it blue.

Lichens may even prove to be a good indicator of air pollution. Quite recently, people living in the British Isles noticed that the lichens had almost disappeared from places where they were formerly abundant. The cause of their disappearance was traced to badly polluted air. Perhaps it would be a good idea for us to keep a close watch on our own lichens. If they seem to be decreasing in abundance, we should heed the warning.

Liverworts, the First Real Land Plants

THE COMMON names of many plants end with the suffix "wort." This is derived from "wyrt," an old Anglo-Saxon word which meant herb or plant. Liverworts got their name long ago because people thought they were shaped something like the human liver. People also once thought that any plant shaped like an organ of the human body was intended to cure the ailments of that organ, so liverworts were used to treat all kinds of liver trouble.

The ancestors of today's liverworts lived hundreds of millions of years ago. They developed from some of the green algae that left the water and began to grow on the damp earth. Thus the liverworts were the first real land plants.

The plant body of a liverwort is just a thallus, with no true roots or stems or leaves, but it is not as simple as the thalli of green algae or of fungi. It is made up of several layers of cells. The outermost layer forms a skin which prevents the loss of water from the cells within. Fine hairlike threads grow from the bottom of the thallus and anchor it to the soil or rock.

Liverworts show a marked advance over their algal ancestors in another way, since their reproductive organs are not just single cells, but many-celled structures. Yet liverworts are not

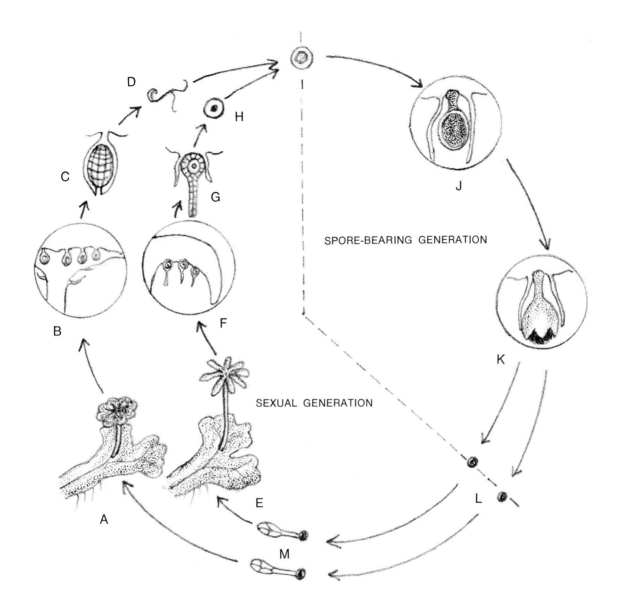

Life cycle of a liverwort (*Marchantia*)

A. The familiar liverwort plant (male). B. Male organs on upper surface of umbrella-like structure. C. Single male organ. D. Sperm. E. The familiar liverwort plant (female). F. Female organs on lower surface of umbrella-like structure. G. Single female organ. H. Egg. I. Fertilized egg results from union of egg and sperm. J. A growing spore-bearing plant. K. A mature spore-bearing plant opening to shed spores. L. A pair of spores. M. Germinating spores.

altogether freed from their watery past. In order for reproduction to take place, the plants must be wet. The sperms produced by the male organs are still swimmers, although they need just a thin film of water to swim in because they are so tiny. But water they must have, for they must swim to the egg lying within the flask-shaped female organ.

After the egg is fertilized by a sperm, it divides and begins to develop into a new plant. Although this new plant remains attached to the parent thallus and gets all its nourishment from it, it looks nothing at all like its parent. It is much, much smaller, and it is a little bag or boxlike structure full of spores. It is these spores which will grow into plants with green thalli like those of the grandparents.

In liverworts, as in all of the seedless and seed plants above them, there is this same alternation of generations. One generation of plants has male and female organs producing sperms and eggs. The next generation of plants produces spores. These spores develop into a new generation of plants with sex organs. The cycle goes round and round.

On a patch of moist soil which has recently been disturbed, perhaps where someone had a campfire or has burned some brush, you may notice what seem to be bits of flat green ribbon which are an inch to a few inches long. Stooping to pick some of them up, you discover that they are not pieces of ribbon. They are fastened to the soil by many fine hairs; their upper surface is dotted with minute pores, and many of them are forked. What you have found are the thalli of *Marchantia* (mar-KAN-sha), one of the commonest of the liverworts.

Some liverworts have male and female organs on the same plant, but in *Marchantia* these organs are found on separate plants. Thus we may say there are male and female plants. When *Marchantia* is ready to reproduce, it sends up slender stalks, with a disk at the top of each one. They look very much like tiny opened umbrellas. On the female plants the disks are deeply divided into fingerlike lobes, at the bases of which are tiny flask-shaped structures too small to be seen with the naked eye. Each of these contains an egg. The "umbrellas" of the male plants have shorter stalks and the disks are only scalloped. On their upper surface are the male sex organs, which produce the microscopic sperms.

Since the sperms are so tiny, a few inches is a tremendous distance for them to swim—and part of that distance is vertical. But somehow one of them usually manages to make its way to the flask and fertilize the egg within it.

After the egg is fertilized it begins to develop into a tiny spore-bearing plant. These plants look like little bags hanging from the undersides of the "umbrellas" of the female *Marchantia* plants. When they mature they will release microscopic spores. These will grow into new *Marchantia* ribbons.

Marchantia, however, does not rely entirely on sexual reproduction. Small cups often appear on the upper surface of the ribbonlike thalli (on both male and female plants), and within them are tiny buds, or gemmae (JEM-me). They remind one very much of minute bird nests full of eggs. These little buds can grow directly into new *Marchantia* ribbons.

On wet rocks in a shady ravine, or on stones bathed by the spray from a waterfall, you are likely to find *Conocephalum* (cone-o-SEF-a-lum). Its thalli, too, are like flat, forking ribbons, but they are much larger and coarser than those of *Marchantia.* Often they will cover an area of several square feet. During most of the year there are no "umbrellas" on *Conocephalum.* For a short time in the spring the "umbrellas" go up, but then only on the female plants. The male plants have warty spots on the upper surface of the thalli, and the sperms are produced in these.

A few of the liverworts float on the surface of quiet waters, but if the water should disappear they will continue to grow

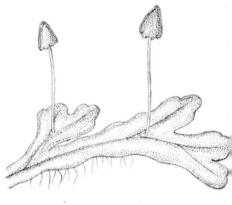

Conocephalum

Riccia

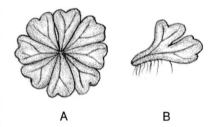

A   B

Ricciocarpus
A. Land form
B. Floating form

on the mud. One of these is the little *Riccia* (RIX-i-a), whose forking ribbons are barely one twenty-fifth of an inch wide. Another is *Ricciocarpus* (rix-i-o-KARP-us), the lobed thalli of which form pretty rosettes, often an inch across, on muddy shores. When *Ricciocarpus* floats on the water, the rosettes break up into small triangular pieces. Neither of these liverworts ever puts up umbrellas. Their minute male and female sex organs are on the same plant, and the second-generation spore-bearing plants are sunken in the upper surface of the thalli.

Not all the liverworts have flattened thalli that might suggest a human liver, or the liver of any other animal, for that matter. A great many of them belong to a group with thalli that look for all the world like higher plants with stems and leaves. They are called the leafy liverworts.

Leafy liverworts often grow thickly in moist or wet places. They are found on the soil, on rocks, or clinging to the trunks of trees. Decaying logs along the banks of streams are frequently covered with a pale green, lacy network of these delicate little creeping plants. Most of us have seen leafy liverworts many times, but we may have thought they were some kind of moss.

How can one tell a leafy liverwort from a moss? The best way is to take a good careful look at the "leaves." Those of the leafy liverworts are arranged in only two rows near the upper side of the "stem," show no midrib, and are often notched at the tip, lobed, or deeply fringed. Moss "leaves" are equally spaced about the stem or arranged in two opposite rows and commonly show a midrib. They are never notched at the tip or lobed, but the margins are sometimes minutely toothed. The spore-bearing capsules of leafy liverworts are very short-lived and usually so short-stalked that they appear to be seated directly on the parent thallus. Unlike the capsules of mosses, they split into four parts to release their spores.

On a moist claybank by the side of a road, you may meet

Leafy liverworts

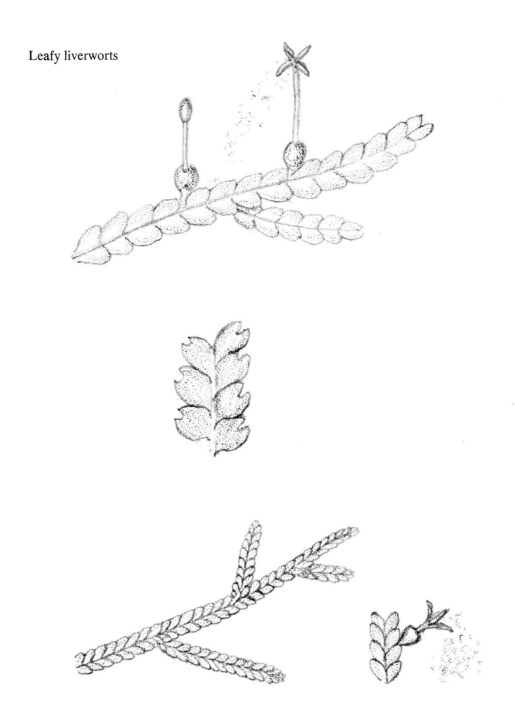

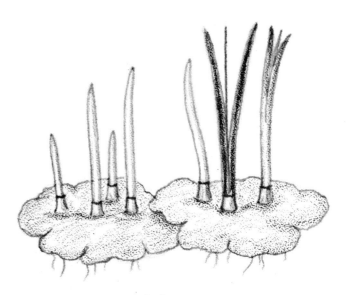

Anthoceros

an unusual liverwort called *Anthoceros* (an-THAHS-a-rus). You may, that is, if you have a keen eye and a great deal of curiosity, for its thallus is not very striking. It is just a flat little green thing that might easily be mistaken for a bit of leaf that some insect had been eating. Most people would never notice it. It never puts up "umbrellas," for its tiny male and female organs are both sunken in the tissues of the thalli.

At times several rodlike "horns" appear on the little thallus. Each one rises from a cylindrical sheath, and eventually they may become an inch or more tall. These are the spore-bearing generation of the *Anthoceros* plants. Although they are not very big, they are real giants compared with other liverwort spore bearers.

At first the "horns" are green, for they contain chlorophyll. They are able to make food, but they are still dependent upon the parent thallus for water and dissolved mineral matter. As they grow upward from the base, the spores within them begin to mature, from the tip downward. As the spores ripen, the "horns" gradually split downward into two halves, which turn black. At this stage *Anthoceros* could easily be mistaken for a tuft of burned grass.

Anthoceros is a very "progressive" liverwort. Its thallus is simple, but the rodlike capsules which produce the spores are quite complicated many-celled structures. Scientists suspect that higher plants, such as the ferns and ultimately the seed plants, developed from just such a horned liverwort as *Anthoceros*.

The Mosses

MOSSES are such common and familiar little plants that most people just take them for granted. We never have to look very far to find them, either, for they grow in our dooryards and between the stones and bricks of our walks, on rocks and on the trunks of trees around us. But there are also mosses in tropical jungles and on the tundra beyond the Arctic Circle, and there are mosses by the seashore and on bleak mountain peaks two miles or more above the level of the sea.

Most mosses are found on land, in at least moderately damp places. But some kinds live in flowing streams and in lakes and ponds—one of them has even been found growing about 180 feet below the surface of a Swiss lake. And some kinds thrive in places that are so dry that few other plants are able to exist there at all. Mosses can do this because they have the remarkable ability to suspend all activity when the environment becomes too dry, simply curling up and waiting for the rains to come again.

Although mosses have been on the earth for a very long time, they have never made very much progress. At some point in time they got off the road leading to the development of the higher plants, and today they are much the same as they were ages ago. They have hairlike structures which serve the purposes of roots, but have a far more simple structure than true roots; their leaves are only one or two layers of cells in thickness; their primitive stems do not have any of the woody tissues found in the stems of higher plants. In fact, many botanists are inclined to regard the whole moss plant as being still just parts of a thallus.

When a moss spore soaks up water, bursts its cell wall, and begins to grow, it does not directly become a leafy moss plant. First a slender thread comes out of the spore, looking much like the thread of one of the green algae. But this thread continues to grow and send out branches, until eventually it may cover several square inches, or even square feet, of ground. Sooner or later little buds will appear on the mat of threads, and it is these buds that will grow into the leafy moss plants which all of us know. After they have formed hairlike false roots at their bases, the green threads usually disappear.

In due time microscopic sex organs are produced on the leafy moss plants. The female organs are shaped like flasks, and in the swollen base of each one there is a single egg. The male organs are more or less club-shaped, and each one of them produces a large number of minute sperms. In some mosses organs of both sexes are present on the same plant; in others they are located on separate plants.

Mosses, like the liverworts, have never shaken off their watery past, and the plants have to be wet in order for them to reproduce. The sperms are equipped with a pair of cilia, and they are so tiny that they are able to swim about actively in only a thin film of water. The female organ secretes a sweet substance which serves as a lure, and every sperm that senses it hastens to its source. But only one of the multitude of tiny swimmers will finally succeed in entering the neck of each flask and fertilizing the egg within it.

After the egg is fertilized by the sperm, a new little plant of the next, or spore-bearing, generation completes its develop-

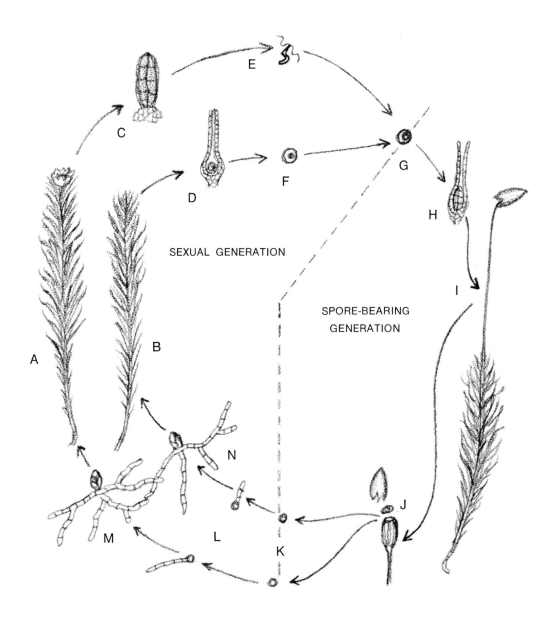

Life cycle of a moss (common hair cap)

A. A male plant. B. A female plant. C. Sex organ of male plant. D. Sex organ of
female plant. E. Sperm. F. Egg. G. Fertilized egg. H. Spore-bearing plant begins
to grow from fertilized egg. I. Spore-bearing plant attached to sexual plant. J. Capsule of spore-bearing plant opens to release spores. K. Spores. L. Spores germinate
to form threads. M. Bud forms to produce a male plant. N. Bud forms to produce
a female plant.

ment within the female organ. Then, suddenly, a hairlike stalk will shoot up from the leafy green parent moss plant. At its tip is a spore case covered with a hoodlike cap, which is a part of the female organ that has sheltered it until now.

The spore cases, or capsules, are usually shaped like little barrels, or urns, or balls. Each one has a tight-fitting lid; when the capsule matures and becomes dry, the little lid falls off, exposing a ring of tiny teeth around the capsule's rim. When it rains or when the humidity is high, these teeth dip down into the capsule. When the weather turns sunny and dry, out they come again, bringing with them some of the spores to be carried away by each breeze.

All of the mosses do not follow this life cycle in every detail, but most of those that we are apt to notice do. The green threads of some mosses are perennial, and the stalks bearing the spore cases appear to rise directly from the ground. The spore cases of some mosses have no stalks at all and appear to be seated directly on the leafy plants or on the ground. With mosses, as with everything else, there are exceptions to the rules.

Mosses vary greatly in both appearance and size. Some are so tiny that they are barely visible; others may be as much as a foot tall. One of the most familiar of the larger mosses is the hair-cap, or pigeon-wheat moss, which is found all over the world in moist spots in fields and open woods. Its stems are often six inches tall or more, and are crowded with slender, green leaves. This moss often forms dense beds many feet across.

In late spring or early summer, many of the plants in a patch of hair-cap appear to have starry-looking flowers at their tips. But mosses, of course, do not have flowers. The "flowers" are really clusters of colorful leaves growing on the male plants, and within the clusters are organs which produce sperms. The female plants have only a pointed cluster of green leaves at their tips, and hidden within these leaves is a flask-shaped organ containing an egg. Later each of these female plants will be topped with a hairlike stalk bearing a four-sided capsule. When the capsules are young they are covered with a hairy cap, which is why these mosses are called hair-caps. When the capsules are fully mature, they are the shape and color of grains of wheat, which accounts for their other name, pigeon-wheat.

One of the commonest mosses found on patches of bare soil, particularly where a fire has occurred, is called the cord moss. At first glance all one usually sees are a host of hairlike stalks with lopsided capsules at their tips. The leafy moss plants from which they arise hug the ground like little buds. If the weather happens to be dry, the long stalks will be curled and twisted; if it is raining or there is enough dew to moisten them, they will be straight.

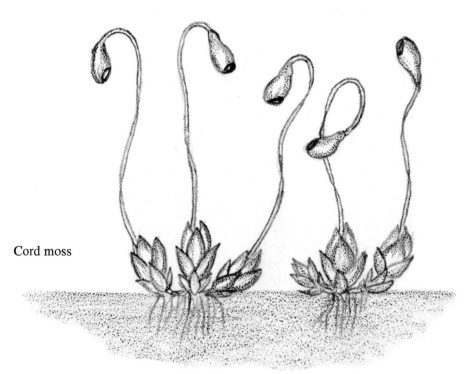

Cord moss

The cushion moss

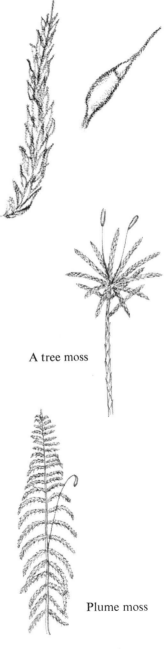

A tree moss

Plume moss

The cushion moss always attracts attention because it forms pale green or whitish mounds, only an inch or two high but often six or more inches across. These "cushions" are seen in rather dry, open woodlands and are made up of a great many moss plants packed tightly together. The cushion moss seldom produces spore-bearing capsules, but when it does, they are usually seen in the autumn.

The American tree moss is common in moist woodlands east of the Rocky Mountains. Although its slender, creeping stems grow beneath the ground, other stems rise from these like the trunks of trees, and toward the top of these stems are clusters of spreading branches covered with minute leaves. These mosses look like a forest of tiny trees.

Plume mosses and fern mosses, on the other hand, have a feathery sort of branching that makes them resemble miniature ferns growing in a dense mat. In cool, moist woodlands, particularly in the mountains, they often form a carpet covering rocks and the trunks of fallen trees. Such moss carpets provide excellent places for ferns, and even many of the seed plants, to grow.

87

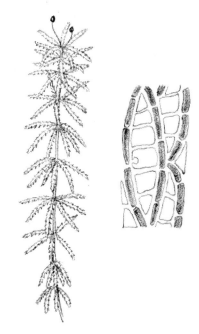

Sphagnum moss:
Plant (left) and magnified portion
of leaf showing
large empty cells (right)

The sphagnum or peat mosses, which grow in water and very wet places, are not true mosses, but seem, rather, to form a connecting link between the liverworts and the mosses. When a sphagnum spore germinates, it doesn't grow into the usual branching moss thread, but instead becomes a flattened and branching ribbon, something like that of many liverworts. Buds which form on this thallus grow into the leafy sphagnum plants. The spore-bearing plants of the sphagnum appear as rather short-stalked, tiny black balls. When the spores mature, the capsules literally blow off their round lids, just as if there had been an internal explosion.

Sphagnums are easily recognized. They are pale green or whitish, though often tinged with red or purple at their tips, and their branches, covered with minute leaves, grow in whorls along the main stem. As the stem dies at the bottom, it keeps on growing at the tip, but it is much too weak to stand erect. Thus we usually find sphagnums closely crowded together, supporting one another in dense clumps or in extensive beds.

Quite often sphagnums will begin to grow in the shallower water of lakes and ponds, close to the shore. But gradually they move out into the deeper water, forming a floating mat which builds up farther and farther out from the shore. Other plants, such as sedges, cranberries, blueberries, and leatherleaf, soon begin to grow on the bog mat, and eventually it is invaded by larger shrubs and some trees. In time the sphagnum and the other plants will completely fill in the basin, and the lake will then be converted into a bog. This has happened to many of the smaller and shallower lakes and ponds formed by the Ice Age glaciers, which once covered the northern part of the North American continent.

If you have never visited a floating sphagnum bog, you have missed an unusual experience. When one steps upon it, the "earth" trembles. Bushes and trees begin to bob and sway in a weird sort of way, and one soon realizes that terra firma is not so firm here. It is a soggy place where water often quickly fills one's footsteps. But the floating mat of plants sustains one's weight, and there is really little to fear. To the naturalist, such bogs are veritable treasure houses. In them he often finds trees, shrubs, and herbaceous plants far south of their usual range, and others that are usually found only in coastal regions. Lovely orchids and fascinating insectivorous plants, such as pitcher plants and sundews, frequently await the bogtrotter.

Sphagnum mosses are able to hold an amazing amount of water, and one can learn the reason for this by examining them under a microscope. Their leaves have a network of tiny green cells; between them are larger cells, which are empty. These empty cells have openings in their cell walls which admit water. Sphagnums are always very "thirsty," so as a rule they are well saturated. Wringing out a handful of them is like wringing out a cellulose sponge.

Because sphagnum is able to hold so much moisture, it is widely used by nurserymen to pack plants for shipment. Dry sphagnum, much more absorbent than cotton, was used during World War I for surgical dressings. Pulverized sphagnum makes an excellent medium for starting the seeds of garden plants, because it eliminates the "damping-off" disease of seedlings which is caused by certain tiny fungi. And the dead remains of sphagnum, and other bog plants, become peat.

Peat is the first step in the formation of coal. It is formed in bogs because a lack of oxygen in bog water, along with its high acidity and its cold temperature, hinders the activity of bacteria and other organisms which bring about decay. Thus the plant debris in the bog only partially decomposes; instead, it becomes peat.

In Ireland and in the Scandinavian countries, dried peat is used extensively as a fuel. There are extensive peat deposits in North America, too, but here we use peat mostly as a soil conditioner for lawns and gardens. Sphagnum peat, as it is usually called, is particularly valuable in growing azaleas, rhododendrons, and other plants which need an acid soil.

Sphagnums, indeed, are extremely useful mosses.

The Small Descendants
of the Coal Age Giants

Horsetails and Scouring Rushes

Early in the spring queer-looking plants with cone-shaped tips often appear by the roadside, in low wet fields, or along railroad embankments. They are pale brown or pinkish, and they may be anywhere from a few inches to a foot tall. Their stems are hollow and jointed, with fine ridges running up and down between the joints, and at each joint there is a sheath which ends in a dozen or so pointed, dark-colored teeth. These are the spore-bearing stems of a plant called the field horsetail.

If you will take the time to examine one closely, you will find that the cone at its tip is made up of separate plates, each of which has a short stalk and is shaped rather like a shield. On the underside of each plate there is a circle of what seem to be tiny bags. These are spore cases which are full of spores. After the spores are shed, these stems will wither and disappear. Their job for the year will be done.

The spore-bearing stems of the field horsetail are quickly followed by other very different stems, which rise from the same creeping underground rootstocks. These stems are green,

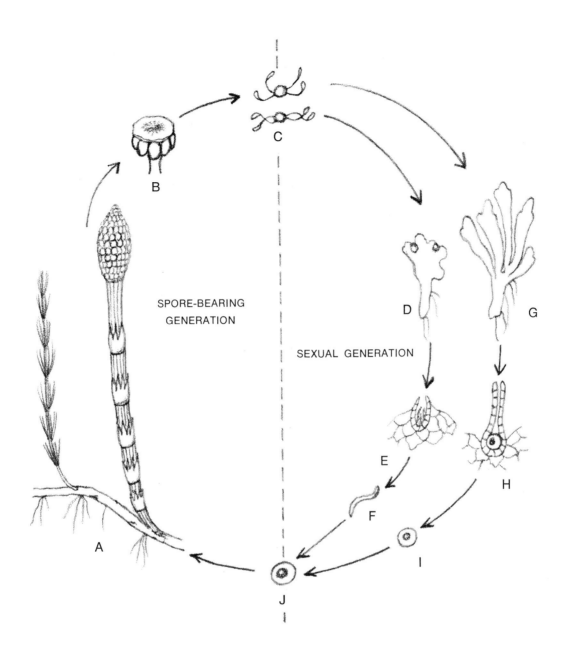

SPORE-BEARING
GENERATION

SEXUAL GENERATION

Life cycle of the field horsetail
A. The familiar horsetail plant. B. Scale of cone showing spore cases on under
surface. C. A pair of spores. D. Male plant. E. Sex organ of male plant. F. Sperm.
G. Female plant. H. Sex organ of female plant. I. Egg. J. Fertilized egg.

Fossils of Coal Age forest plants

Calamites

Lepidodendron

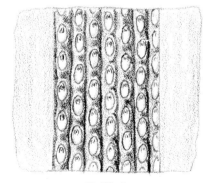

Sigillaria

and, unlike the spore-bearing stems, they remain green all summer. They keep growing until they become a foot or more tall. Around each joint there are circles of very thin, jointed branches, and they really do look quite a lot like green horses' tails.

Not all of the close relatives of the field horsetail produce two kinds of stems. The great scouring rush, for instance, has only green stems, which grow to a height of five feet or more, and which stay green even in the winter. They have narrow, pointed, spore-producing cones at their tips, and they are usually without branches. The stems of the great scouring rush contain minute particles of silica. They were often used by pioneer families to scour their pots and pans, hence the name "scouring rush."

Spores of the horsetails and scouring rushes are quite unusual. For one thing, they contain chlorophyll and are green in color. Also, they are provided with four elastic, ribbonlike appendages which twist and untwist depending on the humidity. Often they get tangled up, and then the spores are carried away in bunches.

The generation of plants which grow from these spores look nothing like the parent plants which produced them; they are just inconspicuous little green ribbons or lobed thalli which lie flat on the ground. They are often of two different sizes; when this is so, the larger ones have female organs which produce an egg, and the smaller ones have male organs which produce sperms. As in the case of the liverworts and mosses, the sperms are swimmers and must have water for fertilization to take place.

Today's horsetails and scouring rushes are mere midgets compared with some of their Coal Age ancestors. One of these ancestors lived about four hundred million years ago, and is called *Calamites* (kal-a-MY-teez). Fossil impressions of its stems are often found in rocks associated with coal deposits, so we know that many of these plants were sixty to ninety feet tall, with stems as much as two feet in diameter. Except for their gigantic size, they probably looked very much like the scouring rush we still see today in wet places.

Club Mosses

The present-day club mosses—which are not real mosses—had giant ancestors too. Among them were the odd-looking *Lepidodendrons* (lep-i-doe-DEN-dronz). These huge trees had hundred-foot trunks, which divided into forked branches thickly covered with narrow leaves. When the leaves fell, they left scalelike scars in a spiral arrangement, giving them the name of "scale trees."

Other ancient relatives of the club mosses were the *Sigillarias* (si-jill-AIR-i-uz), which also grew to be a hundred feet or more tall. Their trunks, which were sometimes five or six feet in diameter, seldom branched, and they were covered with stiffly erect leaves arranged in vertical rows.

Most of the club mosses we see on woodland rambles today are less than a foot tall. They have long stems which creep beneath the ground or trail over its surface and at intervals send up evergreen branches covered with small leaves. Most, but not all, club mosses produce spore cases in the axils of scalelike leaves. These leaves are crowded into clublike cones at the tips of the plant or its branches. It is because of these "clubs" and the fact that the plants resemble large, coarse mosses that they are called club mosses.

The shining club moss, a species which often grows abundantly in cold, damp northern and mountain woods, does not have these cones. Its stems bristle along their length with narrow, pointed leaves, which are a shiny dark green. Usually

Shining club moss

Running-pine

it has alternate zones of long and short leaves, and the budlike yellow spore cases can easily be seen in the axils of the short leaves. So the shining club moss is a club moss which is not a moss and which never has "clubs."

But during a day's outing you may often find several different species of club mosses which do have the clublike cones. In damp or swampy northern and mountain woodlands, one may come across the running club moss, also called the running-pine. Its creeping stems bristle with narrow leaves too, but they are a lighter green and usually much shorter than those of the shining club moss. At the top of other sparsely scaled stems, two to five inches tall, it may have two or three or sometimes even four slender "clubs."

You may also find, perhaps in the same woodland, another club moss which is altogether different. The aerial branches rising from its underground stems are so bushy that they look like miniature trees. And these branches are crowded with

94

small, narrow, and often twisted dark green leaves. Its spore-bearing clubs, unlike those of the running club moss, have almost no stalks. This, of course, is called the tree club moss, or sometimes the ground-pine.

In a drier woodland, or perhaps in some old field, the chances are good that you will see a club moss called the trailing ground-pine, or trailing Christmas green. Its trailing stems often form dense mats close to the ground, and the numerous forked aerial stems rising from them have flat, spreading branches. These are densely covered with tiny leaves, which overlap like the shingles on a roof. Several long, yellowish spore-bearing clubs are held aloft on stalks standing well above the matted plants.

Large quantities of the trailing ground-pine and the tree club moss are gathered each year to make Christmas wreaths and other decorations; for this purpose, they are usually dyed a deeper green. In some places the plants have been so heavily picked that they are no longer as common as they used to be. We should guard against overpicking of these plants, or they may disappear altogether.

The tiny and usually sulfur-yellow spores of club moss have found commercial uses too. They are sold in drug stores as "lycopodium (ly-ko-PO-di-um) powder," for the treatment of certain skin ailments. Since lycopodium powder burns quite explosively, it has been used in fireworks, and also on the stage to give the effect of lightning flashes.

The generation of plants which grow from club moss spores are so small and so inconspicuous that, before 1915, nobody had ever found any of them, at least in North America. Since that time a number of patient people have discovered them. They grow beneath the ground with a nearly microscopic green disk showing at the surface. On this disk both the male and female organs are produced, and water is necessary for reproduction to take place. It is believed that these tiny plants always form a partnership with fungi.

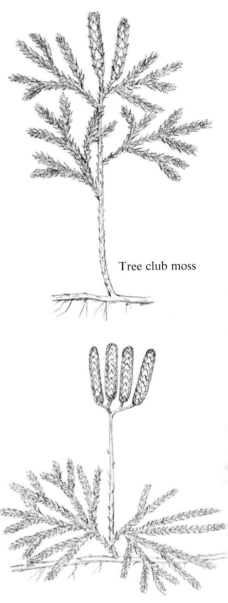

Tree club moss

Trailing ground-pine

95

Selaginellas

Selaginellas (sell-a-ji-NELL-az) are closely related to the club mosses. Most of these small, mosslike plants live in tropical regions, but a few are found quite commonly in the United States and Canada. Several of the tropical kinds are grown in greenhouses, as pot plants, or in terrariums.

Like most of the club mosses, the selaginellas produce their spores in cone-shaped clusters of small, flat leaves at the tips of their branches. But in the selaginellas, the scalelike leaves which hide these spore cases form four-sided "cones" which never have stalks. These cones give the branch tips a spiked appearance, which is the reason why the selaginellas are often called "spike mosses."

In each selaginella "cone," there is a single spore case at the base of each leaf, but they are not all alike. The spore cases in

Creeping or meadow selaginella

the axils of the lower leaves have four lobes, and each of them will produce four large spores. In the axils of the leaves above, the spore cases are smaller, and have no lobes. Each of these will produce a very large number of tiny red spores.

What happens after the spores are formed is most interesting. When the smaller spore cases rupture, the red spores begin to fall out. Some of them will, by chance, come to rest close to or even upon the larger spore cases. Within each of these tiny red spores, a male plant develops and completes its growth. It has only two cells, one of which produces a number of microscopic sperms.

In the meantime, each one of the four larger spores develops into a female plant. Although the female plants are much bigger than the male plants, they are still very tiny. The female plants finally grow large enough to split the walls of the spores and peep through the resulting openings.

When a mossy-looking selaginella plant is wet by rain or dew, the tiny male plants release their sperms, which swim about in a film of moisture. Eventually one of them finds its way to the opening in the wall of a large spore. It swims inside and fertilizes the egg within the imprisoned female plant. Thus a new selaginella plant of the spore-bearing generation is born.

For some time the new spore-bearing plant develops within the old spore wall and finally protrudes from it. Then the large spore is shed and drops to the ground. The young plant feeds for a while upon the tissues of the female plant within the spore wall, but shortly it sends its own roots down into the soil and becomes an independent plant.

Selaginella, indeed, comes very close to producing what could be called a seed.

The creeping selaginella, or meadow spike moss is a delicate and pale green little plant which creeps over the ground. It commonly forms flattened mats in wet meadows and along the margins of ponds and streams. Most people would mistake

· it for a moss, but close examination shows widely spaced leaves of two sizes along the slender stem. The larger ones are arranged along the sides of the stem, while smaller ones grow from both the upper and lower surface. And there are four-sided spikes at the tips of the branches, which are typical of all the selaginellas.

Not all the selaginellas are so delicate, though. Some, like the rock and sand selaginellas, are tough and leathery little plants with overlapping grayish-green leaves. They are able to grow on the driest of exposed rocks or in dry sands. When there is no moisture present they curl up and seem to be dead, but when it rains they open again and turn greener. One of them, which grows in the desert regions of the Southwest, curls into a tight ball when it is dry. When it is moistened it quickly uncurls and "comes alive" again. These selaginellas are commonly known as resurrection plants.

A quillwort

Quillworts

Quillworts are among the most unusual of the spore-bearing plants. All quillworts look quite alike, with their long, hollow, and quill-like leaves growing in tufts. They are found both in water and on mud flats, and when the water level of reservoirs is lowered, extensive beds of quillworts are often exposed. They look like meadows of grass or rushes.

In the swollen base of each quillwort leaf there is a single large spore case. The spore cases in the outer leaves of the tuft contain a great many small spores, as fine as powder. The spore cases of the inner leaves have fewer and larger spores, sometimes large enough to be seen with the naked eye. Intricate markings can be seen on these large spores with the help of a microscope. Since these microscopic marks provide

98

the only means of distinguishing one species of quillwort from another, most of us will be perfectly satisfied if we are able to say "That is a quillwort" when we see one, and leave it at that.

The plants which develop from these spores are very small. Like those which grow from selaginella spores, they complete their growth within the walls of the spores. Only when reproduction is about to take place do the spore walls open a little, allowing the swimming sperms to escape and gain access to the female plants within the larger spores.

The Upward Path

Among the liverworts and mosses, the plants that we see and notice are the plants of the sexual generation. The generation of spore-bearing plants are relatively small and quite inconspicuous. This situation is completely reversed in the case of the scouring rushes, the club mosses, the selaginellas, and the quillworts. In all of these the large and familiar plants are those of the spore-bearing generation, and the generation of sexual plants is often unbelievably tiny.

This reversal of the alternating generations is a definite step upward toward the higher plants. Another important upward step is the fact that these plants have acquired roots, stems, and leaves, as well as a vascular system, composed in part of woody tissue, which distributes water and sap throughout the plant body. In all of these respects they are like the ferns and the plants which bear seeds.

The Ferns

EVERYONE knows and admires the ferns. The delicacy and grace of their leaves and their refreshing greenness give them a distinct beauty. They and their close relatives represent the highest development among seedless plants. Unlike the leaves of other plants, fern leaves unroll at the tip.

One day, while you are on a walk through the woods, you may come across little heart-shaped bits of green leaves, each one barely a quarter of an inch across, lying on a mossy bank. But if you pick one up and turn it over in your hand, you will find that there are tiny rootlike hairs on its lower surface. These are not bits of leaves after all. They are fern prothallia (pro-THALL-i-a), a stage in the life cycle of a fern. Very few people have seen fern prothallia. If we walk the trails through the forests, we pass them many times, but since most of them are so tiny, we just don't notice them.

A fern prothallium is an independent little plant which grows from a fern spore. It is a fern plant of the sexual generation, for on its lower surface it has both male and female organs, too small to be seen with the naked eye. The microscopic sperms produced by the male organs swim about, and eventually one finds its way to the egg within each flask-shaped female organ. Here again, water, even if only a thin film of it, is essential for reproduction to take place.

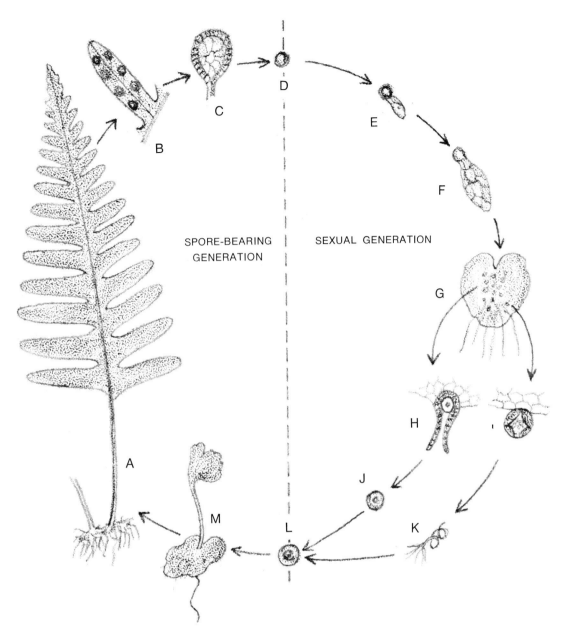

SPORE-BEARING
GENERATION

SEXUAL GENERATION

Life cycle of a fern

A. The familiar fern plant. B. Lower surface of pinna with sori or clusters of spore cases. C. A single spore case or sporangium. D. A spore. E & F. The spore germinates and begins to grow. G. It develops into a small prothallium with both male and female organs. H. Female organ. I. Male organ. J. An egg. K. A sperm. L. Fertilized egg results from the union of egg and sperm. M. It develops into a small fern plant which will produce spores when it matures.

After the egg is fertilized by a sperm, it begins to divide and eventually develops into a little plant quite unlike the parent prothallium. For a while, its foot remains anchored in the little prothallium, which supplies it with food and water. But before very long, it sends a root of its own down into the soil, and its own green leaf will begin to make its own food. It becomes an independent little plant and the parent prothallium withers and disappears. When this plant matures it will be one of the familiar ferns—a plant of the spore-bearing generation.

Fern leaves, called fronds, are usually cut or divided into a number of small leaflike parts, or pinnae (PIN-ee). In most ferns the pinnae are arranged along a common stalk extending to the tip of the frond. As the fronds grow, they gradually unroll from the base upward. The unrolling fronds are so much like the neck of a violin, or fiddle, with the scroll at its end, that they are commonly known as "fiddleheads." Our common ferns grow from a rootstock, or underground stem, but the tree ferns of tropical lands have trunklike stems, sometimes as much as forty feet tall, with a cluster of big fronds at the top.

When dark-colored or rusty dots or lines appear on the lower surface of a fern frond, it means that the fern is about ready to produce spores. These "fruit dots," or sori (SAW-

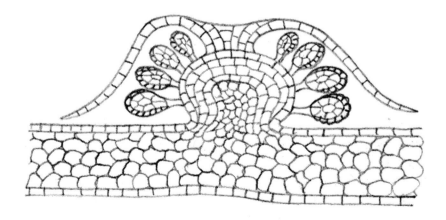

Highly magnified sorus of a fern

rye), are made up of clusters of spore cases or sporangia (spor-AN-ji-a). Each one is a sort of tiny stalked box full of microscopic spores. Quite often these spore cases resemble the helmets worn by soldiers in the days of ancient Rome. Until the spores are ready to be shed, each cluster of spore cases is often protected by a thin cover, or shield, called the indusium (in-DEWS-i-um).

When a fern spore germinates, it grows into a tiny green thread, much like the threads of green algae or those which grow from the spores of mosses. It continues to grow, but not as a thread. As new cells are formed, it spreads out and finally becomes the flat little heart-shaped prothallium—and the fern cycle begins again.

Most of our familiar ferns produce spores on the pinnae of their ordinary fronds, but not all of them do. Some, like the big cinnamon fern of swamps and wet woodlands, devote entire fronds exclusively to the production of spores. In early spring, these rusty-brown spore-bearing fronds are shedding spores while the sterile green ones may still be in the "fiddlehead" stage. By the time the handsome sterile fronds are fully developed, the spore-bearing ones may have withered and even disappeared. A close relative, the interrupted fern, devotes only a few pinnae near the middle of the ordinary fronds to spore production. After the spores are shed, these pinnae shrivel up and drop off, leaving a noticeable gap, or interruption, in the frond.

Another relative of the cinnamon fern—although it looks nothing at all like it—is the royal fern, which is also at home in swamps and other wet places. Its fronds look more like the foliage of a locust tree, and they are tipped with a cluster of spore-bearing pinnae which resemble brown blossoms. For this reason it is often called the flowering fern.

Two other ferns, also found in wet places, devote entire fronds to the production of spores. They are the sensitive fern and the netvein chain fern. Their sterile fronds look very much alike—and not particularly fernlike, since they are long-stalked

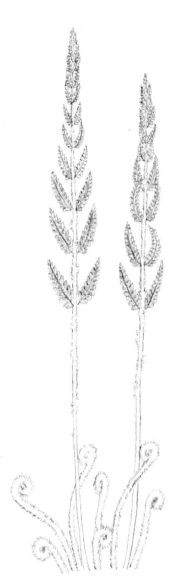

Cinnamon fern (in spring)

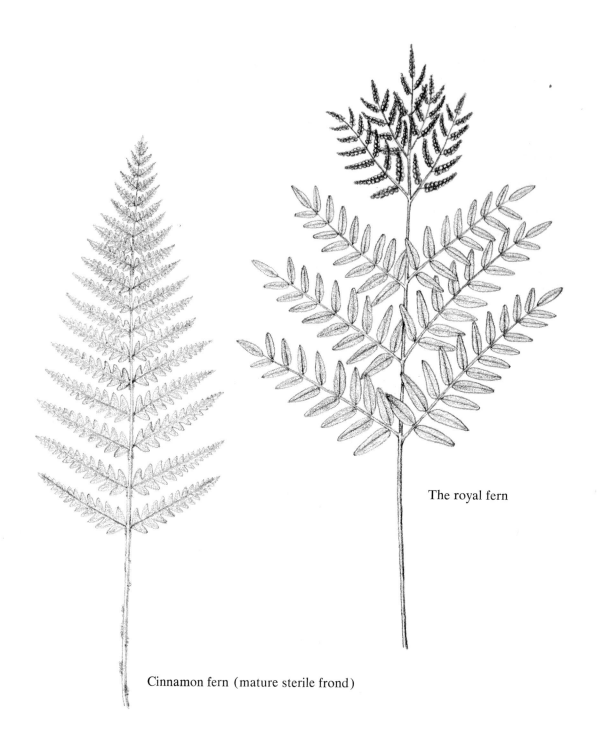

The royal fern

Cinnamon fern (mature sterile frond)

and the pinnae of their triangular fronds are joined at the base by a broad wing running along the stem.

The spore-bearing fronds of the netvein chain fern have narrow pinnae, with two rows of elongated sori resembling trains of tiny boxcars. Those of the sensitive fern, on the other hand, are rolled up into tiny balls which look like beads or berries in rows. Early in the season they turn dark brown, and long after the sterile fronds have been killed by frosts and have vanished, these spore-bearing fronds of the sensitive fern still stand erect. All through the winter, the balls remain tightly closed; only when spring arrives will they open to release their spores.

A few of the ferns do not rely altogether on spores for their reproduction. The bulblet bladder fern often forms tiny bulbs on the lower surface of its fronds, and these drop off to grow directly into new fern plants of the spore-bearing generation.

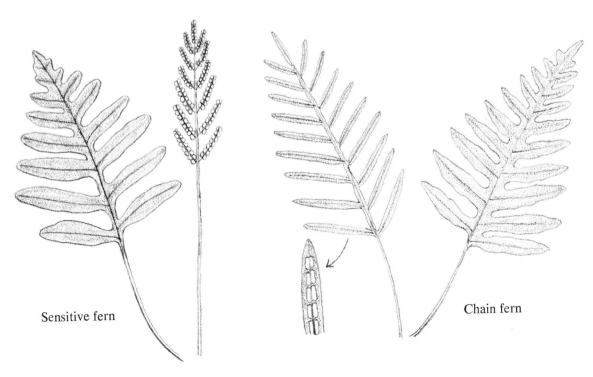

Sensitive fern

Chain fern

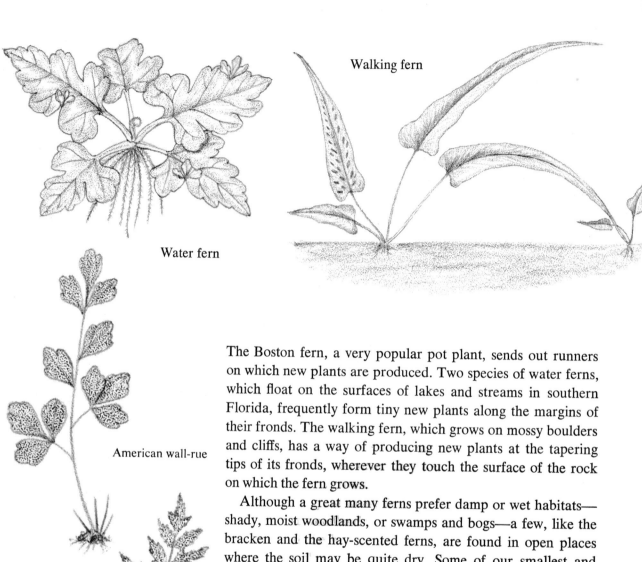

Walking fern

Water fern

American wall-rue

Mountain spleenwort

The Boston fern, a very popular pot plant, sends out runners on which new plants are produced. Two species of water ferns, which float on the surfaces of lakes and streams in southern Florida, frequently form tiny new plants along the margins of their fronds. The walking fern, which grows on mossy boulders and cliffs, has a way of producing new plants at the tapering tips of its fronds, wherever they touch the surface of the rock on which the fern grows.

Although a great many ferns prefer damp or wet habitats—shady, moist woodlands, or swamps and bogs—a few, like the bracken and the hay-scented ferns, are found in open places where the soil may be quite dry. Some of our smallest and daintiest ferns—among them the mountain and maidenhair spleenworts, the purple cliff brake, and the American wall rue —have a definite liking for rocks and can be found only on boulders or rocky cliffs.

The floor of the summer woodlands, particularly in the mountains, is frequently carpeted with many kinds of ferns. Most of them disappear after the first killing frosts of fall, but a few have evergreen fronds which are easily seen when the

106

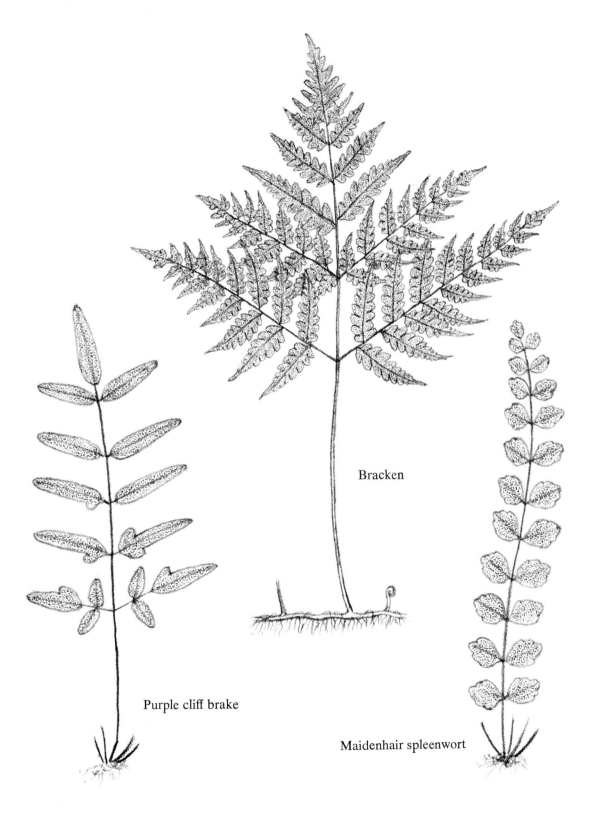

Bracken

Purple cliff brake

Maidenhair spleenwort

Maidenhair fern

ground is not covered with snow. One is the Christmas fern, and its dark green, leathery fronds are often seen on steep, rocky, wooded hillsides. The pinnae on the upper third of its fronds, on which spores were produced the summer before, are often abruptly reduced in size and are rusty-looking beneath. Both the lacy common shield fern and its coarser relative, the marginal shield fern, also have fronds which remain green all winter.

The fronds of the common polypody (POL-ee-poh-dee), or rock-cap fern, also look almost bright green in wintertime, against the rocks where they grow, as they do during the summer, and big, round, brown sori may still be seen on some of the pinnae.

Its smaller relative, the little gray polypody, is found on the trunks and branches of trees, and sometimes on rocks. It grows in our southern mountains but is much more abundant along the coast of the Southeast, where it forms dense colonies on the live oaks and other trees, along with the Spanish moss. When the weather is dry, its fronds curl up and seem to be dead; when it rains, they uncurl and become fresh-looking again. This is often called the resurrection fern.

Some species of ferns are rare, and several grow in only a few localities—or even a single locality—within a state. Many of the places where these rare ferns might occur have still hardly been searched. Ferns also have a way of turning up in unexpected places, far from where anyone might expect to find them. In 1935, a most unusual fern, called the Tunbridge filmy fern, was discovered on damp granite rocks in a deep gorge in northwestern South Carolina. How it got there is a mystery. It has been seen there and nowhere else in North America since. The nearest place its spores could possibly have come from is in the West Indies.

More recently a second species of West Indian fern was

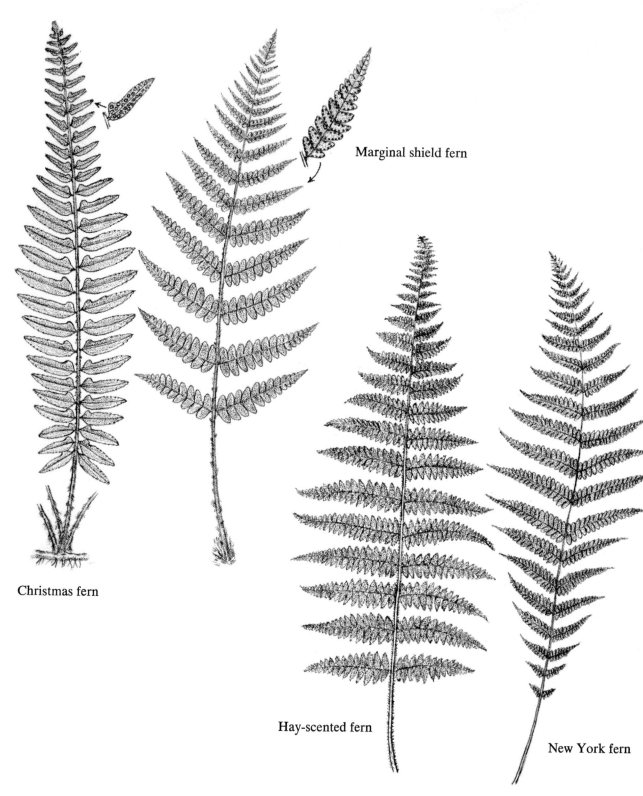

Marginal shield fern

Christmas fern

Hay-scented fern

New York fern

Two common summertime ferns

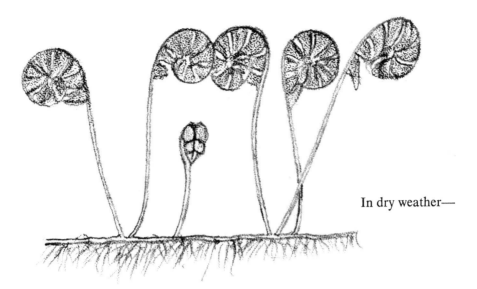

In dry weather—

The gray polypody or resurrection fern

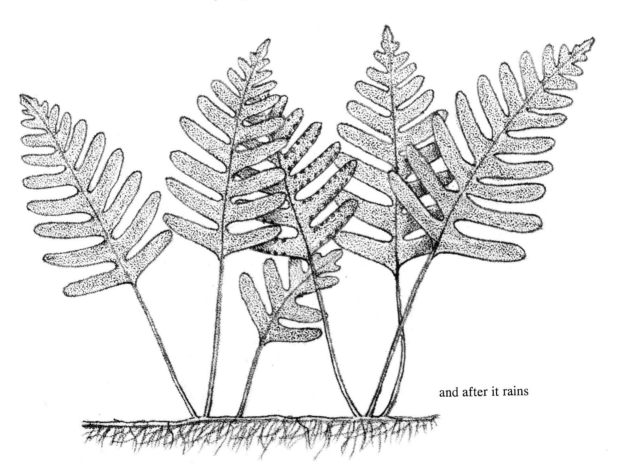

and after it rains

discovered in the mountains of North Carolina, not very far as a crow flies from the site where the Tunbridge filmy fern was found. But there it was, growing on a wet, mossy rock ledge. It, too, was previously unknown in North America. The only possible explanation is that spores of the ferns were carried to these places by hurricane winds.

Florida has a wealth of unusual ferns, many of which are found elsewhere only in the West Indies or tropical America. One of the oddest of them is the shoestring fern, a plant most people would never suspect of being a fern at all. It is an air plant, or epiphyte (EP-i-fite), and it grows on the branches of trees, with long, narrow fronds which resemble dangling green shoestrings. The spores of this fern grow into a generation of sexual fern plants which are unusual, too. They are branched and ribbonlike and could in fact easily be mistaken for liverworts.

Some very unfernlike ferns may be lurking in places close to home. Few people would recognize the climbing fern, for instance, as a fern. It climbs and twines like a vine over other vegetation in wet and usually sandy places where the soil is acid. Its pinnae are scattered along the slender stems and are divided into two fan-shaped, leaflike parts, the lobes of which suggest a widespread hand. The pinnae on the upper portion of the climbing frond are divided into more numerous but smaller segments. On their much narrower fingerlike lobes are rows of spore cases.

One of the most unfernlike of all our ferns grows abundantly in the Pine Barrens of southern New Jersey and, to some extent, in the coastal areas of Newfoundland and Nova Scotia. It is an inconspicuous little plant with threadlike sterile fronds which grow in a dense tuft and are twisted and curled. In midsummer it sends up equally slender fertile fronds, an inch to four inches tall, which are tipped with four or more pairs of fingerlike pinnae bearing spore cases. The plant looks much

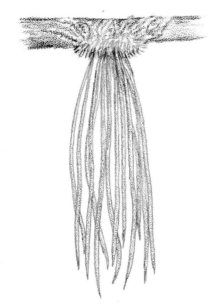

Shoestring fern

112

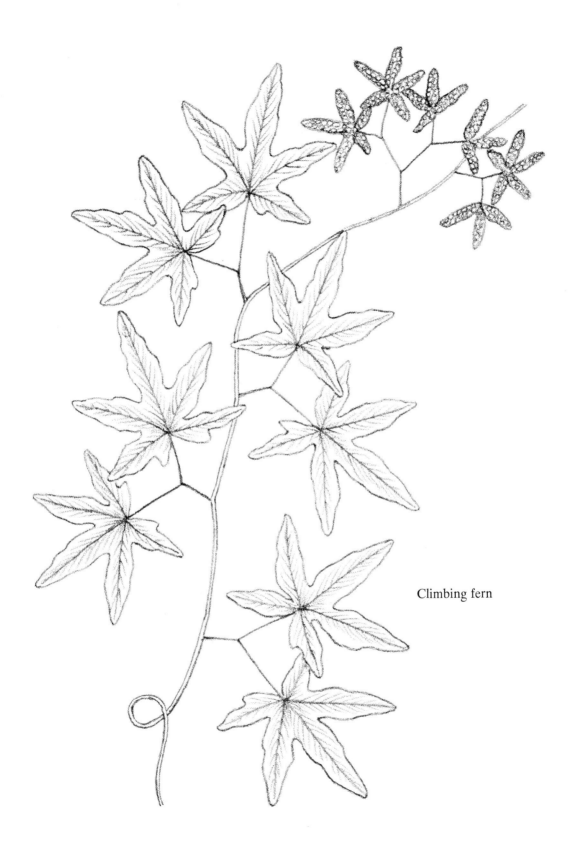

Climbing fern

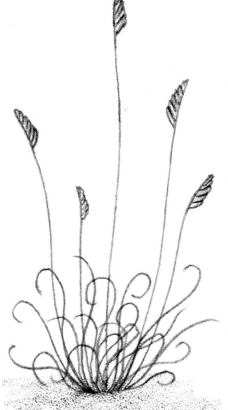

Curly-grass, one of the oddest of ferns

Adder's-tongue

more like some kind of grass than a fern and is in fact commonly known as the curly-grass. All of its close relatives are found only in the warmer parts of the Southern Hemisphere; the curly-grass fern is isolated far to the north of its kin.

Moist meadows and boggy thickets are good places to look for some very primitive ferns called the adder's-tongues. They are rather inconspicuous plants, a few inches to perhaps a foot tall, and they don't look anything like ferns. Above ground they have a fleshy stem on which there is usually a single, nearly oval "leaf." The stem continues upward beyond the "leaf" and ends in a double row of beadlike spore cases. Both the "leaf" and the cluster of spore cases are really just parts of a single frond. When a spore of an adder's-tongue germinates, it doesn't grow into a flat little prothallium as do the spores of most ferns. Instead it develops into a tiny body with merely a hint of green lobes showing at the surface of the ground. And this body, like those produced by club moss spores, always forms a partnership with a fungus.

During the summer months, the rattlesnake fern is usually much in evidence in woodlands across America. From a few inches to sometimes thirty inches tall, well above the ground, it bears a quite fernlike, much divided, triangular "leaf." Some distance above the "leaf" it has a branched cluster of spore cases. As with its relatives, the adder's-tongues, the "leaf" and the portion bearing spore cases are parts of a single frond. Other relatives, the grape ferns, have fernlike "leaves," too, but they are close to the ground, and, unlike the rattlesnake fern, grape ferns keep their "leaves" all winter. Their clusters of spore cases look a little bit like tiny bunches of grapes.

Like the spores of the adder's-tongue, those of the rattlesnake fern and the grape fern grow into very tiny plants of the sexual generation and also form a partnership with fungi. Botanists regard all of these ferns as being of a primitive type.

The most advanced sexual reproduction among members of the fern tribe is found in some ferns which live in the water

Rattlesnake fern

or float on its surface. These ferns look nothing at all like our familiar land ferns. They produce spores of two sizes as the selaginellas do. The large spores develop into female plants and the small ones develop into male plants, both kinds so small that they are extremely hard to find.

One member of this unique group of ferns is *Marsilea* (mar-SILL-i-a), commonly called the water clover. Its slender stem creeps in the mud of shallow ponds and slowly moving streams. Along this stem are clusters of fronds, each having a slender stalk and two pairs of pinnae at the top. Quite often the pinnae float on the surface of the water, looking very much like four-leaf clovers. In the clusters of the fronds, and sometimes attached to their bases, are short-stalked spore cases resembling beans.

Azolla (a-ZOLL-a) is a delicate and mossy-looking little fern less than half an inch across, varying from bright green to a rather deep red. *Azolla* often grows in dense mats on the surfaces of ponds, canals, and sluggish streams. The plants increase very rapidly; they frequently cover the water so completely that mosquitoes are unable to get through. Many people therefore call them mosquito ferns. Spore cases of two sizes are produced on the lower, underwater leaves. The larger ones are like a ball full of many very tiny spores; the smaller ones are egg-shaped and contain a single large spore—comparatively large, but still microscopic.

Salvinia (sal-VIN-i-a), the water spangles, is a somewhat bigger floating fern found in Florida and the American tropics. It is quite popular as an aquarium plant. *Salvinia,* like *Azolla,* grows so fast that the surface of the water becomes covered with a mat of plants. The fronds of *Salvinia* are divided into two roundish parts which resemble pairs of leaves covered with bristly hairs, and they float on the surface of the water. A third part of the frond is divided again, into dangling, hairy, threadlike segments which look like roots. On them the little spore cases are produced.

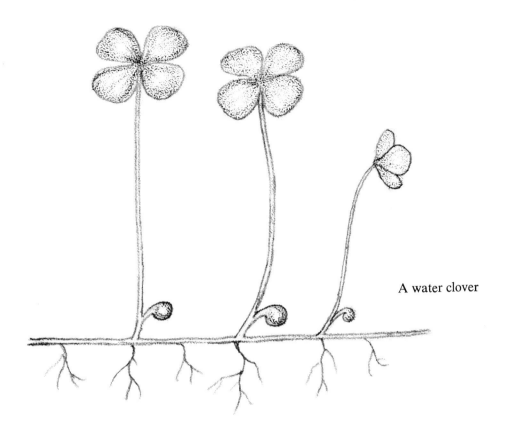

A water clover

Azolla

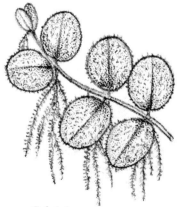

Salvinia

Ferns are still common in the world today, and we still have a number of scouring rushes and club mosses. All of these plants, however, had their "big day" in the Coal Age forests, two to three hundred million years ago. Huge tree ferns and smaller terrestrial ones flourished there, along with the tree-like ancestors of the scouring rushes and club mosses.

But in these same forests appeared some plants rather like ferns except for one special difference: they produced true seeds on their leaves, instead of spores. They have often been called the "seed ferns," but in reality they were the first primitive seed plants. In time they became extinct, but they were almost surely the ancestors of the seed plants which dominate the land areas of the world today.

Bibliography

FOR IDENTIFYING SEEDLESS PLANTS

Algae

Dawson, E. Yale. *How to Know the Seaweeds*. Dubuque, Iowa: William C. Brown Co., 1956.

Prescott, Gerald W. *How to Know the Freshwater Algae*. 2nd edition. Dubuque, Iowa: William C. Brown Co., 1970.

Smith, Gilbert M. *The Fresh-Water Algae of the United States*. New York: McGraw-Hill Book Co., 1953.

Mushrooms

Hesler, L. R. *Mushrooms of the Great Smokies*. Knoxville, Tenn.: University of Tennessee Press, 1960.

Krieger, Louis C. C. *The Mushroom Handbook*. New York: Dover Publishing Co., 1967.

Smith, Alexander H. *The Mushroom Hunter's Field Guide*. Ann Arbor, Mich.: University of Michigan Press, 1963.

Thomas, William S. *Field Book of Common Mushrooms*. New York: G. P. Putnam's Sons, 1948.

Lichens

Hale, Mason E., Jr. *Lichen Handbook*. Washington, D.C.: Smithsonian Institution, 1961.

119

Mosses and Liverworts

Conard, Henry S. *How to Know the Mosses and Liverworts.*
Dubuque, Iowa: William C. Brown Co., 1956.

Ferns and Their Allies

Cobb, Broughton. *A Field Guide to the Ferns.* Boston, Mass.:
Houghton Mifflin Co., 1956.

Durand, Herbert. *Field Book of Common Ferns.* New York: G. P.
Putnam's Sons, 1949.

Parsons, Mary E. *How to Know the Ferns.* New York: Dover Publishing Co.

Wherry, Edgar T. *The Fern Guide.* Garden City, N.Y.: Doubleday & Co., 1961.

Wherry, Edgar T. *The Southern Fern Guide.* Garden City, N.Y.:
Doubleday & Co., 1964.

General

Shuttlesworth, Floyd S. *Non-Flowering Plants.* Racine, Wis.:
Golden Press, 1967. (A guide to over 400 mushrooms, mosses,
lichens and ferns.)

FOR FURTHER READING

Ahmadjian, Vernon. *The Lichen Symbiosis.* New York: Blaisdell
Publishing Co., 1967.

Christensen, Clyde M. *The Molds and Man: An Introduction to the
Fungi.* Minneapolis, Minn.: University of Minnesota Press, 1965.

Corrington, Julian D. *Exploring with Your Microscope.* New York:
McGraw-Hill Book Co., 1957.

Fenton, Carrol L., and Mildred A. Fenton. *The Fossil Book.*
Garden City, N.Y.: Doubleday & Co., 1958.

Hutchins, Ross E. *Plants Without Leaves.* New York: Dodd,
Mead & Co., 1966.

Kavaler, Lucy. *Mushrooms, Molds, and Miracles.* New York: John
Day Co., 1965.

—— *The Wonders of Algae.* New York: John Day Co., 1961.

—— *The Wonders of Fungi.* New York: John Day Co., 1964.

Bibliography

Schlichting, Harold E., Jr., and Mary S. Schlichting. *Algae.* Austin, Texas: Steck-Vaughn Co., 1971.

Sterling, Dorothy. *The Story of Mosses, Ferns, and Mushrooms.* Garden City, N.Y.: Doubleday & Co., 1955.

Walford, Lionel A. *Living Resources of the Sea.* New York: Ronald Press Co., 1958.

Glossary

CAPSULE—A closed boxlike vessel containing seeds or spores.

CELLULOSE—An organic compound found in the cell walls of most plant cells.

CHLOROPHYLL—The green pigment found in plants.

CHLOROPLAST—A small body containing chlorophyll present in certain cells of most green plants.

CILIUM (plural, cilia)—A microscopic hairlike projection of a cell.

CONJUGATION—Sexual reproduction resulting from the uniting of two similar cells.

EGG—The female sex cell.

EUTROPHICATION—The process by which a body of water becomes overly rich in dissolved nutrients, causing an excessive growth of algae and hastening the aging of water.

FERMENTATION—Chemical changes brought about by yeast plants in which sugar is changed into alcohol and carbon dioxide.

FERTILIZATION—Sexual reproduction resulting from the union of an egg with a sperm.

FLAGELLATE—A one-celled plant (or animal) having one or more flagella.

FLAGELLUM (plural, flagella)—A long threadlike or whiplike projection from a cell.

MYCELIUM (plural, mycelia)—Fine and usually whitish threads which make up the main plant body of fungi such as molds and mushrooms.

NUCLEUS (plural, nuclei)—A definite rounded body within the cell which controls its functions.

123

PARASITE—An organism that takes its food from another living organism, living on or within its host.

PHOTOSYNTHESIS—The process by which green plants use sunlight to manufacture carbohydrates from carbon dioxide and water.

PLANKTON—The free-floating mass of minute plant and animal life in a body of water.

PLASTID—A small body containing a pigment present in the cells of plants.

PROTHALLIUM (plural, prothallia)—The minute thalluslike stage in ferns and their allies which bears sex organs.

PROTOPLASM—The translucent and somewhat jellylike living substance of plant and animal cells.

ROSETTE—A more or less flattened circular cluster suggesting a rose.

SAC—A baglike structure.

SAPROPHYTE—An organism which lives on dead or decaying organic matter.

SEED—A many-celled reproductive body resulting from a ripened ovule which contains an embryo or young plant.

SPERM—The male sex cell.

SPORANGIUM (plural, sporangia)—A spore case.

SPORE—A simple, usually single-celled reproductive body.

THALLUS (plural, thalli)—A plant body which shows no differentiation into roots, stem, and leaves.

VASCULAR SYSTEM—A continuous system of specialized tissue which conducts water or sap throughout the plant body.

Index

Index